A View from the South

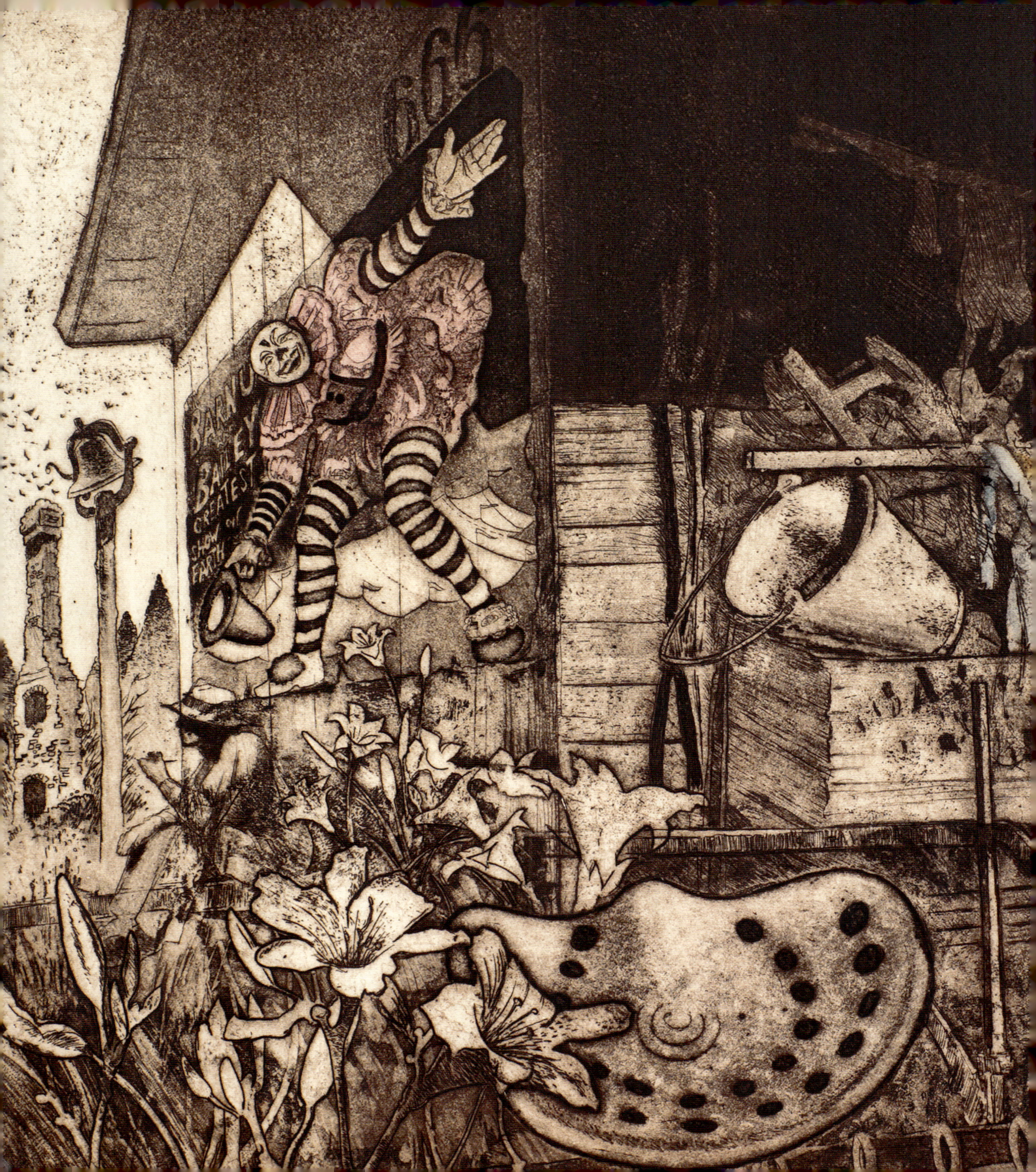
665
BARNU
BAILEY
GREATEST
SHOW ON
EARTH

A View from the South

The Narrative Art of BOYD SAUNDERS

Thomas Dewey II

THE UNIVERSITY OF SOUTH CAROLINA PRESS

Published by the University of South Carolina Press
Columbia, South Carolina 29208

www.sc.edu/uscpress

Manufactured in Korea

28 27 26 25 24 23 22 21 20 19   10 9 8 7 6 5 4 3 2 1

Library of Congress Cataloging-in-Publication Data
can be found at http://catalog.loc.gov/.

ISBN: 978-1-61117-912-5 (cloth)
ISBN: 978-1-64336-020-1 (ebook)

Frontispiece *The Scarecrow* from the *Blackberry Winter* suite of etchings

For my children: Amy, Aaron, and Will

Contents

Foreword

Boyd Saunders is unquestionably one of America's premier printmakers. He is a master craftsman who handles burin and brush with technical virtuosity and who, as a visual communicator, has much to say at a variety of levels. His multilayered prints explore issues of universal concern—issues of place, time, memory, relationships. If this country followed the Japanese practice of designating certain artists as "national treasures," there can be little doubt that Boyd Saunders would be one of those named. Professor Tom Dewey's book, the first monograph to be devoted to Saunders and his art, makes its appearance just as the artist is achieving his greatest successes and attracting the most attention. The publication of *A View from the South: The Narrative Art of Boyd Saunders* is most timely.

Although his prints have received national and international recognition, Boyd Saunders remains true to his roots in the land and people of the agrarian South. If you did not have the good fortune to have been born below the Mason-Dixon Line and are desirous of knowing just what makes the South so different from the rest of the United States, I can think of no better or more rewarding way to do this than by studying Boyd Saunders's prints. Tom Dewey's book goes a long way in providing access to the complex and gifted individual whose art (both visual and verbal) expresses those qualities that can be identified as characteristically southern.

I met Boyd Saunders soon after I joined the faculty of the University of South Carolina's Art Department in 1970. He was an "old-timer" in this newly expanded department, having taken his place on its faculty roster five years earlier. At first I didn't know quite what to make of him. On the door to his office was plastered an iconic poster of John Wayne at his gritty best, and Boyd cultivated a Wayne-like persona. Despite the antiwar sentiment prevalent on campus at that time, which was especially strong in the art department, Boyd proudly acknowledged his prior service in the U.S. Marine Corps. Yet it was obvious that his students had not only profound respect for him but a deep affection as well. It soon became clear to me that his "tough guy" image was but a façade—an example of his love of the theater and of role-playing as well as a manifestation of his penchant for storytelling.

I have just made reference to *his* students, and the printmaking majors did, indeed, stand apart from those who were concentrating on painting, sculpture, or ceramics. His students actually seemed more akin to the apprentices in a Renaissance-era workshop (with Boyd as the maestro) than they did to the everyday art studio major. This, and the fact that his classroom was set up like an old-fashioned printmaking workshop with its assortment of salvaged presses and giant lithography stones, impressed me.

Boyd was able to attract a sizable following of students despite the fact that his use of realistic subject matter ran counter to the mainstream canon of the art establishment. Remember that these were the days of abstract, minimalist, and performance art. Traditional artistic approaches were in disrepute. The overall relevance of the visual arts to contemporary society was even being called into question by some. Yet Boyd continued to turn out visual narratives filled with naturalistically rendered representations of people and places. During this period of nonobjective dominance, it was in Boyd's studio-workshop that successive generations of USC students learned to draw and to express their ideas and emotions using the traditional modes of artistic expression.

The work that Boyd was producing at the time certainly did fly in the face of what was expected of modern artists and set him apart from his studio colleagues. His prints were thought by many to be anachronistic or, even worse, "decorative" (that term being the ultimate disparagement of the day). But times do change. The human figure and his natural environment are back in favor and have resumed their proper place as a legitimate means by which an artist may communicate with the public.

As Boyd and I got to know each other as colleagues, we discovered that we shared a number of experiences, ideas, and values. We were both military veterans and held unpopular, hawkish views concerning America's proper role in southeast Asia; we both had spent time in Florence and had an abiding affection for the surrounding Tuscan countryside; we also shared a profound love of horses; we each had a respect for history and for the traditional role of art in society; and furthermore we were both southerners in a Yankee-dominant department and saw things somewhat differently from our fellow faculty. And, a little later on, we each came to play activist roles in our region's art associations—SECAC (Southeastern College Art Conference) for us both, SGC (Southern Graphics Council) for Boyd, and SESAH (Southeastern Society of Architectural Historians) for me.

SECAC meets annually at the invitation of one of its regional institutional members. In addition to presenting and hearing professional papers and watching a variety of demonstrations, attendees get to see other campuses throughout the Southeast; but getting to the far-flung conference sites often entailed car or van rides of more than fifteen hours. It actually was on these long and tedious road trips that I really came to appreciate Boyd's considerable talents as a storyteller. Thanks to his gift for narration, the miles passed by all the more quickly.

The fact that Boyd and I seemed to be reading from the same page when it came to the visual arts encouraged us to develop a team-taught course simply entitled History of Printmaking. This upper-level course was intended for both studio students and art history majors, and provided those enrolled in it with not only a historical survey of the various printmaking media and their principal practitioners but also with the opportunity to see the printmaking techniques demonstrated "live." Our jointly taught course was designed to appeal to both sides of a student's brain. In general, I would handle the historical progression with Boyd interjecting his commentary on technical aspects and presenting discursive and lively vignettes on various artists or aspects of their production (for example Dürer's *Melancholia* and *The Revelations of St. John,* Gustave Dore's *The Wandering Jew,* Thomas Nast's graphic battles with Boss Tweed and Tammany Hall, the story of Currier and Ives, the Japanese woodblock print, Toulouse Lautrec and the poster). There always is a risk to team teaching, but Boyd and I complemented each other nicely. We enjoyed the collaboration, and the course was well received by both studio and art history majors on each occasion that it was offered.

As I read through Tom Dewey's manuscript in preparation to writing this foreword, I was pleasantly surprised to see how much space he had allocated to the literary side of Boyd Saunders's creative abilities. That, I felt, was as it should be. Boyd's friend and fellow artist the New York–based South Carolinian Sigmund Abeles recently has observed that if Boyd had not developed his talent as a printmaker, he most assuredly would have become a writer. In any case many of Boyd's prints display a very fine line between visual content and implied text. The images are meant to be "read."

It is to Tom Dewey's lasting credit that he decided to include so many of the stories that Boyd delights in telling. Without Dewey's intervention, it is likely that these stories would have remained unrecorded and unpublished and been, in effect, lost. Preserved in this book, they not only complement and enlighten Boyd's work as a printmaker, but they are now available for integration into the existing body of southern folklore.

We encounter Boyd's skill as a raconteur throughout Dewey's book, especially at the conclusion of the second chapter ("A Stallion Named Dan" and "The Saunderses' Red Mule") and in chapter 15, "The Storyteller's Art."

I am particularly pleased that the extraordinary tale "The Return of Miss Dixie" was included in the book, both because of its complexity and because I had not heard it before (perhaps it was too lengthy for even our longest SECAC journey). As one reads through it, the sequence of episodes progresses so smoothly that it is easy to forget, at its conclusion, that you have actually been entertained by four or five stories gathered under a single heading. The construction is intricate, the pace leisurely, and the words carefully chosen to produce the most lasting impact. The ending could have been reached far more quickly than it was—but that is just the point. In telling these stories Boyd Saunders lures us into accepting their fictional truth through elaborate details and tangential information. Actually, the pleasure we derive from "The Return of Miss Dixie" comes more from the way in which the tale is told than from any punch line or revelation at the finish. Just how much of "Miss Dixie" is grounded in fact and how much stems purely from Boyd's imagination is unclear, but the story was meant for public consumption and it is quite consciously embellished to perfection.

Another fine example of Boyd's narrative ability comes from the artist's personal journal, which is cleverly used by Dr. Dewey in chapter 5 to enhance his discussion of Boyd's etching *The Cistern.* The basic elements of this journal entry, which is entitled "The Old Nuckhall Place," are simple enough and involve a visit he and a brother made to a nearly abandoned farm and the thoughts it provoked concerning the changing realities of people, time, and place. But Boyd's recollection of this event takes on added significance through the descriptive passages encountered along the way that turn what might have been a run-of-the-mill diary entry into a masterful tale: "The road unfolded before us, past cotton fields and farm houses and many pastures of motley cows and groves of many hued oak trees, many even older than the road which had cut itself into the red earth until, in places, it formed a great ravine that was colonnaded with the hanging, groping roots of those same trees." Or at another point, "A large red-tailed hawk glided between the tops of the giant old cedar trees, hesitated for a brief encounter with the bats and swifts swirling about the dim chimneys and passed on, a gray cat awoke from his nap on this cistern cover and ambled towards the house." The word imagery is vivid, and each descriptive step in the narration (even in something as informal as a journal entry) is well considered. This is the way stories are told in the South. This is also the way in which Boyd Saunders presents his art.

Boyd deliberately avoids getting directly to the point with his imagery; instead he eases into it. Rather than marching us straight through the front entry, he guides us around to the back door allowing us to appreciate the property in its entirety. As he said, when describing a recent series of prints, *The Return of the Wanderer,* "I have little interest in simply making a picture of what this or that looks like." Just as the real value and enjoyment in his stories is to be found in their telling, the aesthetic rewards in his prints come from the depicting. The abundance of detail forces us to slow our viewing pace and to savor each pictorial passage in the composition. This is a southern experience, after all.

In the second chapter of Dr. Dewey's book, Boyd Saunders describes waging make-believe Civil War battles as part of his childhood play: "the fields and woods around our farm house regularly yielded up Civil War bullets and a host of other weapons and artifacts of that great struggle. Indeed, every part of that land seemed saturated with ghosts and memories of all that had gone before." True to his word, his prints seem impregnated with the ever-present shades of past events, never quite brought into focus but always lurking about in the layered textures of his compositions. Unlike the ubiquitous barn paintings of the Carolina piedmont or the equally numerous swamp paintings of the lowcountry, both categories rendered with generic southern realism and even differing from the rather quaint, Charleston street scenes of Elizabeth Verner, Boyd's prints go beyond what the eye sees to reveal what the mind imagines. Despite the differences in their backgrounds and the locations chosen, one can see similarities between Saunders and Andrew Wyeth.

The mind's eye of this artist has, in fact, created a generic and mythic country community of small farmers and simple merchants, situated, perhaps, in the west Tennessee of his youth or in the adopted South Carolina midlands of his maturity. Wherever it is, the place is quintessentially southern both in its origins and in its present-day character. Through a close observation of the imagery and how Boyd has slowly and painstakingly manipulated the visual content, we come to acquire a sense for the "rhythm of the South."

In a commentary on his masterful etching *The Wedding Party,* Boyd inverted that famous line from

Shakespeare's *The Tempest,* "all past is prologue," and suggested instead that "perhaps the present is a prologue to the past." This is key to understanding his use of layered meaning. One must take the time to peel away the palimpsest of complex images. It becomes almost an archaeological undertaking. But the slow-paced revelation and absorption of each layer of imagery is, in the end, as rewarding as a sip of sweet, southern-style iced tea on a sultry summer's day. And again, the real genius lies in the "telling" of the visual tale.

In illuminating the accomplishments of Boyd Saunders, artist, storyteller, musician, and cultural contributor, Tom Dewey has performed a singular service. He has given greater exposure to an extraordinary body of work by one of this county's most talented printmakers and storytellers and has placed that work within an appropriate cultural context. Along the way, Dewey's book also takes us all that much closer to understanding just what is really southern about the South.

Charles R. Mack

Acknowledgments

A significant number of individuals have contributed greatly to the realization of this book project, and I will be forever grateful to them. Therefore I offer thanks and recognition herewith.

To Dr. Robert Khayat, chancellor of the University of Mississippi at Oxford (1995–2009) and longtime friend, for thoughtful advice when I was searching for grants and related funds to launch aspects of this project.

To Boyd Saunders, distinguished professor emeritus (the University of South Carolina–Columbia) for his constant accessibility, cooperation, patience, and special service as a critical proofreader for factual information—one of the blessings possible when working with a living artist. Thanks also to Boyd's beloved wife, Stephanie, likewise a retired educator, who continues an earlier profession as a painter and designer, for the gracious hospitality and many other kindnesses shown me during my working trips to the Saunderses' home, and when attending annual print conferences.

It is with a special debt of gratitude that I thank art historian Dr. Randy Mack, professor emeritus (USC-Columbia), for providing the book's impressive and sensitive foreword. Dr. Mack is quite knowledgeable regarding the history of printmaking and in particular, Saunders's prints.

To the University of Mississippi for awarding me a sabbatical leave for spring semester 2008, during which formal and sustained writing produced the first drafts of this book.

To my faithful wife, Alta, for her steadfast support during this multiyear project and especially for allowing me to use the dining room table for months at a time to spread out anything, everything book-related.

To Allan Innman and Ross Turner, visual resources curators with the Art Department at Ole Miss, and painters, for digitally scanning many, many images of Saunders's artwork for chapter draft mockups.

Finally it is with great pride that I introduce to the readers of this book some extraordinary Ole Miss students interested in art history beyond the classroom. For varying lengths of time and in varying numbers between roughly 2007 and 2011 they contributed tremendously to the realization of this manuscript. Almost immediately they became fascinated with Saunders's images, the ideas behind them, and his gift as a writer. Then they proved to be tireless workers at innumerable tasks and technical issues. I especially appreciate their perseverance in addressing my endless chapter revisions. That was most admirable. Their names, academic emphases, and hometowns follow:

Jennae Johnson, managerial finance, Oxford, Mississippi
Jamie Johnson, imaging arts, Poplarville, Mississippi
Miles Ginn, modern languages and art history, Columbia, Mississippi
Jerri Fountain, English, West, Mississippi
Nicholas Davis, marketing, Charleston, Mississippi
Amy Rives, art history, Brandon, Mississippi
Irene Matthew Parker, printmaking, Metairie, Louisiana
Amber Williams, printmaking, Wesson, Mississippi
Angelina Mazzanti, imaging arts, Little Rock, Arkansas
Devin-Lindsay Dillon-Maginnis, graphic design, Oxford, Mississippi
Lydia Cross, English and art, Falkner, Mississippi
Sara Lowery, printmaking, Oxford, Mississippi

Chapter 1

Fateful Introductions and the Beginnings of This Book Project

A Personal Recollection

In the spring of 1977, I traveled to Florida State University–Tallahassee to attend a conference with John Winters, head of the printmaking program at the University of Mississippi–Oxford. John was the first friend I made arriving there the previous August fresh from the University of Wisconsin–Madison with a Ph.D. in art history.[1] I was hired to teach twentieth-century art and especially contemporary art, plus the usual foundation survey courses. However since my narrowest focus in graduate school was contemporary American printmaking and drawing, which included a minor in printmaking and drawing through the UW Art Department, John and I immediately had some things in common.

Not surprisingly John encouraged me to accompany him and a couple of graduate students to the Florida conference, informing me during the long drive about the Southeastern Graphics Council (SEGC), a young organization comprising almost entirely artists and artist-educators who primarily made prints and drawings. Those enthusiasts generally met for about two days at a host university or college, observing demonstrations in the techniques and explorations of printmaking across a wide range of media, listening to academic papers, and discussing pressing topics to their field in panels. He said there would be evening receptions at several print exhibitions, and they proved to be exciting. John's description did not disappoint. There was more; for example, looking at member artists' new work brought rolled up into mailing tubes or in large portfolios, which were then spread open across hotel-room beds. The prints ranged in quality from school assignments to professional work.

Perhaps best of all was meeting so many people dedicated and enthusiastic about their graphic work and their desire to increase print and drawing connoisseurship throughout the region. John introduced me to just about every SEGC member he knew and made sure that I met the founding members and current officers. From those introductions came some life-changing consequences. Kenneth Kerslake of the University of Florida became a staunch supporter of my efforts to document graphics council members. Bernard Solomon, Georgia Southern University, partnered with me in organizing several touring print exhibitions of national and international scope through about 1985. Norman Wagner, Atlanta College of Art; Tom Hammond, the University of Georgia; William Walmsley, Florida State University; Roger Steele, University of South Carolina–Beaufort; Beauvais Lyons, University of Tennessee; Juergen Strunck, University of Dallas; and Conrad Ross at Auburn University all influenced my future activities in the council in continuous, meaningful ways, and I remain in their debt.

At that conference John Winters likewise introduced me to the subject of this book, who was not only a founding member of the Southeastern Graphics Council but who also conceived the whole idea and closely oversaw its development to fruition. Our first meeting was absolutely unforgettable as the moment was rather charged when we were facing each other. He was distinctive in appearance: tall, broad shouldered, of good posture, possessing an authoritative voice, an energetic demeanor, and a penetrating gaze. First impressions raced quickly through my mind, for example here's a take-charge person, a force, and again he is one of the founders of this group. I hope I make a good impression on him considering I was from Illinois, a northern state, and my highest educational background was the University of Wisconsin–Madison, a liberal college. I was met with a scrutinizing gaze, and anxiety gripped me. Did I mention that he was also a former Marine? I feared Mr. Saunders was thinking: Great, just what we need, another long-haired, Yankee carpetbagger. Fortunately the preceding assumptions were without validity, but once more I wanted to be accepted, not rejected outright as another northern opportunist before I had a chance to prove myself.

When Bernie Solomon and I began working in earnest on our first project, the First National Invitational Color Blend Print Exhibition 1978–1980, I brought up the subject of outsiders moving to the South to begin their careers or spend their whole careers here and their prospects for acceptance or rejection. Professor Solomon, short and stout, with wildly curly, thick, black hair and beard, a loud voice, and an extroverted manner, was from Chicago, but he might just as well have come through Ellis Island before 1900. With his obvious ethnicity, he paused and told me that he followed the direct practice of trying to make sure that he always gave more than he took.

I thought about that idea, took it to heart, and have tried to live by it while adding other elements. It is not enough to just be in a place to work; one should certainly be objective but also become part of that place, meaning embrace a department, a university, and the wider community in which it resides. If the department, or library, or so on have inadequate resources, one should build them, and never stop!

The 1977 conference featured technical demonstrations in printmaking by noted specialists. For example John and Claire Romano of the College of Manhattanville–New York, and the Pratt Institute, respectively, demonstrated collograph techniques featured in their then-new publication *The Complete Printmaker.* Other featured specialists demonstrating were Arthur Deshaies, FSU-Tallahassee (plaster relief); Byron McKeeby, University of Tennessee–Knoxville (lithography); and Juergen Strunck (relief color blend with conical shaped rollers), University of Dallas.[2] I was amazed that they and the other headliners were so approachable and friendly. In fact that was my impression of almost all the printmakers and drawers that I met. Furthermore it wasn't a fluke, because that impression has held up all these years. Printmakers aren't just friendly; they're eager to share techniques, materials, and approaches to problem solving and the like with others.

On the long drive back to Oxford, my mind raced through possible ways that I might be of service to this new organization. At that summer's graphics council board of directors meeting in Birmingham, Alabama, I proposed the creation of an archives to document the Southeastern Graphics Council, its individual members' activities, and its annual conferences and to begin a print study collection as a repository for council members' artwork, plus other projects. The proposal passed and was ratified at the members' meeting of the 1978 conference. For more about the archives' history visit the Southern Graphics Council International Archives website at www.sgciarchives.org. For a colorful history of SGCI, see chapter 10, "Service to the Field."

I had little contact with Professor Saunders until that 1978 Southeastern Graphics Council Conference in Birmingham, Alabama, when our paths crossed owing to a shared interest. Boyd Saunders recognized a seasoned printmaker from the region (chosen by a committee) for exemplary work and outstanding contributions to the field by designating Elizabeth O'Neill Verner the first recipient of the Printmaker Emeritus Award. She was further honored with a pewter medallion and a one-person exhibition.[3] Since the elderly recipient was unable to attend owing to a stroke, a documentary videotape of her life and work was shown to the conferees. The credit for conceiving and overseeing all facets of the award goes to Boyd Saunders. Even before the conference we communicated about the award process. Boyd was eager to have an example of her work and a copy of the documentary videotape sent to the archives after the conference as long as I thought it was appropriate. I was thrilled, though he hardly needed my approval. That was the beginning of a wonderful thirty-plus-year working relationship and a growing personal friendship between us.

The Elizabeth O'Neill Verner videotapes documented the 1977 Florida State University conference to become the beginning of the graphics council's video and audio tape collection of annual conferences, individual artist workshops, technical demonstrations, interviews, and so on.

Artist-donated prints—from the touring National Color Blend Exhibition, for example—became the nucleus of the graphics council's print study collection. Additional donations followed from more traveling exhibitions, one of which was titled Printmakers in the South 1860 to the Present. It was codeveloped by art historian Dr. Richard Cox at Louisiana State University–Baton Rouge and me and sponsored by the Southern Arts Federation, Atlanta. I was immediately struck by Saunders's etching *The Commissary,* its sound draftsmanship, and its equally deft ability to create an arresting mood with soft grounds and collage fragments of graphic design. Much later I realized that those were some of his trademarks as an artist. They may at first seem placid and crisply ordered in *The Commissary,* but in the broad areas of soft ground shadows, one finds ghostlike images of vintage advertising, another of his muses.

At the 1978 Southeastern Graphics Council Conference, I proposed a name change to the Southern Graphics Council. It passed and later practically doubled the organization's initial territory and membership. Thereafter conferences were held in many new territory cities including New Orleans, as well as west of the Mississippi River, in Tulsa, Oklahoma; Kansas City, Missouri; Austin, Houston, Waco, and Fort Worth, Texas; and Tempe, Arizona. At the majority of those conferences, Boyd and I stayed in touch mainly about graphics council business or illustrated brochures, catalogues, and flyers regarding his exhibitions of new suites of prints and other accomplishments.

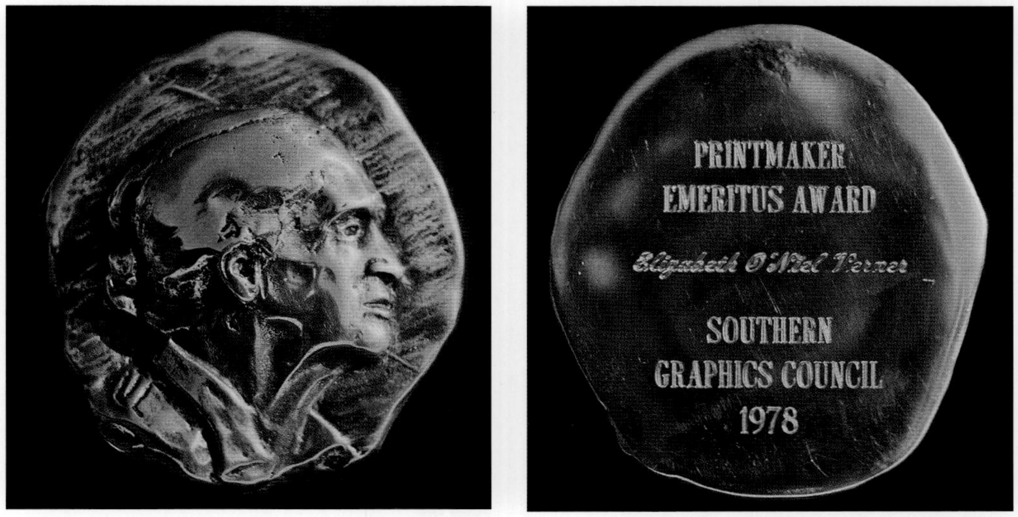

Printmaker Emeritus Award

However, 2001 proved to be a year of major revelations! The annual Southeastern College Art Conference (SECAC) meeting was hosted by the University of South Carolina–Columbia that year, and Boyd, nearing retirement after thirty-six years, was honored with a retrospective exhibition at the McKissick Museum on campus. The exhibit filled several galleries and much of a hall. I was aware that he was a productive printmaker but did not realize that he was also a painter and sculptor. The exhibit was also didactic with copper plates and other printmaking materials and tools on view in exhibition cases surrounded by framed prints on the walls. I left that exhibit with a sense of awe at the diversity of his media as well as the strength of his themes and techniques and then experienced the first thoughts, perhaps only as a fantasy, of being lucky enough to produce a book documenting Saunders's work. The 2002 SGC Conference called "Print Gumbo" was in New Orleans, the Louisiana city where the Southeastern Graphics Council had been born as an idea thirty years before. At that conference Boyd Saunders became the recipient of the award that he initiated twenty-four years prior. The next day I met briefly with Boyd and his wife, Stephanie, in their hotel room, where they gave me a ringed notebook containing Boyd's acceptance speech, commentary on decades of his art, and sheets of selected color transparencies that illustrated his remarks. If nothing else had transpired after that moment, the notebook was a valuable addition to the archives, and I was grateful.

The next two to three years were characterized by correspondence and phone calls of varied topics including the concept of a book. Boyd was by then officially retired from USC-Columbia (though not from making art) and thus possibly had the luxury of time to devote to a book. We both, however, had a lot on our plates.

We met again in 2005 at the annual conference of the Southern Graphics Council, this time in Washington, D.C., at the Capital Hilton. Conference attendance had swelled by the mid- to late 1990s. The two conference sites before D.C. were Boston, Massachusetts, 2003, and Rutgers University, New Brunswick, New Jersey, in 2004, and those conferences were absolutely national in scope with visitors also from Canada, South America, Great Britain, Japan, the Middle East, and Africa.

Boyd and Stephanie attended the session I chaired concerning the SGC Archives and its new website, www.sgcarchives.org, which was publicly launched at that session thanks especially to Ole Miss student Mary Warner, from the Tampa, Florida, area, who is one of the finest students with whom I've ever collaborated. Later a time and a quiet place in the conference hotel were found, and Boyd and I had fruitful discussions regarding a book project. Content subjects were addressed as well as the possibility of a visit by me for a three-to-four-day work sessions at the artist's home and studio on the outskirts of Chapin, South Carolina, hence close to USC-Columbia. The trip came to pass in early August 2005.

My visit was indeed a work session but was also a dream come true. We spent many enjoyable hours camped in his home-based studio discussing approaches to constructing and ordering the flow of the book. We looked at trial proofs from various suites, series, and folios. We discussed a myriad of things, and those discussions went into the nights usually ending at 11 P.M. I initially took notes, about sixteen pages on August 4 and 5 alone, and while that was well meaning, I was missing too much, way too much! Some artists have little to say about their work; not so with Saunders. He was relaxed and seemed to like conversing, talking openly about everything. He also wove stories of his experiences into explanations of context, composition, or technique and did so with ease. Furthermore there was a fine quality to his voice, strong but not grating; a distinguished, natural southern accent. Thus I began taping our exchanges, and though my stay could not be extended, he informed me that a lot of material we were not able to cover existed on videotapes made mostly by Media Services of the University of South Carolina. Those tapes were subsequently copied and later nearly a dozen were sent to me. A heavy teaching schedule, plus prior conference research paper projects, caused me to delay working with the tapes until the summer of 2006, at which time the slow task of transcribing them began. Believe it or not, that process never became drudgery; in fact just the opposite. Imagine an artist standing in front of his exhibited work patiently discussing paintings and prints in his major series thematically, technically, and in terms of intentionality, including his interpretations of Faulkner's works "The Bear," "Spotted Horses," and *The Sound and the Fury* through sensitive, illustrative compositions, many of which could stand on their own merits. On some videotapes Saunders discussed his work in front of a group of people rather like a "walk-through" gallery talk, sometimes in front of a seated audience, a couple of times amid young students, and other times just with a videographer. Yet regardless of the situation, there was one constant: Saunders fully informed his audiences with honesty, thoroughness, articulation, and passion. None of his audiences were listening to the artist for academic credit; it's just that Saunders is a natural teacher and a gifted communicator, and he never talks down to anyone.

One by one the videotapes continued to yield surprises. For example one tape contained the awards ceremony at a Memphis State University (University of Memphis) alumni banquet in 1993. Accepting the award of Distinguished Alumnus, Saunders came to the podium microphone, humbly thanked the awards selection committee, offered greetings to those assembled, and voiced a broad concern for the humanities in crisis. That was a presentation of the quality expected of the keynote speaker at a major conference. After listening to the address and transcribing it, I realized that another talent this artist possesses is oration.

The August 2006 work session visit to the Saunderses' South Carolina home and studio was every bit as productive as the 2005 experience and with additional discoveries. During a discussion of Saunders's original lithographs for the USC Press publication of the Faulkner short story "Spotted Horses" (1989), the subject of mules came up and especially with the illustration of the character Tull driving a wagon containing his wife and four daughters onto a narrow bridge. There they are met head on by a wild, crazed, mustang that smashes into the mules, the travelers, and their wagon. Saunders then began to talk about mules in a wider sense, for example their prominent place in southern farming, the Mule Day Festival in Columbia, Tennessee, and their valued presence on the Saunderses' family farm in west Tennessee. Within a few minutes Saunders was telling me a stranger-than-fiction tale about mules he grew up with and their special relevance to the citizens of Rossville, Tennessee, just a mile from the Saunders farm. When Saunders finished that yarn, I had another revelation. He is a natural storyteller, something quite evident in interviews and other statements. For example Boyd once said, "My art is very much a storyteller's art, and the mixing of text and pictures is quite natural to it and me."

When Saunders told me the story was true and he worked with mules growing up, I felt privileged to have the story on an audiotape. The American South has long been recognized for its writers, but it also has a rich tradition in oral history and storytelling, which Saunders continues. Is that in the water down here?

Another personal discovery of the 2006 trip was seeing a large acrylic painting titled *The Battle of Hanging Rock* about a Revolutionary War skirmish at a rural site in the South Carolina colony (see chapter 9, "*The Battle of Hanging Rock*"). It was a Saunders commission around the year 2000 and was soon acquired by the South Carolina State Museum, Columbia, and installed in its Revolutionary War exhibit area. The standoff confrontation between Tory and Patriot forces is startling and impressive, but so too were a couple of preparatory studies displayed nearby, which also caught my eye and curiosity. Thus I inquired if there were any more, and I was soon ushered into a museum storage area by Saunders and museum employee Jim Knight to a sizeable archival box, which when carefully opened revealed small treasures protected by interleaving papers. There were about thirty graphite studies, red chalk drawings, and outline renderings on tracing paper, and that was only one box. Those preparatory works of single figures, individual armaments, foliage, and so on sometimes appeared near finished though were probably not meant to be exhibited. However, I was overjoyed and blurted out, "Some of these just have to be in the book!" They were so sensitive and so characteristic of Saunders's humility in front of any subject and his determination to achieve authenticity or correctness in any project. Indeed his Catholic tastes and adventuresome spirit recall the likes of Charles Willson Peale, Benjamin Franklin, John James Audubon, and Albrecht Dürer.

Returning to the artist's home and studio, more audiotapes were filled (on August 13, 2006) with data about another commission, this time from about 1986–91, that is, *The Aikenhead Collection.* That commission involved a suite of eight color lithographs and two small bronzes that paid tribute to the stature and tradition of harness horse-racing training in Aiken, South Carolina. As one might expect there was a dramatic, down-the-stretch, neck-and-neck composition, but the majority were poignant, behind-the-scenes glimpses of horse-care chores plus pre- and postrace training rituals, rather in the tradition of the great nineteenth-century French artist Edgar Degas (see chapter 7, "*The Aikenhead Collection*"). Before the work-visit ended, Saunders showed me some of his most recent prints, which were of beach houses in profile elevated high above sandy stretches of the South Carolina coast. All were treated as if loose watercolor paintings and ethereal in spirit. The title for that new series is *September Folly.*

We next met in Kansas City, Missouri, in March 2007 at yet another Southern Graphics Council Conference. Much of my time was consumed by trying to document conference panel and print demonstration sessions for the archives with a new digital camcorder. However, Boyd and I found time to discuss the book project especially in its various subject areas. All such discussions have been special opportunities and have usually gone deep into the night.

The pattern of August work sessions in South Carolina was interrupted in 2007 because of major renovations to the Saunderses' home and the removal of several towering pine trees following from severe drought conditions. However, my proposal to Boyd and Stephanie of a working trip to South Carolina, beginning the weekend before Thanksgiving, was warmly accepted, and they invited me to attend the Marion DuPont Scott Colonial Cup Steeplechase Races, Springdale Race Course, Camden, South Carolina, November 18. The Saunderses' numbered tailgating spot on the outside rail of the track put us close to both the full racing program as well as the paddock area, where under a brilliant azure sky Boyd and I photographed horses, jockeys, and handlers on their way to post time. Perhaps, just perhaps, there will be a Carolina Cup suite of prints in the artist's future.

While at the Saunderses' home, I spent two days and nights going through a footlocker and large boxes of biographical-, career-, and extracurricular activities–related data, which, however, made only a small dent in the materials yet to be sorted. Still that process has been made easier with the completion of a new 18 × 30 feet (c. 540 square feet) metal storage building twenty yards from the artist's home and studio. Since Saunders's retirement in 2001 many of his personal papers, inventories of prints, paper stocks, and much more have been stored in high-security commercial storage units at two different sites around Columbia, plus crowded into his studio. When the moves are completed, the new metal building will become fully organized and handy. Likewise the studio will no longer be cramped and once again be more of a joy in which to work. In 2007 I was awarded a sabbatical leave for spring semester 2008 to work on this project. It proved to be a terrific and productive experience.

There have been at least two more personal discoveries or realizations regarding the artist Boyd Saunders, and one is that he is a published author. In 1982 Boyd and Stephanie Saunders coauthored *The Etchings of James Fowler Cooper* published by the USC Press, Columbia, and in 1990 he and Ann McAden coauthored *Alfred Hutty and the Charleston Renaissance.* In what might be termed compassionate publishing, Saunders and his coauthors essentially rescued the art and careers of two South Carolina printmakers from an earlier era, saving their valuable work and histories for future generations and ensuring their respective places in the history of American printmaking (see chapter 11, "More Service to the Field: James Fowler Cooper and Alfred Hutty").

Most people of accomplishment tend to have specialties in one field, say chemistry, corporate finance, education, medicine, opera, real estate, architecture, and so on, and in the visual arts, one medium, usually painting. There are exceptions, and Boyd Saunders is one of those! The printmaking world, though usually marginalized by the mainstream art world, acknowledges Saunders as a master, but he is also a master of drawing and illustration, a fine watercolorist, a sculptor of small bronzes, and a competent painter in oils and acrylic.

Now add to those exceptional abilities the following gifts in other fields, which he often relates to his visual work. Saunders is an extremely good communicator orally and as a writer, gifts usually not possessed nor thought necessary to develop by visual artists. His presentation speeches annually honoring the Printmaker Emeritus Award recipients at the annual Southern Graphics Council Conferences have become legendary. He received more than one Outstanding Teacher of the Year Awards at USC-Columbia, and to top off his thirty-five-year career there, he was selected as the number one professor, that is, art educator, in the state of South Carolina in 2001. Not surprisingly he has been much loved by legions of his students over the years.

During my interviews with Saunders in 2005 and 2006, I realized he also possessed a natural gift for storytelling, sometimes humorous, mostly heartwarming (though not sentimental mush), intriguing, captivating, never cynical, and usually true from personal experiences. Thus in developing this book project, it seemed a shame to restrict it to an ordinary monograph focusing only on his printmaking and only in the standard chronological manner. Instead this artist needs to be showcased across the spectrum of his talents. As an aspiring art historian and art documenter I treasure an artist's intentions for his or her works. Thanks to a number of remarkable videotape interviews and lectures plus audiotape interviews involving the artist and his prints, paintings, illustrations, preparatory drawings, and sculptures, a significant body of privileged information exists. In academia such things are called primary sources, and they are usually rare. I call these golden sources. They belong in this book and are paired wherever possible with the artwork to which they refer. While they are special, they need not deprive viewers of their own interpretations. Consider that art history, by definition, addresses art of the past, usually a past distant enough to put an artist's work in perspective historically, stylistically, and so on. Yet speculation regarding intentionality is too often an academic game of proposing compelling theories, something necessary to some art historians but, in the end, often inadequate to get to the heart of an artist's purposes and thoughts. Intentionality is also not the silver bullet to art appreciation or understanding art, but it is, at the very least, a well-grounded starting point. Though one may enjoy or otherwise experience artwork without an artist's commentary, again I think a person may realize a more important beginning of a dialogue with the art, especially with an artist's thoughts in hand.

I believe a great many people will be significantly touched by looking at Boyd Saunders's artwork, by reading his commentaries about his own art and about the art of the printmakers whom he documented, and by his stories. However, the overall purpose of this publication is to document Saunders's productivity and accomplishments, to chronicle his varied interests, and to explore the mysterious realm known as the creative process. An artist's intentions, inspiration, experiences, experiments, and basic technical abilities in media may be major contributors to the final artwork, or they may represent only a vague beginning. Art viewers are often clueless regarding art-making processes, especially for printmaking, which can be quite complex. Thus to balance the artist's visual work and discussions, some information regarding techniques will be woven into at least a few discussions about Saunders's works.

There are at least two more talents to mention regarding Saunders, and the first is his talent as a singer. Having been taught to sing at an early age by his mother, he continued to cultivate that talent as an adult. Saunders auditioned in the early 1980s for a prestigious men's choral group, the Palmetto Mastersingers, based in Columbia, South Carolina, and he has been a member since then. These talented gentlemen have performed at Carnegie Hall and have toured the globe (see chapter 13, "Saunders and Music").

The other unexplored talent possessed by Saunders is that of intellectual curiosity. As with the Palmetto Mastersingers organization, Saunders was invited in 1984 to join the prestigious literary entity known as the Loblolly Society of Columbia, South Carolina. Members regularly research and present topical papers at monthly gatherings (see chapter 14, "Saunders and the Loblolly Society of Columbia, South Carolina").

It is hoped that the factors that have led to this book project and the time that it has taken to finish it do not sound academically insincere like the casually indiscrete tale of a movie decades ago titled *Same Time Next Year.* It is certainly not the case! Boyd and I are workaholics, though he works much smarter than I do. Only since about 2007 or later have we been able to think about a steadfast dedication to this project. Since then it has been a blessing to work on it. I hope it has been the same for Boyd, and we both hope the readers of this joint effort will find our efforts justified and stimulating.

Chapter 2

Boyd Saunders

Early Life

James Boyd Saunders was born June 12, 1937, on a farm in west Tennessee close to Rossville, a small town about thirty miles east of Memphis. By the time of his birth, the working farm of several hundred acres had been in the Saunderses' family for at least three generations, and it has influenced this artist in profound ways from early youth to the present. Boyd Saunders's father, Shirley Nebhut Saunders, began to operate the family farm after his father's death in 1941.

Boyd Saunders's mother, Maggie Irene Kee, was born in 1915 in Somerville, Tennessee, one of five children, but she lost her mother two years later during the birth of the youngest son, Herman. Her father, Luther Farris Kee, died during the influenza pandemic of 1918. After those tragic deaths the children were adopted by family members and reared in the Somerville area. Saunders's mother, called Irene, was adopted by two great aunts, Mollie and Victoria Boyd, both unmarried, and Clay Boyd, her bachelor uncle. Irene Kee was not a troubled or unruly child, nor too much to handle; she was just the opposite. Boyd Saunders much later recalled, "These three unclaimed blessings were all over 60 years when this little girl came into their lives. What an awakening it must have been. They adored her and she was very happy with them."[1]

The Boyds lived in a large Victorian home in Somerville, the administrative seat of Fayette County. Miss Victoria Boyd was a school teacher in that community, and the Boyds owned a dry-goods store plus other properties all on the town square.

At an early age, Irene Kee's mature or self-driven tendencies allowed her to skip two grade levels in school, advance quickly through piano instruction, be drafted as a pianist for the local Methodist church, and even acquire piano students by age sixteen. Then Irene's high school principal encouraged her to seek training in Memphis for group music direction, which led to her offering music instruction at the Somerville High School. Such early interest and preparation in music served her well as she later became the organist for the Rossville Methodist Church for life. She also served as organist at St. Andrews Episcopal Church in Collierville, Tennessee, for many years and was a member of the Memphis Chapter of the American Guild of Organists. Additionally she was appointed pianist for summer revival meetings at Danceyville, Tennessee, taught music to thousands of students through private lessons, and still found time to instruct all her children in music.[2]

About 1935 or early 1936, Irene Kee met her future husband, Shirley Nebhut Saunders, a farmer about ten years her senior, at a Methodist church youth fellowship activity. They were married by October 1936 and began life together on the Saunderses' family farm close to Rossville, which is about twenty-five miles south of Somerville and a considerably smaller town. Within a year Mrs. Irene Saunders became the mother of James Boyd Saunders, the first of four children, all boys. The brothers and the years of their birth are: Clay 1939, Lanny 1941, and Lee 1947.

Although there were farm workers (some just seasonal) at the Saunderses' farm, a family farm tends to mean the talents of the entire family are put to work, and this was especially so during the 1940s and 1950s. Thus in addition to the daily routine of chores and tasks, Irene Saunders prepared large meals for the field hands and, when needed, drove a tractor.[3] While farming primarily field crops is seasonal, farming field crops plus livestock (especially dairy herds) or beef cattle, swine, horses, mules, flocks of chickens, and so on tends to own one 24/7. Animal lives and land cultivation investments are dependent on human dedication, adequate financing, the weather, and luck. Vacations are rare, and one's own preferred schedule and biological clock are forced to the rhythms of field crops and creatures with four legs. There is also no guarantee that a family farm will turn a profit, but it's unlikely that a farm family will starve, not even during the Great Depression, during which Boyd Saunders was born and still small when it waned.

Young Saunders was probably not oblivious to the international economic Depression or to personal deprivation, but he fondly remembers his early years of farm life. "I had three younger brothers and parents and chickens and pigs, horses, mules and woods and fields and dogs and cats. But most of all I had Pap-paw! My grandfather [Shirley House Saunders, who was called Mr. Big Shirley by the farm workers] had been widowed shortly before I was born, and he lavished his gentleness and love upon me, and I adored him. Summer days I dogged his steps around that farm and on winter evenings I sat on his lap near the fireplace while we made popcorn and he read to me. It doesn't get any better than that!"[4]

Young Saunders also had a close boyhood friendship with Philip, another farm boy who lived a few

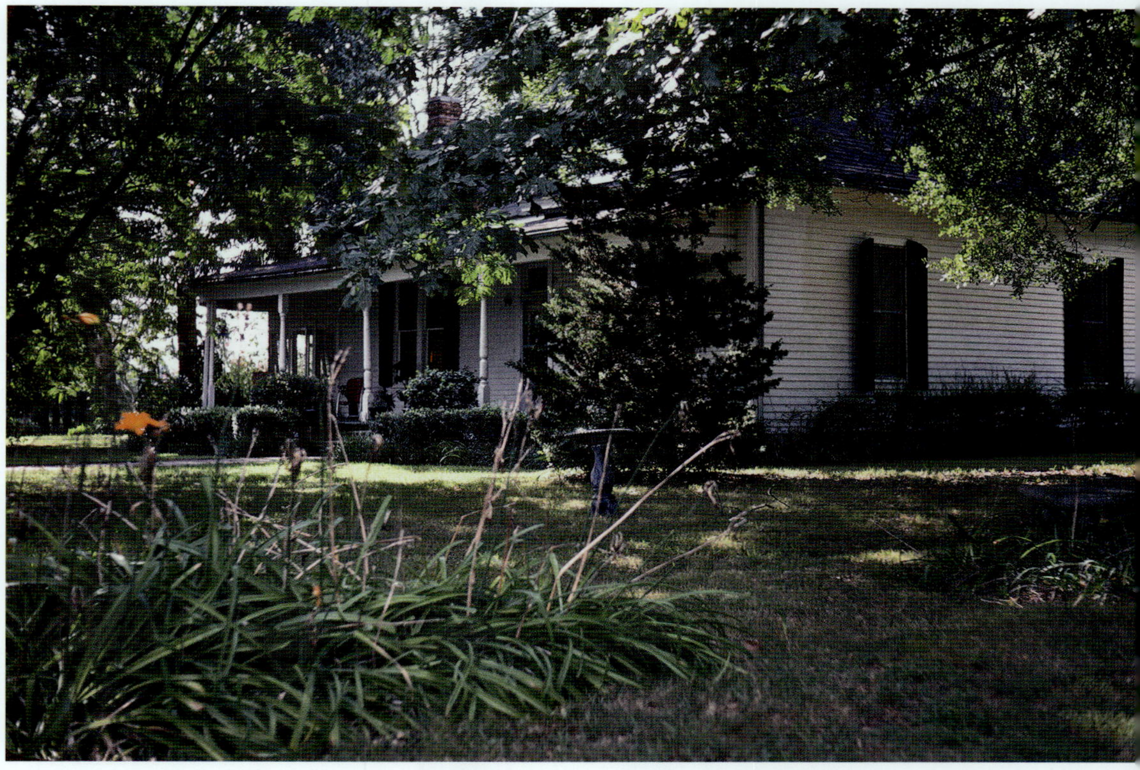

Old Saunders Homestead, Near Rossville, Tennessee

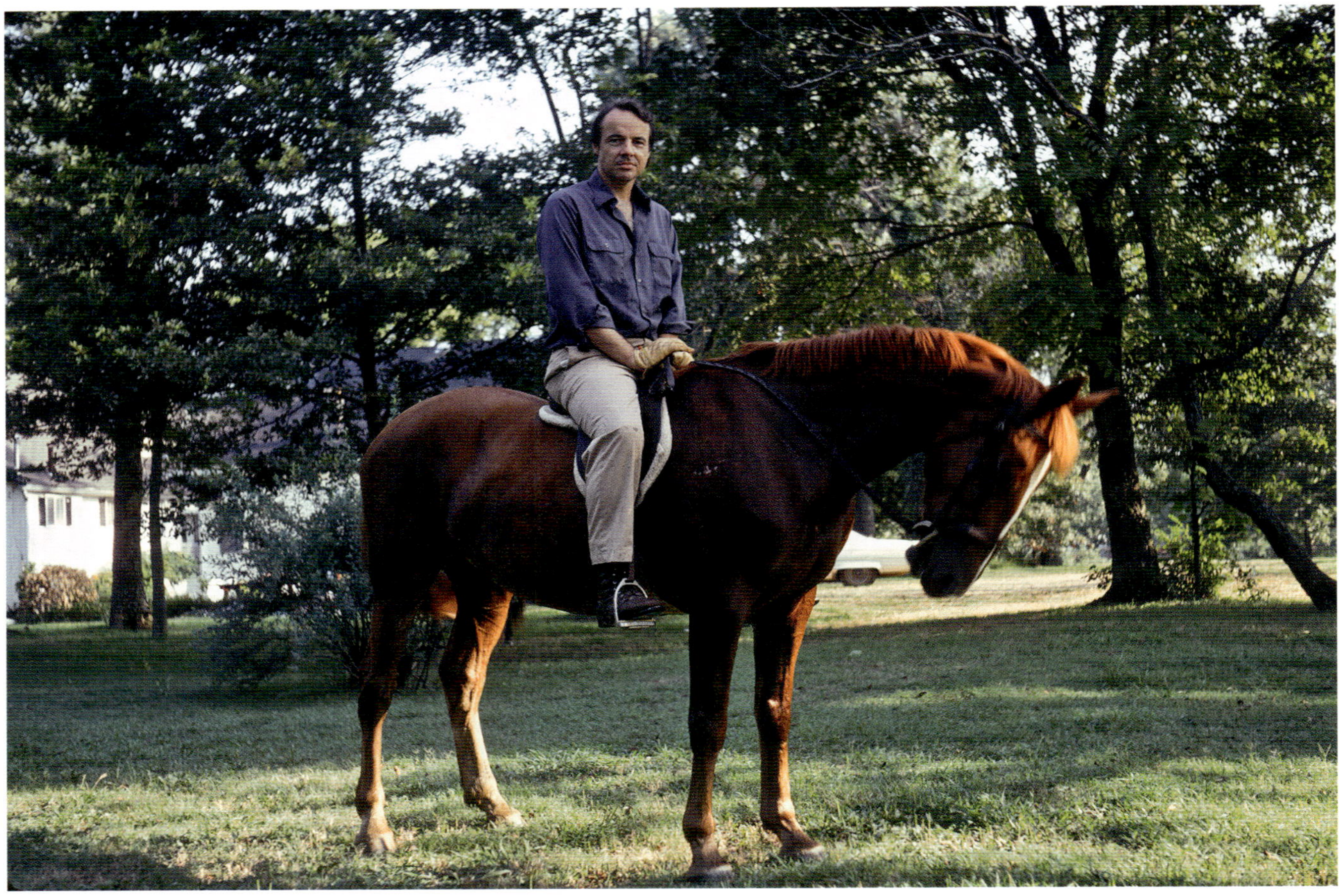

Saunders aboard Charlie

miles away, and their play usually involved horses and reenacting Civil War battles or western stories by popular writers of that genre.

Said Saunders, "On special weekends I rode my horse Charlie, the half-dozen or so miles to his house on the other side of town, or he would ride his horse, Allen, to my house to visit, perhaps to sleep over. Sometimes our brothers and relatives or friends would join us and, mounted on every horse or mule available, (sometimes two to a mount) we would play out great epic battles that would range over a vast acreage of woods and fields and last all afternoon. The fields and woods around our farmhouse regularly yielded up Civil War bullets and a host of weapons and other artifacts from that great struggle. Indeed, every part of that land seemed saturated with ghosts and memories of all that had gone on before."[5]

Such idyllic play marked special weekends; otherwise young Saunders worked in the fields and at all other tasks and chores appropriate for a farmer's son. However, a remarkable relationship developed between Saunders as a boy and the horse named Charlie.

> [Saunders] Companion, solace and tormentor of my youth, that big sorrel gelding and I covered more miles together that I could ever hope to recount. More than just a mount, he was an institution in my life.
>
> I had learned early in my adolescence that I no more owned him than he owned me. He never gave up waiting and watching for that supreme moment when he could, with one swift blow, kick my brains all over an acre of ground; and I never gave up trying to prove to him and myself that he couldn't bring it off, that we were going to do things my way or not at all.
>
> Through it all, though, there developed a very real bond of affection which manifested itself many times but most noticeably when he had broken both back legs in a cattle gap and was lying there on the ground thrashing about in pain and the

highway patrolman had his gun out to shoot him and I was standing there between him and the horse with the axe I had used to chop the cattle gap apart to get his legs out and I had announced to any who cared to hear, that the horse would not be shot! And he wasn't. I got him home, somehow, and nursed him for a year. He was never quite the same again but we came out of that bout with an accommodation and understanding which had never existed before.[6]

Saunders, as a boy, already possessed an active imagination, which thrived on his farm, with its woods, meadows, pastures and fields, horses, and the discoveries that environment yielded. Yet his interests were also stimulated by stories read to him, and from stories he read at a surprisingly early age, from which he developed a love for illustrated books.

> [Saunders] I was read to by everybody; father, mother, and occasionally visiting relatives. This was, of course, in the days before television and computer games. By the time I started school, I was doing a pretty good job of teaching myself to read. Once I was in school I read rather easily and soon read beyond my grade level. My parents and relatives, impressed with my reading ability, often gave me books as presents on special occasions which I read avidly.
>
> There was a lady in town [Rossville] who was the sister of one of my teachers. She had been a teacher herself before a car accident broke her back and paralyzed her. Then she had a stay-at-home job as county librarian. Her job consisted of ordering and cataloguing the library books for all the schools in the county. Knowing of my love for books she gave me the opportunity of borrowing and reading books during the summers before they were sent out to the schools. Once a week I rode Charlie to her house, stuffed my saddlebags with books, then took them home and read them. I liked the ones with pictures the best! Sometimes she asked me to write short reports of my favorites, which then were published in the local weekly paper.[7]

Saunders's friend Philip shared many of his playful interests, but reading was difficult for him perhaps owing to dyslexia. Young Saunders felt compelled to share the stories with Philip, so he read to him. Many of those stories were westerns written by Zane Grey and Will James, and Saunders was immediately affected by their illustrations. The stories were then sometimes acted out by the boys or used as starting points for their own tales. The countryside proved to be the best venue for their innocent theater. Continuing it in the classroom or at recess got the boys in trouble and ostracized.

> [Saunders] At school we got around on make-believe horses, which caused us to have a rather particular loping gait and convinced everyone that we were just a mite peculiar. In class we spent many hours making drawings of the epic battles and tales we imagined and acted out. Those drawings, which we secretly worked on instead of arithmetic workbooks, were passed back and forth (secretly you understand) erased and re-drawn and improved until the pulp notebook paper they were drawn on was virtually disintegrated. Few of the drawings survived because usually they were discovered, confiscated and we were held up to ridicule and made to stay in at recess thus reinforcing our social isolation.[8]

By his own admission Saunders related that he sorely lacked social skills and was rewarded for his schoolyard and classroom antics through about the seventh grade by being tormented, mocked, and shunned by the town kids. His response, for better or worse, was to retreat into a comfortable imaginary world of strong men and impressive horses directed by him and his close friend Philip.

The tangible stage for Saunders's comfortable world was usually his family's farm, especially its topography. An identification with that specific landscape became a bond that increased with his age and distance from it. In a taped interview of the artist at the McKissick Museum at the University of South Carolina–Columbia in 2001, Saunders reminisced about his affinity for the farmland of his youth and specific landmarks:

> Several years ago my brothers, Clay, Lanny, Lee, and I were back there [the family homestead] and started talking about developing some of the

> property. We talked about it and drank a little whiskey and talked about it some more. Eventually we decided to go together in a van through the fields and over to a particular hillside vantage point, where we got out of the van and visually surveyed the area.
>
> We stood out there; waved our arms about like we knew what we were talking about . . . we'll have a road coming down here. No, let's do such and such and so on. After a while it got dark out there and we were [by then] talking about a road that should come by a gum tree [sweet gum]. I said brothers, do you realize that it has gotten dark and nobody can see the gum tree? We all then realized that we were pointing to a gum tree because it had been there all of our lives. We had plowed around it. We had rested beneath it. We had hung our water in the gum tree and what have you. That [gum tree] became a symbol for me of an affinity for the land. I've been away from that [land] for a long time but it is still very much a part of me.[9]

Another important factor in the development of this artist's body of work was his attraction to woodcut or wood-engraved images primarily in books and his affinity to drawing. As a precocious reader, Saunders soon developed a respect and fondness for certain illustrators including the nineteenth-century American political cartoonist-illustrator Thomas Nast and several others.

In the later 1950s Saunders essentially began his formal higher education in art when he entered Memphis State University (University of Memphis) to major in painting and graphic design. While at MSU he also served as editorial cartoonist for the student newspaper the *Tiger Rag.* In addition he was much sought after as a designer of posters for various political and social causes. He graduated from MSU with a bachelor of science degree in 1959 and then began graduate school studies in art at the University of Alabama–Tuscaloosa. While there Saunders met a young coed named Stephanie Stedman from St. Petersburg, Florida, who was pursuing an undergraduate degree in art with an emphasis in graphic design and painting. Before long Saunders and Miss Stedman began seeing each other, and a friendship bloomed.

Unexpectedly, sometime during Saunders's first year of graduate school in Tuscaloosa, he left and returned home to reassess his goals and options. Then Saunders ventured to Oxford, Mississippi, whereupon he applied to, was accepted to, and restarted graduate school in art at the University of Mississippi (affectionately known as Ole Miss) concentrating in painting and printmaking. During the early part of Saunders's school experience in Oxford, Miss Stedman remained in Tuscaloosa, where she worked as a graphic artist. However, the separation was likely too uncomfortable for them, and after a time, Miss Stedman moved to Oxford, where she worked toward teacher certification at Ole Miss. Gradually the Saunders-Stedman friendship became a committed relationship.

Saunders completed a master of fine arts degree in visual art, specifically painting and printmaking in the spring of 1962 and soon the mid-South would no longer be his home.

The following stories told by Saunders are true; the first two are derived from his childhood. The last one has been passed down through his family.

A STALLION NAMED DAN

On the farm where I grew up we bred livestock, mainly horses. We also had a stud and three jacks. We did not have a bull standing at stud. We just bought cattle, fattened them, and sold them.

The horse in question was a big black stallion named Dan, and he was all that a black stallion is, which is fiery and temperamental and strong . . . almost unmanageable. I was a child at the time, and my father had strict instructions that we children were not to mess with the stud horse. We had other horses. I had Charlie but . . . the horse Dan . . . I was not to be around except in the most limited fashion. Dan had a long, long, curly mane and tail, and when he was in his stall at night he would toss his head and fret and worry and stew so that by morning his mane would frequently plat itself into sort of pigtails and dreadlocks, not tight, but certainly there. The African

American hired hands on the place were convinced that the Devil had platted the horse's mane and tail and were very reluctant to go into the barn at night, which had its benefits and its liabilities.

There was also a hired hand who was with my family for a long time by the name of Bo or Bodick as they liked to call him. He was idiosyncratic and would say to my father, especially in wintertime: "How bout I take old Dan out for a little exercise this afternoon or Sunday afternoon?" My father would say, "Sure, he needs the exercise." So Bo would saddle up old Dan, and on rare occasions I might go with him riding my horse, Charlie. Bo and I would talk about many things as we rode through the back country together . . . but he would ride [ahead]. He was in charge. He was a grown man, and I was a boy, and we would ride from sharecropper house to sharecropper house in the backcountry there and tie up to them and socialize.

Bo would ride into the yards. Sometimes he would get down off the horse, sometimes he would just sit in the saddle, and the family would come out, and they would visit around for a while. The tenants might bring him a little refreshment or a snack or something and they'd chat about the weather and the crops. After a while they might bring out a child or an infant with the croup or a cold, and they would hold their infant or child up in front of Dan, in front of his nose . . . and Dan, being the fiery stallion that he was, would arch his neck and reach his nose out and loudly sniff the little child. Then they'd say thank you, press money into Bo's hands, and then take their child back inside. We would say goodbye and ride away.

I asked Bo, "What was that all about?" "Well," said Bo, "the stud horse, he got the power." I said, "What power is that?" Bo said, "He got the power. He suck that sickness out of the child. When he go snuffing around like that, he snuffing the sickness out of the child."

What Bo was doing was making house calls, medical house calls, and they were paying for it. So we went from house to house with people availing themselves of the healing powers of that stud horse to suck the sickness out. I thought it was amazing! Bo thought it was very profitable. He did very well with it.

THE SAUNDERSES' JACKS OF ROSSVILLE

We had on our farm three jacks standing at stud. A jack is a kind of donkey, an ass that is used for breeding purposes. A mule is a hybrid. It is the product of a cross between an ass and a horse. A mule cannot reproduce itself. It is completely sterile, and so it must be the product of this cross. Now you've seen burros perhaps. A jack is a lot like them but usually long legged, tall, and unusual looking with a tiny waist, a large head, and a short tail.

People would bring their mares to be bred by our jacks. We had jacks of different configurations, different varieties depending on what you wanted. Anyway those jacks existed on our farm for one reason. They did not pull plows or wagons; they were lovers. They knew that when a strange horse came in that barnyard, it was party time. They would sing *hon-ee-hon-ee-hon-ee-hon,* and they had huge voices. When one of them sang, you could hear it a quarter of a mile away, and when all three of them sang, they could be heard in Rossville, a mile away. I'm not joking.

I was a little boy at the time, and in the summertime we had as many as ten men working horses and mules in the fields, before we had tractors. My job was to ring a large iron bell many times exactly at noon, which told the fieldworkers to stop work, double up the reins of their horses and mules, and come to the barn and house area to eat lunch.

At exactly one o'clock my duty was to go in the yard and hit that bell just once or twice, which meant to go back into the fields. But when I rang that bell, especially at noon, the jacks at the barn knew that there was going to be livestock coming into the barnyard. So the minute they heard that bell, they'd start singing *hon-ee-hon-ee-hon.* After a while the people of Rossville got so used to hearing the mules singing at noon, they would set their watches by it. Saturdays and Sundays when the bell didn't ring, the jacks still knew somehow when it was exactly noon, and they'd start singing. Some towns have a church whose bell rings at noon, or a weather siren or a fire siren, which is sounded at noon. Rossville, Tennessee, had the Saunderses' Farm Jacks.

THE SAUNDERSES' RED MULE

I am told I was named after my great-grandfather James Lee Saunders. (My first name is actually James, but only the government and health providers and people who want to aggravate me use it.) Family lore has it that he was a mere boy of maybe thirteen or fourteen when he decided to join the Confederate Army to fight in the American Civil War.

It seems that marauding bands of Yankees had repeatedly plundered the farm and killed or run off most of the livestock when young James took matters in hand. He threw some gear and provender in a sack, climbed aboard the only mount left, which was a tall red mule whose name has been lost to history, and rode off to join General Nathan Bedford Forrest and his Confederate cavalry. James had hand-raised the mule from a colt, spent many hours plowing the fields with him, and now they were off together to help fight in the war. In truth the red mule was as much a pet as it was a beast of burden. The Confederate cavalrymen usually supplied their own horses. If a man had a horse and could ride it, he was likely to wind up in cavalry. If not he was destined for the infantry. Their weapons and gear were also quite haphazard; some self-supplied, some provided by the CSA government. The Union Armies, on the other hand, were equipped completely by the federal government.

General Nathan Bedford Forrest's cavalry was extremely irregular but notoriously effective; however a mule did not seem to be an appropriate mount for a proper cavalier, certainly not in the southern chivalric tradition. As soon as possible, young James Saunders appropriated a Yankee cavalry horse whose previous owner had been shot off him in battle, and loaded his gear onto the red mule, who happily followed close behind without the need of a lead tether.

The arrangement would prevail until James was unhorsed in battle; then he would transfer back to the mule until he could liberate another horse. And so this switching back and forth continued throughout the war. He equipped himself for battle in much the same manner. Training was strictly on-the-job.

With General Forrest as his tour guide, young James saw much of western Tennessee and Kentucky as well as the northern regions of Mississippi and Alabama, engaging in unfriendly encounters at such places as Brice's Crossroads, Tupelo, Memphis, Nashville, and Murfreesboro. He was fighting with a cavalry saber at the time in his life when he was still too young to grow a decent beard or moustache.

About dusk one winter day, Saunders was crossing the Tennessee River with his horse of the moment swimming under him, the sounds of the gunfire of the most recent unpleasantness popping away on the embankment behind them, when the horse under him began to falter and go down, perhaps from a gunshot wound. As he was about to be enveloped by the flood-swollen river, he heard a splashing over his shoulder and turned to see the red mule swimming along behind him. At the last moment Saunders left his dying horse and climbed back onto the swimming mule, who carried him to safety on the far bank.

When the war ended a few months later, a much older and wiser James Lee Saunders came riding back to the home place on the same red mule on which he had departed a seeming lifetime ago.

James Lee Saunders lived a long and fruitful life and is buried among his kinfolk in Pleasant Grove Presbyterian Church Cemetery near Hays Crossing, Tennessee.

The story of the rest of the mule's life can be whatever one wants it to be.

Chapter 3

Saunders's Early Career

Bosque Territory and *The Canyon Wall Suite*

BOSQUE TERRITORY

By the summer of 1962, Saunders had secured a teaching position at Southwest Texas State College in San Marcos, located about halfway between Austin to the north and San Antonio to the south. In Saunders's words: "I wound up with a teaching job at Southwest Texas State College in San Marcos. So, we married that August [1962], piled our things into the car and headed for Texas."[1]

Despite a daunting teaching load, typical at the instructor rank, young Saunders nevertheless was open to opportunities outside of teaching. Thus as if by providence Saunders's illustrational skills were called on relatively soon for an engaging project involving Dr. William C. Pool. Saunders described him as "a delightfully eccentric historian at the college."[2] Dr. Pool had just been commissioned by the Bosque County, Texas, Historical Society to research and write a manuscript-length history of the Bosque Territory, of which Bosque County became a part. Intending illustrations for his history subject, Dr. Pool invited Saunders to collaborate with him on the project by producing drawings. Saunders accepted and began to prepare for the task, but it wasn't by rushing to Texas museums to study art of the Old West. Saunders's nature was then and continues to be as follows: to learn as much as possible about any subject to be illustrated before the first sketch or drawing sees the light of day. He has faithfully followed a humble, straightforward approach that includes, but is not restricted to, respectful background reading, site visits, and documentary photography, with paramount importance given to the study of the land. He believes that he must get an accurate feel for the land or for a place and the effects the land has made on humans who have settled on it as well as the impact of humans on the land. For reading preparation Saunders studied landmark works such as *The Great Plains* (1931) and later *The Great Frontier* by Walter Prescott Webb. He also read works by the author James Frank Dobie, described by Saunders as "an inspiring Texana writer whose book, *The Longhorns* [with illustrations by Tom Lea], was profoundly influential in helping me better understand Texas culture."[3] Saunders's practice of study before drawing rather neatly mirrored Dr. Pool's approach to studying history subjects before writing about them. Pool's methodology can be found in the prologue of his book *Bosque Territory:*

> The historical method used in this study was brought to the University of Texas about the year 1910 by Professor Lindley Miller Keasbey. One of Keasbey's students during the years prior to the first World War was Walter Prescott Webb, who remembered that "it was Keasbey who gave me an understanding for an appreciation of the relationship between an environment and the civilization resting upon it; it was Keasbey who taught me and many others, to begin with geology or geography, and build upon this foundation and the superstructure of the flora, fauna, and anthropology arriving at the last at the modern civilization growing out of this foundation. . . . Dr. Webb, in turn, passed the Keasbey formula on to several generations of students of history at the University of Texas, including the author [William C. Pool]. Hence we begin with this prologue—concerned with the land itself as it was and is—before we turn to a history of the men and women of European heritage who came ultimately to occupy this land and make it fruitful.[4]

A sampling of sections in the book *Bosque Territory* includes "Natural Borderland," "Trailblazers," "Frontiersmen," "Settlers," "Civil War and Reconstruction," "Towns and Communities," and the "Farmer-Stockman's Frontier."[5]

In the nineteenth century the Bosque Territory encompassed a vast stretch of land in north central Texas between the eastern woodlands and the dry grasslands of the high plains of West Texas. The Bosque Territory contained grass prairies and significant river valley systems, especially the Bosque and the Brazos. Within that territory Bosque County was developed in the mid-nineteenth century, and, despite being over nine hundred square miles or about 580,000 acres in size, it was still easily engulfed by the rest of Bosque Territory.

Soon Saunders accompanied Texas historian Bill Pool, as he liked to be called, on weekend trips into Bosque County for the purpose of interviews with local amateur historians and other members of historical societies, with collectors of Texana, with genealogists, and with various local fascinating characters. Those trips yielded small treasure troves of information. Saunders was surprised at the ethnic diversity he encountered on such trips and was equally surprised that in the early 1950s, towns were populated by descendants of Norwegians, Slavs, Frenchmen, Germans, and others, many of whom still spoke their inherited languages as their first language and, at best, spoke English with a heavy foreign accent.

Perceptive and ever eager for adventure and discovery, Saunders immersed himself in the study of the various types of transplanted European settlers who were to fill the chapters of *Bosque Territory,* and when he was suitably prepared, the drawing stage began. One of the first illustrations in the book is of a surveying crew moving through rough terrain in animated fashion, led by a mounted rider yelling back something to the rest of the small party. Behind him, at some remove, a tarp-covered equipment wagon, pulled by a pair of horses, is carefully guided down a steep-graded slope by a veteran driver. The equipment likely included a Jacob staff, a box compass, peep sights, a set of surveying chains, axes, maps, and books for field notes: simple tools routinely used to survey the Bosque Territory for grantees existing by the 1830s. Following the equipment wagon are two men on horseback with at least three pack mules in tow.

A large, engaging illustration of a frontiersman-settler also appears early on in the *Bosque Territory* book. A smaller version of that illustration can be found in chapter 3, "The Settlers," with the name James Buckner Barry (1821–1906) beside the image. The drawing is not meant to be a factual portrait of the colorful Barry. More likely it is a tribute to him and many other settlers who contributed significantly to the defense and development of the Bosque Territory.

James Buckner Barry moved to Bosque County, Texas, and established a farm on the East Bosque River in 1856. He had previously served with the Texas Rangers in 1845 and 1846 and later served in the Texas legislature from 1884 to 1886. Excerpts from a spirited profile of Barry by an unrecorded contemporary follow:

> "He [Barry] was of medium height. His carriage was erect, dignified, and indicated energy while his manner harmonized with his militant decisive bearing. He had dark, long curling hair which he allowed to grow long and fall on his shoulders. His eyes were dark and piercing and his features were firm and regular. After most Texans had forsaken buckskin, Barry chose to wear it. He could never tolerate theft, or cowardice, or attacks on the weak, and he believed in upholding the law, even in the absence of law. Being one of the oldest setters, [he] was called on many times by newcomers whose horses had been stolen. Those who knew him declared him to be fearless."[6]

By the late 1850s, the Bosque Territory witnessed the beginnings of stock raising, primarily cattle. South and west Texas became known for the massive herds of range-fed beef. Nevertheless small herds of cattle became an important factor in the frontier economy of the Bosque Territory. Furthermore, in spite of being far from markets, the cattle industry in this region benefited from the presence of the Chisholm Trail, one of the most important cattle trails of the entire Southwest. Entries in the tax records of Bosque County alone show 3,991 cattle in 1856; 5,725 in 1857; and 14,280 by the spring of 1861, suggesting budding prospects for cattlemen.[7] However, few, if any, enterprises in a frontier region were without hardships, and cattle drives were often fraught with enough danger and futility to test the mettle of the best drivers. A startling illustration by Saunders accompanies the chapter "The Farmer and Stockman's Frontier" and presents a frantic attempt by trail drivers to turn frantic cattle into a circular pattern. Maybe this dramatic illustration was inspired by the heartbreaking account of two cattlemen from Iowa who came to Texas in 1866 to buy a herd of longhorns, which they intended to drive north all the way back to Iowa. Portions of the diary entries of George C. Duffield based just on the days May 1 through May 18 in 1866 might also dispel some of the popular, romantic nostalgia of a cowboy's life on cattle drives. Diary entries are reproduced here exactly in the form as that in historian

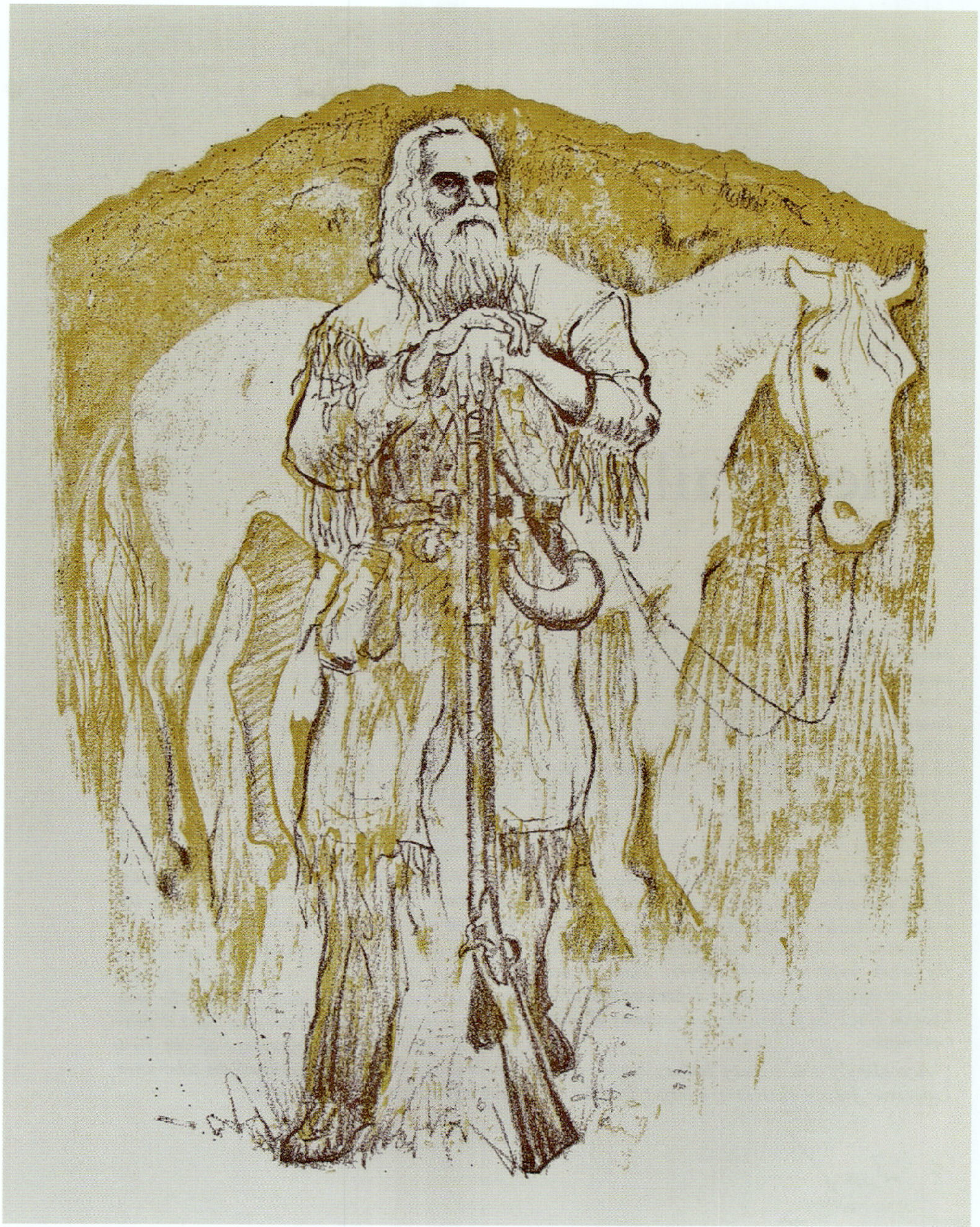

James Buckner Barry, 1964, lithograph, 12 × 9 in.

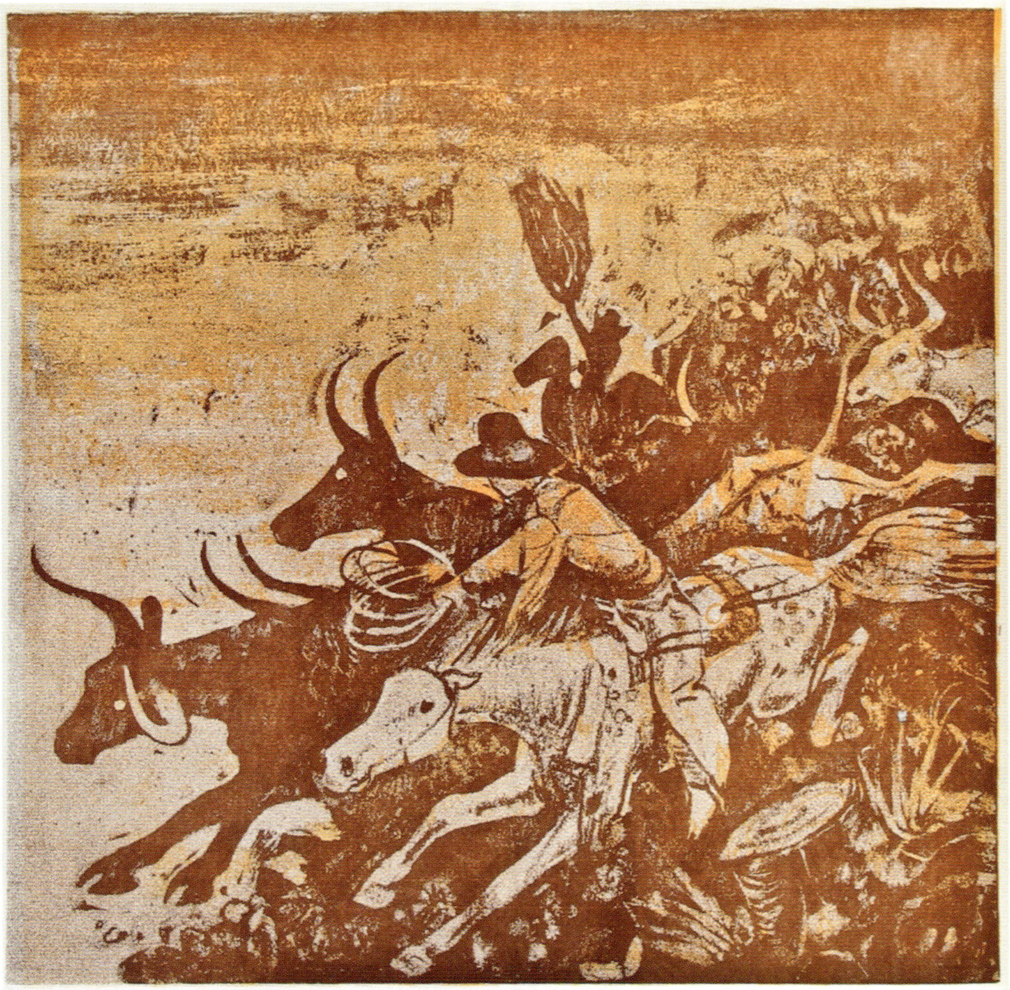

Pool's book. Readers of Duffield's notes will likely be frustrated by a lack of commas, semicolons, and items like odd spacing, misspelled words, and missing words. However consider that Duffield likely recorded much of his data during undesirable circumstances, which may have dictated his brevity. Duffield's entries begin as the herd neared the Bosque Territory headed generally northeast:

> *May 1st* Travelled 10 miles to Corryell County Big stamped lost 200 head of cattle
> *2nd* Spent the day hunting and found 25 head it has been raining for three days. The days are dark for me
> *3rd* Day spent hunting cattle found 23 hard rain and wind lots trouble
> *4th* Continued the hunt found 40 head day pleasant sun shone once more heard that other herd has stampeded and lost 200
> *5th* Cloudy damp morning rode 16 miles and back to see the other boys found them in trouble with cattle scattered over the country
> *6th* Started once more my journey left Cow Houses River and got to Leon crossed and

The Stampede, 1964, lithograph, 12 × 9 in.

Glancing Backward from Mid-century, 1964, lithograph, 12 × 9 in.

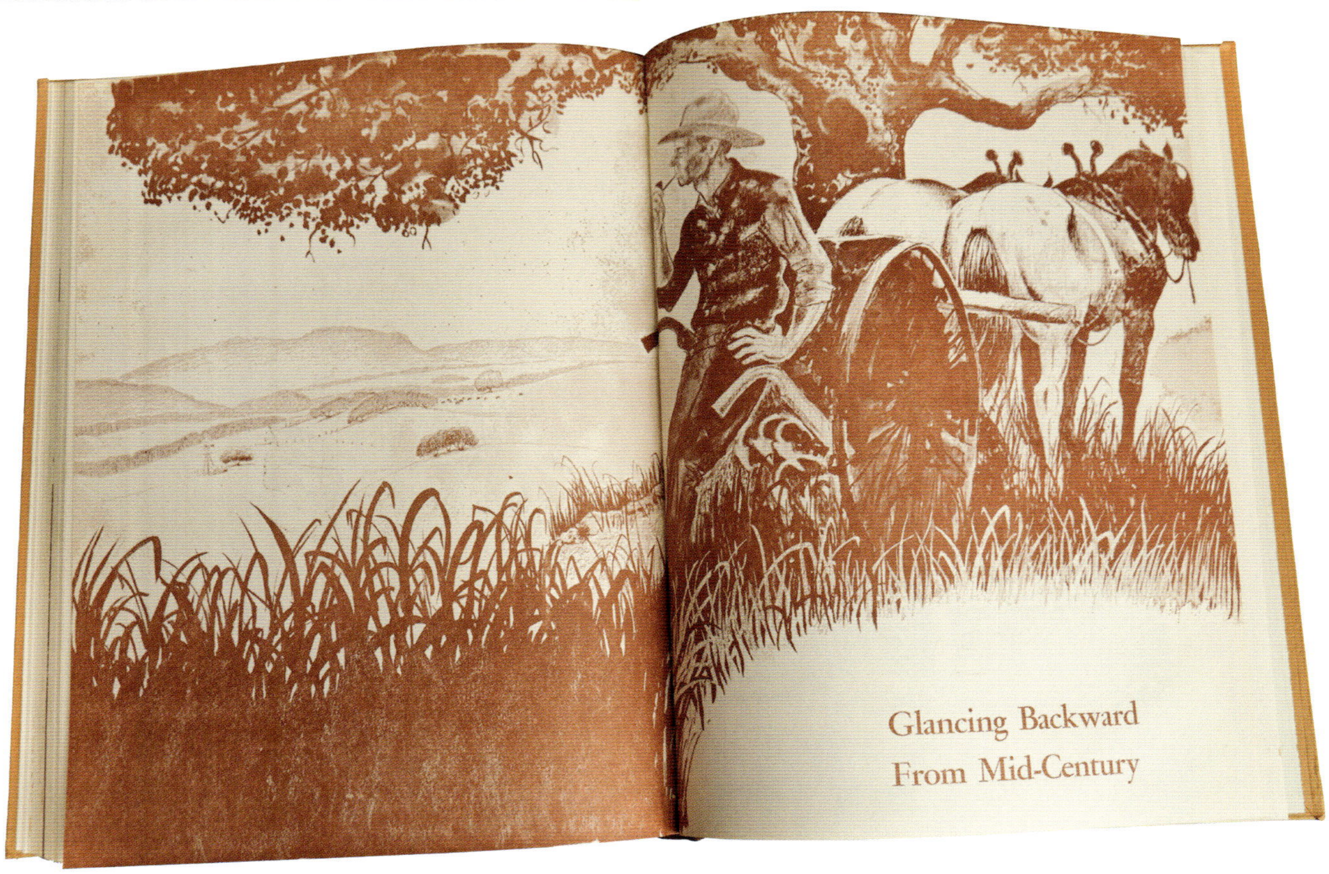

camped prairie 5 miles north of river dark and gloomy night hard rain stampeded and lost 200 head of cattle (Milt's Heard)
7th Hunt cattle is the order of the day—found most of our cattle and drove 12 miles and camped on the large creek in Bosque Co.
8th all three herds are up and ready to travel off together for the first time travelled 6 miles rain pouring down in torrents and here we are on the banks of a creek with a 10 or 12 ft. water and raising crossed at 4 o'clock and crossed into the Bosque
Bottom found it 20ft deep Ran my horse into a ditch and got my knee badly sparained—15 miles
9th Still dark and gloomy River up everything looks blue to me no crossing today cattle behave well
12th lay around camp visited Brazos River and went bathing
13th Big thunder storm last night stamped lost 100 beeves hunted all day found 50 all tired everything discouraging
14th Concluded to cross Brazos swam our cattle and horses and built Rafts and rafted our provisions and blankets and swam river with rope and then hauled wagon over lost most of our kitchen furniture such as kittles coffee pots cups plates canteens
15th Back at River bringing up wagon hunting oxen and other lost property rain poured down for one hour it does nothing but rain got all our traps together that was not lost and thought we were ready for off dark rainy night cattle all left us and in morning not one Beef to be seen
16th Hunt beeves is the word-all hands discouraged and are determined to go 200 beeves out and nothing to eat
17th No breakfast is the word and off is the order all hand gave the Brazos one good dam and started for Buchanan travelled 10 miles and camped found 50 beeves (nothing to eat)
18th Everything gloomy four best hands left us got to Buchanon at noon and to Rock Creek in Johnston Co[8]

The last major illustration in the book spreads across two pages accompanying the concluding chapter, titled "Glancing Backward from Mid-century" (mid-twentieth century). The title is apropos since the imagery is of a farmer, pipe raised to his mouth, who leans against the back of a cultivator hitched to a team of horses. The farmer gazes outward and down across an impressive spread of rolling pastures, grazing cattle, fence rows, and occasional farm buildings.

During Saunders's preparatory drawings that illustrated professor William (Bill) Pool's book *Bosque Territory* in 1964, he had, as stated earlier, accompanied Dr. Pool on several treks through that part of Texas geography. The artist has been marked by, and his art has been shaped by, the landscape and the imprints mankind has left on the land, from the artist's agrarian west Tennessee youth to the South Carolina beach houses of the *September Folly* series in the twenty-first century. The Bosque Territory lies mainly north of San Marcos, Texas, where Saunders lived and taught, but traveling around that big section of the state whetted the artist's curiosity about what might lay to the west of San Marcos. Of this Saunders wrote, "When we lived on the edge of the Texas Hill Country, I discovered the Blanco River Canyon. Those canyon walls provided me with an endless supply of surprises and inspiration. One of the richest discoveries was a shallow cave washed into the wall of the canyon at a bend in the Blanco River. Inside I discovered a fire pit. Closer examination also revealed some curious petroglyphs which I thought may have been made by local kids. However, when I showed photographs of this find to an archaeologist from the University of Texas, he confirmed that this was most likely a Comanche Indian Hunting cave and the fire pit and drawings were probably about 1,000 years old."[9]

One direct result of Saunders's exploration of the Blanco River Canyon in south central Texas was the creation of a suite of etchings. The suite reflects the artist's joyful personal discovery of a cave likely occupied by dwellers long ago, who on more than one occasion left evidence of their presence in a visual form on the interior walls of caves. Man-made marks on walls of many different kinds have fascinated Saunders throughout his long career, be they twentieth-century ads painted across the entire sides of buildings or railroad cars, the white chalk scribbling of children on the exteriors of humble abodes, posters of all sorts, and especially signs with lettering.

Readers of this book will discover that, despite the wide range of the artist's media and subjects, many works carry references to printed language as information and imagery of the commercial world. Having stated that inclusion, such imagery and printed letter forms may not be intended in the literal sense; rather their inclusion may be for compositional reasons. Certainly Saunders's affinity for letter and number images, as well as pictorial advertisements, put him in good company with Picasso, Braque, Schwitters, Carra, Stuart Davis, Sheeler, Demuth, Johns, Rauschenberg, Warhol, Lichtenstein, Estes, and the Guerrilla Girls, to mention a few. However, Saunders's infatuation with a visual commercial vocabulary has a much purer raison d'être.

He began in graphic design, which by its nature is flat, just like the surfaces on which Saunders makes etchings, lithographs, paintings, pastel drawings, and drawings in other media, watercolor paintings, and so on; hence design and composition are nearly synonymous for him.

One of the key prints inspired by Saunders's experiences in the Blanco River Canyon carries a somewhat unassuming title *The Canyon Wall* yet possesses potent imagery. The composition is the result of two separate cut or shaped etching plates, which were inked in several colors, aligned in a centrist composition on a press bed, and printed at the same time. Saunders remembers it thus:

> *The Canyon Wall* was intended as homage to the arid Southwestern United States. Somewhere during the evolution of its concept it changed into a commentary on the transience of mortality. The source was the Blanco River Canyon in central Texas. Through the centuries the river had cut through many layers of rock and sediment. At the same time, the people and creatures that had passed through the canyon, or had come and stayed, had left their own marks, each unique and symbolically significant. The goats, once domesticated, but escaped and once again wild, moving in single file along the sheer precipice with the ease of shadows and the regality of monarchs, suggested the ceremonial procession of deified animals along the frieze of an ancient Roman temple, the Ara Pacis, perhaps. The imagery, then, unfolds from top to bottom like the slow unearthing of layers of an archaeological dig, culminating in the unmistakable symbolism of the human skull to which a mud dauber wasp has irreverently claimed squatter's rights as a fitting place to build its nest and hatch its young. The prevailing mood of the piece is an echo of the poet Shelley's "Ozymandias."[10]

> I met a traveller from an antique land,
> Who said—"Two vast and trunkless legs of stone
> Stand in the desert. Near them, on the sand,
> Half sunk a shattered visage lies, whose frown,
> And wrinkled lip and sneer of cold command,
> Tell that its sculptor well those passions read
> Which yet survive, stamped on these lifeless
> things,
> The hand that mocked them, and the heart
> that fed.
> And on the pedestal, these words appear:
> 'My name is Ozymandias, King of Kings:
> Look on my works, ye mighty, and despair!'
> Nothing beside remains. Round the decay
> Of that colossal wreck, boundless and bare,
> The lone and level sands stretch far away."[11]

Percy Bysshe Shelley's poem of 1819 reminds one that as self-aggrandizement—whether by deeds or physical monuments—may pass away and be forgotten, so too may the person. Saunders has included a human skull in *The Canyon Wall* as a visual parallel to the poem as well as to past human and animal occupants of the river-made canyon on their inevitable mortality. However, the human skull has a considerable history in the art of Western civilization. It was especially popular in western Europe during the baroque period (late 1500s through the 1600s). It contributed to themes or subthemes called memento mori (reminders of death) and were frequently used by Dutch still-life painters in *vanitas* paintings, which balanced images of fine, worldly, goods with reminders of life's transience, something especially stressed by Calvinist morality. Historically speaking, variations of memento mori images may be found as early as 1424–27 in the well-known example of Masaccio's *Holy Trinity* fresco in a chapel of the Basilica of Santa Maria Novella, Florence, Italy. Below the primary imagery, that is, in a predella, the artist painted a

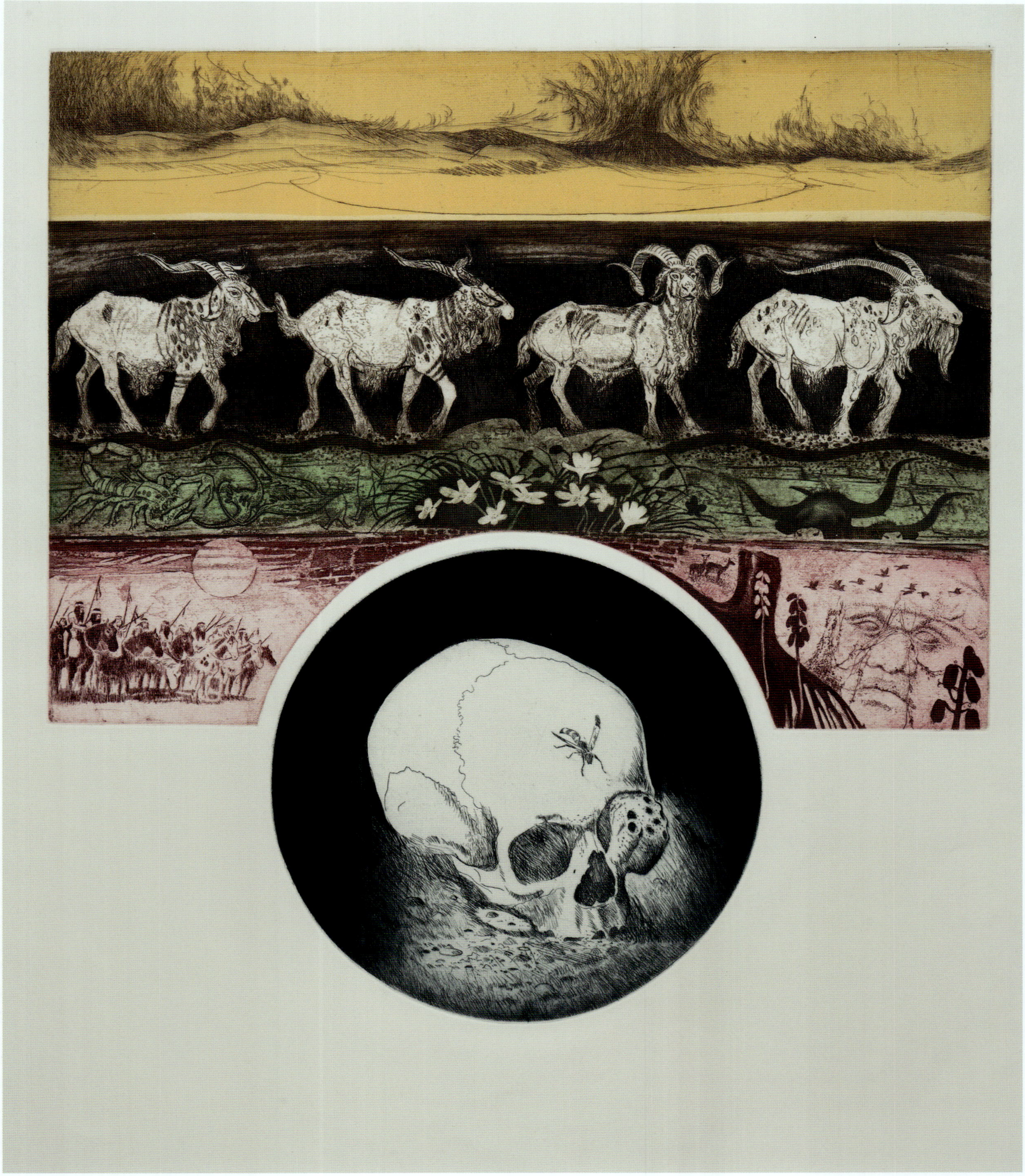

The Canyon Wall, etching with shaped plates, 30 × 28 in.

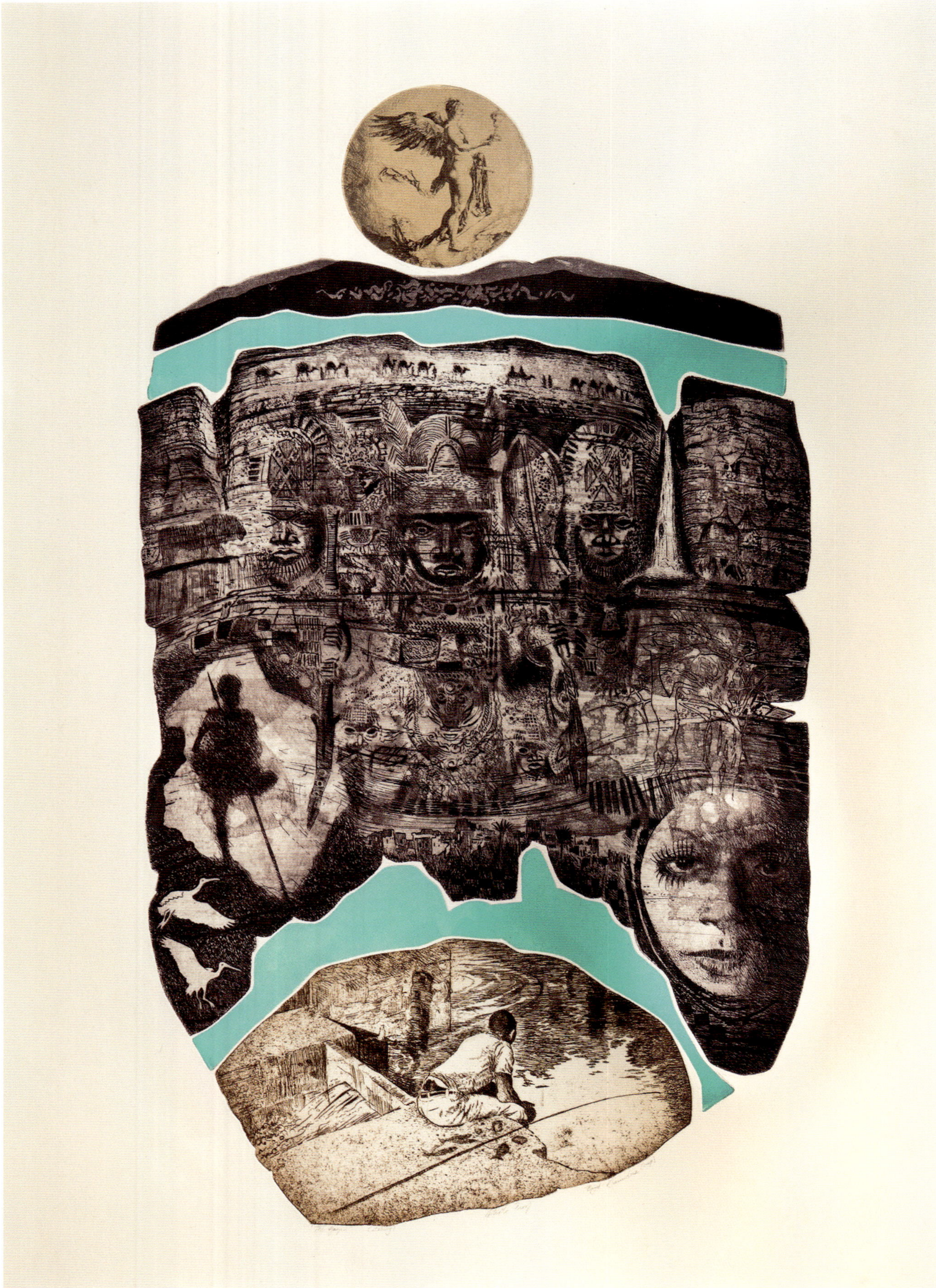

The Gorge, etching with shaped plates, 7¼ × 5 in.

tomb and reclining human skeleton with the sobering inscription "I once was what you are, and what I am you will become."[12]

Another especially remarkable print motivated by the idea of river-made canyons is *The Gorge.* Like *The Canyon Wall* this etching was conceived as a multiplate composition with six separate sections. The shaped plates or segments were inked separately, again as in *The Canyon Wall* (though one segment was inked in several colors by layers), then reassembled and printed altogether in one pass through press rollers. In addition to the colored inks, many areas, read as dark masses as opposed to lines, represent the presence of aquatint. Those visual properties mirror the dense, even surfaces of oil paintings and mezzotint prints. Although the general idea of a canyon wall in *The Gorge* is consistent with other etchings of the series, there are major differences. In this print the canyon wall refers to the Olduvai Gorge in northern Tanzania, Africa (about 150 miles west of Mount Kilimanjaro), where anthropologist Dr. Louis Leakey discovered types of extinct anthropoid apes or paranthropuses. The basic structure of *The Gorge* presents layers of images scratched into the face of geological strata.

> [Saunders] It has historical implications and treats the wall as if it were an archaeological cut through layers of history unfolding as the successive levels. The Central portion is populated with images from the ancient Ibo civilization of central Africa [Negroid tribes of Nigeria]. They achieved a high level of power and sophistication as is reflected in the pride of three kings whose images were taken from certain Benin bronze sculptures [Benin was once a native kingdom of western Africa, later a province of Nigeria].
>
> In the bottom segment a contemporary black fisherman whiles away a spring afternoon at the locks. As the water trickles past him he is mentally or metaphysically transported back over the centuries to another time and place. Or perhaps the three Ibo kings in their glory are able to look into the future and see him at that particular time and place. And Nemesis rides on through the heavens.
>
> The figure in the circle at the top is derived directly from Albrecht Dürer's "Nemesis," a character out of Greek mythology who floats about in the heavens reversing the order of things; elevating the lowly and humbling the mighty.[13]

Nemesis was the goddess of retributive justice or vengeance in ancient Greek mythology. Dürer's corpulent avenger may have been intended as a nightmarish apparition or specter and a universal force with which to be reckoned. Print historian Linda Hults has provided a succinct description of Nemesis's nature that seems to parallel Saunders's inclusion of that character in *The Gorge.* "She looks straight ahead, dispassionately dispensing rewards, represented by the cup, and retribution (or temperance), signified by the bridle."[14]

Boyd Saunders's *Canyon Wall Suite* built on his enthusiasm for the visual and historical character of land as shown in the *Bosque Territory* book project. It adds the human imprint to cave and cliff walls from the basic human need or urge to affirm one's existence and celebrate the hunt, battles, gods, and so on by available skills and materials. This phenomenon has been embraced by Saunders throughout his long, productive career, and it contributes mightily and at times subtly, along with his consistent approach to works in suites, as pictures within pictures and as visual poetry. Images and metaphors change with individual titled works, but his predilection is consistently faithful to discovering new ways of exploring visual poetry.

Chapter 4

Saunders and Faulkner

"The Bear," *The Sound and the Fury,* and "Spotted Horses"

Saunders began seeking a master of fine arts degree in visual art–printmaking at the University of Mississippi in the early 1960s. One winter day the inveterate sketcher and drawer was exploring Bailey's Woods, a secluded area of twenty-nine acres bordering the southeast corner of the Oxford campus. A chance meeting occurred between Saunders, the young graduate student, and William Faulkner, the internationally acclaimed writer whose stately home, Rowan Oak, rests quietly at the southeastern edge of the same woods. The initial meeting between the visual artist and the literary figure was awkward yet led to a fruitful collaboration. As Saunders related, "I was wandering around one day with my sketchbook, as I frequently did in Lafayette County, and I encountered a rather shabbily dressed farmer [I presumed] back there in the woods. We stopped, passed the time of day, then sat on a log and chatted a little while, and just passed pleasantries about one thing and another. After a while, it was time to leave, and at that time we proceeded to introduce ourselves. He allowed how he was William Faulkner. Well, I was kind of blown away because I didn't know who it was. After he told me who he was, I had to tell him who I was. I might have said Hemingway or something like that.

I went on my way but after a time I started haunting those woods again. I ran into him several more times and struck up something of an acquaintance with him. We did not become fast friends or anything like that, but we did have an acquaintance."[1]

Saunders's new friendship produced forthright statements and a determination to learn more about the noted author's work. "I have to confess I had not known his work that well before, but he was from Oxford, Mississippi, which is where the University of Mississippi is, and I was there, so I began reading him voraciously. He's a hard read but I found I identified very much with him and with what he was doing. We grew up in the same part of the country, and I related an awful lot with his imagery."[2]

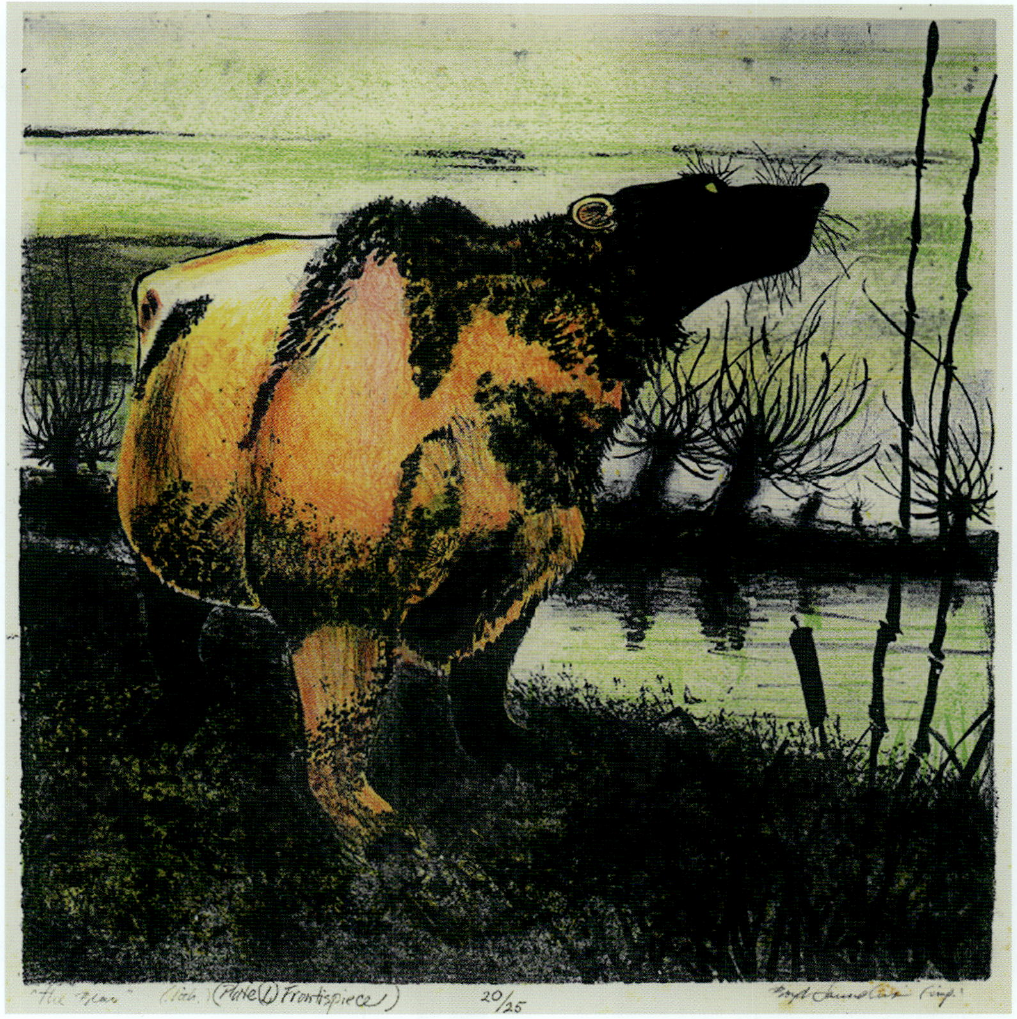

The Bear (plate 1, frontispiece), 1962, lithograph, 15 × 12 in.

"THE BEAR"

In time the graduate student and the celebrated author decided to collaborate on the production of a limited edition version of "The Bear," a short story with original lithographs by Saunders inserted as illustrations with handset type on handmade paper with leather binding. Saunders had read several but not yet all of Faulkner's short stories and novels by the project's startup, but "The Bear" was clearly his favorite at the time. Saunders said, "*The Bear* was one of his great novellas. It was an exciting project and I set forth to work on it."[3]

Sadly, collaborative input from Faulkner ceased before the publication could be completed owing to his untimely death in July 1962. Unwilling to walk away from the project, Saunders finished and printed the eight lithographs in the Art Department printmaking studio of the University of Mississippi. He then grouped them into portfolios titled: *William Faulkner's "The Bear": A Portfolio of Narrative Lithograph Prints.* This project became the centerpiece of Saunders's M.F.A. thesis exhibit, and at an appropriate time Saunders began to sell the portfolios, mainly to Faulkner collectors.

Saunders's eight lithographs included three color and five black-and-white images. What follows is Saunders's interpretive summary of and commentary about the bear hunt in Faulkner's short story.

[Saunders] This was an epic bear hunt, a sort of legendary, ritualistic bear hunt in which a group of hunters went to the woods every year to hunt, and while they shot many things, it was basically a particular bear that they were after. They may have shot deer and things like that, but "the bear" was a big old rogue bear that had been around longer than anybody could remember. He'd gotten huge, he'd outlived all of his progeny and somehow he seemed to be indestructible. This tale was sort of a Moby Dick on land, if you will, but instead of the great white whale, we have this great bear that everybody was after.

Of course, the bear took on mythic and symbolic proportions. One of the things he symbolized for Faulkner was the wilderness idea or

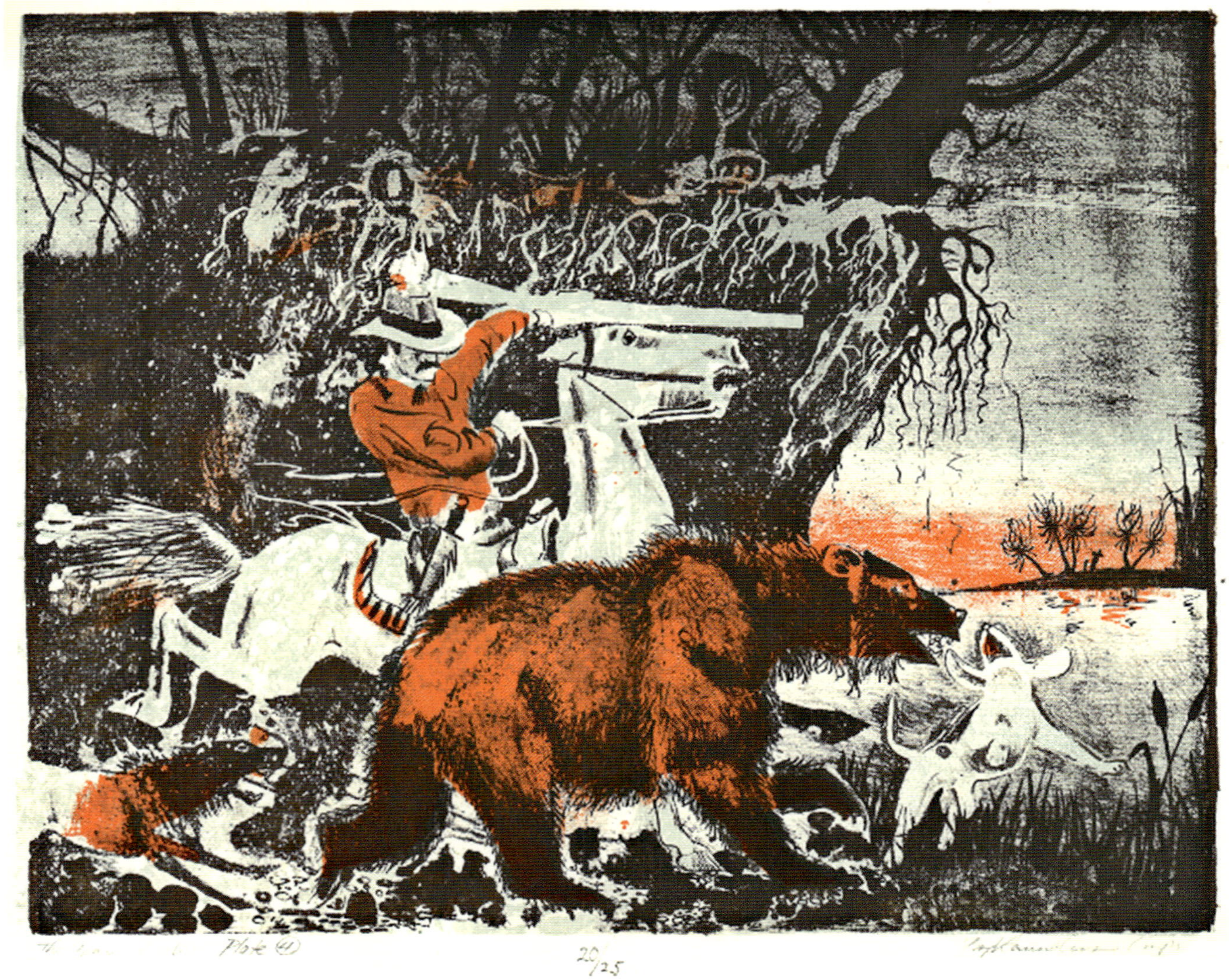

The Chase, plate 4, lithograph, 1962

wildness, a sort of primeval or primordial wildness which these petty and flawed humans chased endlessly and tried to destroy. Ultimately, in the story, they realize that the only way they can bring it to bay is with something special because he tore up their dogs, he tore up everything. Many times they jumped him but he tore up their dogs and got away!

[Saunders] Well, they decided to try to catch a wild dog, and finally managed to do so, a big vicious dog which would be able to stand against the bear. Then they half trained it so that they could chase the bear with him. Finally, there was this cataclysmic battle and the bear was killed and the big, wild dog was killed and old Sam Fathers, who seemed to have spent his life chasing that bear, went over to one side of the bear and laid down and died. He was not injured in the fight or anything; he just seemed to run out of a reason to live now that the bear was gone.[4]

While Saunders was working on *"The Bear"* portfolio lithographs, he ventured around Lafayette County often with sketchbook in tow to try to get a feeling for the lay of the land where a lot of those stories took place. In time Saunders gained a reputation for finding possible Faulkner story settings and occasionally guided Faulkner scholars and devotees to them. Through his contact with such experts, he expanded his knowledge regarding Faulkner in general, but more specifically in the concepts of land, locations, and so on. The friendship and collaboration with

William Faulkner, however brief, in 1961–62 as well as contacts with Faulkner scholars, ardent fans, and collectors of *"The Bear"* portfolio have collectively been regarded by Saunders as a determining juncture in his development. Saunders said, "I enjoyed getting to see Mr. Faulkner's work, getting to know much about him and then I fell in love with his work; a love affair that has been with me from that time forth. Over the years I've come back to Faulkner themes again and again."[5]

Some years later Saunders read William Faulkner's Nobel Prize acceptance speech and was so affected by its power and intensity he decided to produce a bold black-and-white lithograph portrait side by side with the equally bold restatement of the author's acceptance speech. Both works were infused with starkness and an abruptness appropriate to Faulkner's vital message.

Saunders said of this, "I consider this acceptance speech to be one of the great landmarks in the English language, one of the most powerful and affirming pieces I've ever read. I treated this piece [large lithograph portrait and acceptance speech] as if it were the Rosetta Stone which was uncovered in Egypt [1799] . . . and I like the visual texture of the piece so I treated this texture in much the same way, jamming it together here rather tightly to make a body of text."[6]

Saunders's personalized lithograph replication of William Faulkner's Nobel Prize acceptance speech delivered in Stockholm, Sweden, December 10, 1950, is arresting visually, but its tightly packed aesthetic can make reading the address challenging. Therefore Faulkner's lauded remarks are reproduced below the paired images.

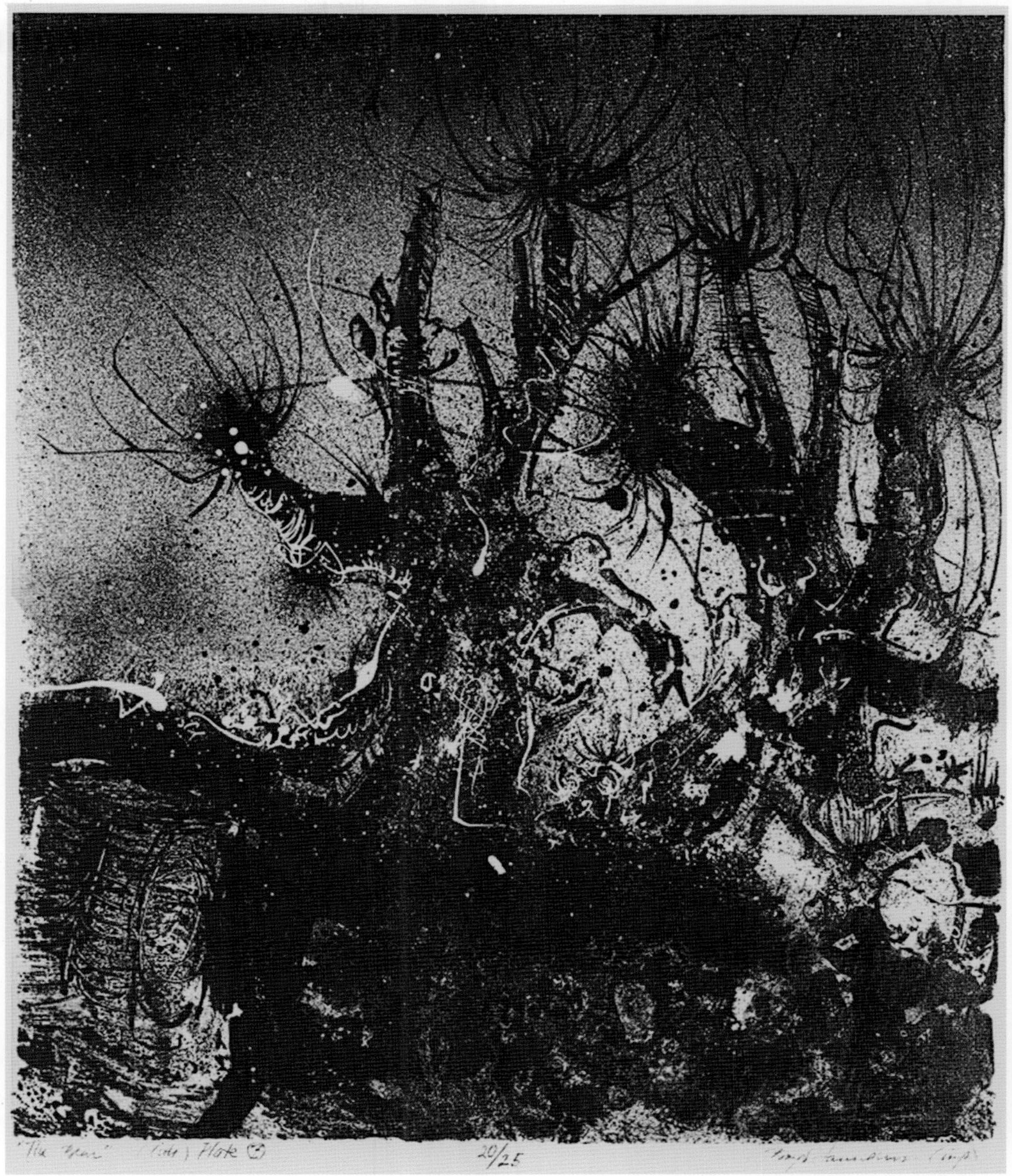

Landscape, plate 7, 1962, lithograph

William Faulkner's Acceptance Speech for the Nobel Prize in Literature, December 10, 1950

I feel that this award was not made to me as a man, but to my work—a life's work in the agony and sweat of the human spirit, not for glory and least of all for profit, but to create out of the materials of the human spirit something which did not exist before. So this award is only mine in trust. It will not be difficult to find a dedication for the money part of it commensurate with the purpose and significance of its origin. But I would like to do the same with the acclaim too, by using this moment as a pinnacle from which I might be listened to by the young men and women already dedicated to the same anguish and travail, among whom is already that one who will some day stand here where I am standing.

Our tragedy today is a general and universal physical fear so long sustained by now that we can even bear it. There are no longer problems of the spirit. There is only the question: When will I be blown up? Because of this, the young man or woman writing today has forgotten the problems of the human heart in conflict with itself which alone can make good writing because only that is worth writing about, worth the agony and the sweat.

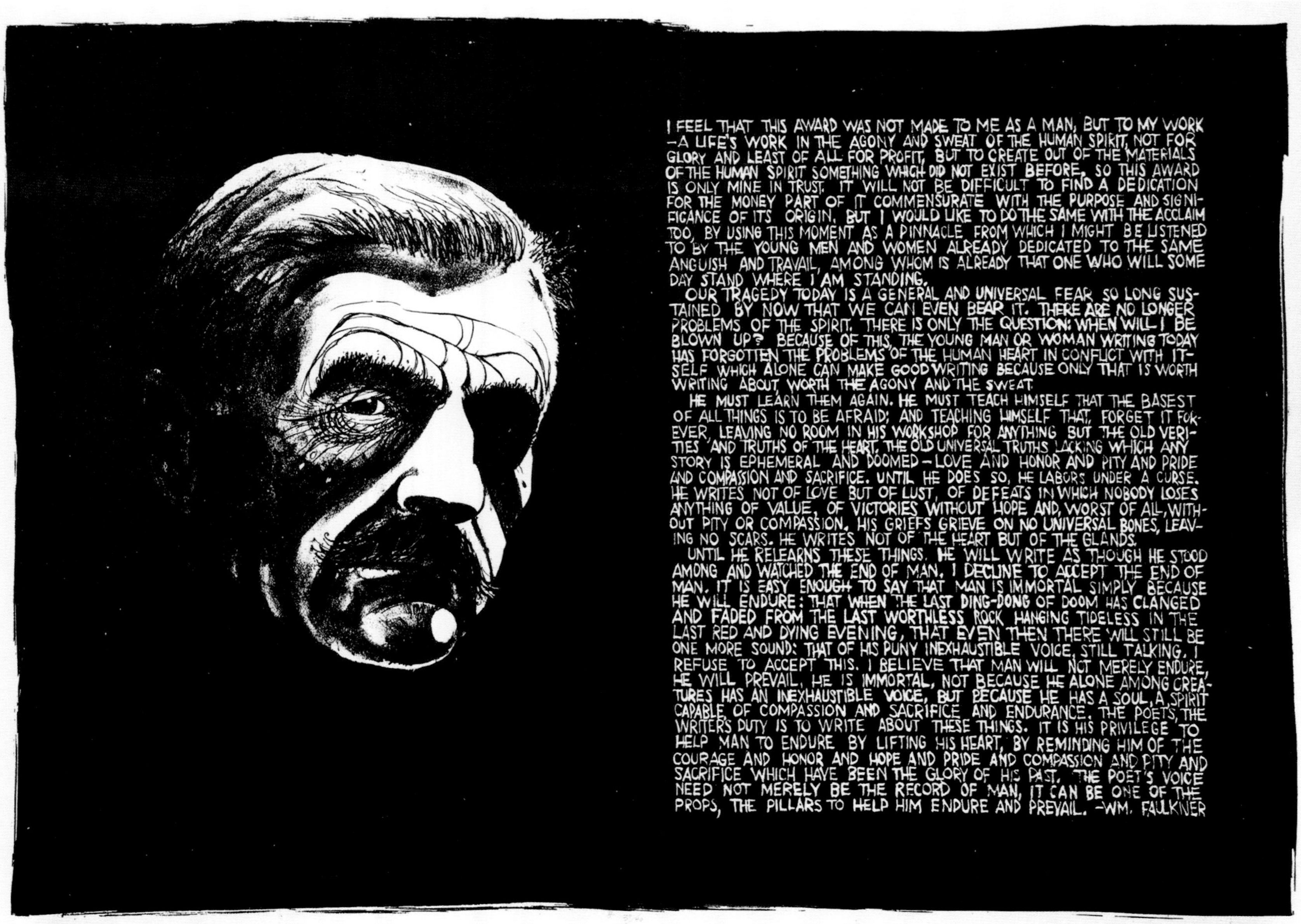

William Faulkner's Acceptance Speech for the Nobel Prize, December 10, 1950

He must learn them again. He must teach himself that the basest of all things is to be afraid; and, teaching himself that, forget it forever, leaving no room in his workshop for anything but the old verities and truths of the heart, the old universal truths lacking which any story is ephemeral and doomed—love and honor and pity and pride and compassion and sacrifice. Until he does so, he labors under a curse. He writes not of love but of lust, of defeats in which nobody loses anything of value, of victories without hope and, worst of all, without pity or compassion. His griefs grieve on no universal bones, leaving no scars. He writes not of the heart but of the glands.

Until he relearns these things, he will write as though he stood among and watched the end of man. I decline to accept the end of man. It is easy enough to say that man is immortal simply because he will endure: that when the last ding-dong of doom has clanged and faded from the last worthless rock hanging tideless in the last red and dying evening, that even then there will still be one more sound: that of his puny inexhaustible voice, still talking. I refuse to accept this. I believe that man will not merely endure: he will prevail. He is immortal, not because he alone among creatures has an inexhaustible voice, but because he has a soul, a spirit capable of compassion and

> sacrifice and endurance. The poet's, the writer's duty is to write about these things. It is his privilege to help man endure by lifting his heart, by reminding him of the courage and honor and hope and pride and compassion and pity and sacrifice which have been the glory of his past. The poet's voice need not merely be the record of man, it can be one of the props, the pillars to help him endure and prevail.[7]

Saunders said, "The wonderful thing about it [Faulkner's speech] is that it is as timely today as it was more than a half a century ago and I find the words to be as powerful and as meaningful as they were then."[8]

THE SOUND AND THE FURY

Saunders felt compelled to pay tribute to William Faulkner in awe of his Nobel Prize acceptance speech, but he was often confounded by the challenge of perceptively understanding the character profiles of the protagonists that he was developing as a suite of eight etchings for the writer's novel *The Sound and the Fury* of 1929.

According to literary experts of fiction, this novel has the dual distinction of being one of Faulkner's best efforts while simultaneously being one of his most difficult works to comprehend. Saunders said of it, "It's a very strange piece of writing. It is a very hard read. If you have ever read this novel, perhaps you can sympathize when I say that I found the 'stream of consciousness' or mental ramblings of the idiot Benjy to be very baffling. And he wasn't much more confused or confusing than the other, supposedly normal, members of the Compson family. I read and re-read the work. It took me several times through to begin to grasp what the story was about. I read critical essays by American and French scholars; hell, I even studied Cliff Notes. Finally, it began to come together and make sense. I must confess that I was maybe more concerned about myself when it DID make sense than I had been when it DIDN'T."[9]

The Sound and the Fury centers around an invented family, the Compsons, in the imaginary town of Jefferson, Mississippi, in the late 1920s. Apparently in some time past the Compson family had been of considerable means thanks to an ancestor from Scotland who built a fortune as a planter in the countryside that surrounded Jefferson.

The present senior generation of the Compsons and most of the Compsons' offspring live in an imposing home but in much reduced circumstances. That predicament grates on Mr. Compson's wife, Caroline, referred to as Mama. She is unstable, contributing little if anything to the family's well-being, yet is class conscious and demanding of others. Mr. Jason R. L. Compson III, the patriarchal head of the family, leads a dissolute life as an alcoholic and is only of minor importance in the story. For example his graveside service, interpreted by Saunders in one of his eight etchings, is included mostly because of the presence of other family members and their actions.

The title of Faulkner's novel *The Sound and the Fury* was borrowed from William Shakespeare's play *Macbeth.* Macbeth's lament upon hearing that his wife has died contains the following outcry regarding life itself. "Life is a tale told by an idiot, full of sound and fury, signifying nothing."[10] Macbeth's raging frustration is somewhat parallel to the raging, incomprehensible, utterances of Faulkner's mentally handicapped and confused character Benjy, who is author of the first of four sections of the work.

As mentioned above by Saunders, *The Sound and the Fury* contains some of the newly evolved stream-of-consciousness writing as character musings. In the service of that new trend, flashbacks of the recent, distant, or half-forgotten past are stirred into the mix to the point that a rational sense of linear time for the reader is often AWOL (absent without leave).

In the years 2002–4, Saunders set about creating a suite of eight black-and-white etchings (each 7 × 5½ inches, and printed on d'Arches or Copperplate Deluxe paper) as responses to the main characters and events in *The Sound and the Fury.* He especially addressed the characters' mental states, irrational perceptions, malice, instability, varied destructive and self-destructive actions related to and apparently reflecting a collective familial degeneration. Much of such malice, longing, guilt, partially remembered past events, disinformation, unnecessary actions, and predatory behavior is vented by the three Compson sons as monologues offered in turn by Benjy, Quentin, and Jason. Their monologues became potent springboards for Saunders's visual responses. Additionally, while

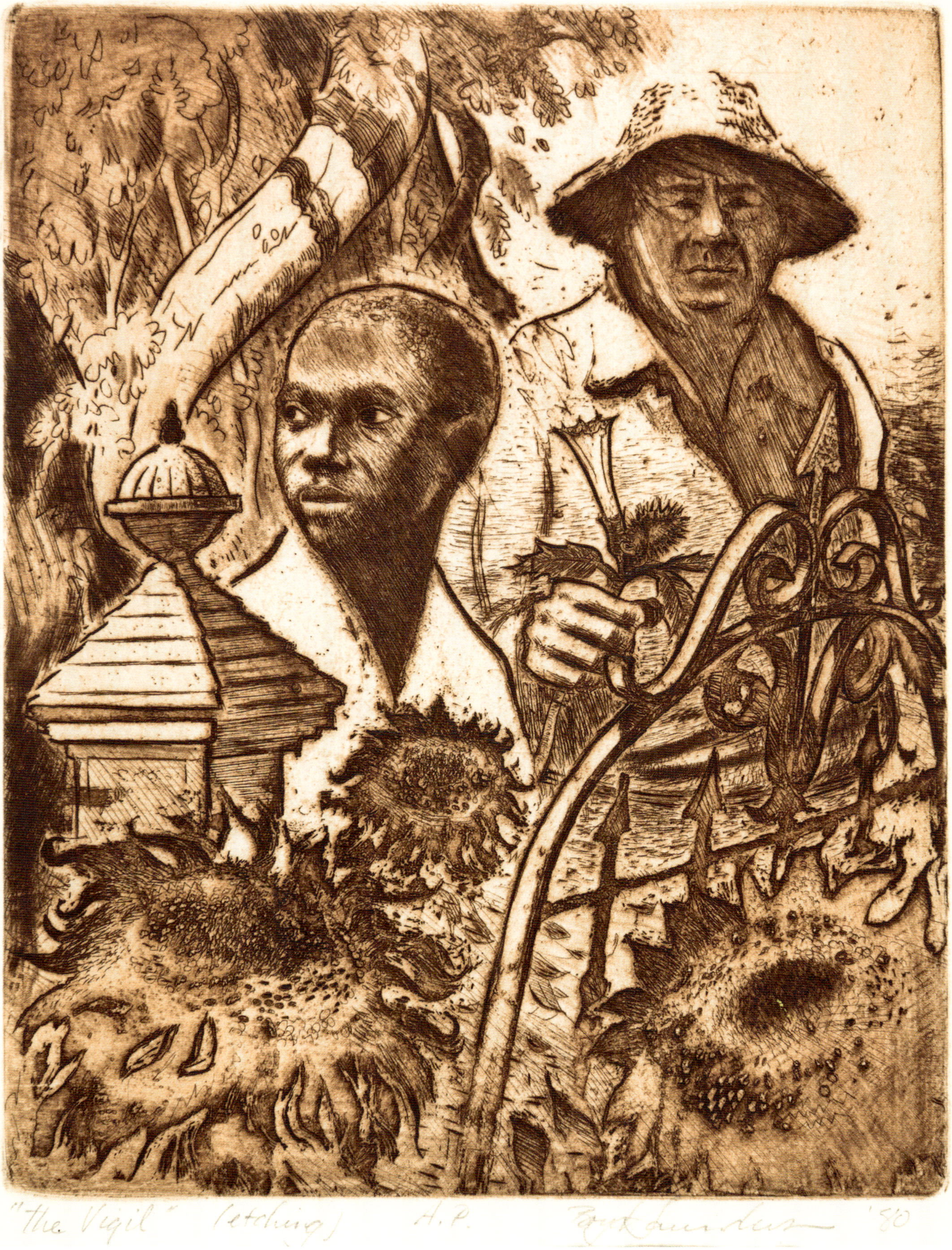

The Vigil, 2002–4, etching, 7 × 5½ in.

those monologues are offered by different Compson sons, they are related by their unwholesome obsession with a fourth character, their sister, Caddy.

Benjy Compson, the youngest of the four Compson children, is the major figure in the first monologue, one in which he recalls situations back to his childhood. He also appears prominently in Saunders's first etching, titled *The Vigil,* which finds Benjy, jimson weed in hand, waiting by the front yard gate of the imposing family home for his sister, Caddy (short for Candace) to return from school, as she did at a certain time. But there is a problem. Caddy does not come because she has grown up and no longer lives at home. Benjy goes down to the gate anyway almost every afternoon to wait for her, and possibly for two reasons. The first may be that Caddy is about the only member of his immediate family to show affection for or spend time with him. The second possible reason may be Benjy's confused state. He is said to be mentally ill, not aware of calendar dates, his age (thirty-three), his own birthday (April 7), not even that his monologue happens on that day in 1928. His incapacities apparently warrant a keeper, though they do not necessarily warrant Luster (probable grandson of the Compson family cook Dilsey Gibson), described by one Faulkner scholar as sadistic.

Not surprisingly Benjy's monologue is difficult to read and to comprehend, and it mirrors incidents from his life that are mixed up. Past recollections are interrupted, others are begun, and then he jumps from one memory to another or babbles about what seem to be irrelevancies, and yet he is clear-headed enough to make longing remarks for Caddy, whom he feels may have abandoned him.

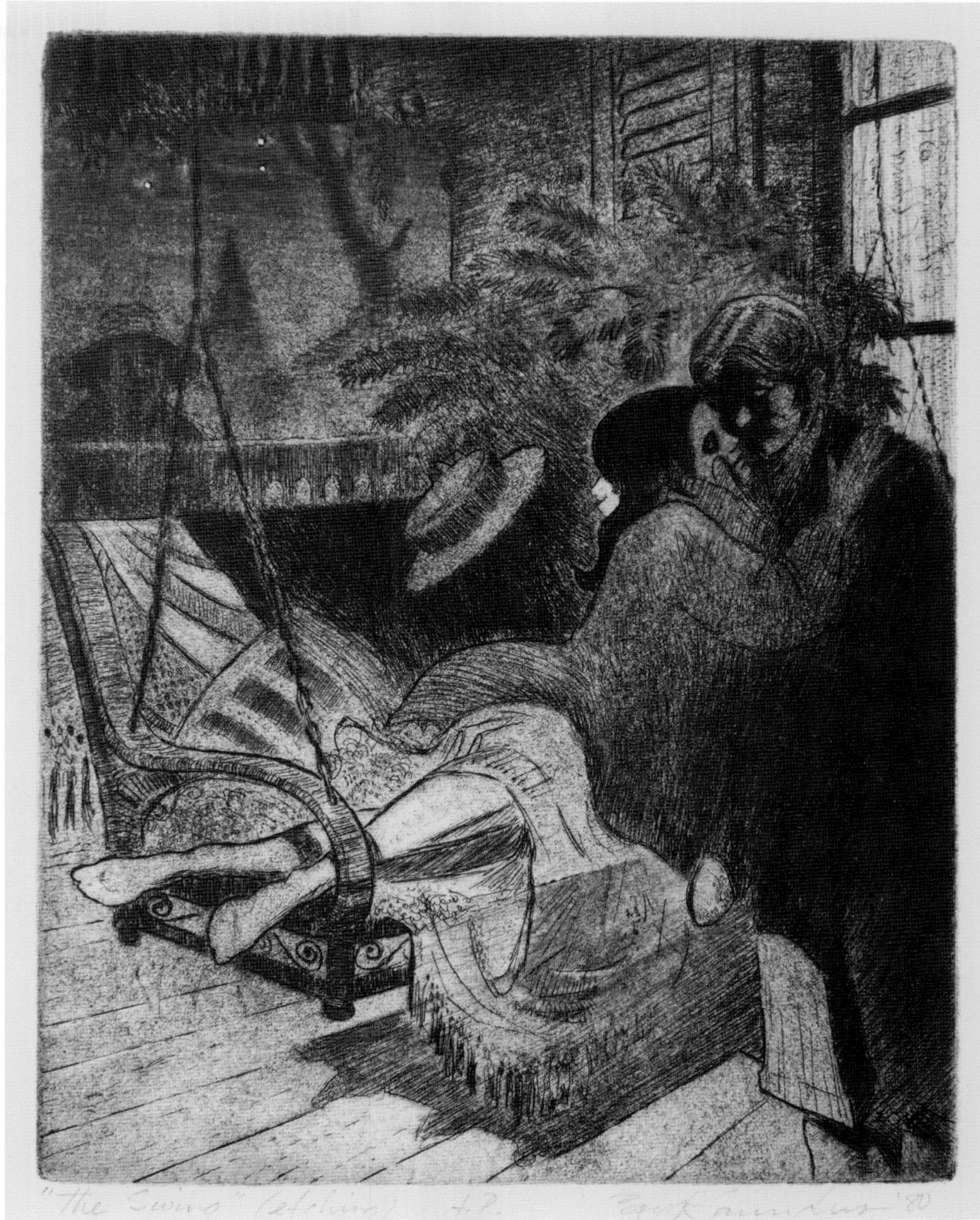

The Swing, 2002–4, etching, 7 × 5½ in.

THE VIGIL

[Saunders] The tale [monologue] is told through the eyes of Benjy, an idiot. This is not a pejorative term in this particular case. It's a descriptive one. Benjy was severely retarded, and could not speak. The story begins with Benjy waiting down at the gate for Caddy, his sister, to come home. Benjy always had a keeper on him, usually a young African-American boy from the neighborhood who would be assigned to Benjy to stay with him all of the time and to be sure that he didn't hurt himself, or wander off or get into some kind of mischief. After a while the keepers sort of merged into one. I worked hard to get a visual description of Benjy's particular character. Benjy is a middle-aged man and still does not comprehend all that is going on around him.

He still goes there every afternoon to wait for Caddy to come home. Benjy loved to carry flowers. His keeper had him carrying a jimson weed. Jimson is a locoweed so there is a little symbolism there. If the keeper gave Benjy the jimson weed as a private joke because it is poisonous [with

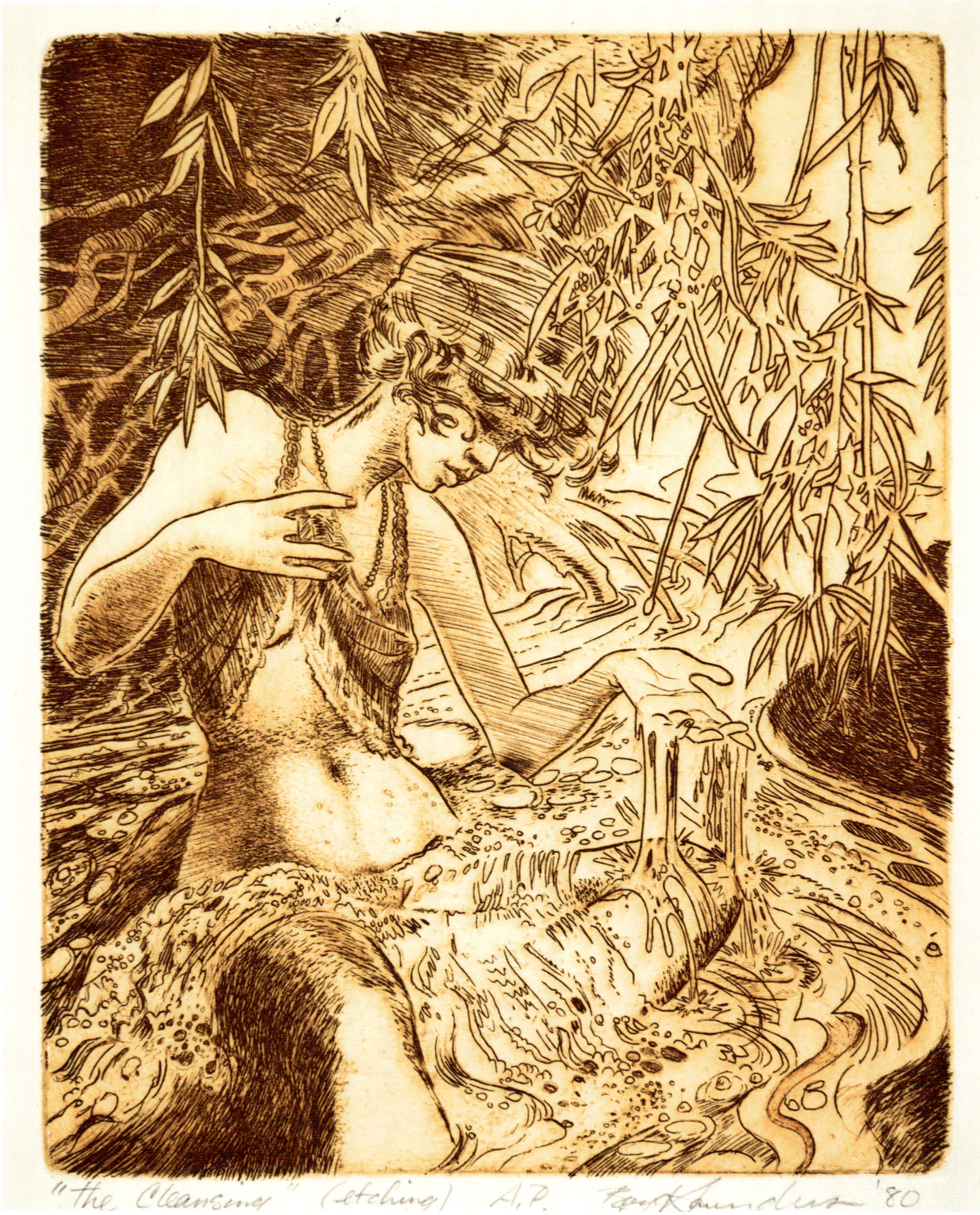

The Cleansing, 2002–4, etching, 7 × 5½ in.

associations of madness], maybe he meant to mock Benjy who was mentally ill.[11]

Since Benjy's mental state was not the result of an injury or childhood illness but congenital and possibly the result of inbreeding, perhaps Faulkner used it as another symbol of the degeneration of the Compson family line.

THE SWING

The relationship between Caddy and her mother Caroline was particularly strained. Mrs. Compson was obsessed with status and seemed cold or aloof regarding Caddy, while her father was stern to the point of being tyrannical. Apparently Caddy sought escape from her repressive home life, found attention and love in the wrong places, and explored promiscuity. Saunders said, "Well, the story unfolds piece by piece of this disjointed, dysfunctional family where everybody is a mess. Caddy tries to make some sense of it as she grows into womanhood."[12] And further, "In this piece we see Caddy with a traveling man she has brought home to the estate. They are in a swing on the front porch. If you look closely back there in the mist of the evening, you see Benjy, just a shadowy figure peering over the porch railing. He just looms up there out of the twilight and he does not approve of what Miss Caddy is doing. He senses Caddy is becoming sexually promiscuous."[13]

> [Saunders] Caddy is sitting in a stream amidst branches of a willow tree. Benjy used to say that he loved Caddy because she smelled like trees and flowers, and then one day, she didn't smell like trees, she smelled like something else, and it bothered Benjy very much. He would push her into the bathroom bellowing at her to wash herself, to cleanse herself of this, what Benjy thought was an abomination.
>
> Caddy knew what was bothering him and it bothered her too, so she would sit in the same stream that they had played in as children. In the etching, she is letting the water run over her loins trying to do a ritualistic cleansing of herself. She spends a lot of time sitting in that stream washing herself. In time Caddy got herself pregnant by an unknown person or persons and she did what was done back in that day and time, she struck up a fast romance with somebody and convinced him that they needed to get married right away. Hopefully he wouldn't realize that the child wasn't his.[14]

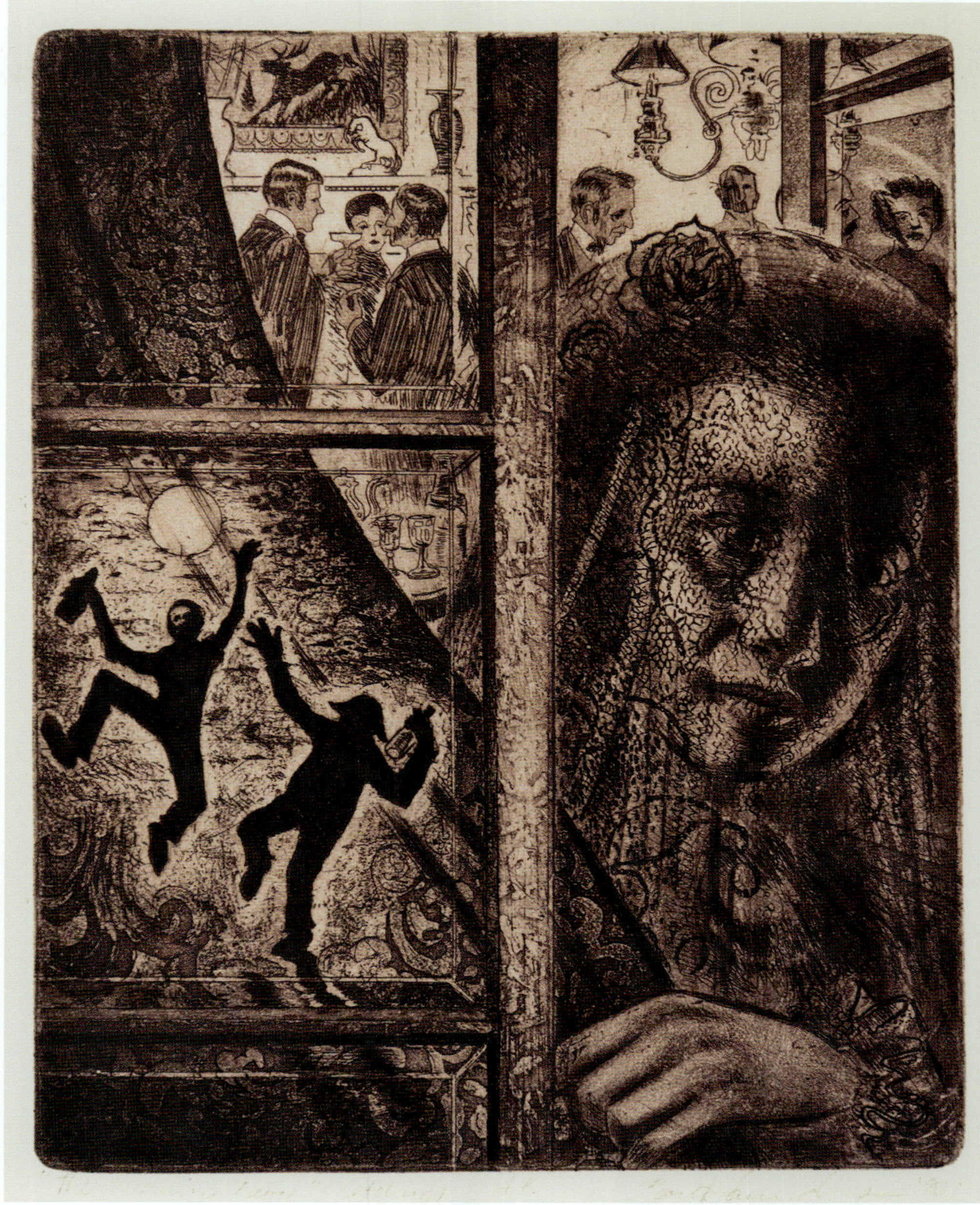

The Wedding Party, 2002–4, etching, 7 × 5½ in.

[Saunders] This is the marriage of Caddy (of about April, 1910). It is called *The Wedding Party.* Caddy is getting married to the Yankee stranger. There is a tremendous amount of information jammed into this small composition. Here, right in the foreground, we see Caddy in her wedding

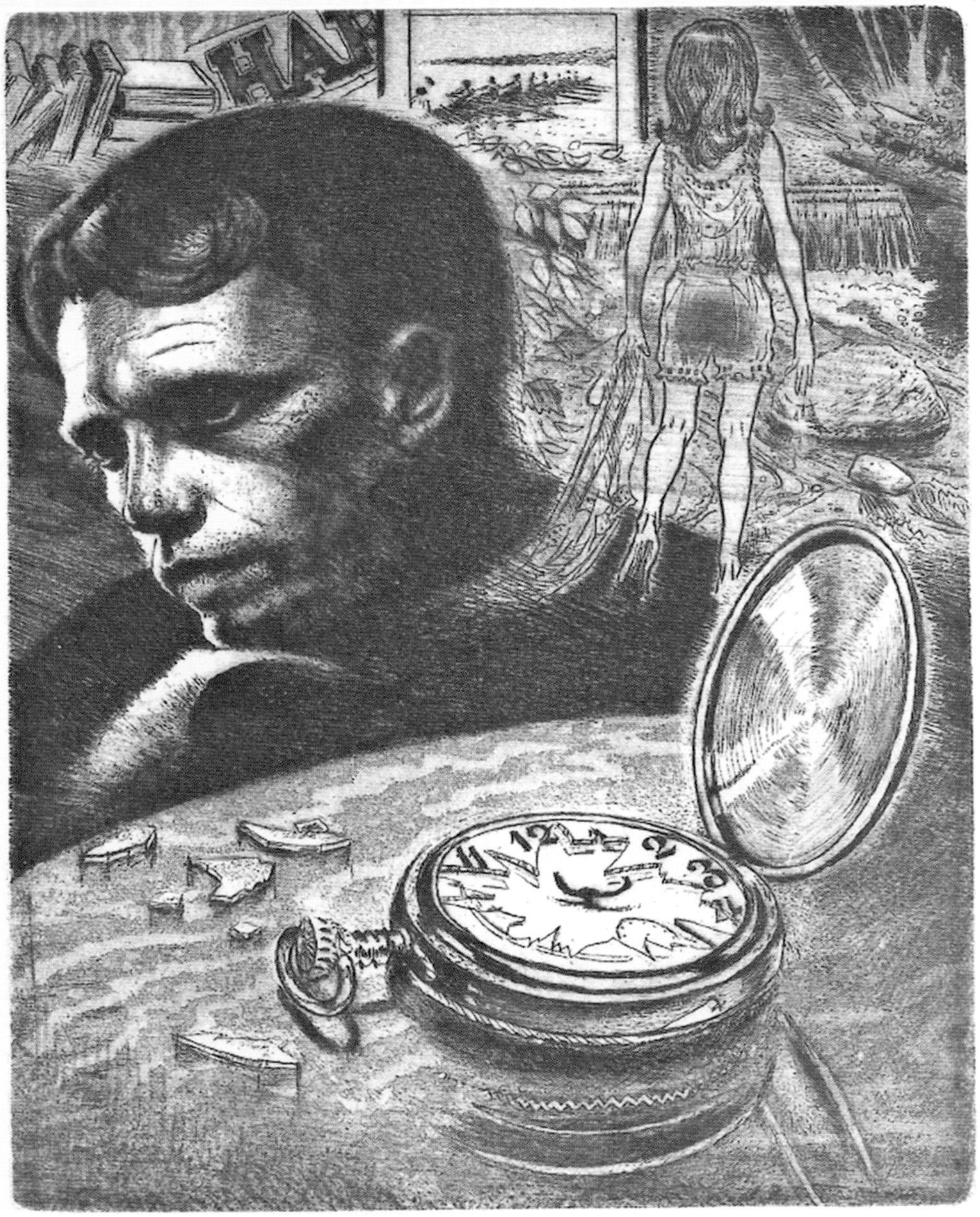

Quentin's Dilemma, 2002–4, etching, 7 × 5½ in.

veil. She has turned her back on the wedding festivities and has gone to the window to peer out almost as if she wished she could get away from all of this. Behind her we see the partiers and the family in the living room. We see on the left side [foreground] the French doors pulled across this space. As Caddy draws back the damask curtains behind the French door, it creates a reflection so that we can see what is going on out in the yard. There we see that Benjy and the keeper have been consigned to stay away from the wedding party so as not to embarrass people. But, in the process, they manage to get into the cellar and into the wine storage. They get themselves as drunk as lords, dancing around having their own party out in the yard. Benjy is described as not knowing what is going on, but he is drinking that good tasting juice and after a while the ground comes up and strikes him in the face. . . . A charming way of putting it, I think.[15]

One of the big challenges of this whole series of images was trying to get all the information that I was dealing with onto these small plates. For a multitude of design reasons, I settled on a vertical format about seven inches high by five inches wide. It was a great challenge again because I had to learn an awful lot about cropping, condensing and abbreviating images so that I could get them down to a certain size. I went through many preliminary pencil sketches, cropping, overlapping, and compressing images to make them work in the space allocated. Compositional design became critical.[16]

[Saunders] "This etching is from Quentin's monologue, and this is Quentin, another brother to Caddy who was in love with her, as was Benjy, but his [Quentin's] love for her was incestuous. It was never realized, never carried out physically. Nonetheless, as far as he was concerned, it was sinful and he worried about it."[17]

The Compson family sold part of Benjy's inheritance (some pasture land) in order to raise enough money to send Quentin to Harvard. According to Faulkner scholar David Paul Ragan, Quentin was obsessed about family honor and time, which resulted in him breaking the pocket watch that was a gift from his father. The broken watch had a prominent place in *Quentin's Dilemma* because of its symbolism and because Saunders's compositional methods stressed a central figure of the story or an important article around which other imagery was arranged.[18]

Quentin's guilt regarding his incestuous feelings toward Caddy did not wane despite his change of environment. A faint figure of her looms close behind Quentin, who looks away. Apparently he became so depressed about his unhealthy feelings for his sister that finally he took his own life while at Harvard.

Coincidentally it was on the same day that he broke the watch from his father. Quentin chose self-annihilation in the Charles River less than two months after Caddy's wedding.

The third section of *The Sound and the Fury* is a monologue narrated by the third Compson brother, Jason, on Good Friday, April 7, 1920. Jason, unlike his two brothers, was less obsessed with his sister Caddy than with her daughter Quentin, who was named in memory of her deceased uncle. Jason scorned his seventeen-year-old niece for flouting sexual behavioral codes and attempted to force her to conform to strict social purity, as he had tried to do with her mother. Further hypocrisy was evident when he betrayed the trust of his absent sister, Caddy, by depositing her monthly child support checks for Quentin into his own bank account.

Jason Compson's monologue inspired the last three etchings by Boyd Saunders: *Dilsey's Charge, The Funeral,* and *The Visitor.* Furthermore Jason's figure is a significant presence in the seventh etching, titled *The Funeral,* which concerns the graveside service of another Compson family member, Mr. Jason Compson III, who until his death was the patriarchal head of this once-genteel family of Jefferson, Mississippi.

Saunders said, "The father was an alcoholic, no account, not of any particular consequence, and not a major figure in the whole story. At the funeral we see Jason in the foreground. Jason was the mean one in the family. He was smart enough . . . but he was mean as dirt! It was not difficult coming up with a characterization for Jason. In fact it was a lot of fun characterizing his illustration."[19] David Paul Ragan described Jason's expression and mindset thus: "Cruelty and greed saturate Jason's face in *The Funeral.* The visage is nowhere softened by grief, only bitterness and lust for revenge upon Caddy."[20] Saunders continues, "In the background we see Mama in a carriage and we see impotent, alcoholic, Old Uncle Maury beside her. It's a kind of classic graveyard scene with a grey winter day and rain falling, the grave with mourners all around, and the horses, and the carriages, and the tombstones."[21]

The Visitor, Saunders's eighth etching in this series, is an outgrowth of *The Funeral* and references a situation at the close of the graveside service for Mr. Compson.

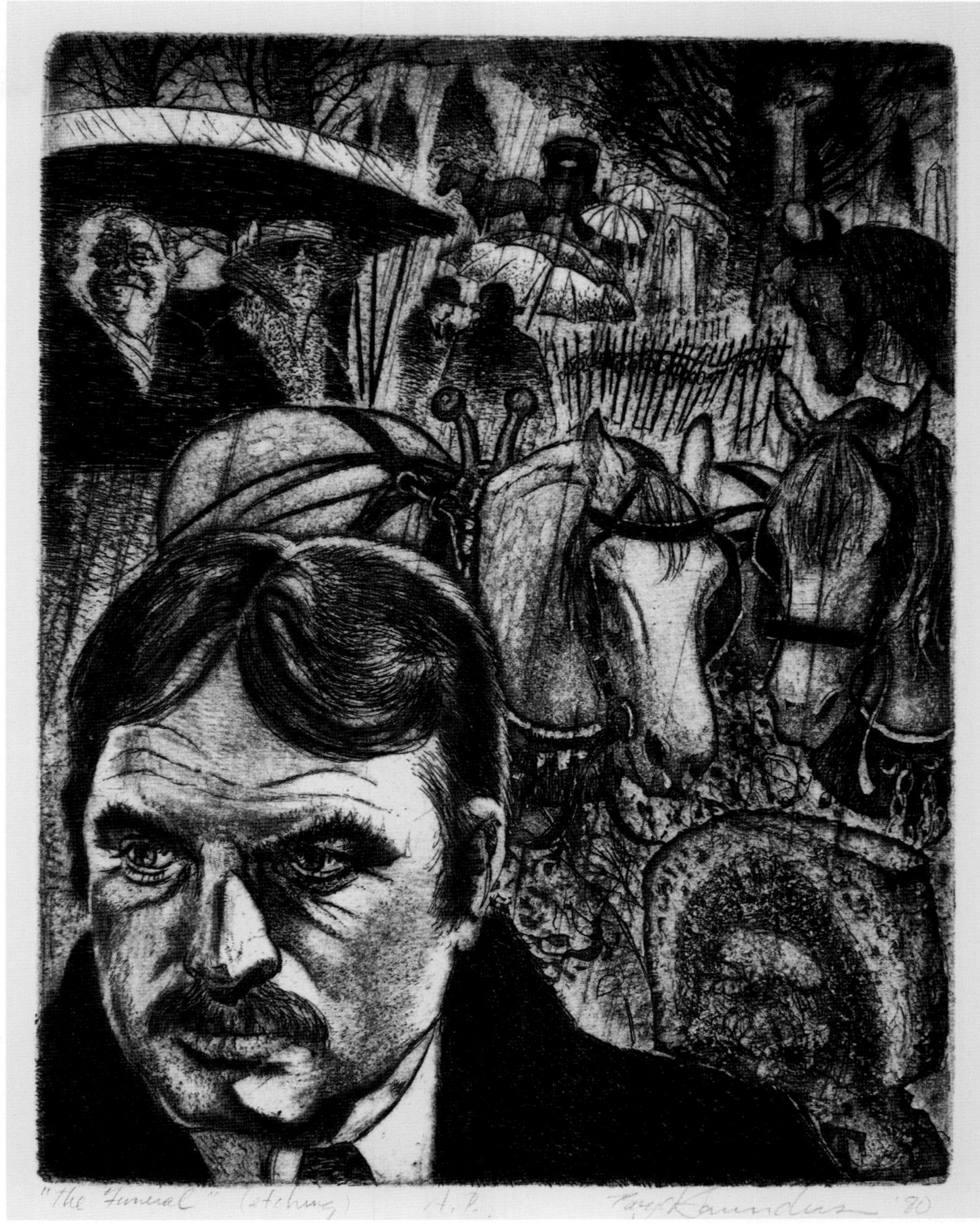

The Funeral, 2002–4, etching, 7 × 5½ in.

Saunders said, "After the funeral was over they [the mourners] looked off to one side where there was a mysterious woman in black. Jason went closer to her and realized it was Caddy. She had been banned from the family and it was forbidden to speak her name in the household. But when she read of her father's death in the Memphis paper, she had come to the funeral. She watched from a distance and placed a rose on the grave stone of her brother Quentin."[22]

David Paul Ragan has suggested that Caddy had an additional reason for coming to her father's cemetery committal service: "The other carriage at the

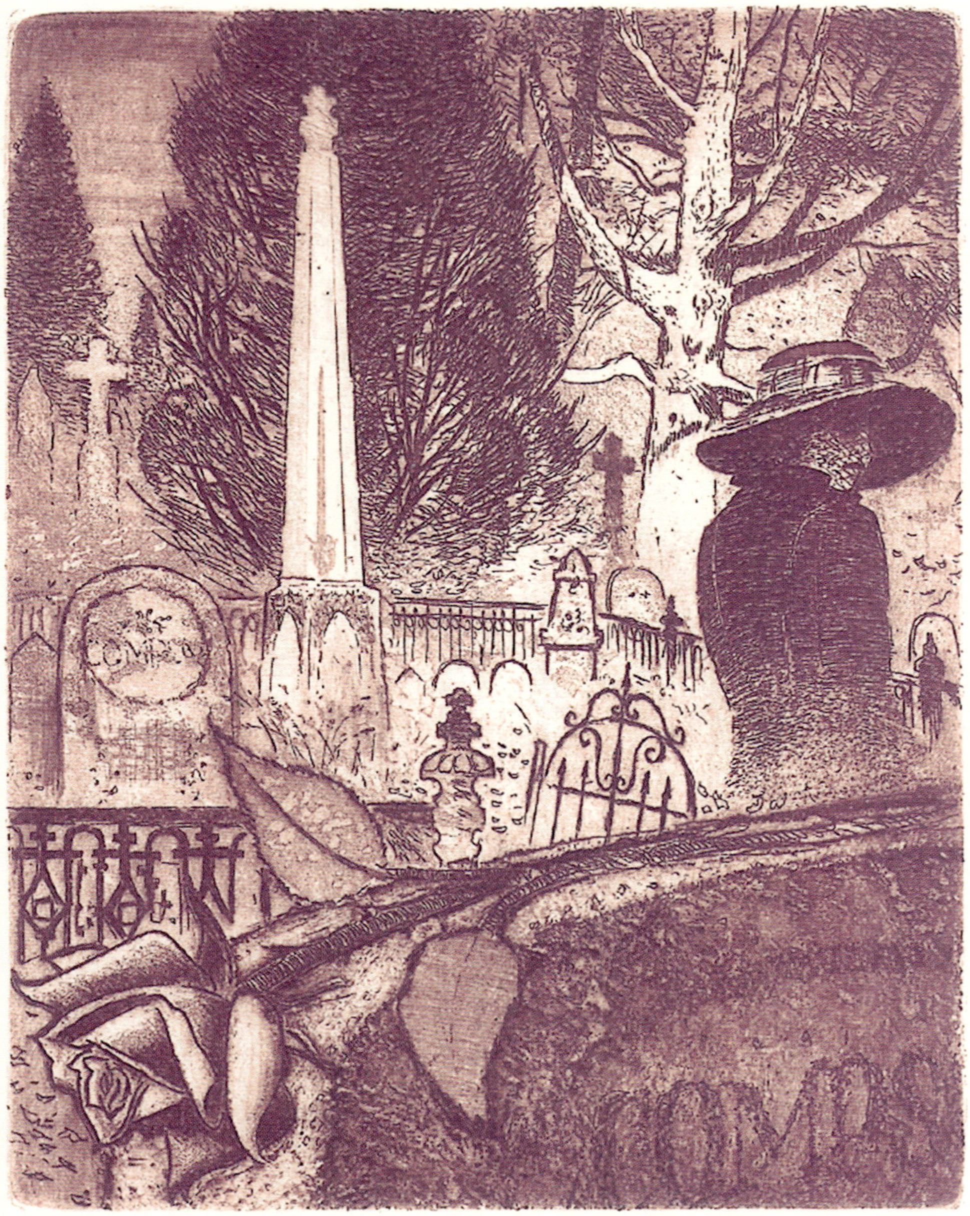

The Visitor, 2002–4, etching, 7 × 5½ in.

graveside service suggests his [Jason's] extortion of one hundred dollars from his disgraced sister [Caddy] for only a glimpse of her infant from the back of a passing carriage."[23]

The last etching by Saunders, for this short story, had its inception in Jason's monologue, but it is not from any situation or event in Faulkner's novel. However, Saunders was so taken by the strength and goodness of one of the story's characters (Dilsey) that he devoted an etching and invented a plausible familial situation to acknowledge her importance in the Compson home.

According to Saunders, "If there was one sane character in the whole family, in the whole story, it was old Dilsey. Dilsey was the African-American woman, the [Compson] family retainer, cook and housekeeper. She was the anchor for the whole family and made more sense than all the rest of them put together. She had raised all [four] of these children. When Caddy had her child and her husband realized that it was much too soon to be his, he threw her out of his house, hence she was sent from the house in disgrace. Then her father banned her from their own house in disgrace, but they had to do something with the child. The father went to Indiana to bring the child home for old Dilsey to raise. Here we see the child [infant Quentin] cradled in Dilsey's loving arms, who becomes the next generation of these children that Dilsey is supposed to raise, as she had raised the previous generation. I think Dilsey is a fine strong character."[24]

Behind Dilsey and baby Quentin stands a shadowy female figure on a grand staircase landing, in glaring indignation that the out-of-wedlock child of her daughter has been brought into her household.

As Saunders said, "In the background we see Mama. Mama [Compson] was a hopeless neurotic who could not function under any circumstances. On the wall behind her is a family portrait of the old progenitor of this whole Compson line, a stalwart Scotsman who had come here and hacked an agricultural empire out of the wilderness."[25]

The painting of the Compson family ancestor in *Dilsey's Charge* is a fiction, and so is the entire scene, but Saunders's perception of human character and core issues can be surgically accurate. His scenario, based on character profiles and actions, seems both plausible and compelling.

SPOTTED HORSES

In the latter part of the 1980s, Saunders collaborated with the University of South Carolina Press to produce an illustrated version of the short story "Spotted Horses," which was originally imbedded in a larger work *The Hamlet,* again by William Faulkner. However, unlike Saunders's small edition of prints for "The Bear," or for the boxed set of prints of *The Sound and the Fury,* the lithographic illustrations numbered

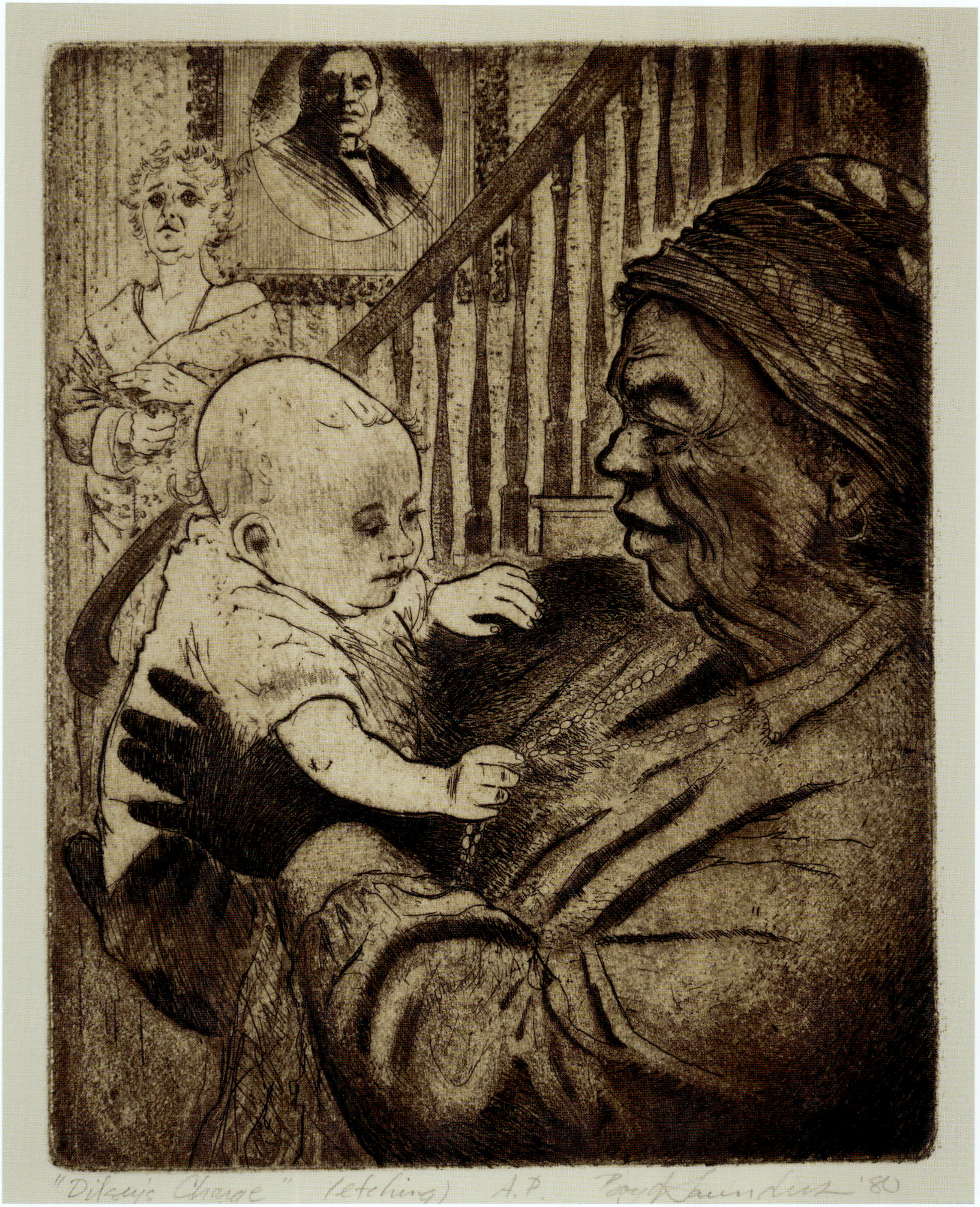

Dilsey's Charge, 2002–4, etching, 7 × 5½ in.

thirty-four for *Spotted Horses*. The project was conceived as a deluxe, hard-cover, bound, limited edition of six hundred copies printed laboriously and slowly on a legendary Heidelberg rotary press by master printer L. A. Munn. This approach necessitated separate aluminum lithographic plates for every color used on an illustrated page, which was run separately six hundred times with careful attention paid to the correct registration of colors on top of other colors, and the overall design of every illustration. An easier option would have been to use a high-speed, computer-controlled, multicolor, high-volume, offset press. Typically that is the choice for large distribution runs, for example newspapers, national magazines and journals, textbooks, catalogues of retail merchandise, and the like. That process uses digital photographs for all pages to be printed. But this book, with its full text, was designed by Robin Sumner and Jan Butler of the USC Press, who worked closely with Saunders and L. A. Munn as master printer, collectively pursuing the conceptual union of images and text with openness and flow.[26]

The conception of an illustrated version of *Spotted Horses* with full text began long before the 1980s. As mentioned at the beginning of this chapter, Saunders stated he began to read another work by Faulkner even before he finished creating the suite of prints for *"The Bear."* Among those stories was "Spotted Horses," and almost immediately upon reading it, the young graduate student at Ole Miss began dreaming about the possibility of illustrating it, especially because of the indomitable spirit of the mustangs in the story and because of Saunders's love of horses in general.

His affection for and bonding with horses has been alluded to in the chapter on Saunders's early life, but it has also continually manifested itself in refreshing opportunities. Excited to begin work on the wild horses of Faulkner's tale, Saunders nevertheless disciplined himself to understand the story thoroughly. Said Saunders, "The first thing I did was simple, read the story over and over and over again until I knew it by heart almost."[27]

The tale of "Spotted Horses" should perhaps be more correctly termed an episode within *The Hamlet* and yet is neither like an introduction nor as an appendix to *The Hamlet.* The main characters in "Spotted Horses" were already well established before the "Spotted Horses" segment. However that is not to say that "Spotted Horses" is not strong enough to be a standalone publication. Faulkner is said to have stated as much, and a short version of "Spotted Horses," possibly the first version, appeared in a 1931 issue of *Scribner's Magazine.*

The story "Spotted Horses" that Saunders repeatedly read involved a scam artist named Flem Snopes who acquired a group of wild, unbroken mustang horses from Texas by way of a Texan cowboy, who, in concert with Snopes, attempted to auction them to gullible farmers at Frenchman's Bend, Mississippi, which, like Jefferson, Mississippi, in *The Sound and the Fury,* is nonexistent.

The next couple of pages offer privileged insight into Saunders's creative process for the development of this extraordinary publication.

> [Saunders] When I was very young I had a horse and I grew up riding that horse. I have known and have loved horses all my life. I've never gotten away from them. I still have a fascination with them. They're big and they're strong. A good size horse will weigh 900, 1,000, 1,200 lbs. and can go 30–35 miles an hour sometimes. They're also not very smart. They can hurt you. Still, they are wonderful animals.
>
> When I was in school I would rather be drawing horses than doing arithmetic problems. I wasn't a very good student. I would daydream and look out the window and imagine myself riding a big horse across the sunset. I stayed in trouble with my teachers for doing that. Yet this fascination stayed with me and when, many years later, I had the opportunity to draw some horses [for *Spotted Horses*] my goodness, I was in good shape.
>
> All the time I was thinking of these horses, running and galloping. When I was drawing a horse (in my mind) I was feeling it under me. I could smell them. I could experience the whole thing. Then I started making preliminary sketches, rough things, just rough black and white sketches on tracing paper. I wasn't sure what the book was going to look like or how the sketches would be used. I just started taking instances from the story and making sketches of them.

I had told the people at the University of South Carolina Press that we might be talking about twelve illustrations of one or two colors. They said that will cost about . . . that much, and yes we could do that. By the time I got finished I had done thirty-four of them, but they stayed with me on it.

After making the initial sketches, I made the book designers [photocopies] to play around with the size and used Xeroxed drawings to make a dummy. The dummy was a clipboard with pages inserted in it. It was what the book was supposed to look like. We took the Xeroxes we had made and ran them up or down [enlarged or reduced] them in size, taped them in and glued them in, mixed them up with type, and pushed everything around a bit. This became our bible as it were, this became our guide. Everything was built around this particular dummy. That was the beginning of the book.

Then we set about thinking about what kind of paper to use. We started looking at paper samples. We tried [laying] the images on the color paper. We tried the images on several different color papers and finally wound up with a beautiful paper by the name of Mohawk's Artemus which is a tan color.

Not only was the color of the paper important, the weight of it was important. It had to be strong enough that it could be printed on and not have it [type and imagery] show through excessively on the other side. It also had to be strong enough and opaque enough that you could handle it without it crinkling or creasing on you all the time. Some papers will do that very profoundly. You just handle it a little and it's got a crinkle in it. Well, you're going to want to handle it and you won't want it going to pieces on you every time.

Then, I started working on the plates. You have to understand that, in this day and time, a lot of commercial printing is done by a process in which a photograph is taken and it runs through a large machine process. Not this book! This book was to be hand done, hand done from the beginning!

The plates used were flexible, grained, aluminum lithograph plates with a sort of egg shell surface. I drew on them with a wax greasy Crayola or crayon-like pencil. When the drawing stage was finished, and the imagery on the plates was etched to establish it permanently, I took the etched aluminum plates to a friend of mine, a Mr. L. A. Munn, who had a commercial [printing] shop in Columbia, and who agreed to print the plates.[28]

Lockard A. Munn (1932–1989) of Laurel Printing was a veteran printer with a reputation for high standards, a critical eye, and patience. For this project Munn used a Heidelberg rotary press, and though not computer operated or high speed, this particular make of press is known for its reliability and durability.

Images were printed first, text last. Colors were in fact printed individually, one color per plate for one entire press run. Hence if an image required six or more colors, the entire edition of six hundred sheets of paper plus extras (in case of mistakes) representing only one page in the book needed to be run one new color at a time, six or more times. At the same time Munn and Saunders needed to make sure that the colors were printed in the correct sequence for the desired effect of the illustrated image and that the individual colors were in correct alignment, called registration.

Each aluminum lithography plate with ink-colored imagery was locked onto the drum of the Heidelberg rotary press, which transferred the lithographic ink to one piece of paper; was reinked; and the process was repeated until the six hundred to seven hundred sheets of paper, designated to carry that imagery only, were printed. However, that still is an over simplification of the Heidelberg rotary offset press printing process. Saunders said of the process, "A plate is prepared in such a way that it is chemically processed, and when it prints, the plate is wet. It has water sponged onto it and then a roller goes across it with oil based ink which is mostly repelled by the wet plate. But the ink sticks only where the greasy drawing is, and then it prints off of that as the roller turns around, and then prints onto a rubber blanket which is on another roller. Then it is printed off that rubber blanket onto a piece of paper, which is passing through under great pressure. That is why it is called offset printing; offset from the lithographic plate onto a rubber blanket, and offset to a sheet of paper.

Once the press gets started, it goes bookety, bookety, bookety, along like that, and it snatches the paper putting it in the printing press, and it works rather well although it takes a lot to get it started."[29]

A brochure accompanying this limited, deluxe edition of *Spotted Horses* contains a thoughtful commentary about Faulkner's story and Saunders's interpretive illustrations, about which professor George Reeves noted: "Saunders shows us the horses much as they are described in the text: Calico-coated and gaudy as parrots."[30]

When Saunders and Munn printed the inked, colored lithography plates, which illustrated the wild story, and enticing imagery. Saunders's illustrations for *Spotted Horses* do not have titles in the limited-edition book. Suggested titles, which begin immediately below, were provided by the author of this manuscript, with Saunders's permission.

> [Saunders] This group of horses just goes on and on and none of them looked like real horses until they were finished. Some of them just looked like spots. An image like this has seven colors in it.
>
> I'd show up at Mr. Munn's shop on a Tuesday morning with a series of plates that I had been

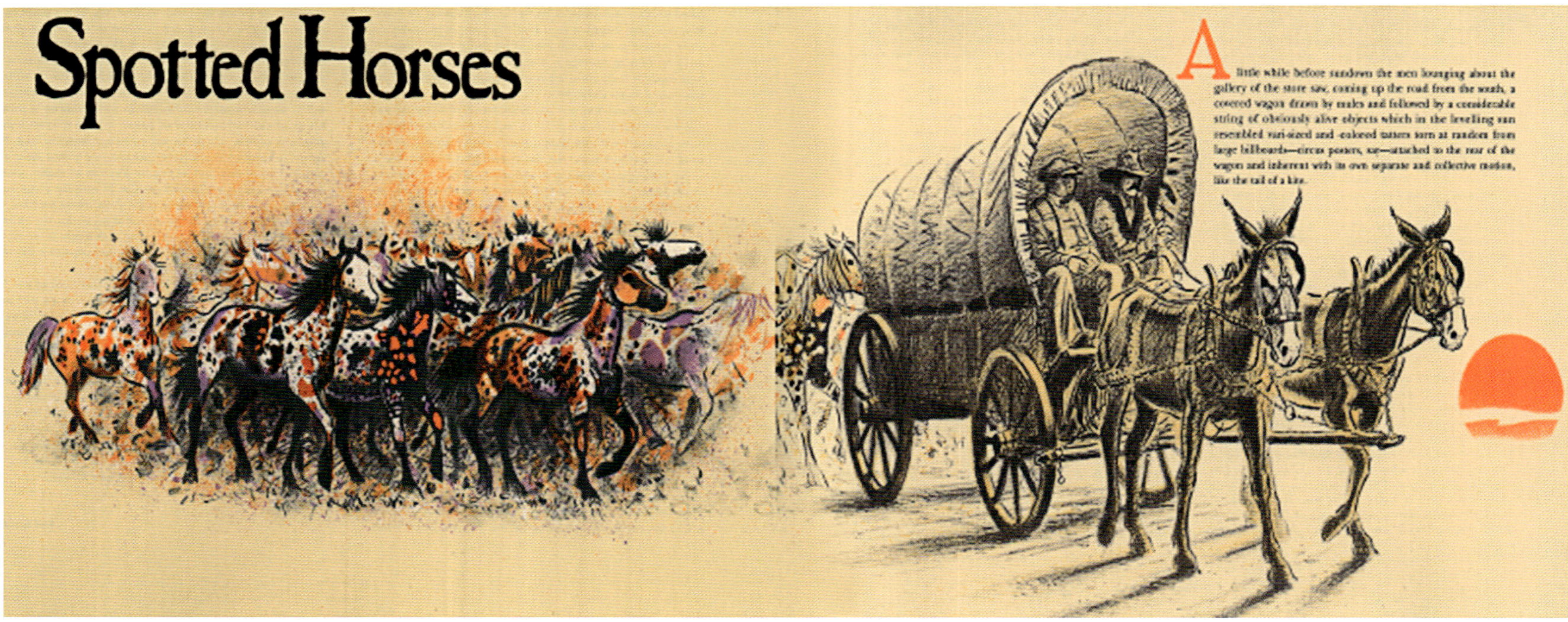

Spotted Horses, double-paged title image

mustangs, some of the color choices for the inks probably seemed crazy, but printed in the correct sequence, they built the desired end colors. The first two pages of the story represent a good example. At least a dozen speckled horses, strung together with wire, move from the left page across the book's gutter to the right page, following close behind a covered wagon. The wagon is pulled by a pair of mules and driven by a Texas cowboy (the Texan) with Flem Snopes seated to his right. The images, which spread collectively over both pages, are startling yet natural and immediately launch the reader into the story with three elements: title, first paragraph of the

> drawing on all week, and had etched, and he would say, "What are we going to print today?" I'd say, "A horse." He'd say, "What color?" I'd say, "Pink." He'd say, "Pink? Pink! Horses aren't pink!" I smiled and said, "Trust me." After the last color was printed, usually black or dark brown, you could see it [the correct colors] falling into place. Then, all the text was printed.
>
> After all the printing runs, we put together a binder's block. The individual pages, in correct order, were sewn together on the left side to see how the book was going to look at that stage. Binding

> the book was no small matter because we could only print one page at a time. You may say, what's unusual about that? The fact is, in most commercial printing jobs today, the printer will print four or eight pages which can be divided on it at the same time. When they're finished printing those, they'll fold them over and cut them into separate pages mechanically and sew them to make a book. But the press we used could only handle one piece of paper at a time, which meant that one could not fold paper across the back or spine of the book, we had to have a sewn binding. That also meant that the book was going to have a deep sort of gutter, i.e., the groove or channel with page margins of an opened book. So, I began to use that gutter as a kind of visual and psychological boundary to divide the parts for the images. For example, the spotted colored image of a horse over there is looked at by a somewhat duller image of the man across the gutter. I used the gutter like this in a number of places.
>
> Then, having finished the binder's block, we were ready to go to the binder itself. A bindery [Sherwood Deluxe Binding] at Kingsport, Tennessee, bound the book. It has a cloth cover over boards with the recessed image of a running, kicking mustang on the cover, and leather quarter binding on the back. A color lithograph of the same image fills one of the last end papers of the book perhaps to suggest that the wild spotted horses remain untamed, or unconquered throughout the entire story.[31]

The *Spotted Horses* story . . . begins now as artist-storyteller Saunders recounts with enthusiasm episodes particularly memorable from Faulkner's story. The incident titled "The Texan vs. The Mustang" is complemented with paragraphs that are direct quotes from Faulkner's text. In addition, Saunders addresses those same passages visually. Approximately one-third of the thirty-four original color lithographs produced by Saunders for the deluxe, limited edition of *Spotted Horses* are included in this chapter section of the book. However, Saunders in effect tells this venerable tale twice; first, through lively commentaries, and second with keenly perceptive and sometimes raucous visual images.

A BRIEF INTRODUCTION

Said Saunders, "He [Flem Snopes] had gotten in trouble back home in Mississippi. He was in Texas for awhile probably to escape the long arm of the law, then time passed and he came back riding in a covered wagon with a tall, rangy Texan and a string of wild mustang ponies coming along behind them. Here he has come back into Frenchman's Bend, Mississippi, in the spring time of the year [perhaps in the 1890s, in April] with these wild ponies. He had gotten the idea of selling them to local farmers to use as plow horses for the coming spring planting season. Now that is ridiculous in itself! If you've ever seen a western mustang, the idea of hooking one of them to a plow is about like trying to tame a hurricane with a willow branch. They are as wild as deer. The idea of hooking them to a plow and making them plow up and down a row all day long is a preposterous idea to begin with. Well, Flem Stokes would have come up with something like that."[32]

THE WILD HORSES ARE CUT FREE AND RUN AMUCK IN A BARN LOT

Flem Snopes had the Texan (also called the cowboy or the tall stranger) pull the wagon, with the mustangs in tow, into a barn lot behind Mrs. Littlejohn's boarding house. Once there the Texan, helped by Eck Snopes, cut the horses free, one by one, from the barbed wire around their necks.

Saunders said, "The minute they cut that barbed wire loose, those horses started running up and down that pen. They'd run over here and run into the fence and fall down, then they'd run over there into the fence and fall down, they'd run over here, they'd run over there. The farmers who had been at the [general] store nearby were all gathered around [the barnyard fence] looking at this spectacle in the pen and saying, what in the world is that? Why, that's them horses he's [Flem Snopes] going to sell us.

"Finally, the horses calmed down and the cowboy was moving around them some. Then the Texan said he was going to feed them so he herded them up into the barn. When he got them all into the [long open hallway of the] barn, he closed the [half-length] barn

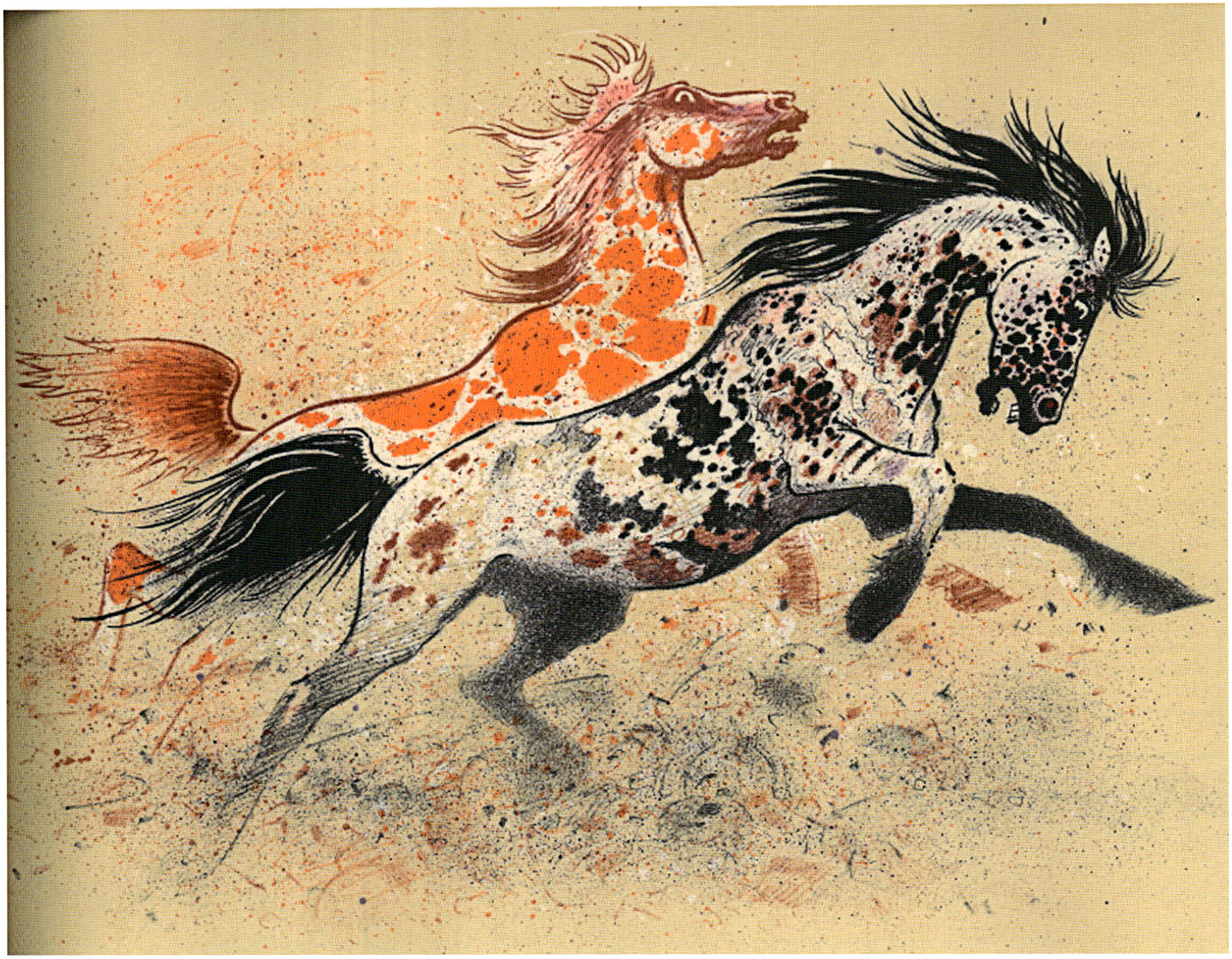

Mustangs Bolt Out of the Barn, lithograph

doors, whereupon some of the farmers began peeking through cracks in the boards. One little boy [Eck Snopes's son] peered through a plank with a knot-hole in one of those half-doors."[33]

The Texan then located a crib and emerged with a large basket of shelled corn to feed the horses. It was probably not his first choice, but the load of hay, supposedly to be sent there the night before by Flem Snopes, had not arrived.

Saunders said, "One of the farmers said: Reckon them horses will eat out of a trough? The cowboy said: Don't rightly know. They ain't ever had a chance to yet. So, he walked over there and poured the corn-pellets into the trough, in a dry wooden trough. Well the sound of that dried corn hitting the long wooden trough rat-t-t-t-t-t was all it took. It sounded like a rattlesnake. The horses panicked and took off right through the barn hall, right through the doors, exploding out all over the barnyard and knocking those

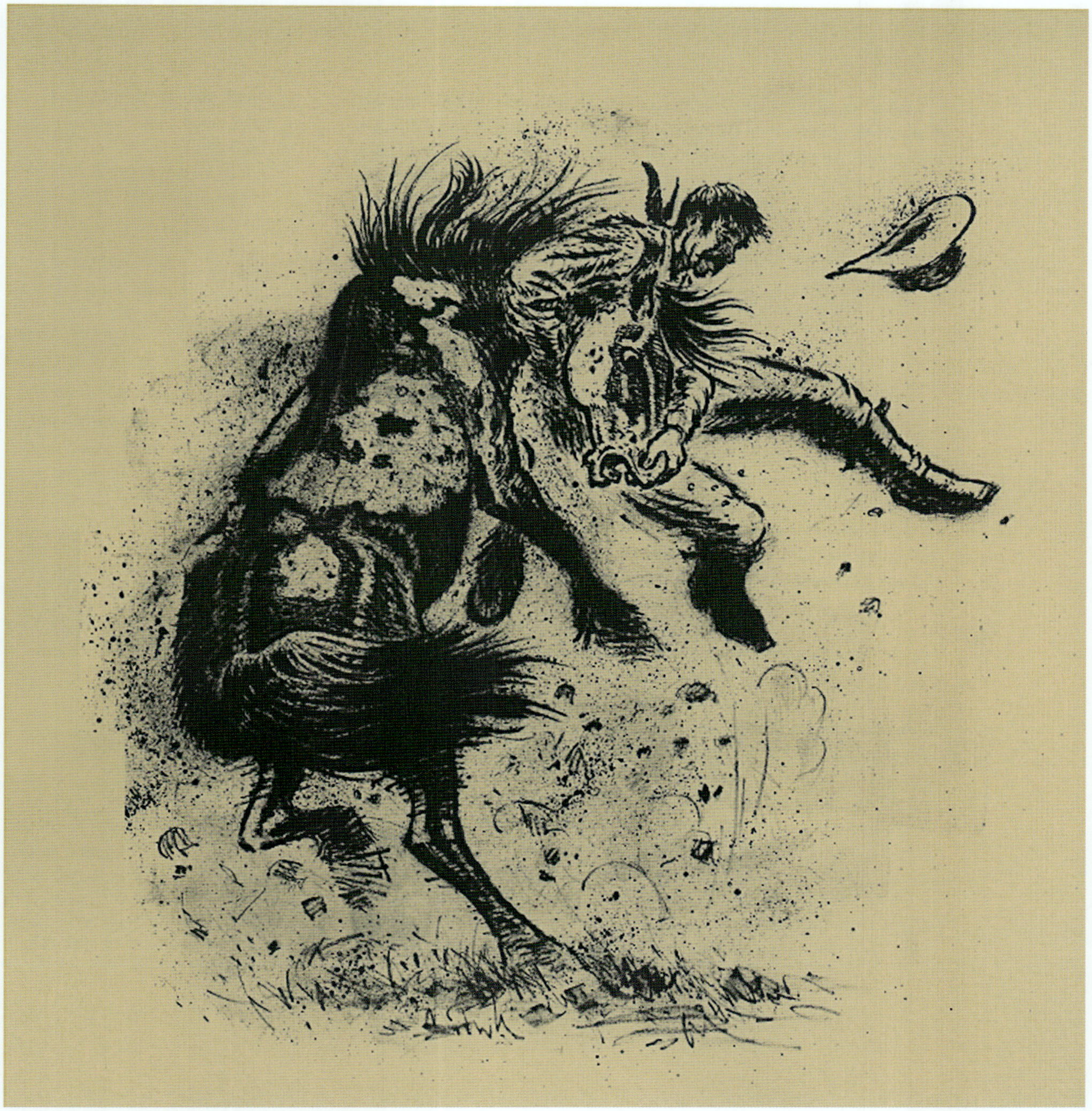

The Texan versus the Mustang, lithograph

farmers over everywhere. That little boy was still standing there [unharmed] with his eye up to the hole that wasn't even there anymore because the door was gone. It was a crazy thing!"[34]

The day of the auction, at the scene of the auction site, but before it was a reality, the Texan was having some difficulty getting it underway. No one was bidding, yet quite a few farmers were standing at the corral fence, and the lane nearby was filling up with wagons. The Texan, frustrated at the nonstart, jumped down from the board fence and proceeded to separate a mustang from the wary two dozen or so other horses, intending to demonstrate again that it was possible to handle such a horse. It would just require a little effort.

> [Faulkner] The ponies huddled, watched him. Then they broke before him and slid stiffly along the fence. He turned them and they whirled and rushed back across the lot; whereupon, as though

he had been waiting his chance when they should have turned their backs on him, the Texan began to run too, so that when they ran to the opposite side of the lot and turned, slowing to huddle again, he was almost upon them. The earth became thunderous; dust arose, out of which the animals began to burst like flushed quail and into which, with that apparently unflagging faith in his own invulnerability, the Texan rushed. For an instant the watchers could see them in the dust—the pony backed into the angle of the fence and the stable, the man facing it, reaching toward his hip. Then the beast rushed him in a sort of fatal muzzle wrung backward over its scarred shoulder while it breathed in labored and hollow groans. . . . "Look him over, boys," the Texan panted, . . . "Look him over quick. . . . The animal exploded again . . . whoa . . . let me get a holt of . . . you blare-eyed jackrabbit, whoa!" They were moving now-a kaleidoscope of inextricable and incredible violence. . . . Then the broad clay-colored hat soared outward; an instant later the Texan followed it . . . and the pony shot free in mad, stag-like bounds. The Texan picked up the hat, struck the dust from it against his leg, and returned to the fence and mounted the post again. He was

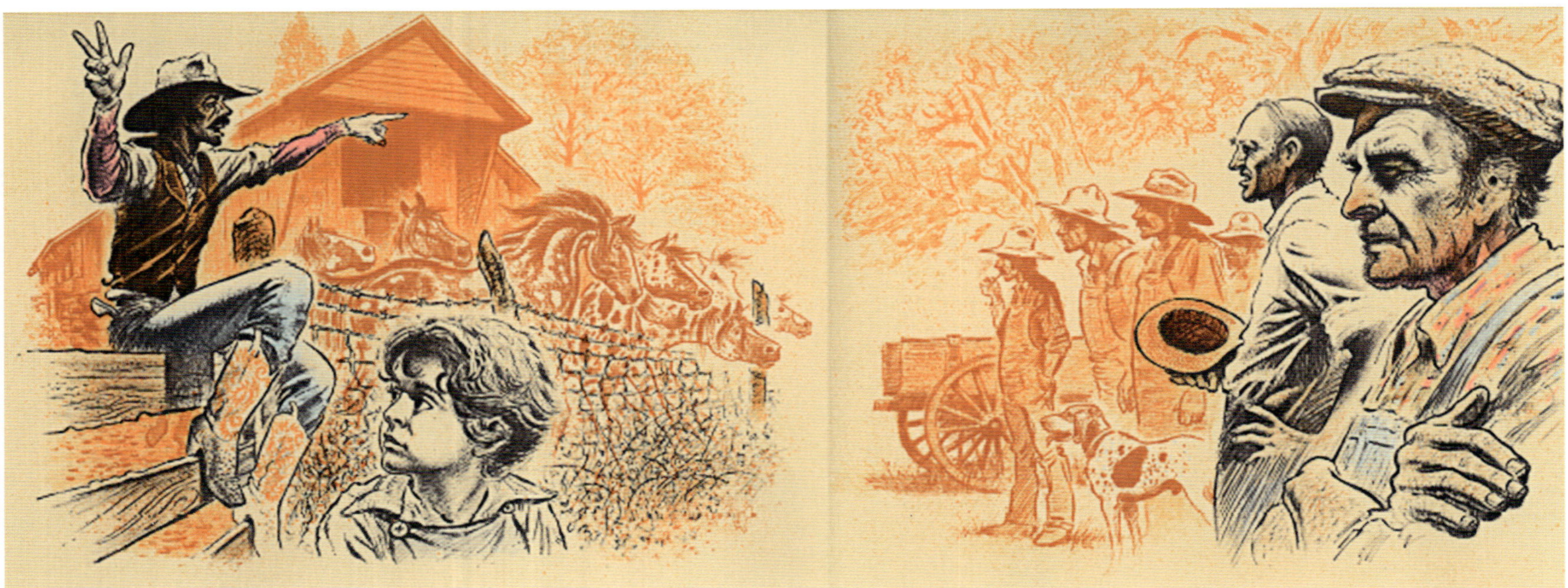

The Auction, lithograph

and hopeless desperation and he struck it between the eyes with the pistol butt and felled it and leaped onto its prone head. The pony recovered almost at once and pawed itself to its knees and heaved at its prisoned head and fought itself up, dragging the man with it; for an instant in the dust the watchers saw the man free of the earth and in violent lateral motion like a rag attached to the horse's head. Then the Texan's feet came back to earth and the dust blew aside and revealed them, motionless, the Texan's sharp heels braced into the ground, one hand gripping the pony's forelock and the other its nostrils, the long evil breathing heavily. . . . He said, "Now, boys," the Texan said. Who says that pony ain't worth fifteen dollars?" You couldn't buy that much dynamite for just fifteen dollars. There ain't one of them can't do a mile in three minutes.[35]

[Saunders] They finally got ready to have the auction. This, to me is the center point of the whole story. There was the cowboy [the Texan] on one side [left page]. He was a rangy, colorful character with a pistol sticking out of his pocket and a big wide brim hat. The cowboy would say to the little boy: [described earlier] Go get me a box of gingersnaps from the store there son, and the little boy brought him some, all the while the boy was eating some of those gingersnaps. The cowboy was sitting over here [left page] on the fence when the auction was happening and he would say to those farmers [right page]: Alright, what am I bid for that horse over there with stocking feet? And somebody would say $2.00. Then the cowboy would say okay that's good. You've got to remember this was 1897 and $2.00 was worth a great deal more than it is now. Maybe the price would be bid up to $5.00. So, the auction went on and the cowboy would say okay the one with the brown stockings is yours. After a while he had sold them all right where they were in the pen.

One of the big challenges of dealing with projects like this is space. Just as you are hearing me telling you this, it's a story that goes all over everywhere. It goes on through time. Imagine this on a big wide movie screen, across a theatre with stereophonic sound. Here I was stuck with a page only this big, and the imagery could not be any bigger and I want you to know that it was a considerable challenge to get everything on that page, especially so right here. Look at all the things I needed to get into that one space. I've got a cowboy sitting on the fence, the little boy, a half-dozen horses, a barbed wire fence, a barn and trees [and wary farmers] all in that space.

I had to crowd them, overlap them, cut them off at the bottom edge, edit . . . notice the little boy. I had to get rid of most of the little boy. That's all that's left of him. There is also a confrontation here of sets of faces. If those horses [left page] had been from Mars, they wouldn't have been any stranger things than those horses were to the farmers [right page]. And the same was true for those horses. They'd never seen anything like those farmers before. Again, notice how these farmers are crowded into this space. I went through drawing and redrawing, moving those figures closer and closer together, overlapping them. I cut almost all of this figure [front right page with arms folded] I mean I had a full standing figure to begin with but I just kept pushing it inward [for the sake of the composition] until that was what was left of him. I hope that I have managed to leave enough of him because there is another confrontation here [between the front two farmers, right page and the Texan cowboy acting as auctioneer sitting on the fence rail, left page]. Also, I have tried to unify this [left-page imagery] with a compositional device, a zigzag line.[36]

That implied zigzag line begins with the young boy's general glance upward to his right toward the animated cowboy on the board fence. The cowboy's outstretched left arm is almost exactly parallel to the canted left edge of the gabled roofline on the barn loft. The gable peaks and descends downward as a line leading the viewer's eye toward the decreasing diagonal of the row of mustangs. Simultaneously another compositional device is working toward the same goal of compositional unity. The composition of the left page has a board fence at the front left. It continues right and back or inward as a barbed-wire fence, and a perspective diagonal line. A similar idea is repeated on the right page with the row of farmers, the dog, and the wagon, which diminish toward the book's gutter. The farmers' faces look across the gutter at the cowboy and the mustangs, and vice versa for the cowboy and the mustangs. Why? Obviously an auction is in progress, but it is an auction with tension and anxiety from elements on both pages. Thus thematic tension is countered or contained, checked by implied zigzag lines and perspective diagonals of the dynamic composition.

[Saunders] While the auction was going on Henry Armstid and his wife drove up in their wagon coming from town. They didn't know about the auction beforehand, but once there, Henry Armstid decided he just had to have one of those horses. However, he didn't have any money. His wife had $5.00 that she had saved from weaving at night [after the rest of the family had gone to bed], selling eggs, sewing and things like that. [She was against buying a wild horse fearing her husband might be hurt by it and also felt they could not spare $5.00 since they were poor.] Henry took his wife aside and beat her until she gave him the $5.00. He was not a nice man and

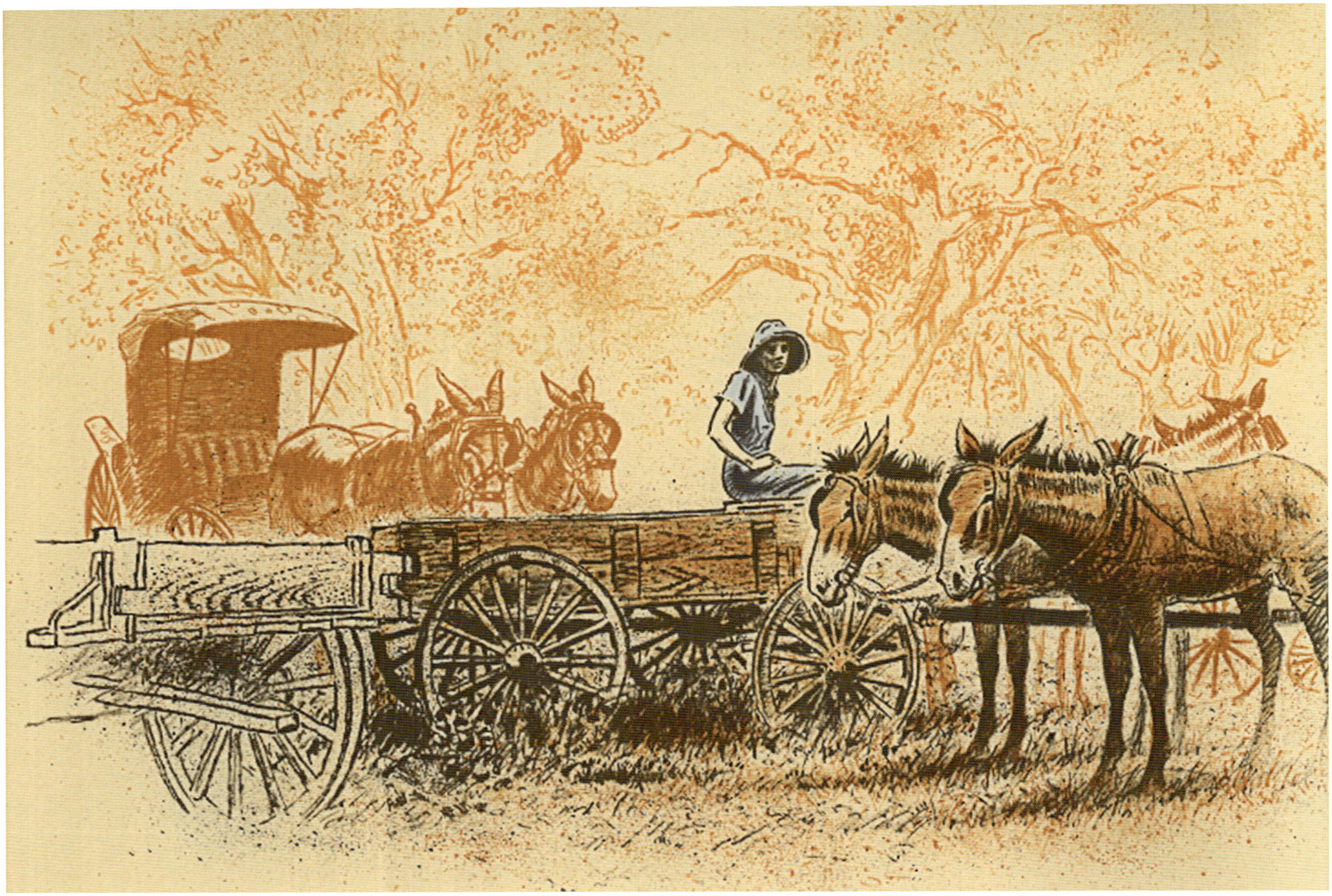

The Armstids at the Auction, lithograph

was determined to have one of those horses. I was trying to capture, in this particular character, the feeling that he was just about crazy, just on the edge of losing it, while his wife was mute after years of abuse and hard times. She was just back on the wagon [trying to reason with her husband] saying Henry, Henry, you ain't got no sense. Come over here. But no he had to have one. The cowboy didn't even want to take his money because he thought Henry was about half-crazy [and may have sensed that Henry was regularly abusive toward his wife]. But Henry insisted on it and he got the thing.[37]

What kind of farmer would purchase a horse, of a historically wild breed, with the intention of converting it into a docile, plow-pulling horse even when reason tells him the task is likely impossible, or that he might be injured badly or killed? Assuming common sense is both an asset and a survival skill, then surely only an idiot would waste hard-to-come-by money on such a life-threatening venture. George Reeves's commentary for Saunders's *Spotted Horses* book offered the following observation: "They are poor whites with varying degrees of frustration and hardship engraved in their features."[38]

Reeves further compared their facial types and expressions to those of tenant and sharecropper farmers documented decades later by Farm Security Administration (FSA) photographers, for example Walker Evans, Dorothea Lange, and Arthur Rothstein. If this story was indeed set in Mississippi in the 1890s, perhaps some of the poor white farmers also endured the aftermath of the 1861–65 war, especially carpetbaggers and other scourges of that ironically termed period Reconstruction. In the "Notes and Reflections" section of Saunders's *Spotted Horses* book, he recalled discussing this topic with his friend and Faulkner scholar at the University of South Carolina Jim Meriwether: "The grinding, relentless poverty of Faulkner's hill country farmers emasculated them. With that insight, it was made clearer to me why those farmers in Frenchman's Bend were so fascinated with the spotted demons. In them the men could sense some hope for strength and mobility and the salvation of their own manhood. It was a futile, irrational notion, but it made a certain kind of sense anyway."[39]

Professor Meriwether's thoughts are compassionate, empathetic, and noble and might apply to a few of the farmers, but it is also quite possible that such eloquently stated concepts would have been a luxury for those farmers. If they had any wits about them, the necessity of survival would hardly have entailed squandering seed money for the spring planting of crops that must carry them through the coming year. The exception might be farmers of the Snopes clan. Some of the Snopes family members had physical abnormalities and mental deficiencies that likely led to repeated bad decisions. Otherwise stated, maybe the biggest problem lay not in their jeans (or overalls as farmers) but in their genes. On the other hand, if they all had been normal, they would not have foolishly bought wild horses, and there would have been no story. However this story is fiction and said to be in the genre of Old Southwest humor, in which exaggeration was liberally utilized and wedded to an equally important American tradition, storytelling and oral history. Part of the tall-tale humor in "Spotted Horses" is the confidence game. The Texan tried to con the farmers as to the virtues of the mustangs for use in farming. Meanwhile his partner in crime Flimflam Flem Snopes, who might as well be called Snopes, generally stayed out of sight but stood to benefit the most from this scam. For the record Snopes essentially conned the Texan cowboy into most of the physical labor of bringing the mustangs to Mississippi, auctioning them, and collecting the money. Both characters duped the farmers and tried to con each other, seemingly as just part of the game.

Saunders briefly described his illustrations of the Texan and Flem Snopes as follows: "The human characters were, by far, the most demanding challenge. The Texan was perhaps the easiest, and Flem Snopes was by far the most difficult, and yet, ultimately the most satisfying visual resolution."[40]

George Reeves's commentary is a good source for a fuller visualization of Flem Snopes. The commentary is below the image:

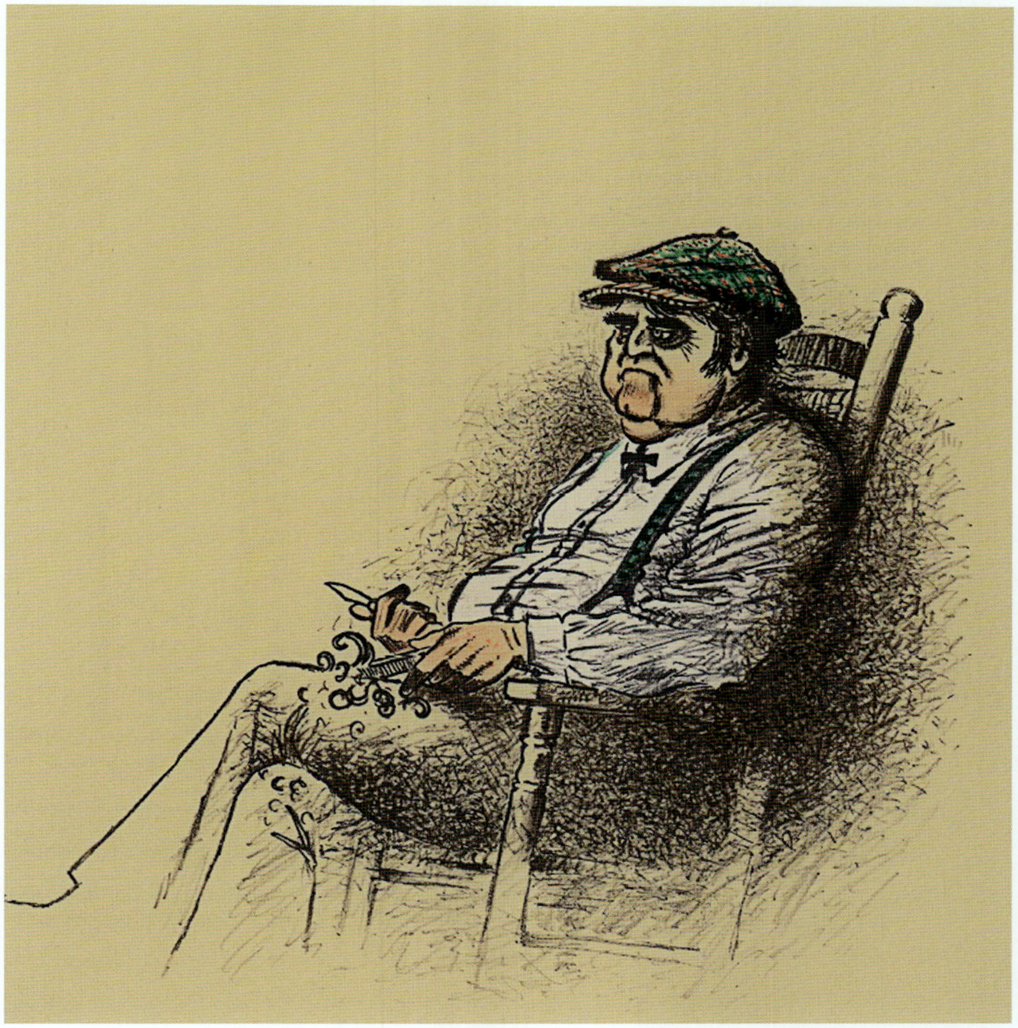

Flem Snopes, lithograph

Reeves said, "His most intriguing portrait is undoubtedly that of Flem Snopes, the predator whose cunning and greed, determine the conditions under which the other characters play out this episode of their story. It is not easy for the reader of 'Spotted Horses' to picture Flem Snopes. Early in [*The Hamlet*] Snopes is described as a thick, squat, soft man of no establishable age between twenty and thirty, with a broad, still face containing a tight seam of mouth, stained slightly at the corners with tobacco, and eyes the color of stagnant water, and projecting from among other features in startling and sudden paradox, a tiny predatory nose like a beak of a small hawk. In another passage his expressionless face is compared to a pan of uncooked dough."[41]

MUSTANGS ESCAPE BARN LOT AFTER SALE; PANDEMONIUM ENSUES

> [Saunders] The auction lasted almost all day. He had sold them all right where they were in the pen. Then they were finished, and the afternoon was about gone, and the money was all collected. The Texan stuck his money into his jeans and said, "Thank you gentleman, that's all." One of the farmers said, "Ain't you going to catch our horses for us?" The cowboy said, "They ain't my horses," and he turned and walked away [from that discussion].
>
> So there they were. They were going to have to catch their own wild ponies out of that pen. They stood around and looked at each other for a while, then got cotton rope. Then they all went into the pen and not quite sure about it, they eased along, trying to hem the horses into a corner, as the horses were running around. Finally, one horse looked toward the gate and saw that the last farmer to enter had left the pen gate open about a foot. That horse made a run for the open crack in the gate. The rest followed, and when they hit that gate, they exploded and ran through those wagons, and all those buggies down that lane knocking them over, mules kicking themselves loose from their traces, people falling over and the horses going everywhere.[42]

Henry Armstid initiated the culling and catching efforts in the pen after the auction, and when his horse got past him, he blamed his wife and lashed her repeatedly with a cotton rope from their wagon. When the third beating began, the Texan stepped up, stopped it, and advised Mrs. Armstid to leave the pen for her own safety. Most of the other farmers had also brought their ropes from their wagons. Farmers there without ropes, because they were unaware of an auction when they came into Frenchman's Bend that day, went the short distance to Varner's store to purchase them and returned. Ropes or no ropes the end result was the same, all the horses escaped as dusk turned into night, and the prospects for catching the mustangs appeared hopeless. There was one bit of justice though, in the escape of the horses. The horse for which Henry paid his wife's five dollars ran over him and broke one of his legs. That said, who then would put in the Armstids' spring crops, Mrs. Armstid? This downtrodden, essentially innocent character seemed to be continually victimized in the story.

Miraculously Mrs. Armstid escaped injury, when the horses bolted back and forth in the corral, when the farmers tried to catch the ones for which they paid, and when those same horses broke out of the pen for good, knocking over people, wagons, and buggies, Mrs. Armstid was found sitting stoically in her wagon without a scratch. Faulkner saved her from death thus but not from an abusive husband or certain scam artists.

The chaos unleashed by the stampeding horses fueled imminent disaster and terror with the force of an F-5 tornado. The improbable and the unimaginable became a real specter. Farmers pursued their horses in all directions well into the night but to no avail. Inexplicably, one of the fleeing mustangs turned around and ran back toward Mrs. Littlejohn's boarding house. It happened to be Eck Snopes's horse, the one given to him by the Texan. Almost immediately Eck and his son Wall chased it as best they could, though not intentionally toward Mrs. Littlejohn's house. What happened next is considered by many Faulkner readers to be the height of hilarity in this much loved short story. Saunders retold the events thus: "One horse ran up onto the front porch of Mrs. Littlejohn's boarding house, then ran down the hallway of the house banging into furniture. Then it ran onto the back porch while she was coming up those steps with her washing in her arms. She had been washing all afternoon. She hit him over the head with a wash-board and told him to get him to get out of there. The horse wheeled, ran back through the length of the house onto the front porch, and went sailing across the railing of the veranda, down the lane to the road."[43]

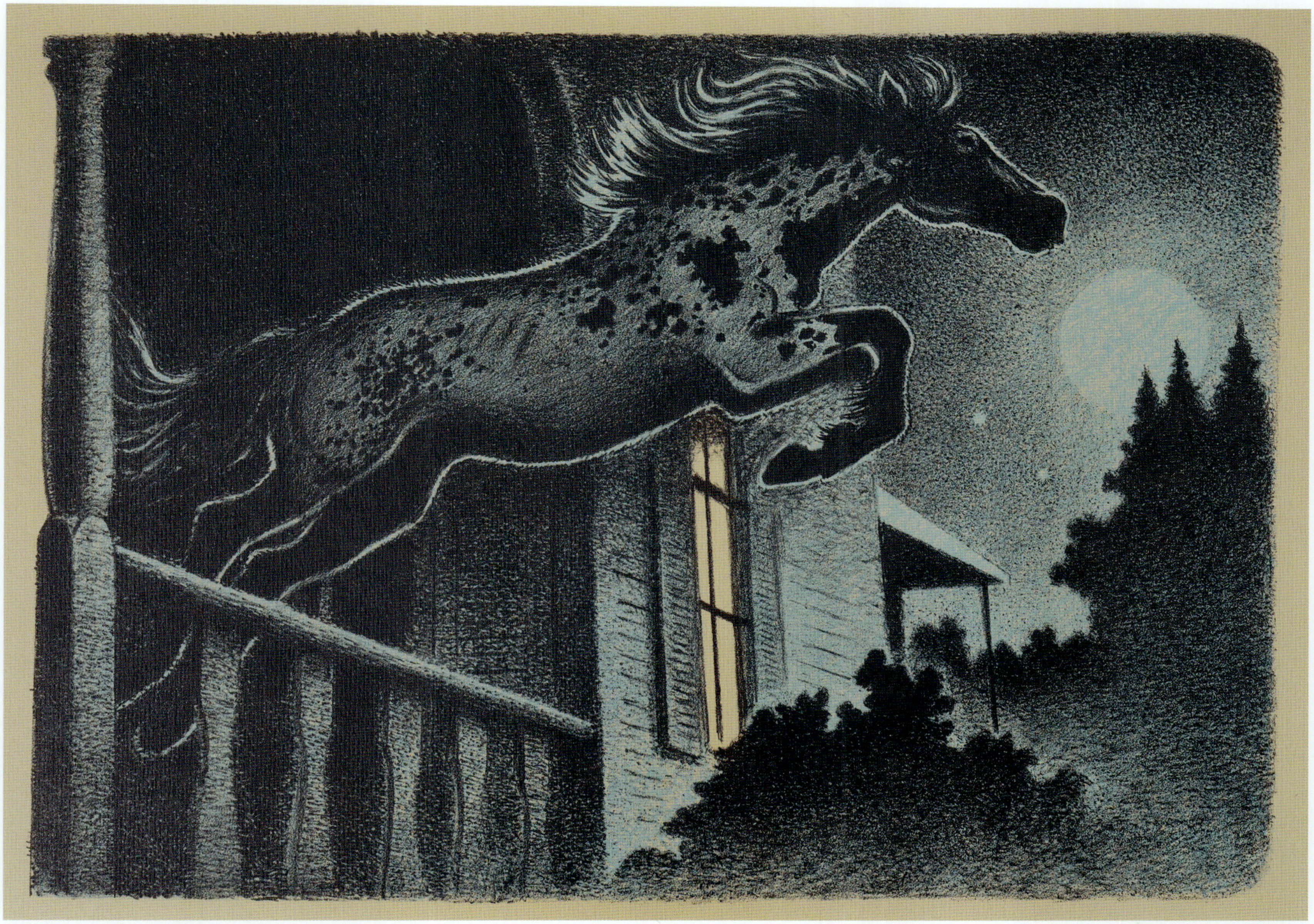

Hobgoblin Horse, lithograph

This wildly humorous slapstick-like incident no doubt appealed to Saunders the first time he read "Spotted Horses" in the 1960s. Perhaps just as simultaneously, Saunders began to dream about someday illustrating a special edition of that short story. If so it is especially tempting to speculate the impact of this mental image of Faulkner's mustang, this virile specimen of horse flesh, soaring effortlessly to its regained freedom on a brilliant moonlit night. If the words "explosively elegant powers" ever go together, this is one of those times. The mustang breed may be ungainly and jug headed, but in Saunders's hands this horse's confirmation and jump is as noble and clean as any the artist has likely viewed over many years at the annual Colonial Cup Steeplechase Races near Camden, South Carolina. As a lifelong equestrian, the artist may have even experienced jumping firsthand. Saunders's handmade lithographic image forever freeze-frames the heroic vault, as if by the most advanced, digital, stop-action photography, to be enjoyed again and again.

Nonetheless the panicked horse soon wreaked havoc to a much greater degree than Mrs. Littlejohn's boarding house invasion, and it was not likely interested in photo ops or a self-image of élan anyway. Next the horse raced through the torn-up lot gate, and among the overturned wagons, and then it was onto the road, which led to a narrow creek bridge.

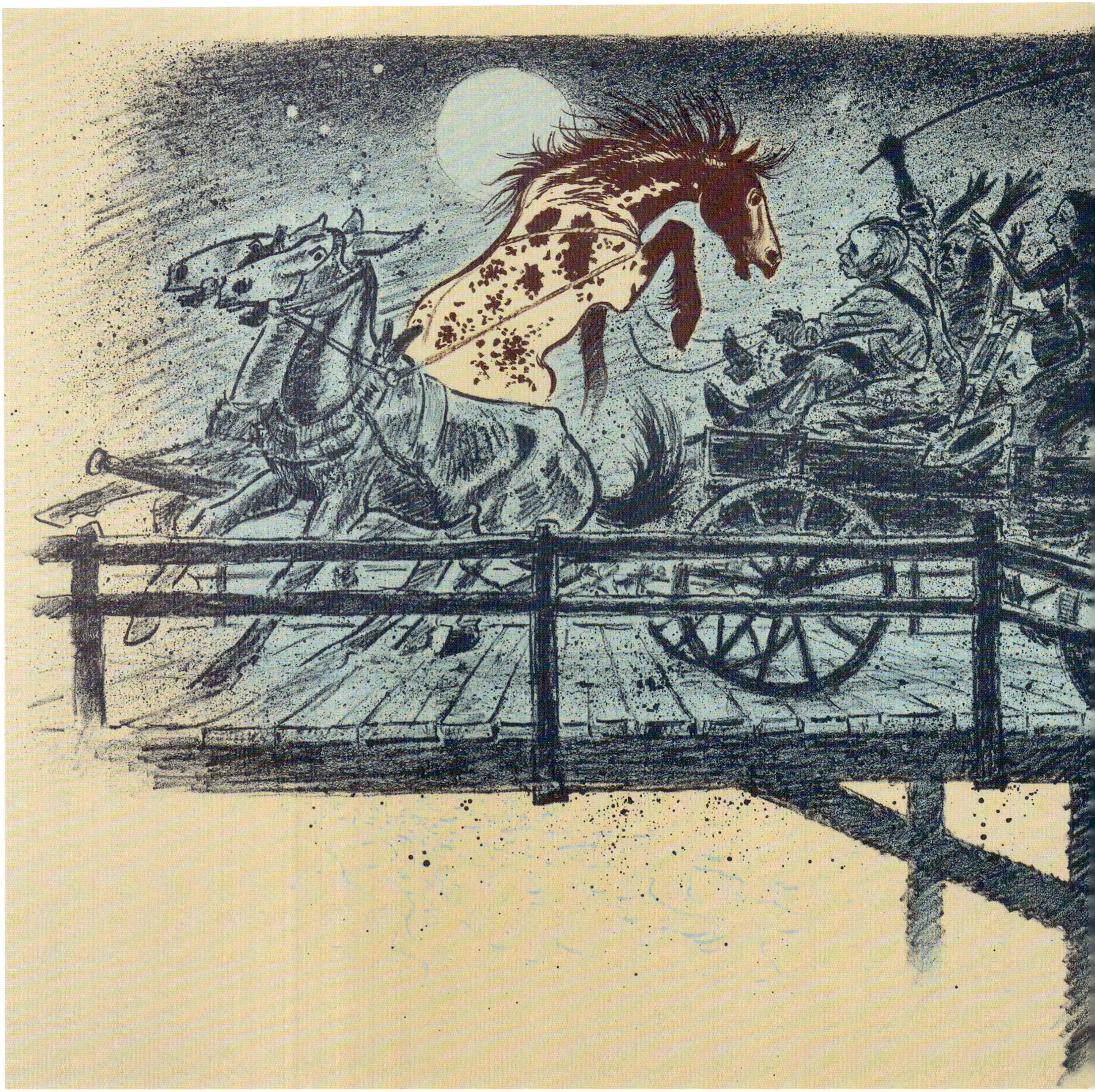

Collision on the Bridge, lithograph

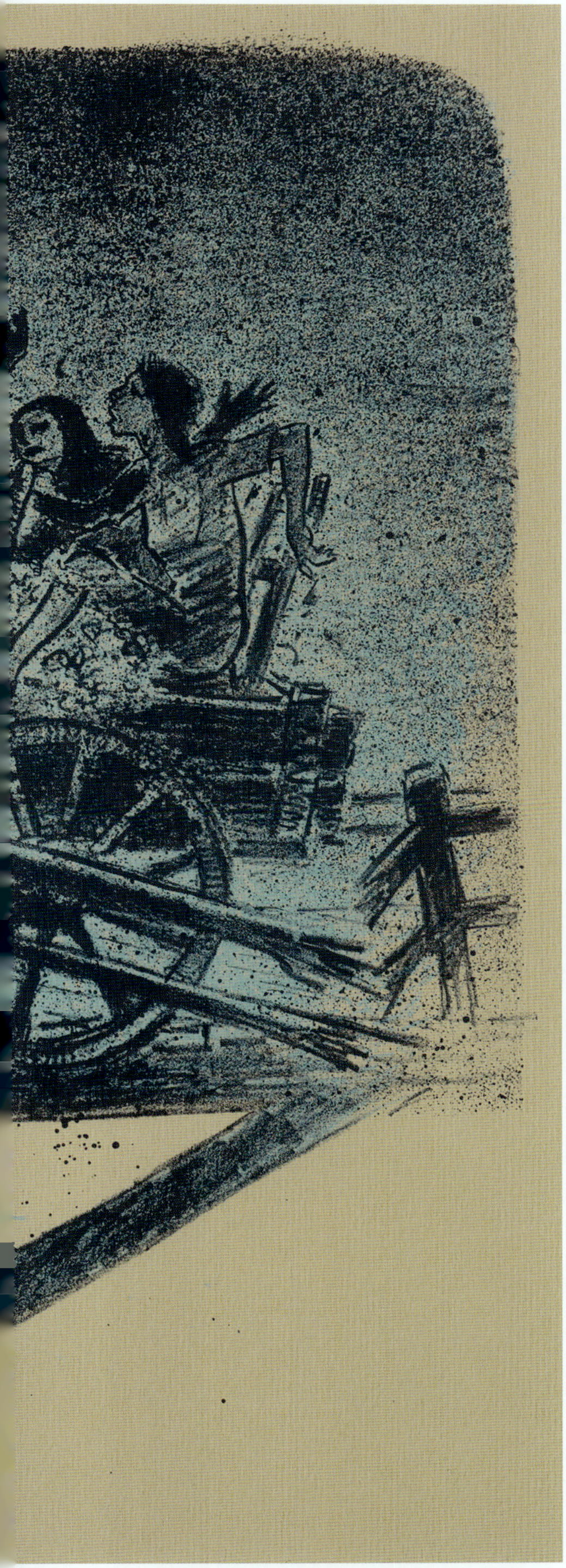

When the fleeing mustang reached the bridge, it was already occupied by a wagon coming from the opposite direction.

> [Saunders] That wild horse was running down the road and it approached a bridge where Mr. Vernon Tull and his women folk were coming home from visiting some of her [his wife's] relatives from somewhere. It was getting dark by then and they were sitting on chairs in the wagon [all but Mrs. Tull who sat by her husband] like country people used to do. The mules were half asleep in their traces, and all of a sudden, here was this wild pony!
>
> There were wild ponies down there running every which way all through the countryside with farmers running after them. Well, the one already mentioned ran up the bridge and suddenly they were all about on top of each other right in the middle of the bridge. That horse ran through the two mules and nearly jumped on top of the wagon tongue. Mr. Tull was beating the horse with his whip saying: "Get out of here!" The mules went crazy and backed the wagon about halfway around and about halfway off the bridge, tossing women folk out, tossing his daughters out. I think he had six or eight daughters, no sons. The mules kicked loose from the traces and took off down the road. Tull had the reins wrapped around his wrists, so the mules sort of dragged him off the wagon, (like you see in cowboy movies), dragged him the length of the bridge and farther, before he broke loose. After that was all over, the wild horses were spread all through the countryside with farmers chasing after them, and you could hear them calling into the night. They never did catch any of them . . . well, that's not totally true. One of the horses did run against a fence, broke his neck and fell down dead. So they did catch him, but he wasn't any use to anybody.[44]

Compared to the previous composition, with its glorious equine leap into a serene, moonlit setting, the bridge collision is a statement in coarseness, frightening confrontation, and startling disbelief. Vernon Tull's team of mules, with ears laid back, dug in their heels, trying to cope with some mysterious force that had crashed into them, ensnaring their reins. Those reins immediately went through the harness guides and pushed the bits hard into the soft parts of their mouths. Vernon Tull hung onto those reins with one hand while wielding his driving whip at the horse with his other hand, kicking and yelling at it all the while. All this caused the wagon to lurch violently, shoving its left rear wheel against a guardrail, breaking both boards. Not surprisingly the Tulls' daughters were jostled about out of their chairs and maybe into the creek.

To render such frantic defensive actions, Saunders used summarized outlines and short, quick marks, generalized shading, distressed faces, and jerky movements. Color also plays a key role in this clash of forces. The Tulls, their wagon and mules, the bridge, and the night sky are all of the same value range, a dark blue-gray-black fog or mist, which, considering the full moon, may suggest the lack of alertness of the Tulls and their mules. Faulkner did mention that the Tulls' visit to Mrs. Tull's relatives lasted all day, that their return was belated, that the two mules were already asleep in the harness, and that their slow pace created a "soporific motion," implying a drowsy mental state also for the entire Tull family. Saunders rendered the untamed, powerfully built horse in a spectacular, aerobatic position, rearing up or leaping almost vertically, all in tan and dark brown. This color contrast enhances the shocked expression of its face-to-face confrontation with the Tulls. In addition, although the leap from Mrs. Littlejohn's boardinghouse presents this horse in flight, the irrationally and desperate athleticism of it on the bridge may also reinforce a behavior trait, that horses are indeed flight animals.

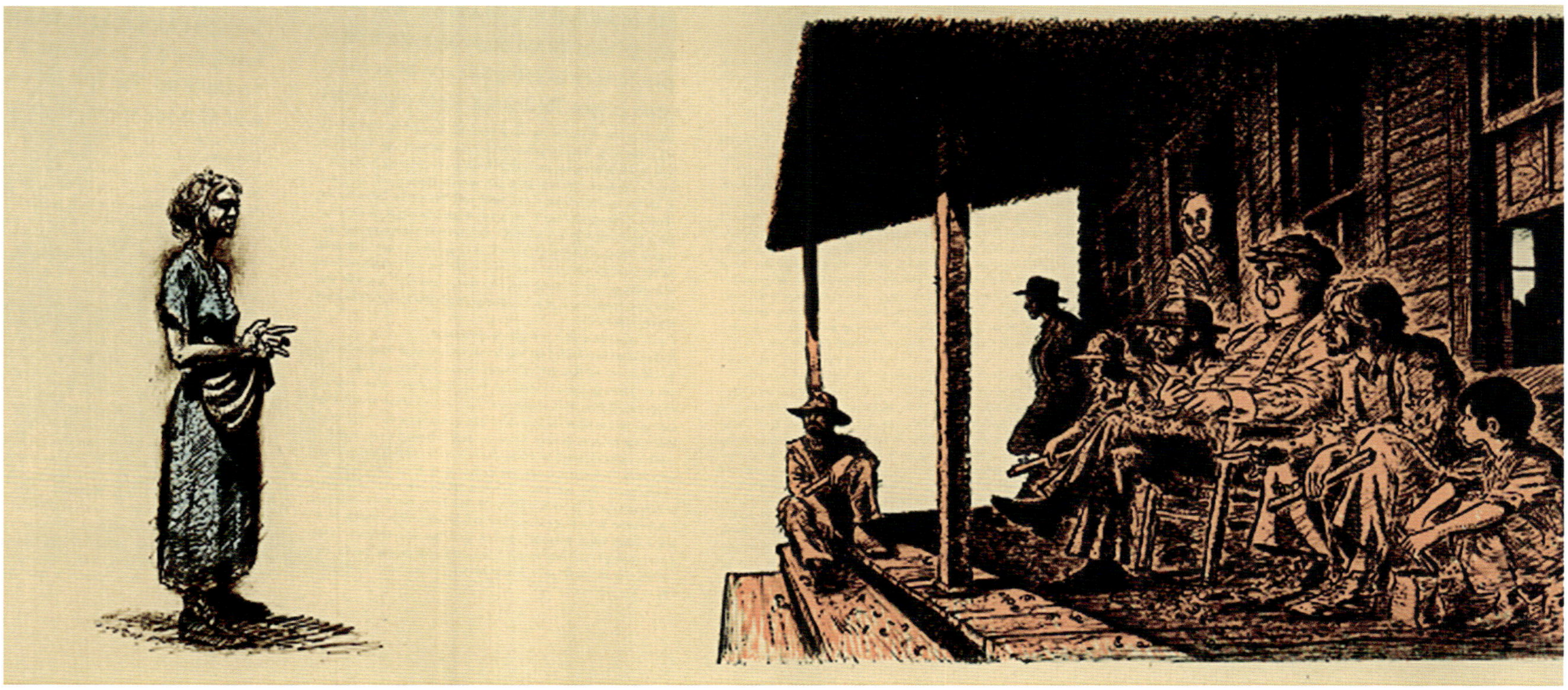

Varner's Store Front Porch and the Five Dollar Confrontation, lithograph

Two or more days after the futile horse-chasing episode, a confrontation of a different kind occurs in front of Varner's store. Initially the day had seemed uneventful with the predictable occupants in place across the porch, including old farmers whittling and chewing tobacco; the store clerk, Ratliff; a sewing machine salesman; and especially Flem Snopes and some of his blood relatives. Snopes is shown considerable deference and admiration by his relatives and others for swindling gullible and trusting people. In return he barely acknowledges his fellow porch squatters. The conversation of the day centers around the question of ownership of the newly scattered horses and liability, if any, for Henry Armstid's broken leg and Mr. Tull's injuries from the bridge accident. Then a lone figure appears in the distance walking slowly toward the store. It is Mrs. Armstid, who has walked from Mrs. Littlejohn's boardinghouse where she now often assists Mrs. Littlejohn with many daily tasks during Henry Armstid's convalescence.

She has come to Varner's store because Flem Snopes has resurfaced after being scarce during the auction. She had talked at length with Mrs. Littlejohn about the possibility of Snopes refunding her five dollars, which the Texan cowboy had given to Flem Snopes for the purchase of a mustang horse. It was as if she was trying to muster courage to do so and sought Mrs. Littlejohn's encouragement too. Said Saunders, "Now, Mrs. Armstid needs her five dollars back because her fool husband was standing in the way when the horses stampeded to escape the barn lot and ran over Henry and broke his leg. So not only did he lose his [wife's] five dollars, he has a broken leg, and crops to put in his field."[45]

In "Spotted Horses," Mrs. Armstid is described as downtrodden, abused by her husband, sitting silently in the family wagon as if "carved outen wood," "not looking at nothing," and other characterizations implying that she was a defeated woman who, however, was spared more than once by rampaging mustangs. Now she has somehow found the nerve to stand up to Flem Snopes and request repayment of the elusive five dollars. According to Saunders, "So she goes to confront Flem Snopes as he is sitting out on the porch. It looks like something from Shane [the movie] at high noon. There she is, standing up for herself possibly for the first time in her life, but wringing her hands in her apron."[46]

It's hard to imagine a more pitiful sight than this woman beginning to take her stand. She faces Flem Snopes (who averts her gaze) and twice tells him that the Texan had told her that she could get the money from Snopes. In Saunders's illustrations of that confrontation, this figure, pathetic and entirely alone on the left page, looks across the book's gutter at Flem Snopes and his cronies on the store front porch, which nearly fills the right page. This composition isolates Mrs. Armstid physically and emotionally, which was Saunders's intent. The composition furthermore stresses that Mrs. Armstid is facing unfavorable odds even before she utters her request for repayment. When she does so, Snopes tells her that the Texan took all the money and left after the auction. Mrs. Armstid is determined and repeats her statement that the Texan said he had given the money to Flem Snopes (presumably less his fee) and that Snopes would give her the five dollars. Snopes repeats his first statement and lies twice. Then in a gesture of insult and contempt, Snopes asks Mrs. Armstid to wait briefly while he goes into Varner's store. When he reappears, he gives Mrs. Armstid a small paper bag containing a few pieces of candy. She thanks him, and after a pause, sensing her polite but persistent effort is failing, she says, in a barely audible manner, that she better return to Mrs. Littlejohn's to help in preparing supper. There is a trial of sorts later to try to determine ownership of the mustangs. It cannot be proved. The case against Snopes is dismissed. Mrs. Armstid is never refunded for her loss. Flem Snopes swindles everyone including some of his relatives and frequent companions who, blind or dense, still admire him.

One point that Saunders repeatedly raised, in his choice of plot segments to illustrate, was the sheer wildness of the mustangs. The mustangs in Faulkner's "Spotted Horses" were descended from domesticated horses brought by Spanish explorers in the 1500s to what is now the American Southwest and Mexico. Some of those escaped captivity, survived in the wilderness, and propagated, becoming feral animals. By the twentieth century, if not before, their numbers had increased to the point of competing for grazing areas with cattle. To protect and increase grazing range for cattle, some mustang herds were thinned out by killings. In response to those shootings, certain horse enthusiasts organized roundups transporting them to the East Coast for adoption, a process that continues to the present. Saunders learned of such an auction to be held at Monroe, North Carolina, and attended it for the opportunity to witness and photograph it firsthand. Monroe is located in the southwestern part of the state. It is about fourteen miles southeast of Charlotte, hence about one hundred miles northeast of Saunders's home.

Saunders said, "I had to see it. So I got up early and drove to Monroe. It was just like the "Spotted Horses" story. There they were. They'd just stand around for a minute and look as docile as anything, but if something happened, they would run against the pen. I still remember the lady from the United States Land Management Bureau talking to people who wanted to adopt a mustang. She said: Now, if you want to adopt one of these ponies, you've got to show proof that you have a pen of a certain size that you can keep the horse in with a fence that is at least six feet high, and that the outside of the pen is of wood or steel. It cannot be wire because the ponies don't understand barbed wire. They don't know what barbed wire is. They'll just run through it and hurt themselves and tear it down. They're wild! These horses don't know how to drink out of a bucket. They've never known a bucket in their lives."[47]

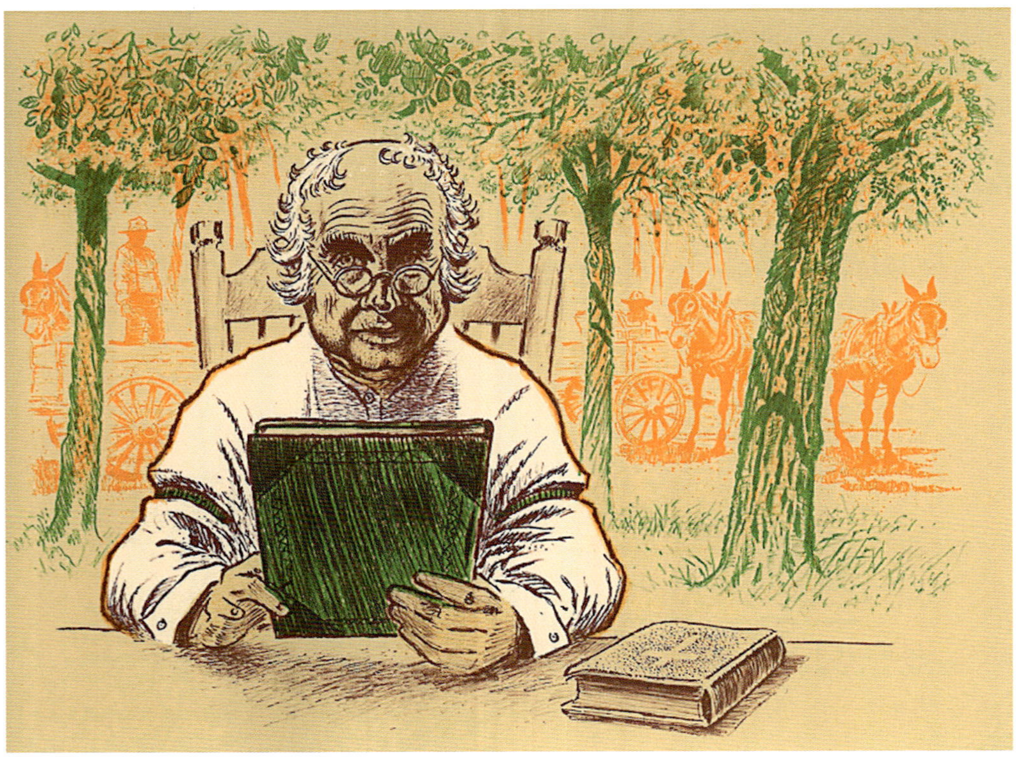

The Last Drama Begins, lithograph

Said Reeves, "That sounds like Faulkner, doesn't it?"[48]

Though wild mustangs are definitely the featured animals of the "Spotted Horses" story, mules have a role too. They appear as victims of a rampaging mustang on a narrow bridge, a team with fancy harness at the trial, and Mrs. Armstid rides one in the next-to-the-last illustration of the story. Mules are not strangers to Saunders. They were a vital part of everyday life at the farm where he grew up. There were mules and horses that regularly pulled plows and wagons. Yet as Saunders was beginning to work on the *Spotted Horses* book project, he felt he needed to refresh his knowledge of mules.

Saunders said, "When I was doing research for this story, I already knew what mules looked like, but it had been [some time] since I'd had mules at home anymore. I went with a friend to Columbia, Tennessee, to study them during its annual Mule Day Festival. At the turn of the Twentieth Century, Columbia had one of the biggest mule markets in the world. It raised and sold mules there and they still have, every spring, a Mule Day Festival. They still have mule teams from all across the country. I spent two days drawing and sketching mules there."[49]

That experience was put to good use for Saunders's illustration of a particular team of mules in *Spotted Horses.* In Faulkner's story it was likely among many other teams of mules and teams of horses pulling wagons, surreys, and buggies, plus saddled mules and horses. They took folks from Frenchman's Bend to the Whiteleaf Store some eight miles distant, because of a change of venue for the trial to determine ownership of, by then, the uncatchable mustangs. This mule team sports a decorative harness quite possibly based on one he sketched at Columbia, Tennessee, in the 1980s. Saunders said, "Many of them [the mule teams] had fancy harnesses. I saw one set with a little heart hanging on its harness."[50]

Mules also appear in the illustration of the magistrate officiating at the aforementioned trial. As it goes in Faulkner's words, "So by the time the Frenchman's Bend people began to arrive, there were two dozen wagons, the teams reversed and eased of harness and tied to the rear wheels in order to pass the day."[51]

The above mules stand quietly at the edge of a grove, in front of which looms the benevolent figure of the justice of the peace at a table. Saunders, faithful to the spirit of Faulkner's written description, created the justice character from the following passage:

"The Justice of the Peace was a neat, small, plump old man resembling a tender caricature of all grand fathers who ever breathed, in a beautifully laundered, though collarless, white shirt with immaculate starch-gleaming cuffs and bosom, and steel-framed spectacles and neat, faintly curling white hair. He sat behind a table and looked at them."[52]

The object of his forensic gaze is everyone in front of him: plaintiffs, defendants, relatives thereof, and lots

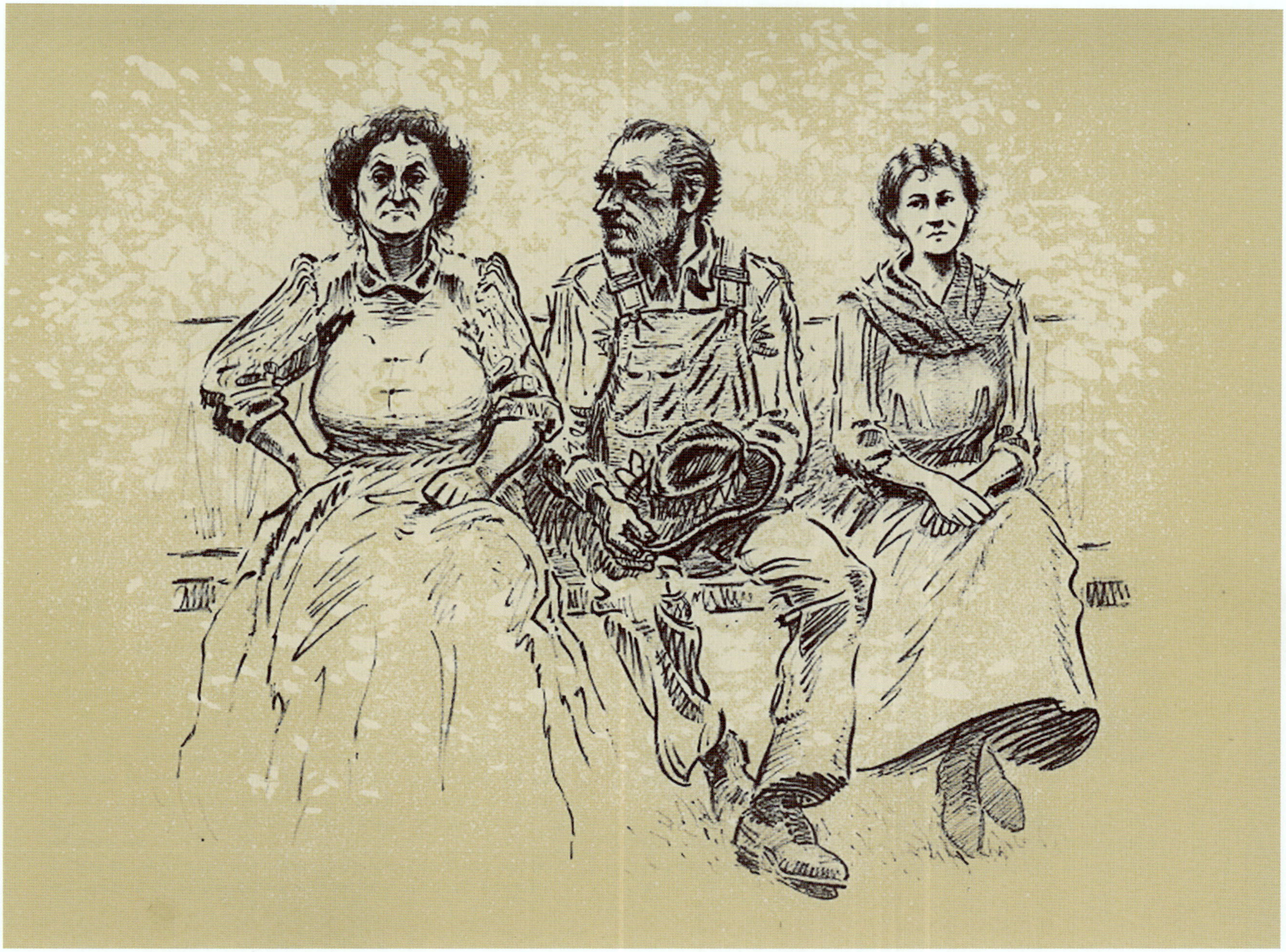

The Tulls at the Legal Proceedings, lithograph

of curious onlookers. Conspicuously absent is Flem Snopes, even though one of the two lawsuits to be heard that day was against him. A bailiff has attempted to serve the proper papers on Snopes, but he refused them. That case, Armstid vs. Snopes, pits Mrs. Armstid against Flem Snopes for the second time in the story and with the same grievance, reimbursement regarding the mustang for which her husband has paid Flem Snopes with Mrs. Armstid's money. Mrs. Armstid pleads her case and does so in a much more forthright manner than when she confronted Snopes on the porch of Varner's store. However once more her efforts come to nothing because the justice declares that she fails to prove that Snopes owns the wild horses. No matter that that judgment is based on the sworn statement by Lump Snopes, brother of the accused, that he saw Flem Snopes give Mrs. Armstid's five dollars to the Texan along with the proceeds of all the other mustangs auctioned. Lump Snopes's statement, under oath, was quite likely a lie and supports the notion that blood can be thicker than justice. It might also suggest that most all the Snopes are amoral and rotten.

The justice then begins to make another effort to help Mrs. Armstid, but she interrupts him in

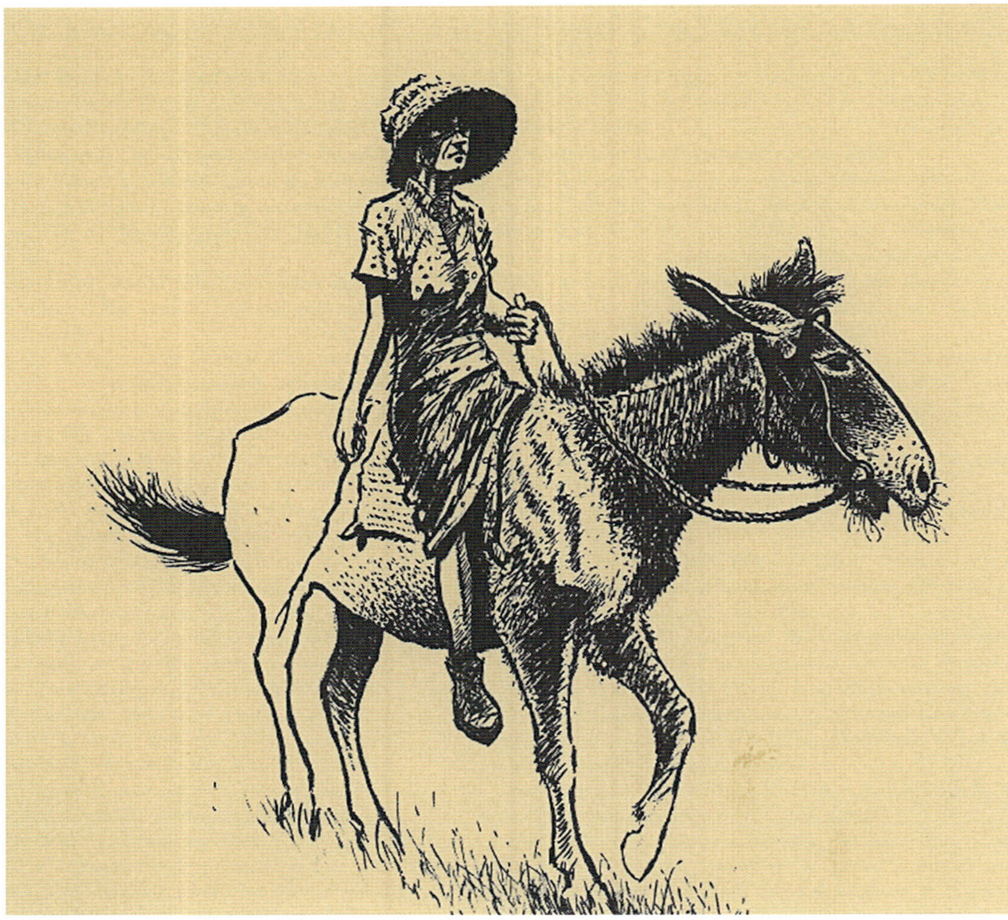

Mrs. Armstid Astride a Mule, lithograph

defeat, frustration, awareness, perseverance, courage, self-reliance, and stoicism.

As just stated regarding the post-trial image, Mrs. Armstid sits on a forlorn, floppy-eared, scraggly whiskered mule. Wearing a simple print dress, a summer straw bonnet, and her trademark well-worn tennis shoes, she guides the mule with a hemp rope, loop-rein in her left hand and a switch in her right. If she was earlier meek and reticent facing Snopes, she appears stoic now. There is fatalism about her as a whole. She may have had little formal education, but she is perceptive. She possesses common sense and a strong work ethic; she quietly assumes major responsibility for her family's needs and is even loyal to her abusive, ignorant husband. Certainly she plays the hand she is dealt in life with resolve to survive and endure for her children while remaining selfless. Yet she is not even accorded a first name in the story.

Saunders may have viewed Mrs. Armstid as an understated heroine, constantly turning the other cheek, and yet by finally standing up for herself against impossible odds and despite losing her legal suit, she gains a little self-respect. Saunders's bittersweet depiction of Mrs. Armstid, on her ungainly mule moving forward rather unapologetically, is more than a dutiful book illustration; it is an empathetic portrait and a tribute to Mrs. Armstid's worth.

The last bound image in this special limited edition of *Spotted Horses* is appropriately one of the uncatchable mustangs running with abandon, kicking its back legs outward, as if emphatically declaring its freedom in front of a large, brilliant-red setting sun. A twin image to this horse graces the front hard cover as an exotic fugitive, a mysterious but recessed image. The illustrations by Saunders for this limited edition of *Spotted Horses,* reproduced and discussed here, are again just some of the thirty-four that grace his book. The purpose has been to introduce a selection of Saunders's illustrations, especially of horses and mules and their dramatic interactions with people, and of course to give visual flesh and bones to Faulkner's main characters in their finest or worst moments, described by him through both keen insight and exaggeration.

midsentence, stating that she had better leave because of the distance to return to Frenchman's Bend. Perhaps she feels the justice of the peace is about to demand the appearance of Flem Snopes but feels Snopes would probably lie again about the matter of ownership, even under oath.

Whatever her reasoning, she leaves the proceedings the way she arrived, mounted on a family-owned mule for the eight-mile trip back to Frenchman's Bend. For the second time in Faulkner and Saunders's illustrated version of the *Spotted Horses* story, Mrs. Armstid is the only human figure on a whole page, facing Flem Snopes and his companions, and as described earlier she is almost swallowed up by the empty space around her, showing her psychological isolation confronting Snopes whittling in his comfort zone. She seems to embody unequal portions of meekness,

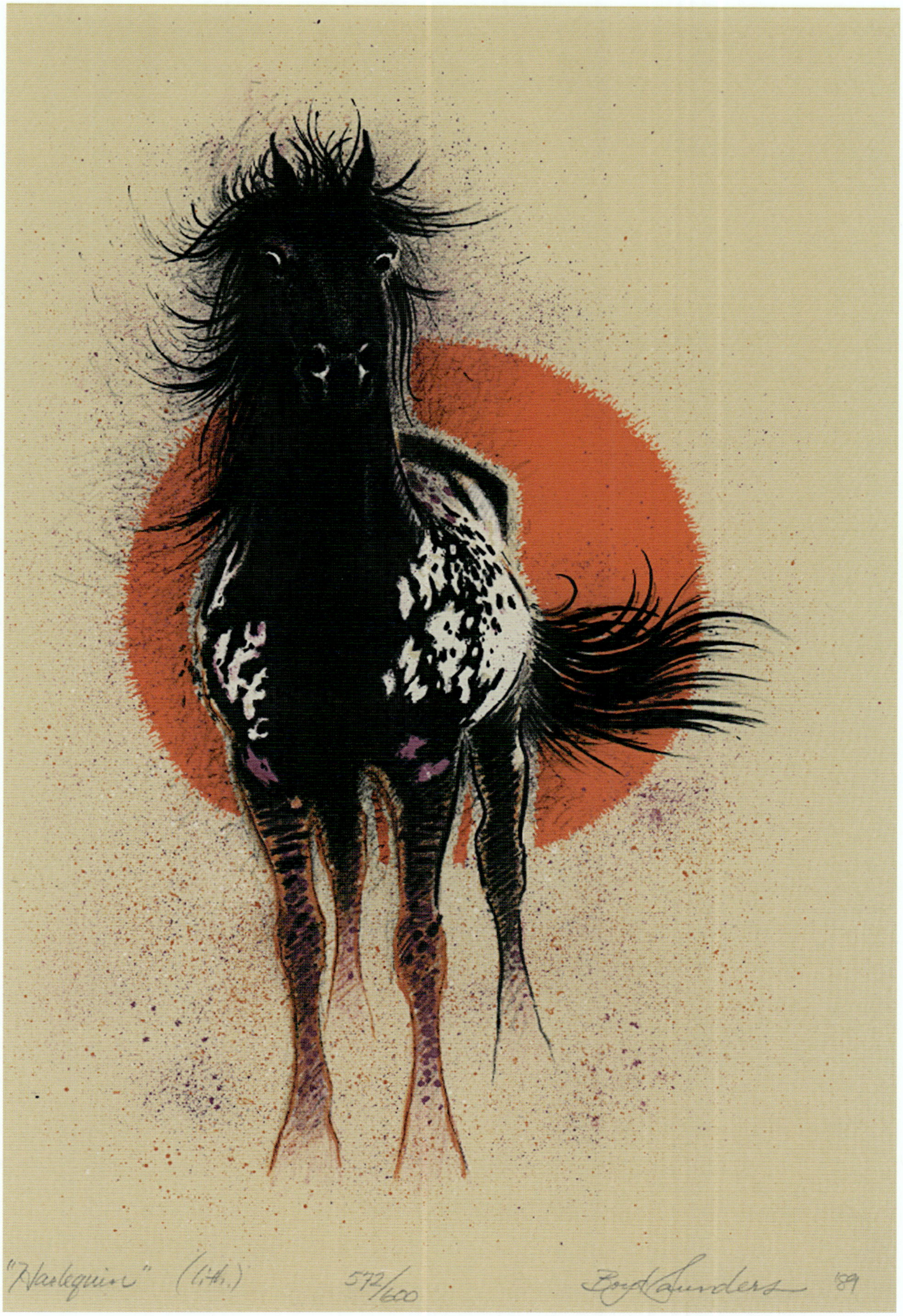

Harlequin, lithograph

Chapter 5

Southern Cross/A Trilogy—The Farm, Blackberry Winter, and *Late Light*

Around the middle of the 1970s, Saunders embarked on an open-ended series of etchings that initially reflected three major forces in his life at the time. They included a fondness for the literary works of William Faulkner and Edgar Lee Masters, a rethinking of the general direction for the themes of his art, and an appropriate response to a personal tragedy. By that time the artist had been experimenting for years with a number of tendencies involving content, compositional structure, color, drawing, narration, geology, poetic vagueness, abstraction, surrealistic passages, and the impact of mankind on the land from the paleo-Indian culture of the American Southwest to the modern era, to name just a few.

By the early 1960s he had become enamored with selected short stories by William Faulkner as well as the poetry of Edgar Lee Masters (1869–1950). Saunders empathized with Faulkner's pessimism ascribing it to the writer's anger with the doomsday scenario of the Cold War during the 1940s and 1950s . . . along with his heavy drinking. Saunders was in the U.S. Marine Corps during part of the 1950s and vividly remembers his own similar fears at that time: "Then there was the Cold War. World War II was the most horrific struggle the world had ever known. It ended in 1945 with a pair of atomic explosions, which were virtually heard

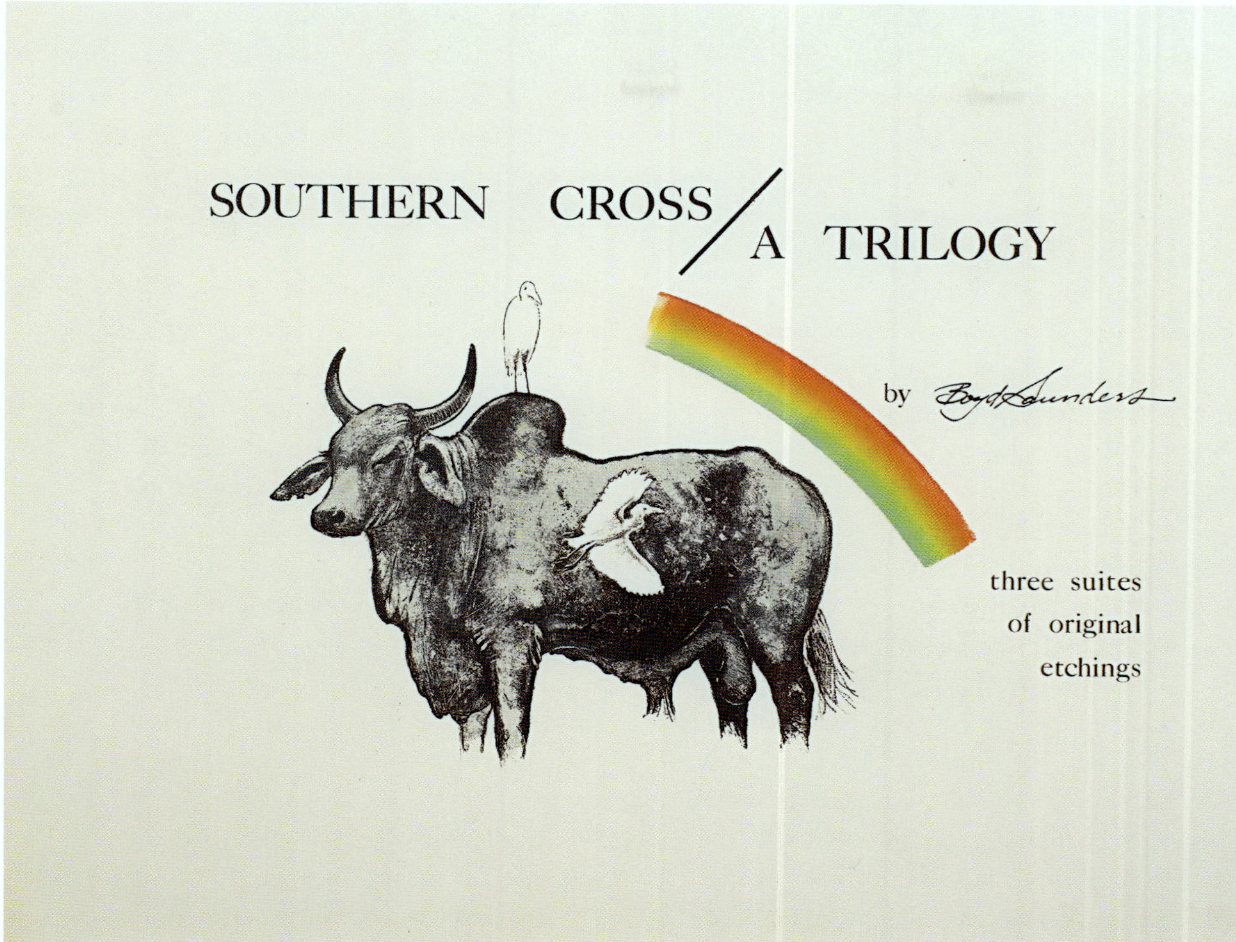

Southern Cross/A Trilogy, cover print

around the world, and which made it clear that one era had ended and another had begun. Even as we reveled in the end of the great struggle, we had to look ahead to the next big war which could begin at any moment, be even more horrible than the last, and which might ultimately mean the end of life on Earth. Like many of my generation, I put on the uniform and shouldered a rifle, convinced that it would happen; that I would participate in the last great Armageddon battle. We just weren't sure exactly when. Incidentally, we weren't as crazy as one might think. A couple of times it nearly did happen."[1]

However, concurrent to reading dark works by Faulkner, Saunders was moved by the poignancy and wisdom from the grave (so to speak) in Edgar Lee Masters's *Spoon River Anthology.* Then Saunders happened to read closely Faulkner's acceptance speech for the Nobel Prize for Literature in 1950 with the resulting response of relief and surprise at its ring of hope for humans and their planet. An intertwining of sorts of buoyancy from the works just mentioned by both major authors seemed to alter Saunders's view of the world and the direction for his own work. Then unexpectedly a personal tragedy in the early 1970s played a highly significant role in the nature of much of Saunders's artwork to come.

In late October 1972 Shirley Nebhut Saunders, father of the artist-educator Boyd Saunders, died of injuries sustained from a farm accident involving a tractor. The artist-son grieved, and in subtle ways he did so for years thereafter: "As far as I was concerned, he had always been an ageless, timeless, indomitable rock. Then suddenly, inescapably, he was no more. That event was a key piece in a puzzle of temporal disorientation."[2]

Southern Cross/A Trilogy began as a loving tribute to him. It is not about the life of the artist's father; it is about, in general, the lifestyle and other memories of living on the family farm where Shirley Saunders played a large role. On the title page of *The Farm,* a small intaglio image of a pair of man's worn work gloves appears at the bottom right corner preceded by the words "for Shirley." The dates of his life ("1906–1972") are positioned just below the gloves imagery. "The title page says for Shirley. Most people think it's a woman. . . . It wasn't. My father's name was Shirley, my grandfather and one of my brothers were all named Shirley. When your name is Shirley, you have to learn to fight early and often."[3] "It was not directly about him, it was simply a tribute to him."[4]

The print series *Southern Cross/A Trilogy* is composed of three suites of intaglio prints: *The Farm, Blackberry Winter,* and *Late Night.* Counting assorted title pages, there are twenty-two original etchings, each 16 × 22 inches in size, with six etchings spread over each of the three sections.[5] All the compositional imagery was developed on copper plates and printed in limited editions. The *Southern Cross* portion of the title of this series came from several sources. First and maybe most important, the Southern Cross is the name of a constellation of stars most visible in the night sky over Earth's Southern Hemisphere, and it has been used by seafarers to navigate for millennia. Its counterpoint in the Northern Hemisphere is, of course, the North Star located at the end of the Big Dipper. A second possible source is found in the title of a painting by another mid-South artist named Carroll Cloar (1913–1993). That title is "*Where the Southern Cross the Yellow Dog*" which was derived from a transportation juncture in the Mississippi delta involving the Southern Railroad crossing a local short-line railroad called or nicknamed the Yellow Dog.[6] The painting's title may sound awkward, but that awkwardness is known as informal English or local color, which is widespread in the South and elsewhere. A third possible source is found in the title of a short story by South Carolina writer William Price Fox, the "Southern" in its title, "Have You Ever Rode the Southern?," again meaning the Southern Railroad.

It is not surprising that Saunders would be drawn to railroad metaphors for such an important body of work. He is fond of railroad imagery. It appears in at least three prints of *St. James Crossing,* a suite that is an extension of *Southern Cross/A Trilogy.* It is ongoing, as of this publication, in a total of seven prints, paintings, or drawings in a further extension titled *The Return of the Wanderer.* He is also particularly respectful of the Southern Railroad owing to its long history in the South and its role in the South's economic rise during the post–World War II era. A fourth possible source is present in the upper right corner of *The Gathering,* a color etching in the *Late Light Suite* where the words "Southern" and "Crossing" are partially visible in all capital letters on a railroad crossing gate.

In sum the title *Southern Cross* was derived from all the just mentioned sources, directly or in spirit. However, a persuasive case can be made for the Southern Cross constellation with its prospect of helping humans in their ocean travels, just as Saunders has made repeated mention that the premise of the trilogy was that the artist and then viewers would be walking (or navigating) around an abandoned farm community, reflecting on human and animal artifacts that have survived. Prior humans, for the most part, have vacated the farms or hamlets, leaving unsettled situations and maybe some raw pain for the artist, too. *Southern Cross/A Trilogy* began about 1976 and was completed by 1984. The prints in *The Farm* and its accompanying suites were published by Fine Art and Publishing, a Division of Transart Industries, Atlanta, Georgia.[7] The premiere exhibition for the *Southern Cross/A Trilogy* series of prints was at the Columbia Museum of Art, Columbia, South Carolina, from February 19 to March 25, 1984.

THE FARM

The trilogy is centered around farm life, though it is not a documentary about the Saunderses' family farm nestled near Rossville, Tennessee. Some of the images are based on the farm of Saunders's youth and refer to the lifestyle he came to know, but Saunders created an imaginary farm as a composite of his family farm plus many other southern farms from stories and vignettes of farms from several different places. For example some of the images are based in general on barns, outbuildings, and farmhouses from the Dutch Fork community, which is a rural area around Saunders's home and studio close to Chapin, South Carolina. However sometimes his sources are a little more specific. "A lot of the images are from one little abandoned farm over close to Peak, South Carolina."[8]

Yet again no matter how convincing or compelling *The Farm Suite* images are in the trilogy, they are not of a specific farm. Saunders's farm imagery functions as a catalyst for viewers to wander about such a place and speculate about what sort of life took place there, to daydream, and to start a journey placing themselves in *The Farm* and so on. That may sound simple enough, but an element of mood or sensibility is also present, by intention, permeating the entire trilogy series. The mood or sensibility also changes, though slowly, from suite to suite beginning with sorrow, loss, and a shadowing emptiness in *The Farm,* to a certain expiation in *Blackberry Winter,* and finally to solace, a spiritual peace, and a regeneration or renewed will to reengage life in *Late Light.* In all three suites there are personal experiences hinted at, a dominance of visual metaphors, and implied questions asked of viewers, reflecting experiences and feelings that are universal.

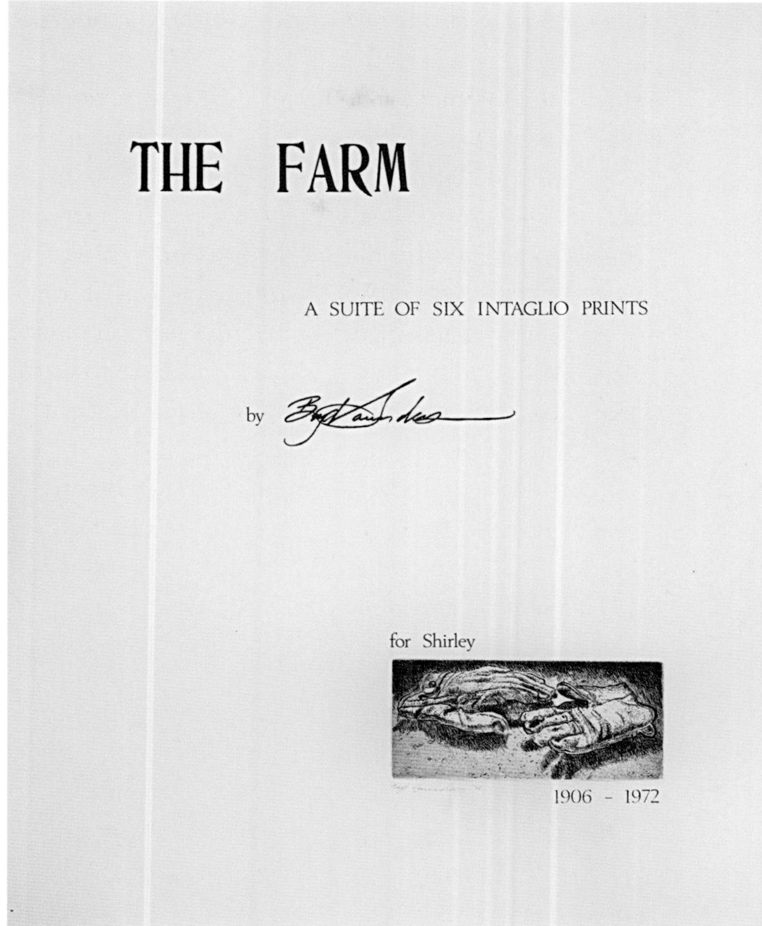

The Farm (cover print), 1976–84, 16 × 22 in.

As mentioned earlier, the most immediate motivation for the beginning suite was the tragic death of the artist's father and dealing with it. Reportedly the artist walked around the farm of his boyhood rather at a loss following his father's accidental death. When doing so he observed a number of interrupted projects and perhaps could see in his mind's eye his father, plus maybe hired help, working through those tasks.[9] Then slowly Saunders started to channel his feelings of sadness into planning a body of prints as a worthy testimony of his love and admiration for his father and as a reflection of the reverence for the land his father possessed and passed on to his children.

The Farm Suite, then, initiates a sober tribute with six hand-wrought, copperplate etchings. All the etchings present exterior or interior views of farm-type structures, though almost none contain a person, the exception being *The Guardian.* There are images of humans and animals on posters, calendars, and signs, and in *The Bedroom* there is the ghostly apparition of a woman. Curiously, though humans are scarce in the various settings, animals are not. *The Guardian* sports two stabled horses and a mare with foal behind a sheltered vintage roadster. Elsewhere there are hounds, a horse, and a cat in *The Cistern,* and a collie dog, the model for which may have been one of a succession of Saunders's family collies, for example Old Jock. If *The Farm Suite* is supposed to be about a farm community of mostly uninhabited structures, why are domesticated animals there? Dogs, cats, goats, and horses will perish or not stay without access to food or water. The answer may be simple. This place, this amalgam of places, exists in the artist's mind. He has lived in, worked around, and visited such places; and he sketched them and surrendered all those experiences and memories to his imagination. Then he began calling forth such imagery as an appropriate tribute to his father's exemplary life and to a way of life in the greater community of southern agrarian culture.

THE ORCHARD

The journey around *The Farm* community with its rundown buildings, left-behind objects, and numerous autographic markings begins with *The Orchard.* The suggestion is that viewers are looking through the eyes of a former resident of a two-story farmhouse,

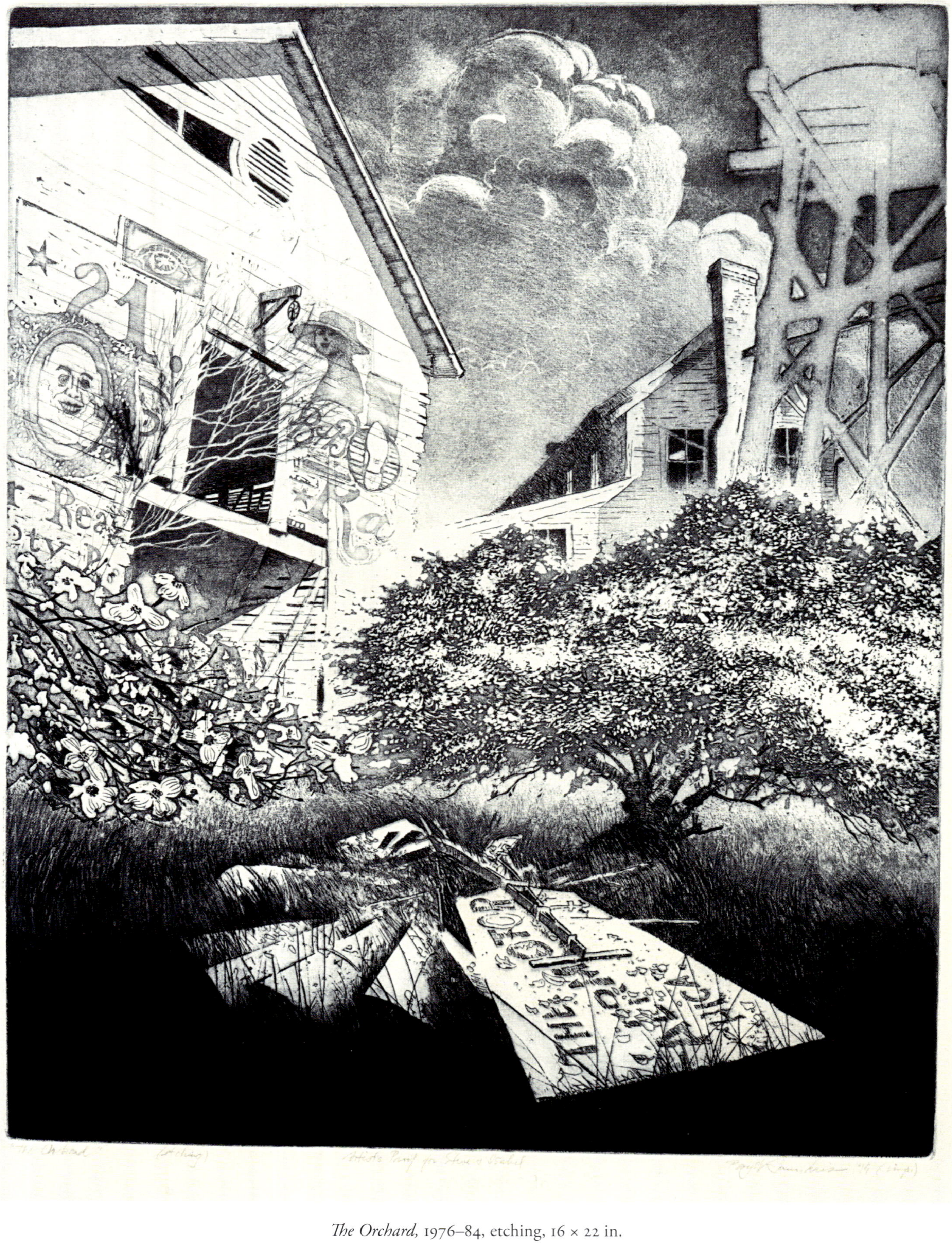

The Orchard, 1976–84, etching, 16 × 22 in.

the home place. Memories of living there with well-maintained buildings and grounds now collide with the realization of a kind of benign desertion. The faded image on the siding of the barn's gable end reveals neglect, and the blades of a windmill lie useless amid tall grasses and weeds in the foreground. The words "Air Motor Company, Chicago" are partially visible on the blade closest to the bottom of the composition. To Saunders the fallen windmill is not a symbol of death only: "Down here lying in the weeds are the ruins of an old windmill, lying there like a dead bird, yet also like a phoenix. Around, trees are blooming again and life has started over."[10]

Writer Steve Harris found this print to be especially unsettling owing to some advertising graphics on the barn's exterior: "The print's forbidding quality is further brought about by the authentic 1917 Gillette Razor Ad with its staring, penetrating eyes faded by the years, but even menacing in its presence."[11]

The traveler to this orchard and homestead in the spring identifies with it because he (the artist) was touched by it or places like it as a youth. He may be saddened by its decaying state; his reactions might be both emotional and physical. Death and rebirth are both present along with rekindled memories of a home place, familiar objects, and special animals, but no one factor dominates. *The Orchard,* like other etchings in *The Farm,* has unsettling qualities. Notice its composition. A case could be made that most of its images are not anchored. They tend to float and overlap like passing thoughts and layered memories, like the unsettled mental state of the artist.

THE GUARDIAN

The Guardian possesses the only substantial human figure of the six etchings in *The Farm,* a half-length study of a person. The individual seen in three-quarter view was a longtime friend of the artist and of the artist's father. Saunders said, "In this print is a friend to my family named Floy; a wonderful person. It's a kind of tribute to him. Sadly, he is no longer with us."[12]

"The solitary human figure was inspired by and modeled after Mr. Floyd Kinner. Floyd, whose name had, over the years come to be pronounced 'Floy,' was a warm and generous man with a close understanding of horses. He took considerable pride in his ability to predict the gender of a mare's foal long before it was born, and had an uncanny ability to know the minds and ways of horses and mules. When he spoke to them it was almost conversational. Suspended above his head is a cotton scale, which can be seen as either a symbol of precariousness or balance, or perhaps both."[13]

The imposing portrait of Floy is positioned just right of center in the composition, which is, overall, a triptych, a composing device popular with Saunders. The triptych has existed since the late Gothic and Renaissance periods in western European art. Diptychs, triptychs, and polyptychs served as formats for small in-home Christian devotional art on a ledge, on a table, or in conjunction with a prie-dieu. They could also be massive, multisection, hinged, painted, and sculpted panels such as the Ghent altarpiece, St. Bavo Cathedral, Ghent, Belgium, by Jan van Eyck (completed 1432) and the equally phenomenal Isenheim altarpiece (c. 1510–15) by Matthias Grunewald for the chapel of the Hospital of St. Anthony, Isenheim, Germany, now in the Musee d'Unterlinden, Colmar, Germany.[14] In *The Farm Suite* alone the triptych format is easily recognized in *The Guardian, The Stable,* and somewhat in *The Dogtrot* and *The Bedroom.* In the first three of these etchings vertical rectangles unequally divide the horizontal format of their entire compositions into spaces that seem near, far, open, closed, or puzzling illusions. Now returning to *The Guardian:*

> [Saunders] In the side panel to the left, one can see a grand automobile, an elegant relic of another day and time, long abandoned to neglect and deterioration, now serving as a roosting place for barnyard chickens. It is easy to imagine that it has a dramatic story of its own. In its day, it replaced the horse as a means of transportation and a symbol of power and status. Now, in a moment of supreme irony, it crumbles in decay as a mare and new foal can be seen walking by beyond, a vital symbol of spring and rebirth.
>
> In the center panel, behind *The Guardian,* is a wall which has, over the years, served as a repository for fragments of newspaper clippings and popular advertising graphics, creating a sort of disjointed montage which takes on its own

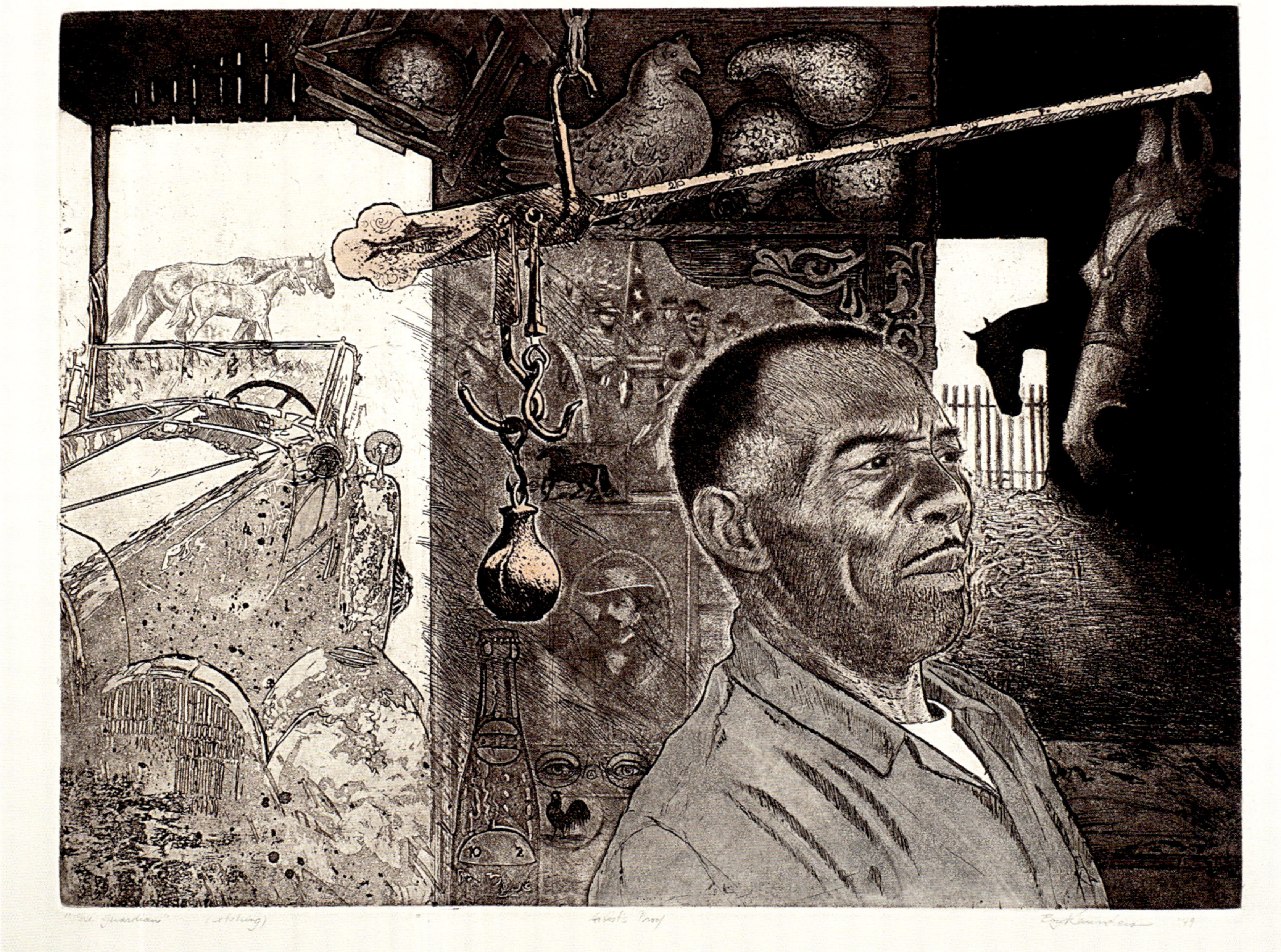

The Guardian, 1976–84, etching, 16 × 22 in.

pictorial character. The viewer is left to wonder what commonality these bits of imagery share and what impulses caused them to wind up together here. One is also caused to ponder their relationship to *The Guardian* and the other pictorial elements throughout the triptych.

This image is as much about the formal elements of art as it is iconography. The somewhat irregular balance of the triptych format, the carefully studied placement and arrangement of the various parts, the wide range of values—from sparkling whites to rich velvety darks, and all the tones and textures in between—the implications of mass and volume firmly stated in the head of *The Guardian,* and the counterweight (pea) of the cotton scale and its repetition like a leitmotif

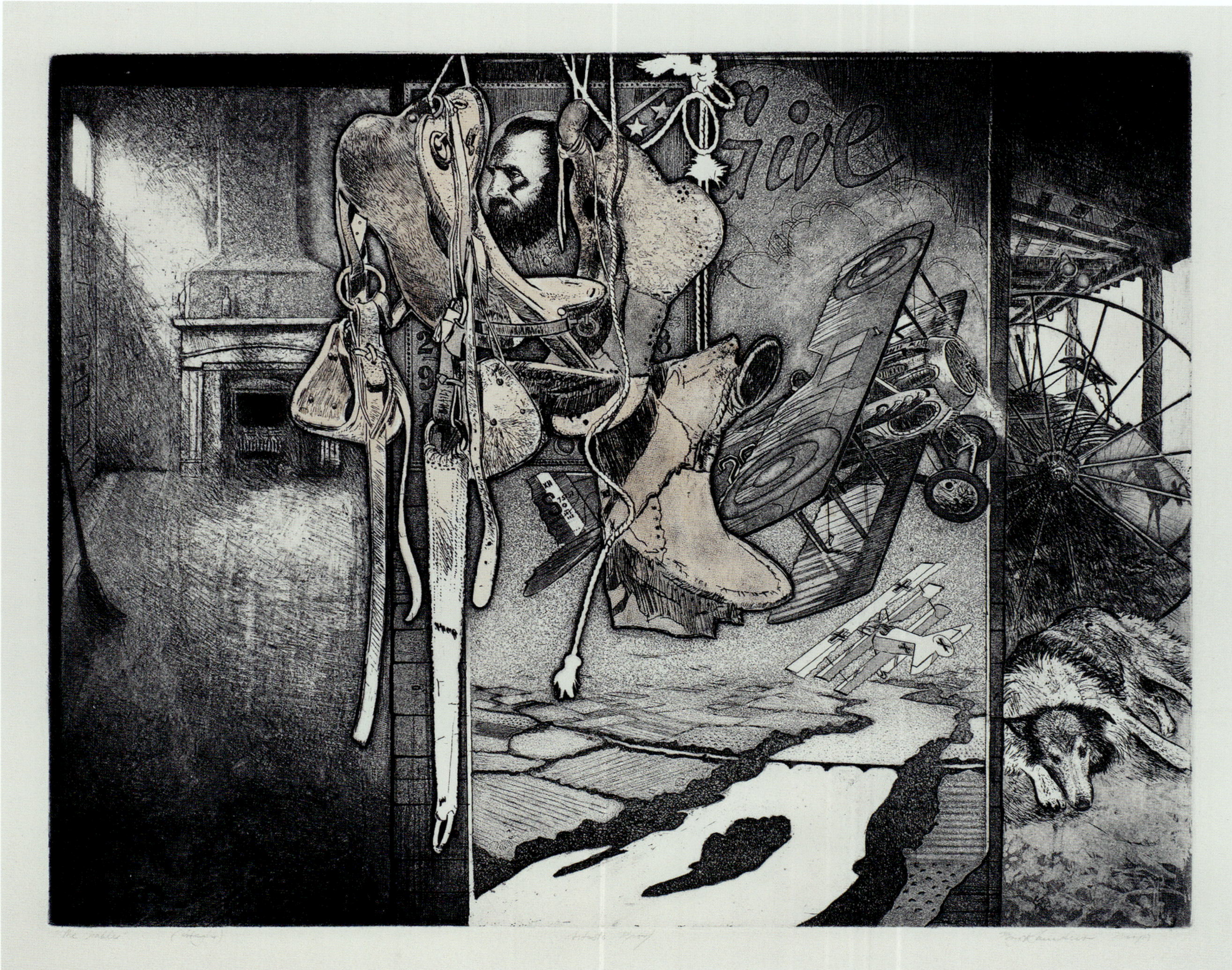

The Stable, 1976–84, etching, 16 × 22 in.

throughout the composition all proclaim this work to be absolutely committed to the classical language of visual design.[15]

THE STABLE

Among other triptych compositions in *The Farm* is *The Stable,* which is rich in metaphors, illusory textures, and dynamic abstract structure. The left and center panels seem loaded with clues or symbols of major historic or tradition-soaked narration, leaving the right panel anticlimactic. In the left vertical rectangle a bare room, with its high-placed window and imposing chimneypiece, recalls the grand but now unfurnished public rooms at homes like Drayton Hall, an eighteenth-century plantation home that survives near Charleston, South Carolina. Overlapping the entrance to the room in *The Stable* is the wooden stirrup of a saddle grouping in front of a wide central panel-wall. The suspended saddles partly obscure a large poster depicting an aerial dogfight between a French biplane and a German triplane over peaceful, tilled farmland during World War I.

The biplane almost flies off the poster as its left wheel extends slightly past the right-side border and in front of the partition wall. What wonderful trompe l'oeil. Actually the poster imagery, in its entirety, is part of a larger illusionistic performance. Traditional Renaissance perspective attempts to convince viewers that the implied depth, in this case, the large empty room and that of the farm equipment shed, need only be measured in feet or yards. The implied depth in the poster is in miles, many miles to a horizon. But that whole illusion is halted at the poster's edges and the flat wall behind it. So, the space that is theoretically the deepest in the entire composition is actually the shallowest. Likewise the three distinctly different sets of images do not exist together in the physical world but may do so in a surreal world of visual metaphors, in visual art, or in visual poetry. After all nothing in the entire composition even looks like a stable except for the presence of the saddles.

Insight into Saunders's creative process reveals that he does not predetermine specific imagery or compositional issues in individual works of a series. His pieces develop slowly with exploration and a kind of testing. The following commentary was written by the artist upon completion of *The Stable* as a reflection of how it turned out, not as some rigid plan in hand before he started even though the first few paragraphs may sound like there was a specific plan that was followed almost to the letter:

> Three saddles, in part or whole, hang from the rafters of a shed. One of them is an army saddle, the other two, are parts of western saddles. Behind them is a wall with a World War I Victory poster on it. A commemorative Civil War calendar honoring Stonewall Jackson has been plastered over part of the poster. Fragments of the calendar image can be seen between the saddles.
>
> To the left is a door opening into an empty room, perhaps at one time a farm or plantation office. To the right, one sees around a corner to another shed with a hay rake, other farm tools, and a dog. The whole presentation forms a sort of triptych somewhat reminiscent of three-paneled altar paintings of another time and, as such, seems to imply a certain votive significance. The primary theme is involved with the old southern triad of agriculture, and equestrian and military pursuits. It seems to reflect on war and peace, e.g., the beating of swords into plowshares and spears into pruning hooks, from the Bible.
>
> On a less didactic level, it explores the assimilation of popular graphic images and their occasional ability to transcend their original functions and become cultural symbols. It also confronts the pervasive conflict between reality and illusion. On a still more formal level, it probes the asymmetrical and eccentric relationship of the three panels—between the sculptural three dimensionality of the three saddles, the flat illusionism of the poster wall, the emptiness of the enclosed space in the left panel, the crowded fullness of the open space in the right panel, and the contrasting points of view they seem to present.
>
> The composition further deals with a visual line of fan shapes beginning with the wedge of light entering the transom window at the left side of the image. It follows to the wings and spinning propeller of the plane and repeats itself over and over in the rafters and the wheel to the right, then in the legs and snout of the dog, finally, to the fingers of land and river shown in the war poster. This outward radial force is arrested and contained by the taut line of the road and bridge, a line which is, in turn, redirected and turned upward upon itself by the broom leaning against the wall in the empty room.
>
> This piece is more concerned with musings and reflections than hard questions.[16]

Additional insight into Saunders's creative process carries the thought of the last sentence from Saunders's commentary even further into receptivity for unexpected directions: "One of the things I enjoy playing with in my work is relationships. I ponder a long time about the exact placement of a particular object or line or mark. I worry about the relationships of these symbols to each other. Some of them I make

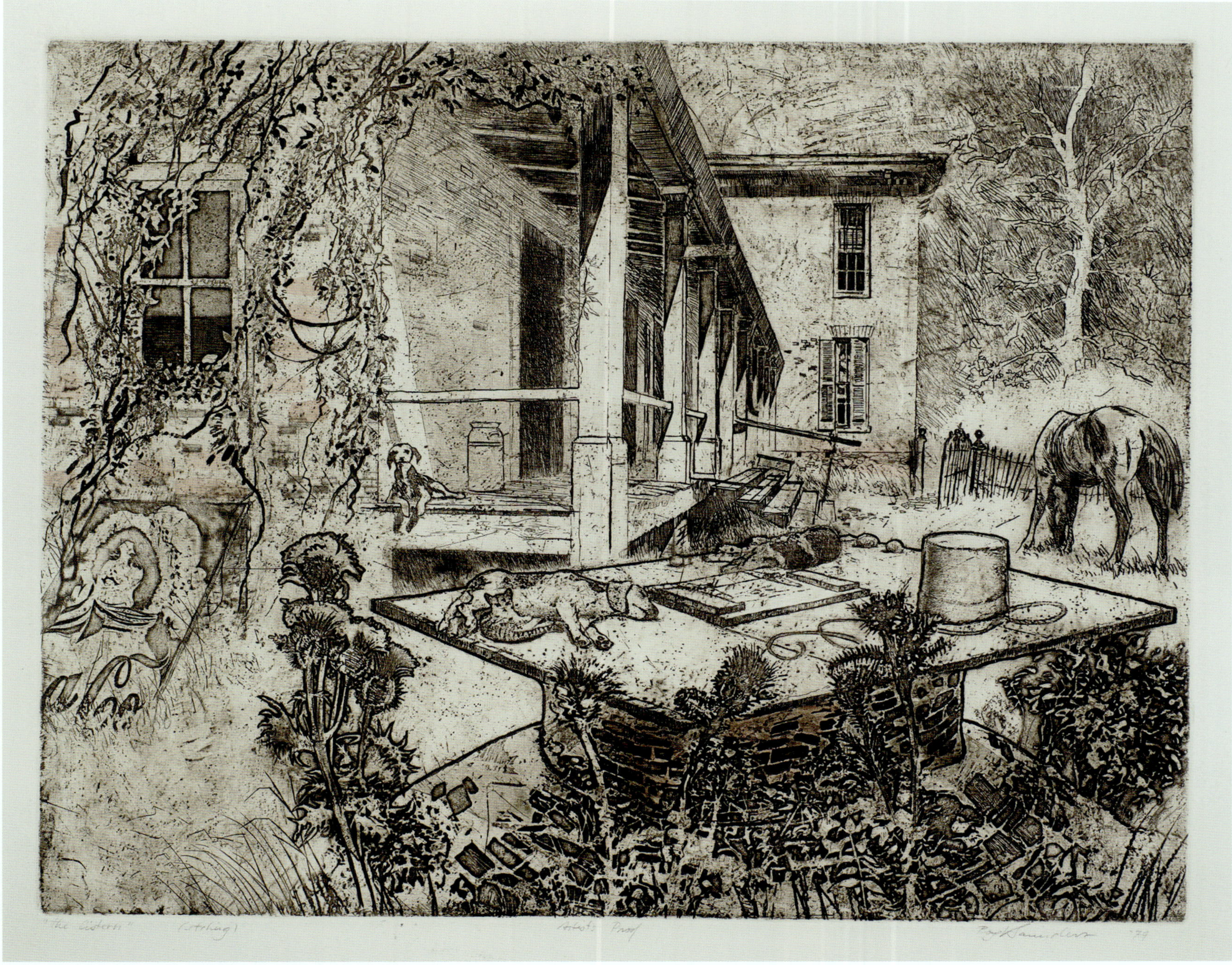

The Cistern, 1976–84, etching, 16 × 22 in.

very close spatially, and very obvious. Then I like to switch off and have some relationships stretched very thin, so that at first glance there seems to be no reason at all for these things to exist in the same space.

"Sometimes, by their disparity, I hope they may prod the viewer to [imagine] why they exist on the same plane. Hopefully, there is a sense of discovery in finding that relationship, and some pleasure in the tension created there."[17]

THE CISTERN

The Cistern presents a partial view of a sizeable country home that appears to have exterior walls of stucco over brick construction with one wall section partially covered in vines. Seen at a rather extreme receding orthogonal view, the porch, with its stately but simple boxed columns or piers, seems to front the entire right-facing façade. A two-story structure with an exterior wall surface similar to the foreground dwelling rises at ninety degrees to the main home and in full sun. A gate and a picket fence take the viewer's eye further back to the right but are partly obstructed by a grazing horse. In the lower foreground is a cistern with a large, flat cover on which rest an overturned bucket in one corner and a sort of odd couple (dog and cat) reclining together in the opposite corner. The cat and dog on the cistern cover near the porch likely take note of viewers before viewers notice them. Mysteriously the bust-length image of a young woman, perhaps part of an advertising sign, covers the entrance to a storm cellar or basement, adding to the eclectic nature of the place.

The house in *The Cistern* is reported to be very much like one near the Saunders's home place. Saunders describes it as "a special place that always surprises one when you come upon it. It practically springs out of nowhere. When I think of this place, I often hear a certain sound which I always associate with it. It could be described as almost a non-sound; one the mind hears and records."[18]

THE OLD NUCKHALL PLACE

> [Saunders's journal entry] We had taken his [Mr. Shirley's] clothing to Floy, which nobody in the family could wear, and we had gotten lost. Well, really, it wasn't us that was lost, it was Floy's house that seemed to be out of place, but then maybe it was our fault, not the house's, because neither Lee nor I had been there but a few times before.
>
> Then, mission accomplished, we started for home. Then it was home that was lost and the little dirt and gravel farm roads wound round and round and intersected just often enough to be even more confusing. The wind blew steadily and the October afternoon took on a strange hazy light, and that light, plus the lingering presence of the man which his clothing we had carried and left in the car, merged with the temporary disorientation to form a strange surreal quality which both of us felt but neither acknowledged.
>
> The road unfolded before us, past cotton fields and farm houses and many pastures of motley cows and groves of many hued oak trees, many even older than the road which had cut itself into the red earth until, in places, it formed a great ravine that was colonnaded with the hanging, groping roots of those same trees.
>
> At some point we weren't going home anymore, but were off on a pilgrimage to see or perhaps experience the Old Nuckhall Place. It was a pilgrimage I had made many times before for reasons not fully understood even by myself but Lee had not and so now it seemed appropriate that he should be initiated to and made spiritual guardian of that elegant decaying fragment of the heritage we both shared. On this strangest of days, even that venerable shrine seemed to have misplaced itself.
>
> At last, as daylight was growing scarce, we stood in awe, watching the house thrust its chimneys high into the gloom of the ancient cedar grove. The slave-made bricks had gotten redder through the years until they seemed to glow with a strange light from within; the carved stone window headers and cornices, imported many decades before from England, had covered themselves with a motley gray and green patina of moss and fungus and the old lead glass windows had warped and discolored until each one gave forth strange hints of images that constantly contradicted whether they were born in the glass or emanated from the darkened interior of the house.
>
> From around back the ancient Negro caretaker appeared. It seemed inconceivable that any living mortal should inhabit this place, but the owner (who kept residence off in Memphis or somewhere) had this man's family living in one wing of the old house for years to maintain and protect the place. He appeared now, looking as if he had somehow been spontaneously generated from the decaying brick and mold. His challenge was polite and insistent. "What can I do for you?"
>
> Though I had been there before, it had been many years and time had taken its toll on all things including his eyesight. I told him who we

were and why we were there. "Sanders?" he said, mispronouncing the name as most people thereabouts do, "I know them. Ain't that the boy who got killed the other day?" "Yes, that's right." "Was that the old man or the boy, Mr. Big Shelly or Mr. Little Shelly?" I explained that Mr. Big Shelly (who stood all of 5'5") had been dead for some time now. "How long?" "About 30 years." "Is that right? Lawd! Well how old was the boy?" As I told him that Mr. Little Shelly (6'1") was 66 he allowed as how that wasn't old at all, I had to agree.

The place had changed little since the last time I was there, which was when I took Clay there before he was married. There was the kitchen house set apart from the main house for reasons of heat, smells of cooking and fire; there was the former slaves' basement dining room, the old smoke house made of hand hewn logs, the cistern and the enormous old oak trees.

The previous caretaker who I had known, and had visited and hunted with from time to time, was many years since dead and gone. But the hounds; the overwhelming presence of the place was the hounds. Contained in a colony of ingenious, jury-rigged enclosures which had seemingly grown, one onto another like something alive as their members had increased. They were a noisy and forbidding lot; strong, arrogant, wearing their sexuality like a badge and secure in the knowledge that their pens kept them safely removed from having to give physical realization to the threats and promises they threw at us.

So we stood there, the three of us, and talked of dogs and night long hunts and how the elder Mr. Nuckhall had met his untimely end many years ago when he had words with a poaching white trash neighbor and had been shot from his horse for his trouble. As we stood there, shouting our tales above the din of the hounds, my mind kept going back repeatedly to that phrase, "Mist Shelly Sanders? Dat's de boy was killed other day, ain't it?" It was the key piece in a puzzle of temporal disorientation which had been building to this point for some time. Certainly this journey today had known its share of interrupted chronology but it had actually begun long before.

Ever since I left home a strange phenomenon had been occurring. I would come back once or twice a year to the home place, this venerable location of my beginnings, and it would seem that I had only left the day before, only in reality many months or a year would have passed. The visit would last a few days or a couple of weeks and then it would be another year before I'd be back, seemingly to take up where I'd left off living. It was like the fictional town of Brigadoon which existed one day every hundred years then vanished into the Scottish highlands' mists to be reconstituted for one more day a hundred years later. In the last dozen years I had spent less than a year's actual time there, so that while the seeming passage of time was negligible, its measureable effects were dizzying. I was frequently reminded of certain movies which attempt to span the lifetime of a character or of several generations in two or three hours. A cruel and whimsical thing to do to any character, I always thought.

Through the years, though, several things had occurred to serve as reminders that certain chapters in the story had ended. One example was Charlie: companion, solace, and tormentor of my youth, the big sorrel gelding was more than just a mount, he was an institution in my life.

Many years later I was home to visit, and they broke the news to me that my faithful horse had died. While I grieved for him, I grieved more for what had been and for the fact that one more door had been closed on my youth. It slips away so insidiously that it is a temptation to believe that it is still around until some token occurrence happens to say that there is no turning back or even lingering for long.

It was like that with Perry, counselor and mentor, second father and friend during all those turbulent years of adolescence and early adulthood, he had seemed ageless, timeless, and indestructible. Though I knew him to be mortal, nevertheless it was somehow surprising and incongruous when he began to weaken with advanced years and emphysema. When news of his death came, I realized all too well that an institution had passed; another door had been closed on a

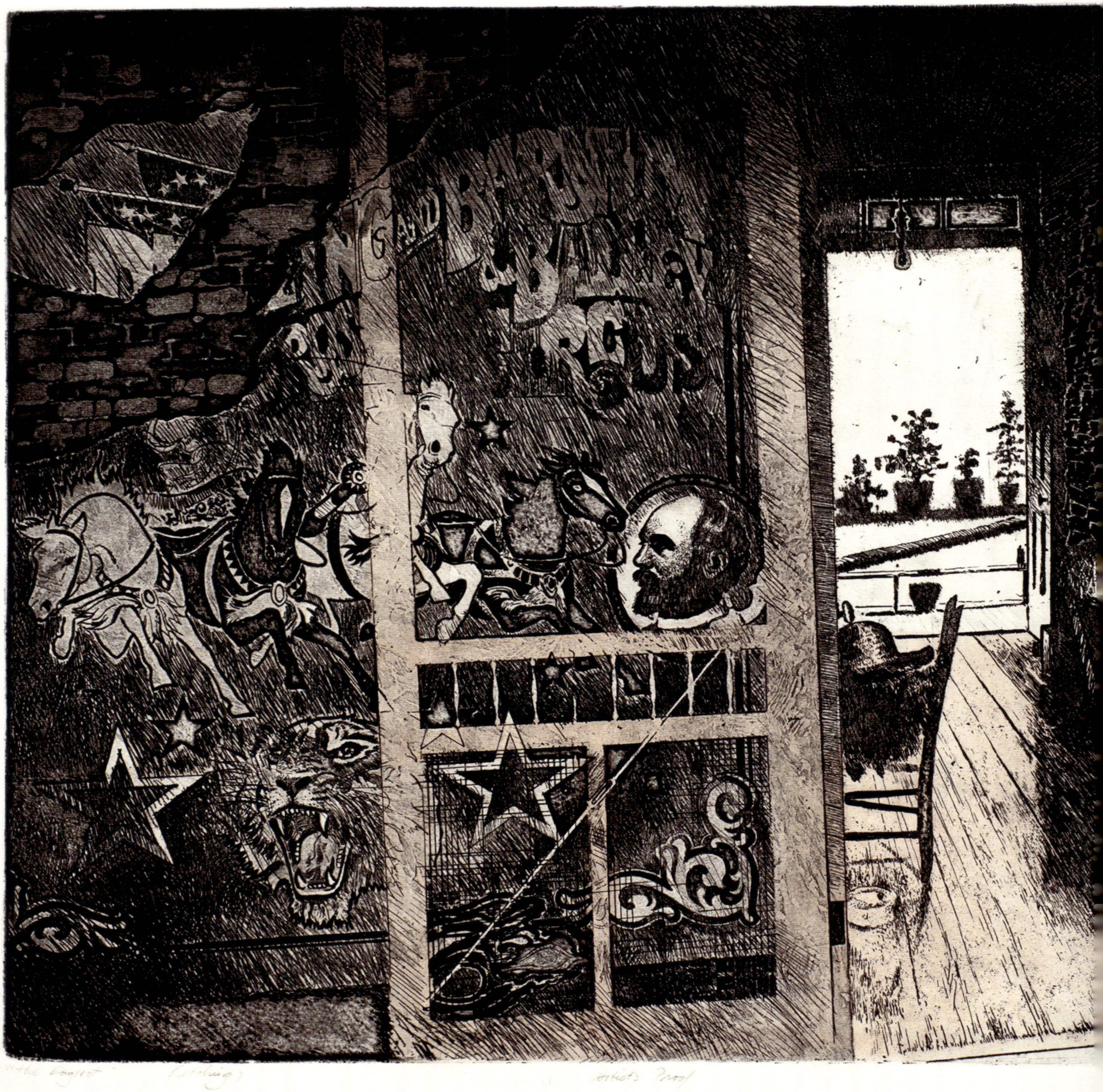
(etching)
Artist's Proof

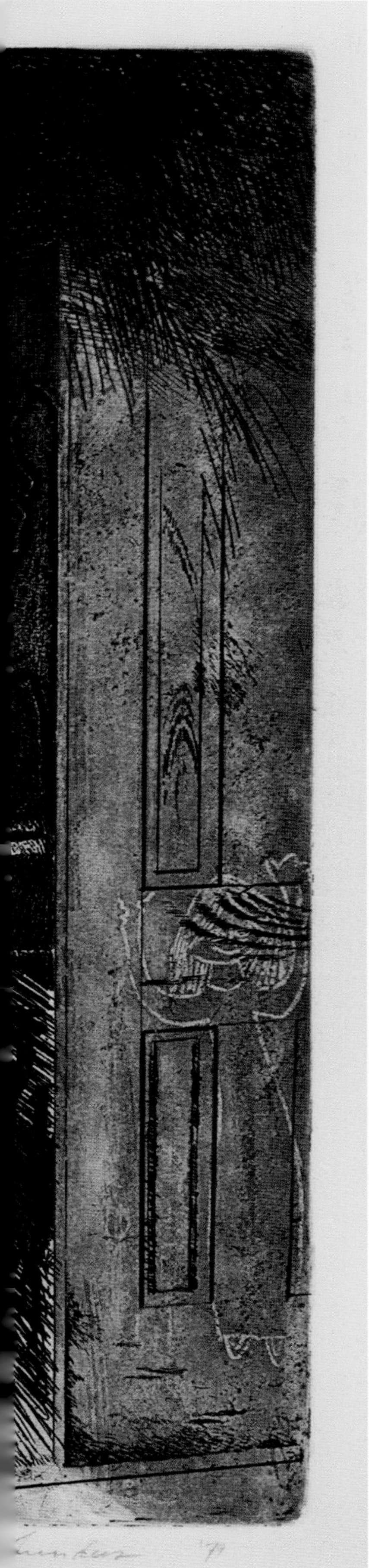

Dogtrot, 1976–84, etching, 16 × 22 in.

time of life, denying forever any hope of the briefest visit or even a lingering backward glance. Even his failing though, was affected by this 'Brigadoon Effect' so that while his decline took place over a period of several years, from my vantage point it seemed more like a matter of days or weeks at most.

Now 'Mist Shelly' was gone. To our ancient host, though, he was "that boy." Then again I saw "Miss Rene," frightened, hurt and grieving, leaving for the cemetery with that little girl handbag and I realized that to her he was also "that boy," then, more profoundly than ever before, came the truth that in most ways, he too probably saw himself as "that boy"; that the years must have flashed by for him the same as for the rest of us, that his ending caught him by surprise as certainly as it would have any of the rest of us. But for me it was the passing of an era, the closing of one more door that could not be passed back through, ever.

The sun was gone, now, and dusk was descending on the old homestead. The hounds had quieted down but the old caretaker talked on, spinning tales which spanned a decade or an hour with equal ease and unconcern. A large red-tailed hawk glided between the tops of the giant old cedar trees, hesitated for a brief encounter with the bats and swifts swirling about the dim chimneys and passed on, a gray cat awoke from his nap on this cistern cover and ambled towards the house. From inside the sound of the voice of the caretaker's old wife, singing or talking to herself came, rising and falling, riding on the rich warm aromas of supper and wood smoke. It was as if, in this strange enchanted place, time had learned to move to a different, arrested beat or perhaps had stopped altogether. For a brief, nostalgic, homesick moment I was gripped with an urge to stay here; to hope that somehow I could be caught in the timeless magic of this place and maybe even be carried back to an earlier happier day. But even as the half-thought was being formed, another harsher conscience was acknowledging that it was already much too late. Then Lee and I walked back to the car and drove silently home to more concrete realities.[19]

DOGTROT

The fifth etching in *The Farm* suite, *Dogtrot,* also evidences the triptych format and contrasts of depth and flatness. However, the vertical rectangles of space are not squared up to the viewer, that is, to the bottom edge of the composition, as they are in *The Guardian* and *The Stable.*

A dogtrot was originally called "two pens and a passage" by seventeenth- and eighteenth-century Scandinavian and German settlers to North America. Two log rooms or pens of identical squared dimensions were erected side by side and in line with an open space between them. The length of the logs tended to determine room dimensions. Eventually both pens and the space between them were roofed over creating a breezeway, and hence, a symmetrical arrangement. If the overhanging roof was generous enough, a full-length porch was created ninety degrees to the open passage between the two rooms. Regardless, the breezeway or dogtrot became a pleasant place to relax or do chores like snapping beans or shelling peas, etc. With screen doors, the space became a sleeping area in hot weather. The breezeway in *Dogtrot* seems to have a couple of simple pieces of portable furniture, which is appropriate. The angled composition of *Dogtrot* provides a glimpse of the porch floor at the lower edge, knowing this allows viewers to see Saunders's triptych as part of a much wider diptych.

Though the porch walls are dark, a bewildering assortment of commercial poster fragments dominates the left half of *Dogtrot*. It is not an accident. Saunders has a fondness for the graphic design profession and its relationship to the farm families of his youth.

> [Saunders] When I was growing up I was surrounded by hard farmers, sharecroppers, and other people like that whose lives did not have much joy. Occasionally, a little circus would come to town and big posters were put on the walls of buildings. What a wonderful incongruity of the drab existence of those people compared with the dazzle and drama, color, and glitter and yet cheap stuff of those circus posters. That is something that has always struck me.[20]
>
> For many, those bright circus clowns, war posters and tobacco signs were the only "art" they knew. Those and the calendars and almanacs celebrated phases of the moon and the times for planting while they spoke to people of the way they should dress and look. I use popular graphics so much because they truly are powerful. People took them to heart and kept them around and made them their own.[21]
>
> . . . The tattered remains of a circus poster, perhaps salvaged from the side of a store in town, and having outlived its commercial function even before it came to this place, can be seen through the opened screen door on the porch wall. Someone, sometimes saw it as a work of art and used it to adorn this otherwise drab homestead. Perhaps over several generations, its color; its wonderful drama and special magic must have brought a new and contrasting dimension into the meager fare, constant labor and endless cycle of the seasons which made up the existence of the inhabitants of this farmhouse. The various layers and fragments of the image seem to reflect the several layers of meaning which this piece conveys. The asymmetrical triptych format of the composition lends stability and again suggests a votive significance.[22]

THE BEDROOM

The etching titled *The Bedroom* is one of the most unusual of all the prints in *The Farm Suite,* in fact, in *Southern Cross/A Trilogy* altogether. Though totally fiction, its compelling imagery, empathetic mood, and surprising inclusion of a written text within the compositional field, make this piece a riveting work. Its genesis is no less absorbing.

> [Saunders] I spent a spring afternoon exploring an old abandoned farm near Peak, South Carolina. As I walked through the rooms of the closed up farmhouse I began to imagine a couple having spent their lives living in that farmhouse. One room was easily identified as having been the bedroom. You could see the marks on the floor where the bed had been and you could see marks

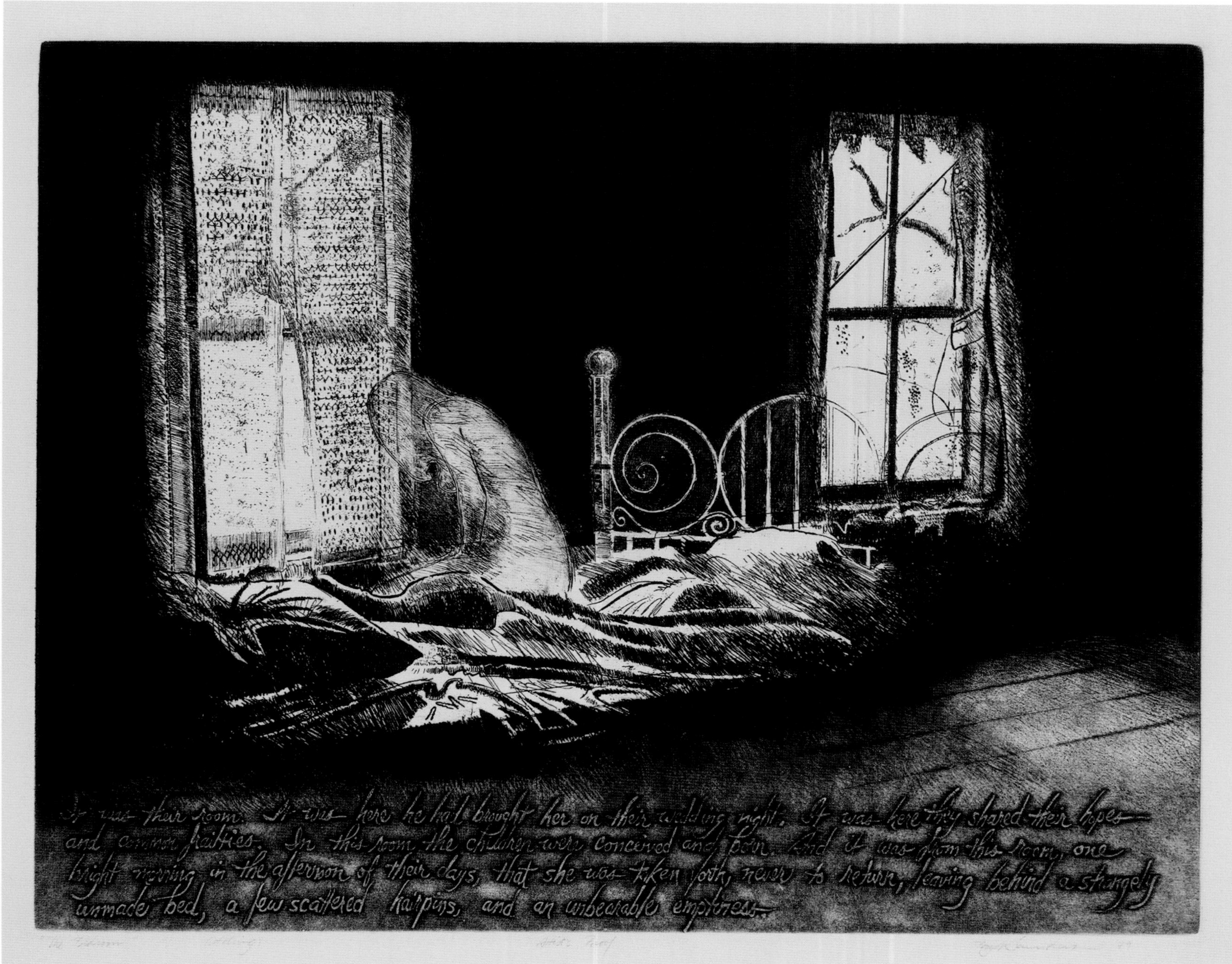

The Bedroom, 1976–84, etching, 16 × 22 in.

around the walls. That bedroom was as dry as a powder house. The windows had curtains hanging in them, which had turned to gossamer because the sun had rotted them. If you touched them or breathed on them, they turned into powder and fell away. Again, although the inhabitants were long since gone and never known by me, I thought of them living out their lives on this farm, returning to this room and each other every night. And I imagined that in living there all their married life, maybe one of them died.

About the same time [that I was making this piece] my friend John O'Neil's wife was terminally ill with cancer. They sent her home and John asked her if there was anything special she wanted to do. She said, "Well, I've always enjoyed

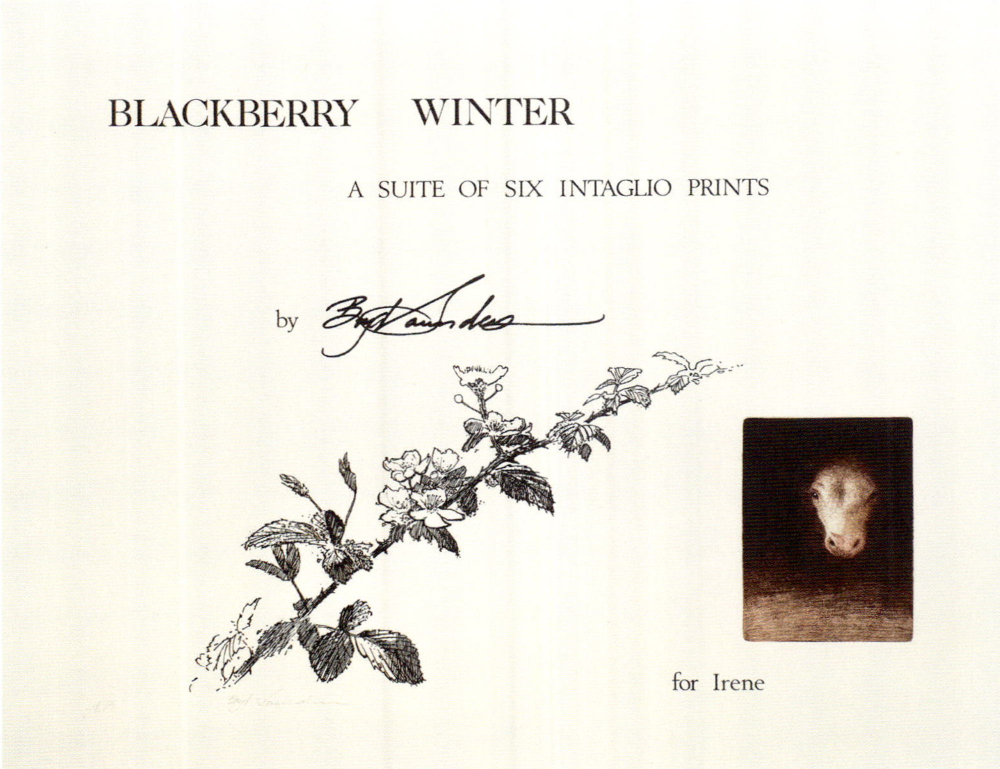

Southern Cross/A Trilogy, Blackberry Winter (cover print)

the cottage down at the beach [South Carolina's coastal beaches]. Could we go down to the beach?" They went down to the beach and spent the weekend. Very shortly afterwards she died.

I've always wondered how you say goodnight to somebody knowing you might not wake up together the next morning. So, I began to deal with that in this piece, *The Bedroom.* Sometime later I remembered the words of an old gentleman, of a different time and place, as he told me of his wife of half-a-century, how she had taken sick in the night, and how, come morning, she was worse. He took her to the hospital where, shortly thereafter, she died. He came back home and walked into the bedroom they had left a couple of mornings before and there was the bed still tossed up and turned back, uncharacteristic of her because she always made the bed. An imprint of her body was still on the bed and he told how, overcome with grief, he had left the room, locking the door behind him, unable to return.

In the etching *The Bedroom,* the ghost of a woman rises up from an equally ethereal bed in an otherwise empty room. The only real thing is the room and yet there was a lot that I could not deal with visually, so I started writing [on the etching plate]. Now, a few lines of blank verse appear across the bottom of the print.[23] It was their room. It was here he had brought her on their wedding night. It was here they shared their hopes and common frailties. In this room their children were conceived and born. And it was from this room, one bright morning in the afternoon of their days, that she was taken forth, never to return, leaving behind a strangely unmade bed, a few scattered hairpins, and an unbearable emptiness.[24]

This bit of sensitive and tender verse not only complements the female spirit rising from the fugitive metal bed; it may also parallel in its incisive tone, the level of sorrow carried by Saunders while conceiving *The Farm Suite.* That suite is a lament, dark and full of irresolutions and strange juxtapositions of objects and spaces. But at times it is also rich and moving like a Bach or Mozart requiem, expressing pain and loss and solemn moods, while simultaneously providing soothing, merciful comfort. A number of people who have seen this print or have heard him tell its story have wept. He was not seeking that response, but he feels that the print has a lot of strength through suggestion or implication. "I think it is a powerful piece. It talks a lot about what existence is all about."[25]

The premiere exhibition of the *Southern Cross/A Trilogy* suites of prints was at the Columbia Museum of Art, Columbia, South Carolina, February 19–March 25, 1984.

BLACKBERRY WINTER

The title page for *Blackberry Winter,* the second suite of six etchings in Saunders's major thematic project of the 1970s, *Southern Cross/A Trilogy,* represents a sparse but effective design aesthetic of sensitively chosen and placed elements. In fact those qualities are present in all three title pages. In each the title is stated clearly and boldly to announce the name of the suite, but it does not dominate the other information. For *Blackberry Winter* staggered, horizontal lines of type are relieved by a signature with flair beneath them. All that is then countered by the strong diagonal thrust of the thorny blackberry bush stem with blossoms that

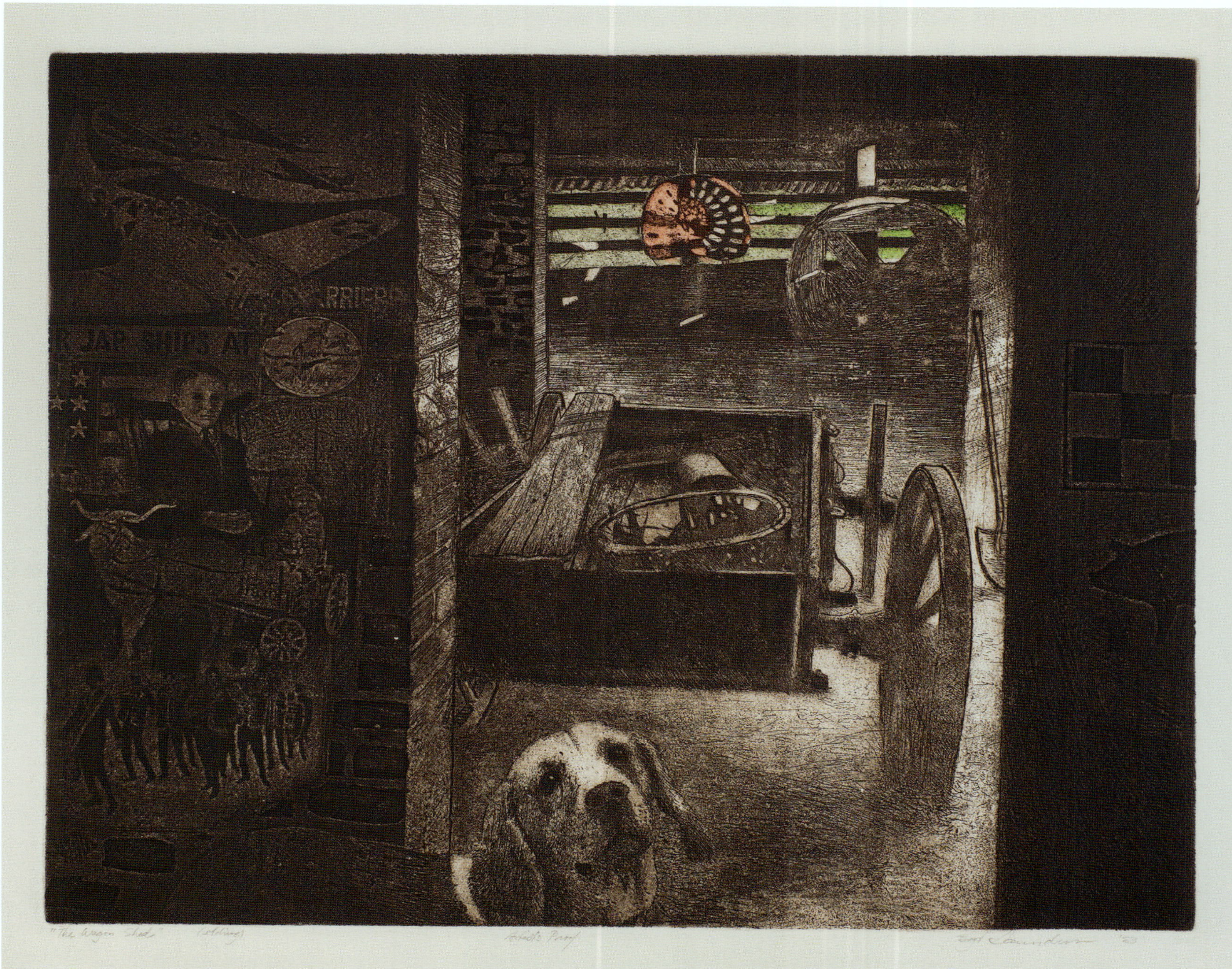

The Wagon Shed, 1976–84, etching, 16 × 22 in.

are checked by the small but bold image of a calf's face and the diminutive but emotionally powerful two-word dedication. All such decisions of layout, message, and design should remind viewers of this artist's foundation in and career-long commitment to graphic design. The three suites have been dedicated respectively to Shirley (Saunders), the artist's father; to Irene (Saunders) the artist's mother; and to Stephanie (Saunders), the artist's wife.

Though the artist's journey around a semimythical, unoccupied southern farm, and his reflections as to what life may have been like there, fuel the three suites, their moods are not the same. The moods of *Blackberry Winter* and *Late Light* slowly lighten, for example, in prints like *The Wagon Shed, The Commissary,* and *Old Pony,* which possess elements of a haunting loss and sorrow, and they represent half of the suite. The phrase "blackberry winter" traditionally refers to a false winter in April, the month when wild blackberry bushes tend to bloom.

THE WAGON SHED

Saunders's effective use of compositions divided into three sections, that is, in the triptych format of late medieval and early Renaissance art in Europe, is explored further in *Blackberry Winter.* In point of fact, the first etching in this suite, *The Wagon Shed,* is composed in three unequal sections and unified by dark brown tones. The artist reflected on this print as follows:

> In *The Wagon Shed* etching, the viewer is placed in the dimly lit interior of an out-building on a small farm somewhere in the American South. In the immediate center of the composition is a farm wagon seen in one-point perspective, back-to-front in a manner that reminds one of the famous Mantegna painting of *The Dead Christ* [c. 1501]. Various odds and ends are in the wagon and light from an unseen door or window off to the right rakes across the scene.
>
> Beyond and above the wagon, a farm implement seat hangs on the wall, its form and volume articulated by a ray of sunlight from another unseen source somewhere off to the right. To either side of the seat, the alternating light and dark horizontal bands of the slats in the side of the building join with the seat to form a stylized image resembling a setting sun and clouds.
>
> Much of the energy of this composition seems to be related to the sense of atmosphere of the viewer experiencing the shadowy chiaroscuro of this dimly lit place. One observer felt that he could actually smell the mustiness of this interior space. As the spectator's eyes grow accustomed to the dim light, the presence of a resident dog takes form and welcomes viewers.
>
> Further examination reveals that the composition is in a format as if an altarpiece with the center panel depicting the wagon and attendant elements, and with dark side panels to the right and left.
>
> From the right-hand section, a graphic [livestock] feed logo emerges out of the darkness. To the left, a montage of image fragments; photographs and newspaper clippings are faintly visible. In the middle of that assemblage is a formal portrait of a young gentleman of perhaps twelve or thirteen. It merges into a fading photograph of a little boy in a goat cart. Around and above him are bits of newspaper articles of World War II fighter planes, flags, and scraps of words such as " . . . Jap ships," and "Battle," etc. The images have been torn and overlapped and decayed so that one sees the fragments in layers. Toward the bottom one sees the tattered image of a New Orleans funeral band.
>
> Slowly, it becomes apparent that some man at sometime has turned this wall in his work space into a private shrine with memento mori to a beloved son who was sent off to a war from which he never returned, leaving behind an emptiness which can never be filled.[26]

THE SCARECROW

Saunders's lifelong fascination with the circus world, circus posters, circus characters, and otherwise magical or mysterious figures comes to center stage in his etching *The Scarecrow.* At first glance the whole work seems to be an impenetrable jumble, an overly complex, convoluted abstraction, a visual assault without a hint of rationalism. Yet in the *Southern Cross/A Trilogy* theme of an abandoned and left-behind farmstead, this spectacle, this place, is far from dead. It simply awaits a viewer to come around.

> [Saunders] Amid the clutter of farm tools and implements in the tool shed on the side of a barn, a strange, anthropomorphic figure takes shape. Moving closer it turns out to be an old weather-worn scarecrow, (or booger) as the local farmers call it. Here it has been stored in seeming retirement from its function of protecting crops. Its clothing has slowly deteriorated until it barely exists. . . . Perhaps it has now taken on a somewhat cross and crucifixion configuration, a religious significance.
>
> The etching could, in a more general sense remind one of the life, death, and rebirth cycles of existence and the annual regenerative cycle of the seasons. In support of that suggestion, several of

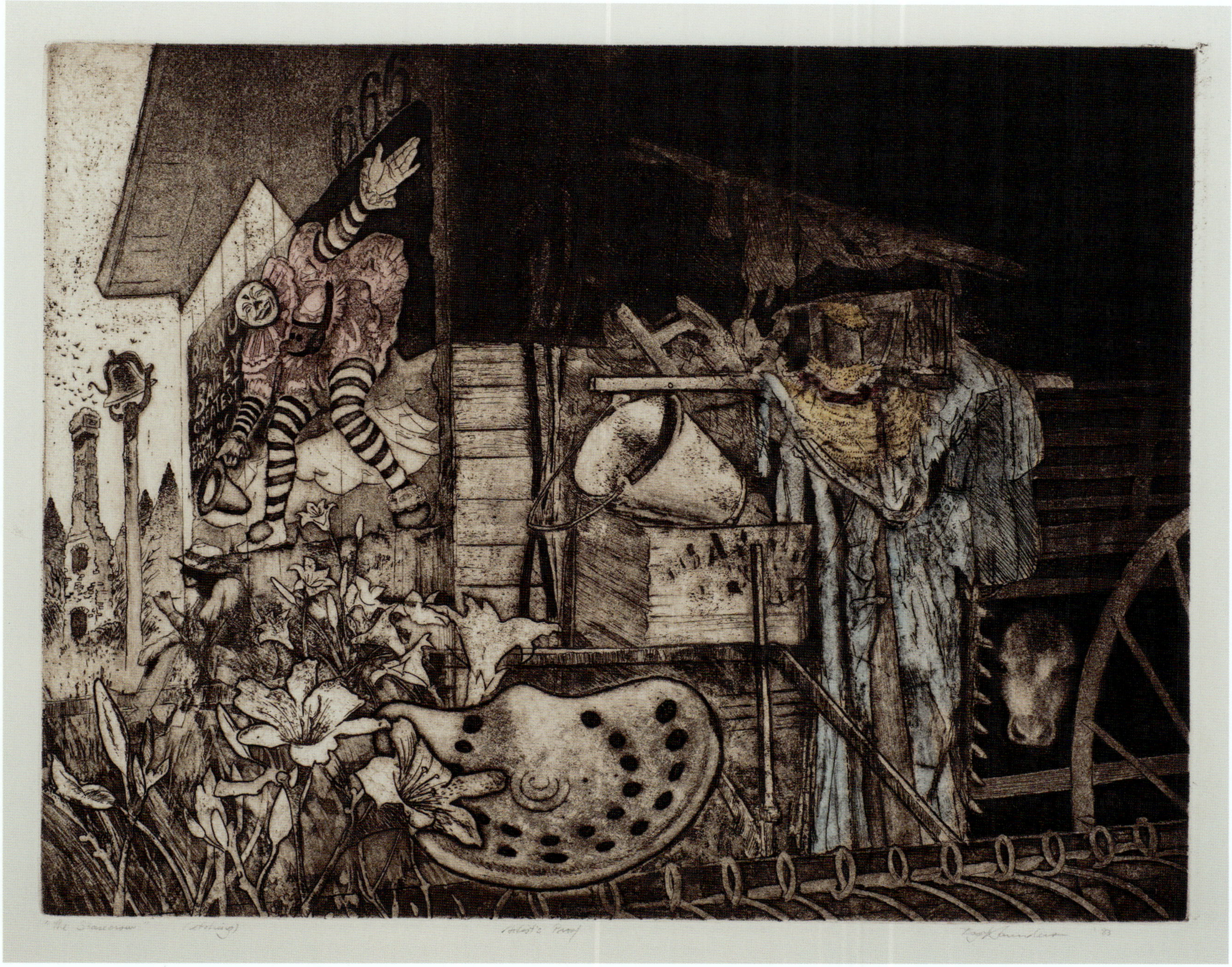

The Scarecrow, 1976–84, etching, 16 × 22 in.

the implements stored in this open shed are tools of reaping, harvesting or gathering-in. The teeth of a hay mower, for instance can be seen just to the right of the scarecrow, and in the immediate foreground can be seen the wheel, tines and seat of a sulky hay rake. To these connections add the lilies in bloom nearby and the presence of a young spring calf peering out from the dark barn interior, both as symbols of rebirth.[27]

Analogies within this carefully constructed etching do not end with the artist's thoughts above. "Around the corner, a circus poster has been applied to the wall of the barn. On it, a clown acting as a master of ceremonies, bends low and sweeps his hand in an exaggerated gesture of introduction as the words on the poster beyond him proclaim this theme to be 'The Greatest Show on Earth.' This almost sinister figure quickly begins to resemble a Shakespearean

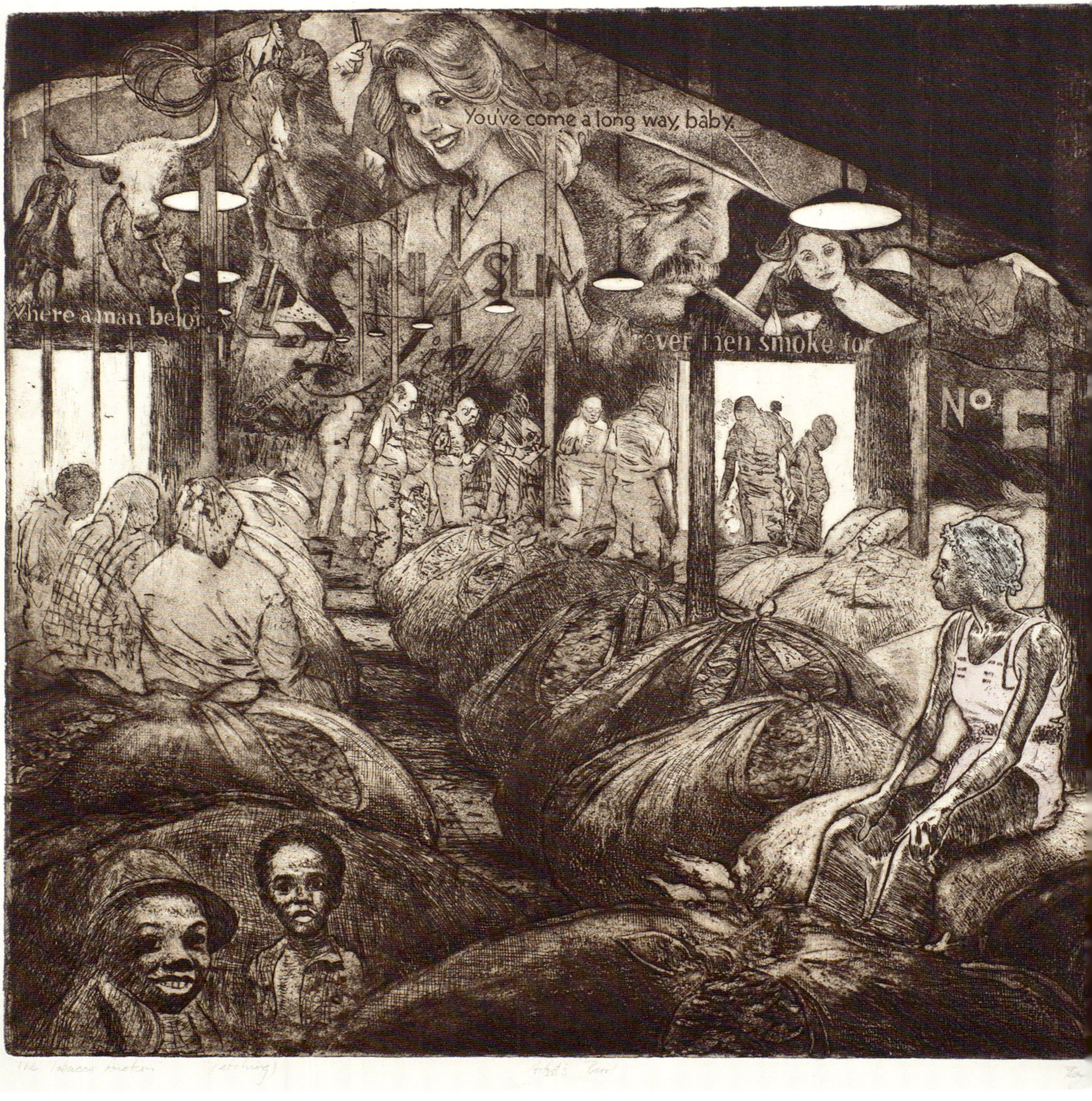
You've come a long way, baby.
The Tobacco Auction (etching)
Artist's Proof

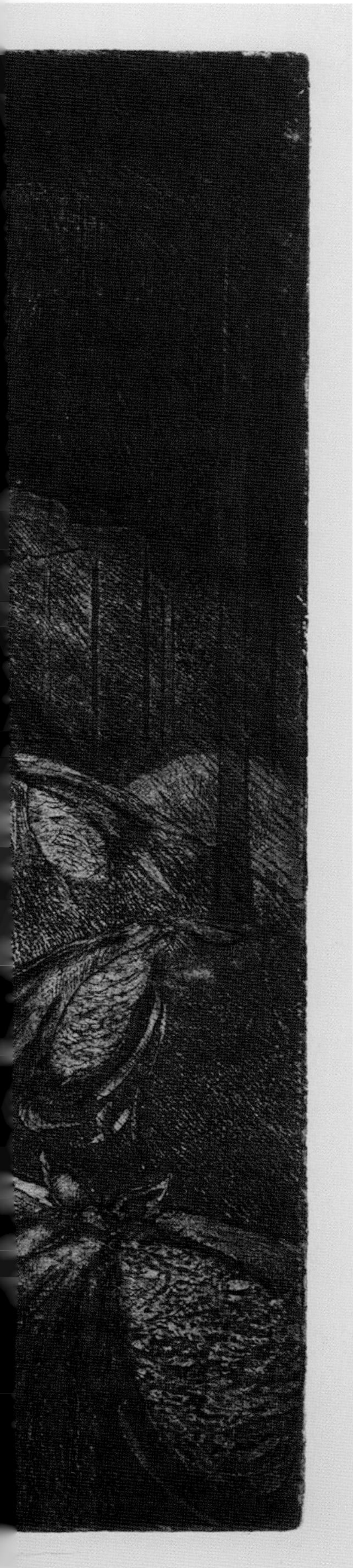

fool or the mocking grim reaper in a Medieval Dance of Death."[28]

Given the rather pessimistic or sinister clown figure metaphor, perhaps Saunders is implying a thematic balance of good and evil forces in life and in the print as a whole. Granted such offsetting thematic elements do not make *The Scarecrow* unique. That basic theme is practically timeless. However most viewers will likely be unaware of the degree of compositional forethought and planning invested in this print. Saunders said, "In this complex composition everything is built around and relates to a strong vertical line which pictorially defines the corner of the building and separates the tool shed containing the scarecrow from the end of the barn containing the clown poster. This off-center vertical line is placed in accordance with the Greek golden section, and the rest of the left side of the composition repeats this proportion several times over.

"These two unequal portions, seemingly in opposition to each other, are unified by the inverted arch of the rake seat at the bottom, and the zigzag horizontal line at the top created by the cast shadow of the roof overhang and the shadow of the roof of the lean-to-tool shed."[29]

Whether or not the subtleties of the ancient golden section of proportion contribute to viewers' comprehension or enjoyment of *The Scarecrow* is hard to predict, but it is indicative of Saunders's approach to searching, testing, experimenting, and evaluating options given the challenge before him for every print.

Almost lost in the discussion of *The Scarecrow* is some poignant imagery on the far-left side of the composition, which is sensitively addressed by the artist. "Below the circus poster, almost overlooked, a solitary figure of a man, almost transparent, like a wraith, sits and gazes reflectively back toward a now silent farm bell and the remains of a brick fireplace chimney; the last vestiges of a farmhouse that is no longer there."[30]

THE TOBACCO AUCTION

[Saunders] It is a small visual drama set in a cavernous tobacco auction barn somewhere in the American south, perhaps South Carolina. It is also late summer, and as the tobacco auctioneer walks

The Tobacco Auction, 1976–84, etching, 16 × 22 in.

up and down between the rows of jute squares of harvested tobacco, he sings the mysterious, staccato cadences of the auctioneer's chant; unintelligible to any but the trained ear. As he goes and chants, he points, quickly and almost furtively to selected jute squares of tobacco. Accompanying him is a small cadre of tobacco buyers who respond to his chant with a wink, or nod or flick of the hand. In this manner, and with a dazzling display of efficiency and dispatch, the fruits of an entire season of the intense, backbreaking labor of small farm families and large landholders alike are bought by tobacco companies to be turned into cigarettes or other tobacco products for worldwide distribution.

On the left side, a group of farmers sits, like an audience or maybe a congregation, backs to the viewer, watching the mysterious ritual play out, unable to take part in this ritual which will determine their financial compensation for the year's labor.

Meanwhile little children play about on the floor [front left side] and, off to one side [front right side] a young black woman sits on a square of tobacco and watches the whole scene with an uncomfortable degree of understanding. She is yet young, lean and sinewy, but has the face of a woman twice her age, from too much hard work, and from too many children, too young. Though coated in sweat and dust, she wears a faded blue lace night cap and wears it as if to defiantly affirm her femininity. In this unlikely setting, this tattered and jaded vestige of feminine delicacy becomes a stark symbol of poetic irony.[31]

Above the din of the auctioneer's rapid voice and the buyers' responses—all, mind you—at the far end of the sale barn, tobacco advertisements fill much of the wall above the entrances. In collage fashion popular tobacco product ads occupy a pediment-like space with proportions deftly close to the pediments of Doric temples of the fifth century B.C. on the Athenian acropolis. One can easily spot the Marlboro Man, a Virginia Slims model, and other iconic images created by Madison Avenue firms to glamorize smoking, especially certain brands of cigarettes.

The Forge represents another dark or murky farm building interior. Like many other prints in this trilogy, it's a still life with narrative potential. As such it continues an important tradition whose initial golden era occurred in Holland and Flanders in the 1600s, that of the quotidian, of middle-class interiors and their contents.

THE FORGE

[Saunders] The setting is the interior of a blacksmith's shop of a small southern farm. The space is filled with the clutter of reminders of the labor of this place; reminders of some simple farmer being occasionally transformed into the mythical Vulcan who then formed iron and steel into the tools that shaped the land of this farm and the people who dwelled there.

The place has seemed to take on the character of the one who labored there. Apparently he has been interrupted in the middle of a job; perhaps called away to supper or a more pressing task, and has not yet returned. The interruption may have been brief or the remainder of a lifetime. No matter, some part of his essential qualities lingers here.

Closer inspection shows that the proprietor has also turned the place into a sort of den, with clippings and photographs and assorted commercial graphics stuck to a wall in a kind of spontaneous collage—what brought these images together?

A shop vise and a large cat have a commanding sense but what about the stag calendar image to the left, the reclining female nude on the right wall and the orchard in bloom seen out the window? Is it small wonder that throughout history, agricultural peoples have created female deities of fertility, and the worship of them has been largely sexual? Might the erotic fold-out image of the reclining female nude suggest such a deity?

The large cat, as the current proprietor, has made this place home. And with typical feline indifference, he allows the viewer's presence with no sign of welcome, rejection, or insight regarding the objects around him or the images on the walls.[32]

Of the eighteen etchings in the epic visual poem *Southern Cross/A Trilogy,* almost half are of building

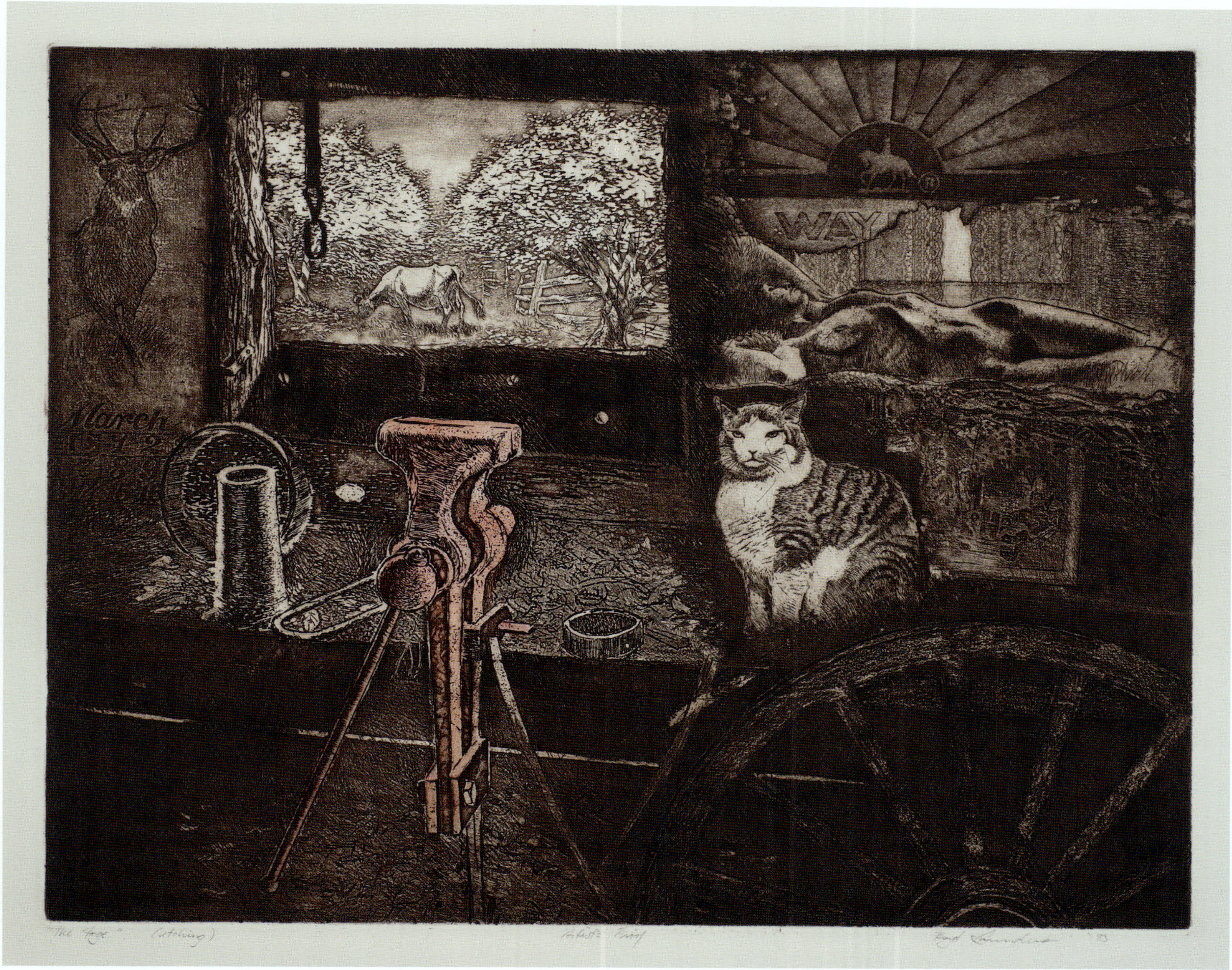

The Forge, 1976–84, etching, 16 × 22 in.

interiors. In this trilogy the artist has written a commentary for three of the eighteen etchings, one per suite: *The Stable* from *The Farm; The Commissary* in *Blackberry Winter;* and *The Wedding Party* in *Late Light.* Two of those three etchings are interior views. The artist's commentaries are printed on pages facing the respective prints in the *Southern Cross/A Trilogy* catalogue (1984), suggesting an importance to those three works and, perhaps again, to the importance of southern interiors for Saunders.

THE COMMISSARY

[Saunders] In *The Commissary* the viewer is introduced to the back room of a country store or

> commissary. A raking wedge of light from an unseen window imparts an almost votive significance to the long-handled rakes and shovels on a wall. The rhythmic placement of these implements along the dust mellowed wall suggests a music or meter of dirge-like marching character.
>
> From the gum machines, pop bottles and general clutter accumulated beneath, a World War II service flag and a "Loose Lips Sink Ships" poster manage to distinguish themselves. One has to wonder why these two pieces of popular graphics from another time have managed to retain a place on that wall for so long. One also feels that the relationship between the flag and the poster is more than mere coincidence. Almost unnoticed, a solitary figure stands in the gloom of the adjoining room and gazes pensively into the midday brightness beyond. Among other things, this piece is concerned with light, space, intimations of mood and silence, and unanswered questions about young men who march away to war and fail to return and of the emptiness they leave behind.[33]

With the artist's identification of the large poster; the World War II service flag; and his written metaphors like "music or meter of dirge-like marching character," "intimations of mood and silence," "young men who fail to return from war, and the emptiness they leave behind," viewers cannot but be left with sadness and empathy for the figure looking out a window in a gloomy attached room. Therefore it is possible to deduce that, no matter how busy and noisy this commissary may be, at times, on slow days or during the fallow season, the cavernous space of the commissary may actually add to the crushing emptiness for the gentleman at the window.

Sadness and emptiness in *The Commissary* are driven home strongly by the artist, but he also explored the elements of light and space. If viewers were unaware of the melancholy commentary for this etching or, if knowing, they concentrated even a little on the formal elements of this work, they would surely praise the use of light and space here. In *The Commissary* light enters the grand interior from multiple sources and then reverberates among fixed objects and a variety of surfaces. The mastery of

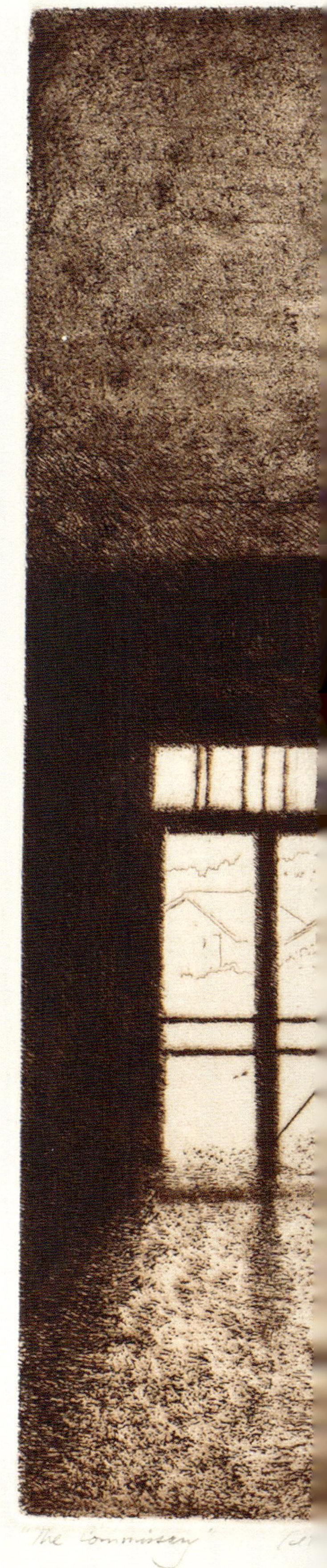

The Commissary, 1976–84, etching, 16 × 22 in.

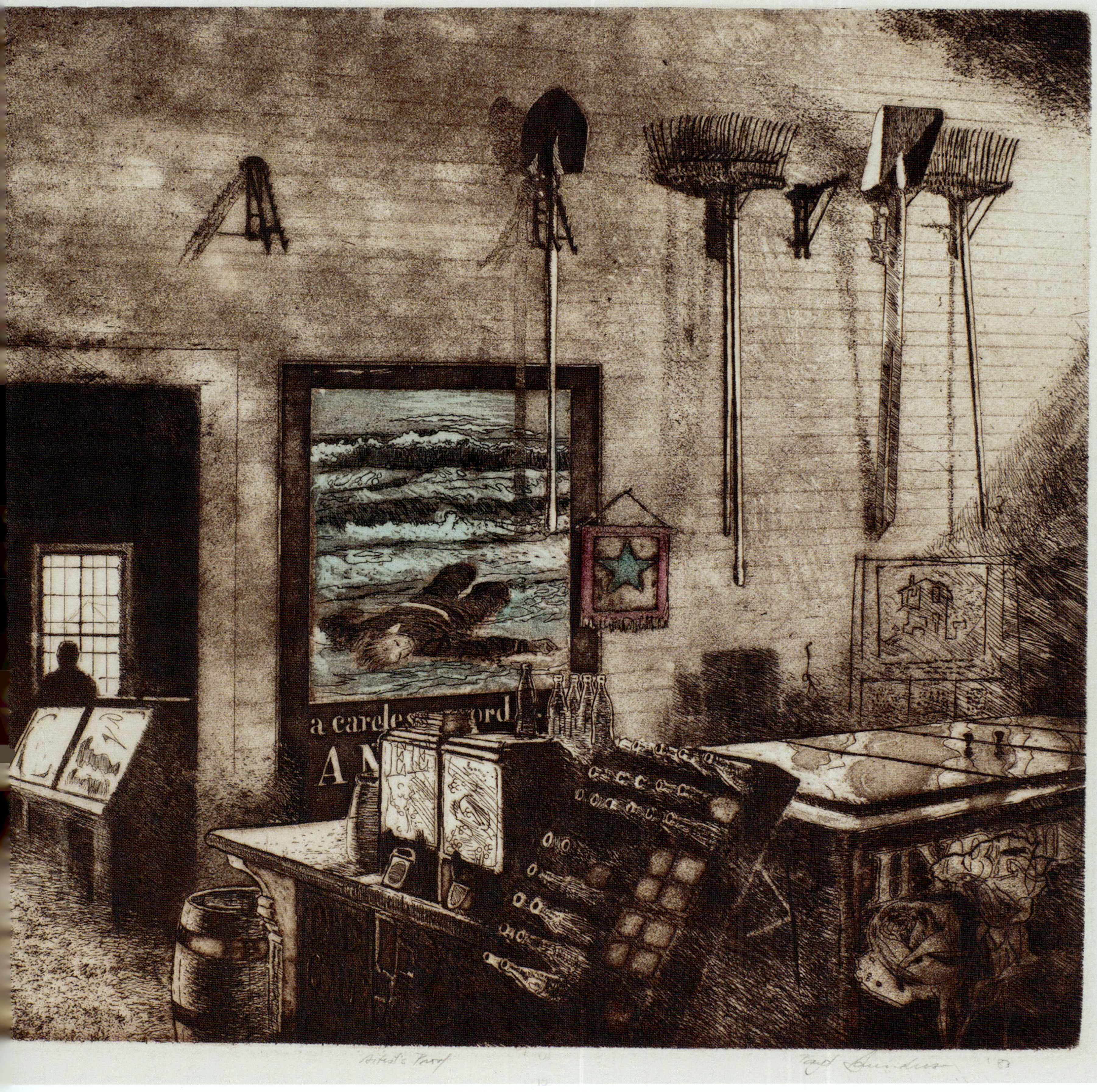
Artist's Proof

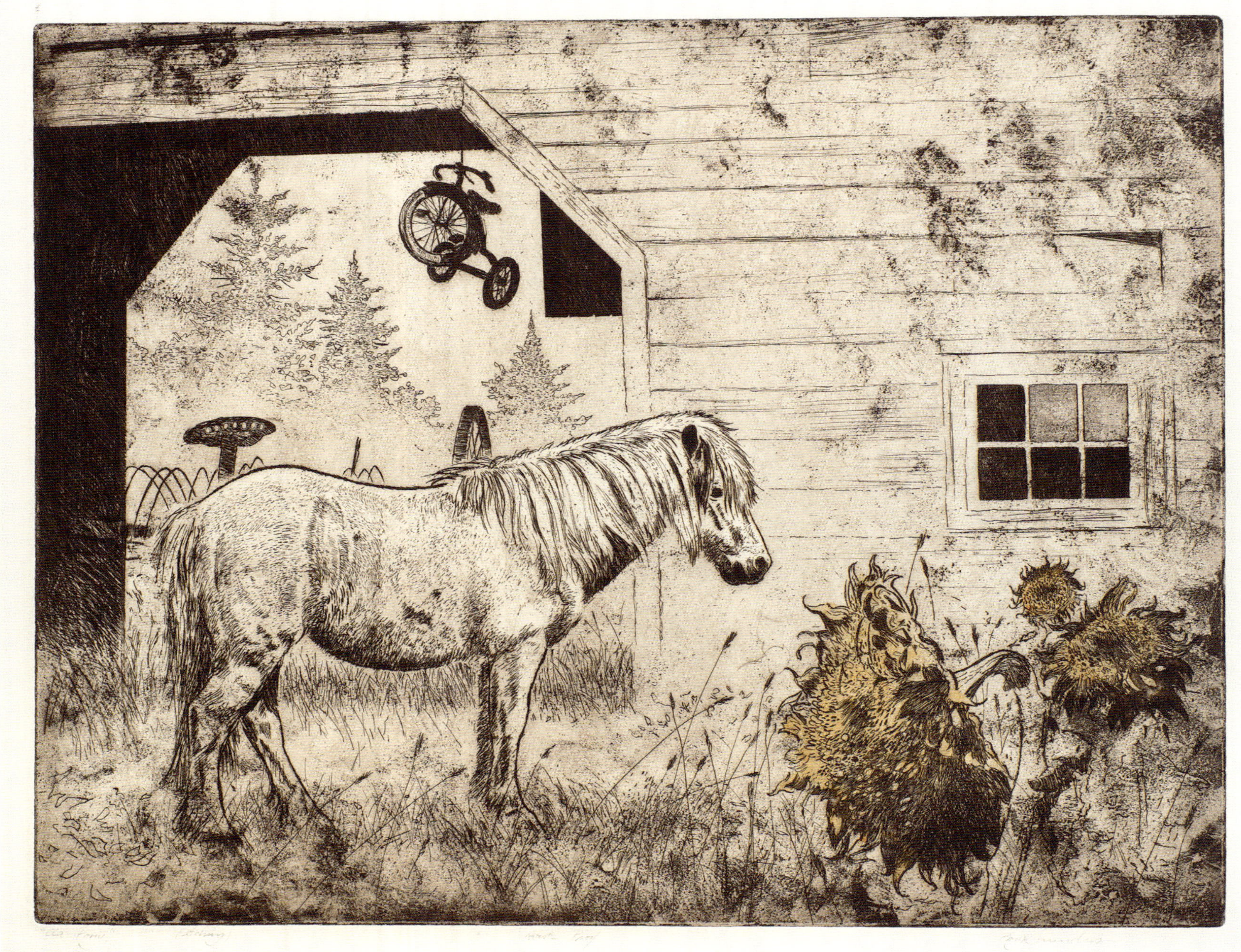

Old Pony, 1976–84, etching, 16 × 22 in.

light-rendered surfaces is breathtaking, and their variety and range recall the signature painting by Diego Velasquez—*Las Meninas* (The Maids of Honor) of 1656—or works by the best Dutch painters of interior light at that time like Vermeer, Steen, and Claesz. *The Commissary* is one of Saunders's signature works regardless of suite or medium.

The last etching in *The Blackberry Winter Suite* is titled *Old Pony,* which presents a Shetland pony standing amid an overgrown barn lot in front of an outbuilding.

OLD PONY

Said Saunders, "*Old Pony* is a tribute to all old ponies who raise little boys who one day hear the distant drums and go away to war, never to return, leaving their one-time servant and master to spend the rest of its days standing, dozing and dreaming, in the barnyard among the dry stalks and memories. May there be a special reward and reunion for them somewhere."[34]

The simplicity and brevity of the above commentary, along with the etching, need nothing further, and in part speak volumes for those fortunate to have had a pony as a youth.

SOUTHERN CROSS/A TRILOGY, LATE LIGHT

The concluding suite of etchings in *Southern Cross/ A Trilogy* begins with the title page, *Late Light,* featuring a sunset and conifer vignette. The dark-red clouds certainly reinforce the sun slipping toward the horizon as dusk approaches. The first *Late Light* print is *The Gathering,* whose subject may be true to one of the connotations of its title, that is, a gradual accumulation (in this case, of men and dogs), a convenient location, and a comfortable porch.

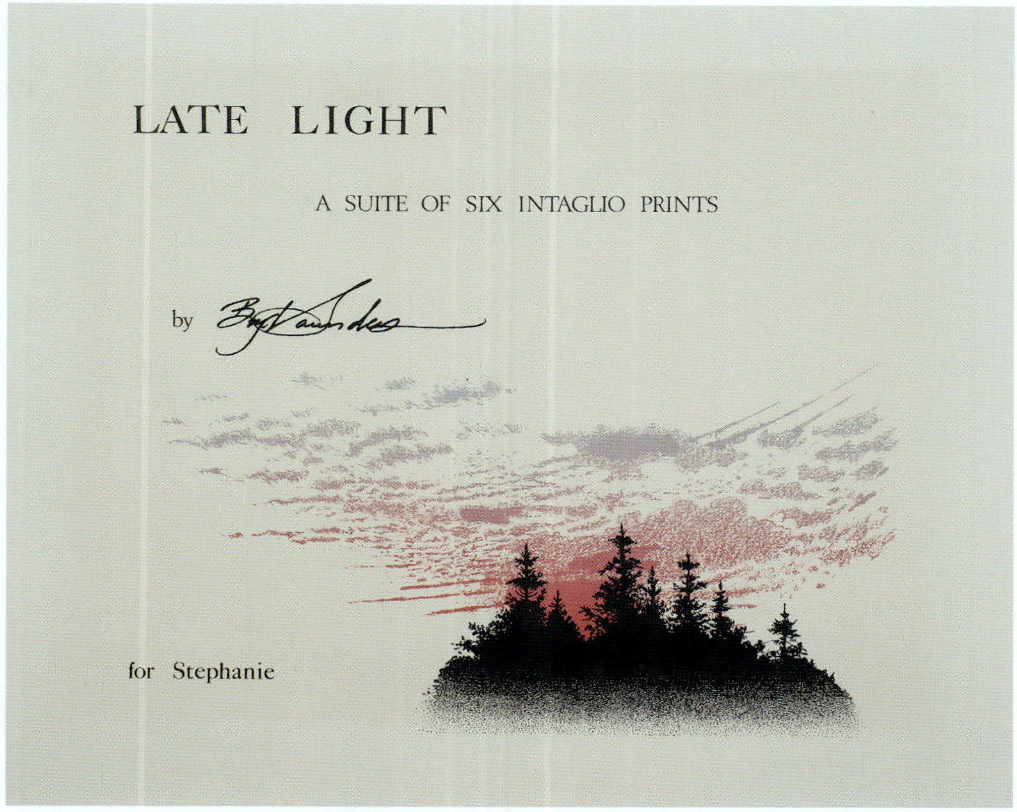

Southern Cross/A Trilogy, Late Light (cover print)

THE GATHERING

[Saunders] In this etching the viewer comes upon a country store at a railroad crossing. The encounter is perhaps, more by chance than by design, and one witnesses, but does not disturb, the languid sociability of a Saturday afternoon.

Four men lounge about on the porch, engaged in conversation about everything in general or nothing in particular. Their postures and positions within the group reveal the hierarchy that exists among them at the moment. The way the dogs are lying or sitting on the ground repeats the arrangement of the men on the porch. Between the men on the porch and the dogs in the foreground, a car is parked parallel to the front of the country store. It occupies the dominant position in this composition, at once part of and yet removed from it.

The store building is an archetype of southern vernacular architecture, with the rustic hominess of the porch standing in symbolic contrast to the trio of fan-shaped windows above and behind it.

Like many of the images in *Southern Cross/ A Trilogy,* this etching explores the use of popular commercial graphics as a decorative element, and as iconic images which have outlived their original functions and have assumed a life of their own. [Compositionally, this print repeats the artist's fondness for the triptych though its use here is more subtle.] In fact *The Gathering* utilizes a duality between threes and fours to help achieve its rhythmic complexity. In the narrow section flanking the store to the right one sees a fragment of railroad track and a railroad station off in the distance. Such buildings seem to define a particular place, and at the same time, point the way to all that lies beyond. In the extreme front portion of that same narrow space is a portion of a Southern Railroad crossing warning sign. It has been cropped and obscured until only the words . . . "Southern Cross" can be seen. Of course "Southern Cross" is also the name of a celestial constellation in the southern heavens, not to mention the title of this trilogy of print suites.[35]

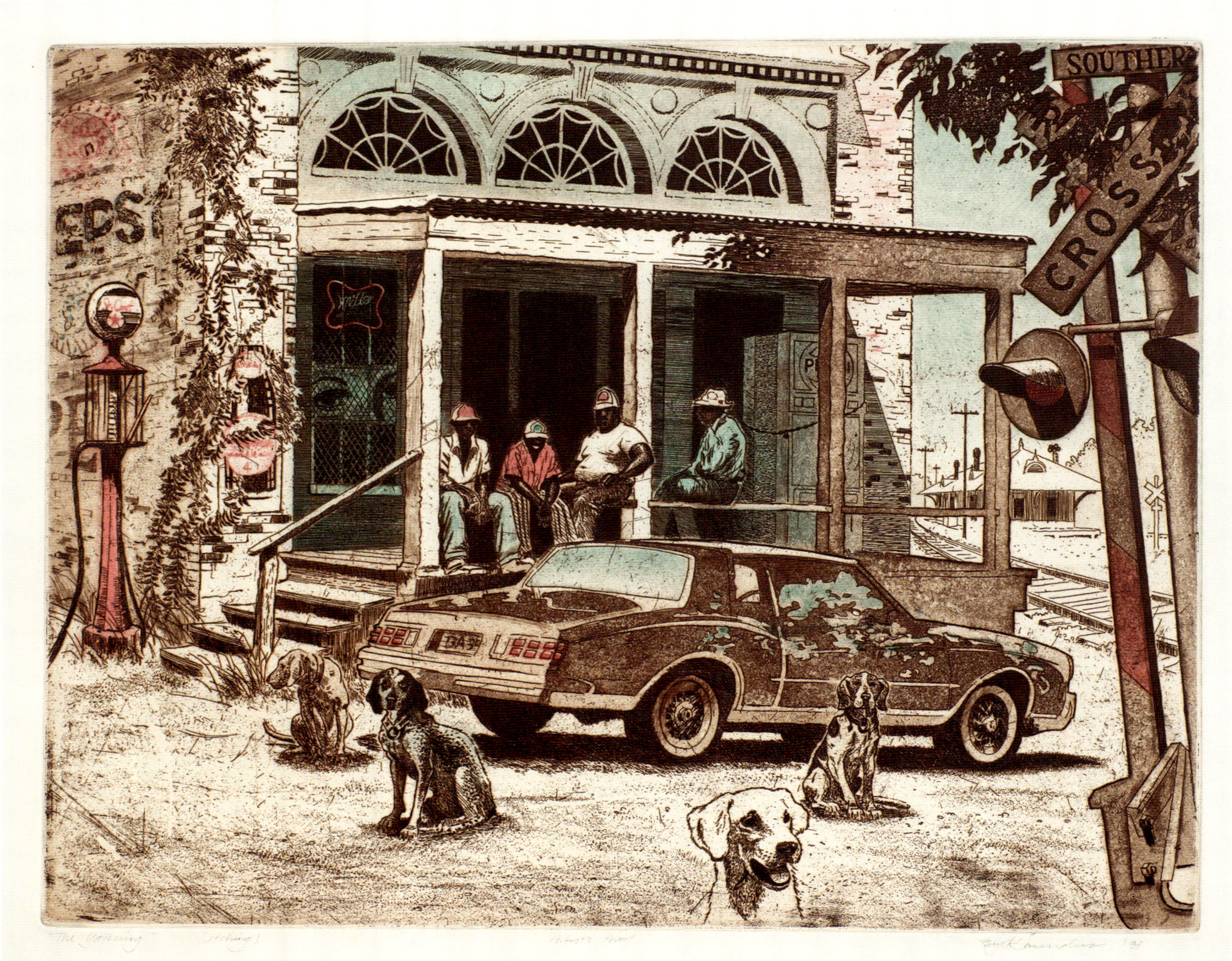

The Gathering, 1976–84, etching, 16 × 22 in.

EARLY EASTER

This work is rich in abstract networks of lines and masses and in its range of tonalities, all of which recall the pioneering efforts of late nineteenth-century English art photographers, especially Carl Frederickson with works like *Morning Mist,* a platinum print from 1905. The composition of *Early Easter* is also dynamic because it is part of something bigger beyond the cropped field of vision. Another noteworthy ingredient is the presence of color tints here, making *Early Easter* perhaps the first colorful etching in the entire *Southern Cross/A Trilogy* series. Saunders said, "Sturdy trunks and brittle, leafless, winter trees stand in a pond or stream. The reflection of a cloudless cerulean sky mixes with the reflections of the screen of trees and animates the surface of the water. Earth, Air, Sky,

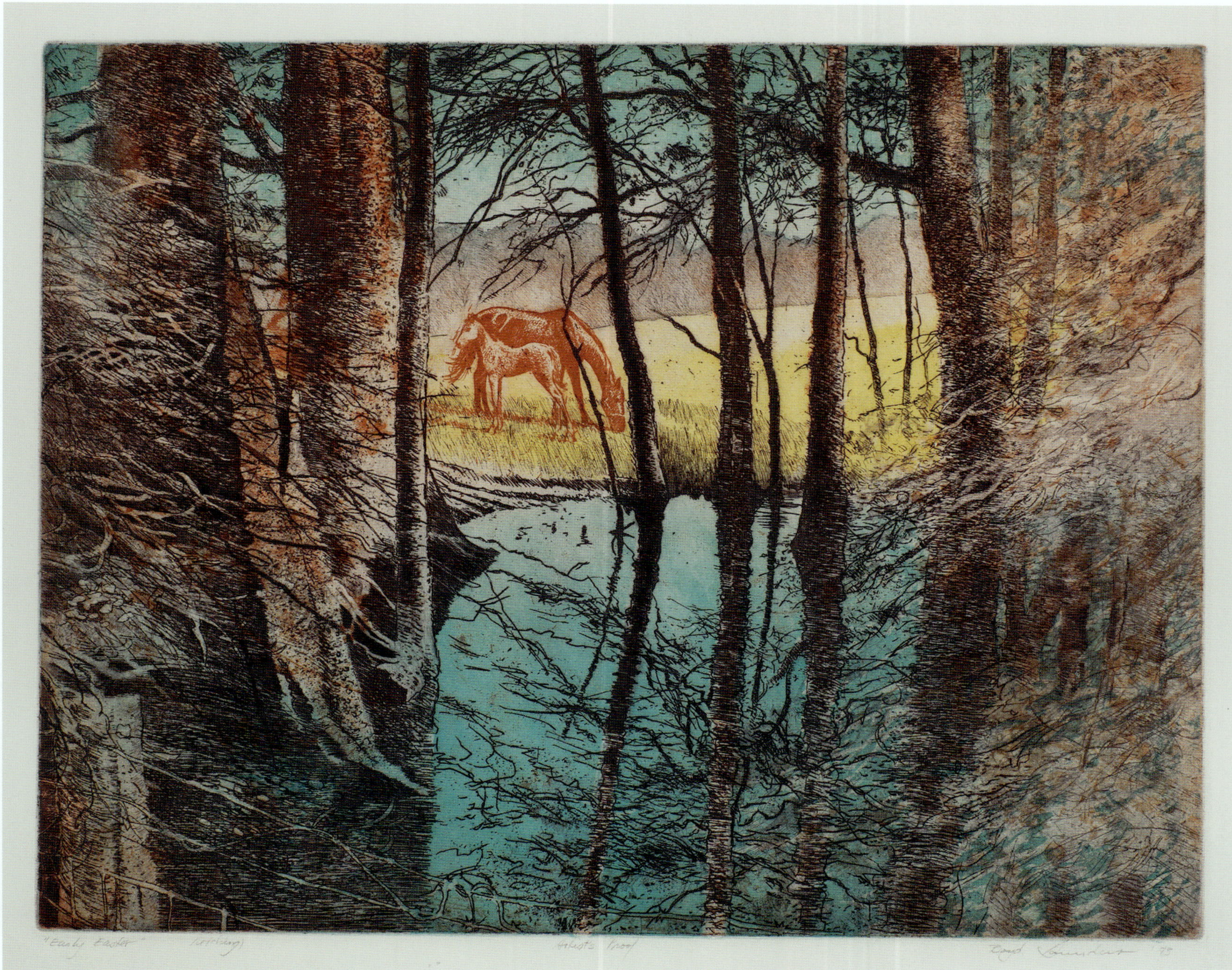

Early Easter, 1976–84, etching, 16 × 22 in.

Water; the fundamental elements are joined. In the middle distance a mare, with her new foal, grazes on new spring grass. Easter came early this year, and the cycle of life has begun again. All is well."[36]

THE WEDDING PARTY

With *The Wedding Party,* the third print in the *Late Light Suite,* Saunders has produced another work with potent, surreal, cinematic imagery with present, past, and future narrative potential.

The artist penned two similar commentaries for *The Wedding Party,* one for the 1984 *Southern Cross/A Trilogy* catalogue and the second one as recent as 2008 or 2009. The following is a combination of both:

> *The Wedding Party* contains a rather straightforward presentation of a large country store

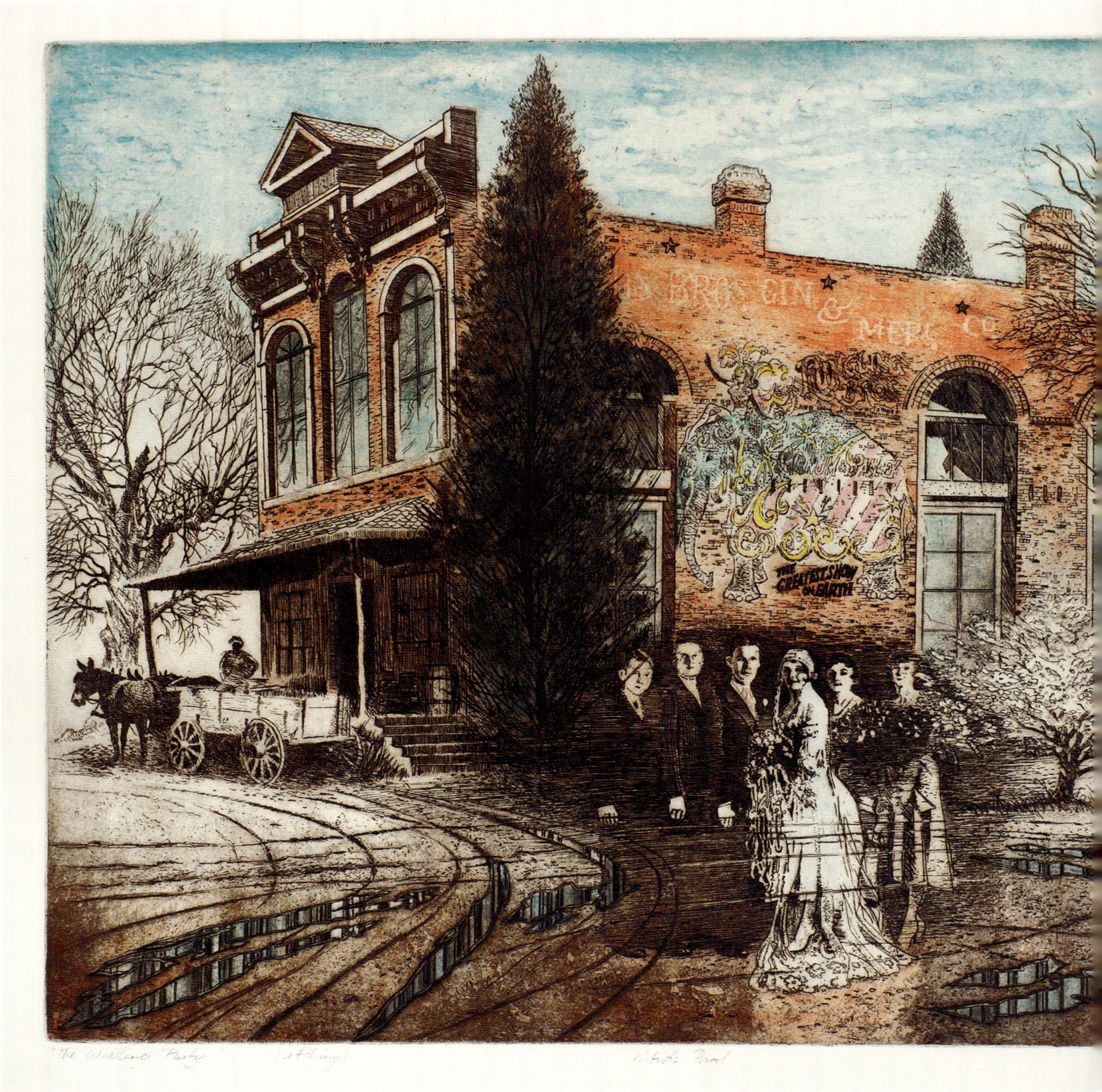
THE GREATEST SHOW ON EARTH
"The Wedding Party"
(etching)
Artist's Proof

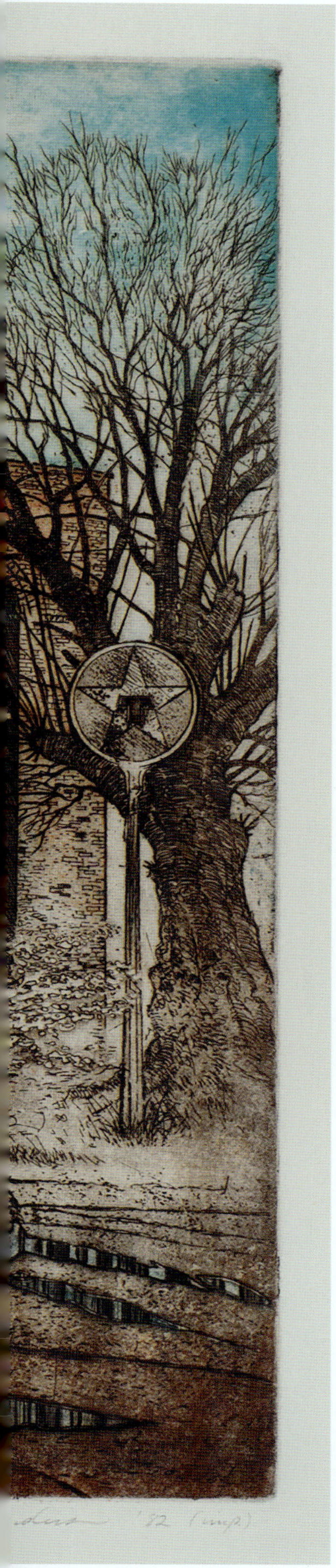

The Wedding Party, 1976–84, etching, 16 × 22 in.

which perhaps dates from around the turn of the twentieth century. This is not just any crossroads clapboard shack, but an imposing edifice with arched Palladian windows and soaring façade. Its scale and its grace, its arches, and collectively, its wonderfully pretentious false front assume a certain heroic self-confidence. This store once had pretensions. It had notions that it would someday be the heart of a nice town or perhaps a very important agricultural empire. Instead, it now stands in solitude; its red bricks and smoky glass having taken on their own peculiar glow.

On the side of the building can be seen the remains of a large circus poster with an elephant being ridden by a beautiful lady, and words which announce . . . "The Greatest Show on Earth." Of course, the circus has long since gone, but the poster remains.

A strange visual phenomenon rather blocks this old country store. It is the partial materialization of a bride, a groom, and their self-conscious attendants posing for a wedding picture. All are dressed in fashions from another time. Closer examination shows them to be transparent and ethereal. The elephant in the circus poster above and behind them forms a ceremonial arch above the group.

It is perhaps late February. Tracks and puddles form patterns in the road. The trees are bare yet a small fruit tree has burst forth into bloom and a farmer has parked his wagon in front of the store to load seed and fertilizer to begin spring planting.

Of course the wedding party is not really there. It is, again, a visual recollection mingling with wagon wheel ruts and pooling water.

Perhaps this store was to be the young couple's life's work. Perhaps the store interior seen in the etching *The Commissary* is the same building. Could the bridegroom be the same man who can be seen gazing out of a window of *The Commissary* still grieving over a son who had not returned from the war? Could this bride be the same woman who can be seen rising from her death bed in *The Bedroom?*

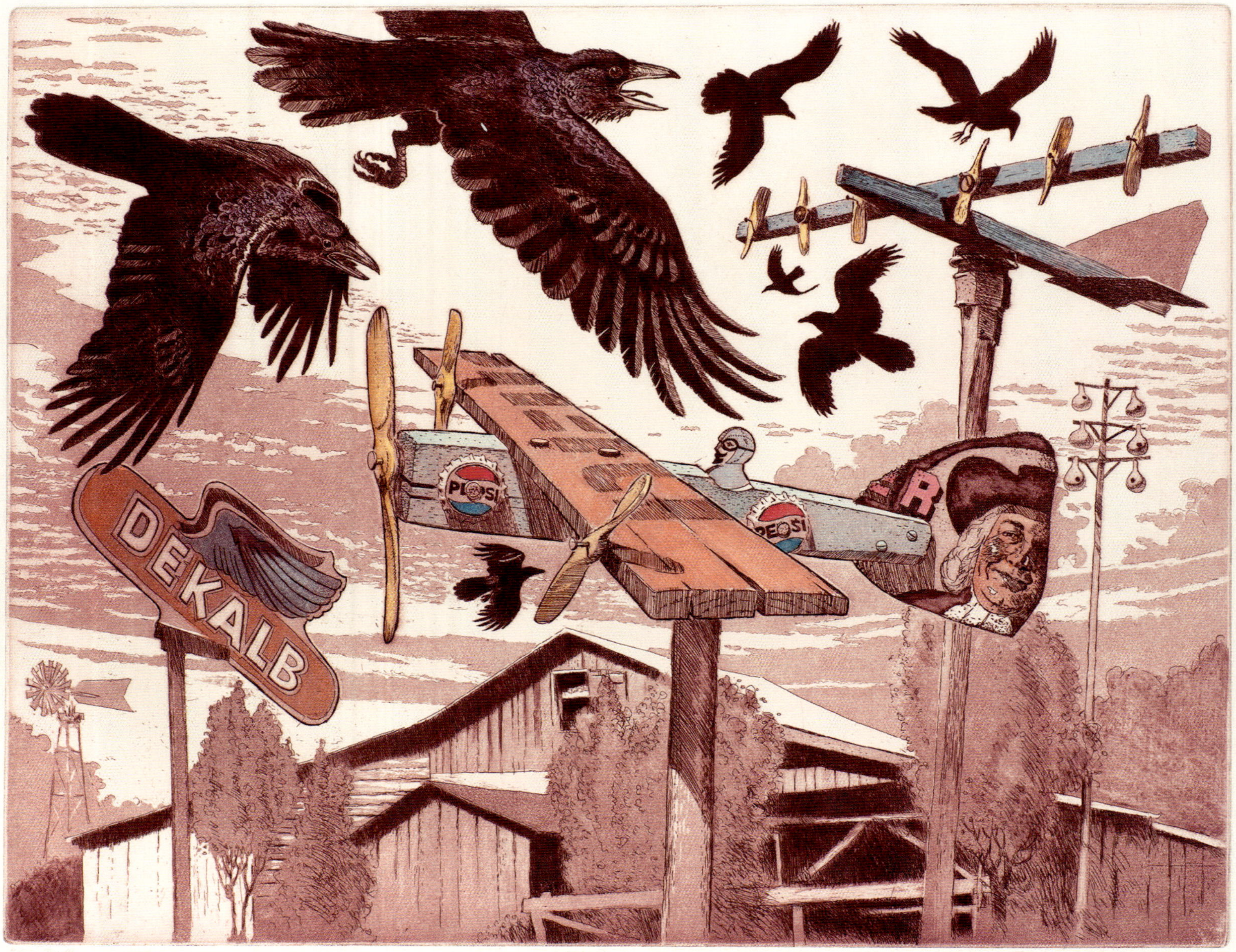

Air Battle, 1976–84, etching, 16 × 22 in.

Whatever the case, like the surviving country store and the determined budding of the young fruit tree, the young couple's attitude is one of courage, faith and hope. Viewers are left having to decide what is real and what is merely an illusion. Therefore, perhaps the present is a prologue to the past.[37]

AIR BATTLE

[Saunders] This etching is a retreat into whimsy and fancy. In the rural South, one can often see fanciful home-made whirligigs in the yards of rustic farmhouses and sharecropper cabins. These creations are made of whatever materials are at

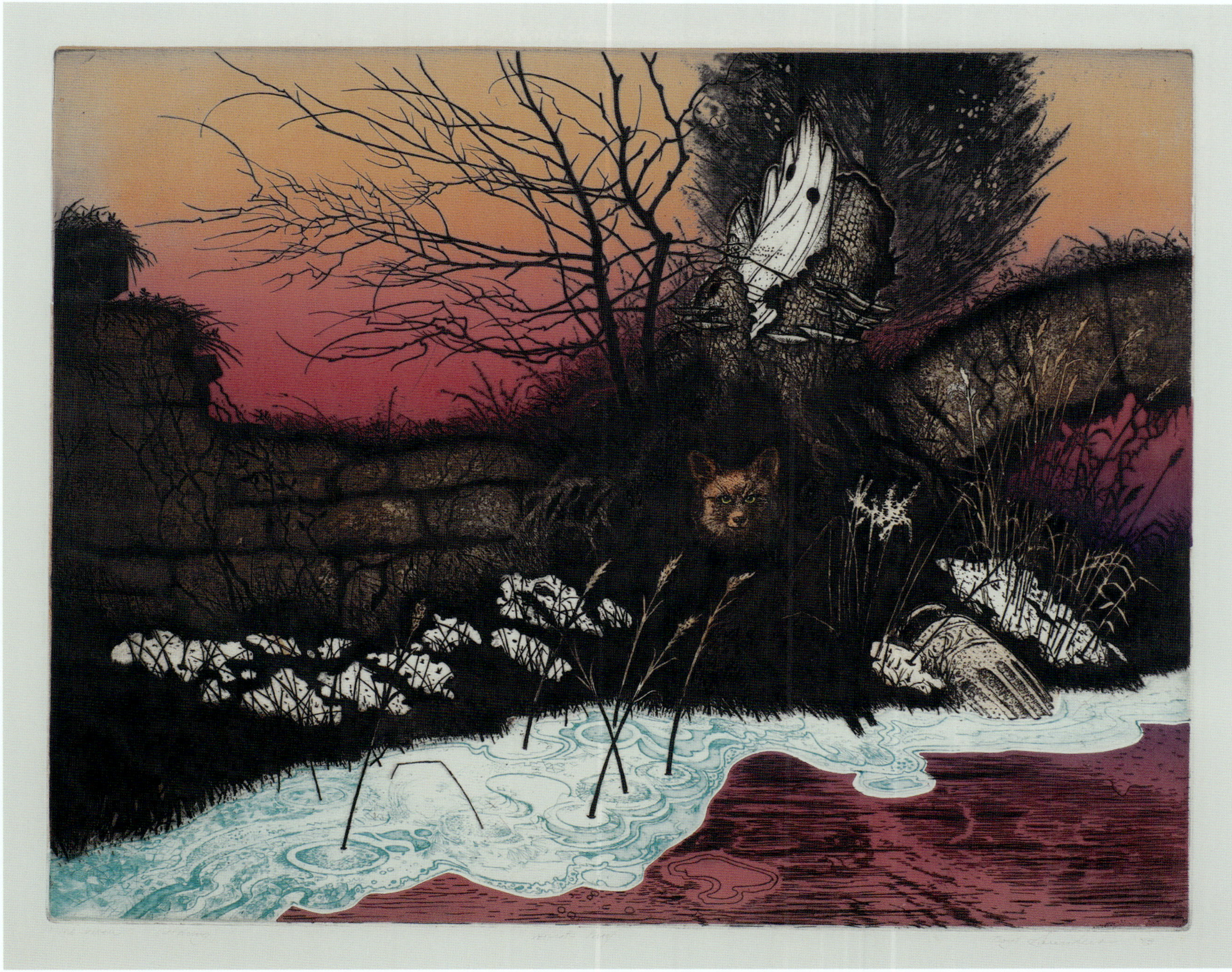

hand with whatever tools the artist-farmer may have.

They are elevated on poles and usually resemble airplanes with tails to turn them into the wind and hand carved propellers to catch the breezes and spin. Sometimes they are painted in whimsical designs and sometimes the materials of their construction retain fragments of the graphic images of their previous use. In the *Air Battle* etching, the tail of one airplane-like whirligig is obviously made from the remains of a Quaker Oats cereal box, and pop-bottle tops adorn the sides of the fuselage.

In this image, an armada of airborne, yet earth bound contrivances that pretend to fly, but don't, is being assaulted by a squadron of crows,

The Vixen, 1976–84, etching, 16 × 22 in.

which do fly, in a mock battle over the barnyard. This late afternoon confrontation between fantasy and reality becomes an almost sobering reminder of the great air battles of World War II.[38]

THE VIXEN

[Saunders] In the etching *The Vixen* [female fox], the viewer has become a wanderer, or hiker, or perhaps a hunter, crossing a stream at twilight on a cold winter day; thigh-deep in icy water, gun or belongings held high and dry. Along the bank, the water has turned into an icy sheet; its surface etched with crystalline designs.

Slowly one realizes that the stream bank is really a man-made stone wall, carefully constructed of hand cut blocks, for some now-obscure purpose by the hands of strangers, at some earlier time. Atop the wall is a gnarled tree stump, attempting to revive itself by sending up surging new canes of growth. Off to the right can be seen the remains of a stone arch. Vines and brambles have almost covered these remains. A classically fluted stone or ceramic vessel lies half-submerged in the icy water nearby at water's edge. . . . The whole scene is almost overwhelmed by the brilliant color blend of a winter sky at dusk. Almost by chance, as daylight continues to fade, one becomes aware of the face of the vixen. At first she is not there. Then without any movement or sound, she has materialized, peering out of the brambles, fixing the intruder in a long, steady, hypnotic gaze. Then, still without movement or sound, she simply disappears. She doesn't leave or walk away; she just isn't there anymore.[39]

The closing print of the *Late Light Suite,* and thus the last etching of the entire *Southern Cross/A Trilogy,* is . . .

MOLLIE'S TABLE

[Saunders] Miss Mollie Boyd was sixty or so years old and unmarried when the great Influenza pandemic of 1918 made orphans of my mother and her four siblings. My mother, who was about two years old at the time, went to live with her great aunt Mollie; Mollie's also unmarried sister, Victoria Boyd, and their bachelor brother, Clay Boyd, in their large old house in Somerville, Tennessee. She brought joy into their lives, and they showered her with love and affection.

In the etching *Mollie's Table,* the dominant symbol is the table that stood in Mollie's house. It is now a cherished part of my home. A tiny vase of spring flowers sets on the table and is illuminated by strong, late afternoon light from an unseen source. The dark wall beyond is a rich mosaic of assorted pictures and glimpses of wallpaper. There are various family photographs, including one of my mother, and one quickly recognizes engravings of a large butterfly and of *The Three Graces* from classical mythology.

Do you realize that this is a very feminine space and that the various elements refer to fertility, nurturing, and nesting? The spring flowers on the table, eternal symbols of beauty and rebirth leave little doubt. Outside the window a young girl plays with her dog in the late light of a spring afternoon.[40]

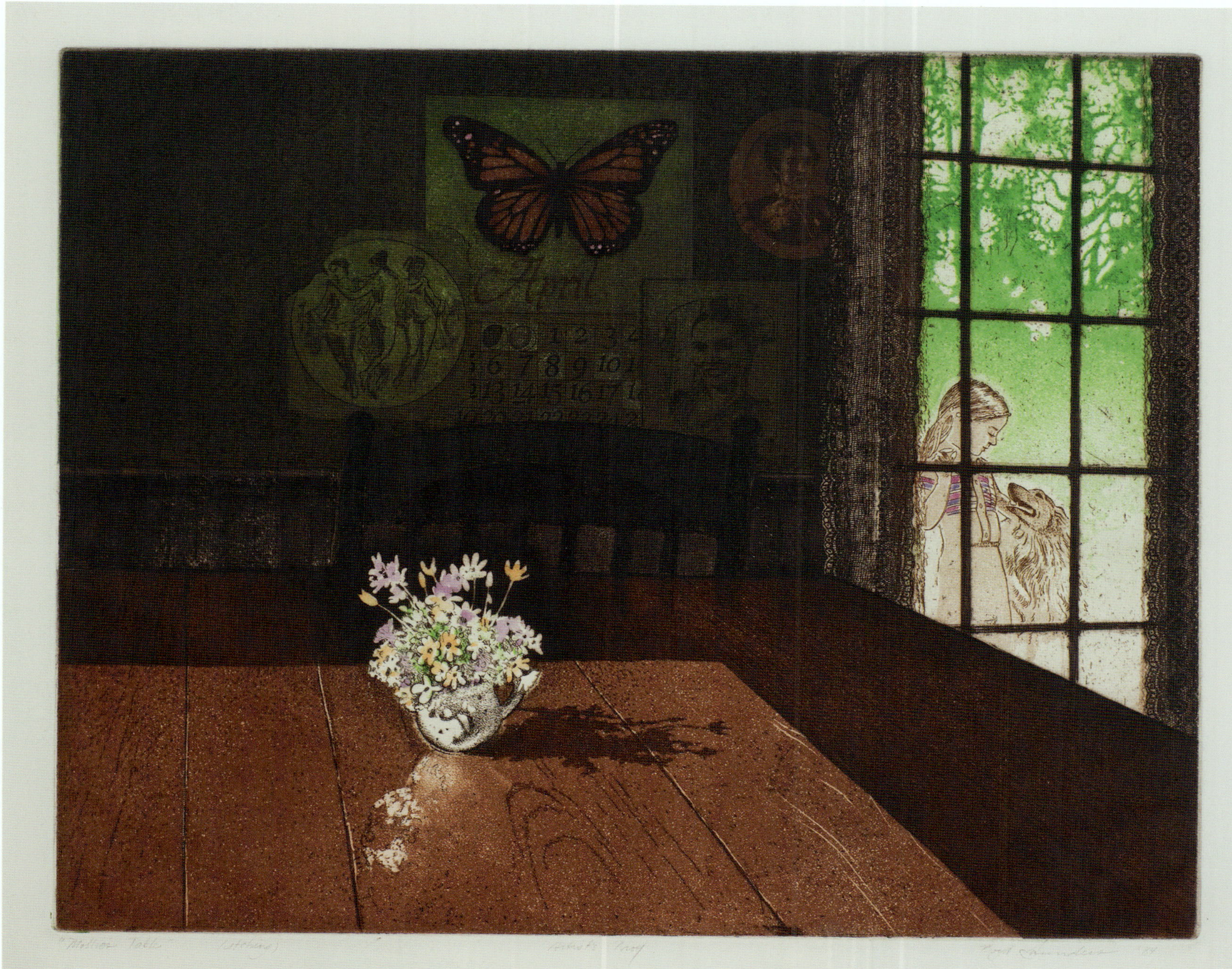

Mollie's Table, 1976–84, 16 × 22 in.

Chapter 6

The Return of the Wanderer, Railroad Muses, and *September Folly*

Saunders finished the epic work *Southern Cross/A Trilogy* in the 1980s, and in somewhat overlapping fashion he embarked on two other projects unrelated to that project, *Spotted Horses* and *The Aikenhead Collection.* But by the early 1990s, he apparently felt a tug to once more contemplate an imaginary person visiting imaginary places, to combine it with his youth in the South, and to realize the subsequent images. Saunders's realization of that direction was gradual, not spontaneous, for example with the title *St. James Crossing* accompanying the appearance of works evoking the southern landscape. That title became a place, an imaginary place, but a place in his statements by the 1990s.

Saunders said, "The *St. James Crossing* imagines that a wanderer returns to where it was that he grew up 30, 40, 50 years ago . . . and in wandering around this place, and this community . . . it's not just a farm anymore, it's a town with railroad boxcars, storefronts, old ruined houses . . . and again engaging in the reflections of how he remembers how it happened so many years ago . . . and he/she remembers it so and so, but it had now taken on a life of its own, in part—a horror of its own . . . and so it is really an end piece to the whole set."[1]

The preceding quotation dates back to a 2001 interview on the occasion of Saunders's *Retro Spectus Exhibition* at the McKissick Museum, University of South Carolina–Columbia,

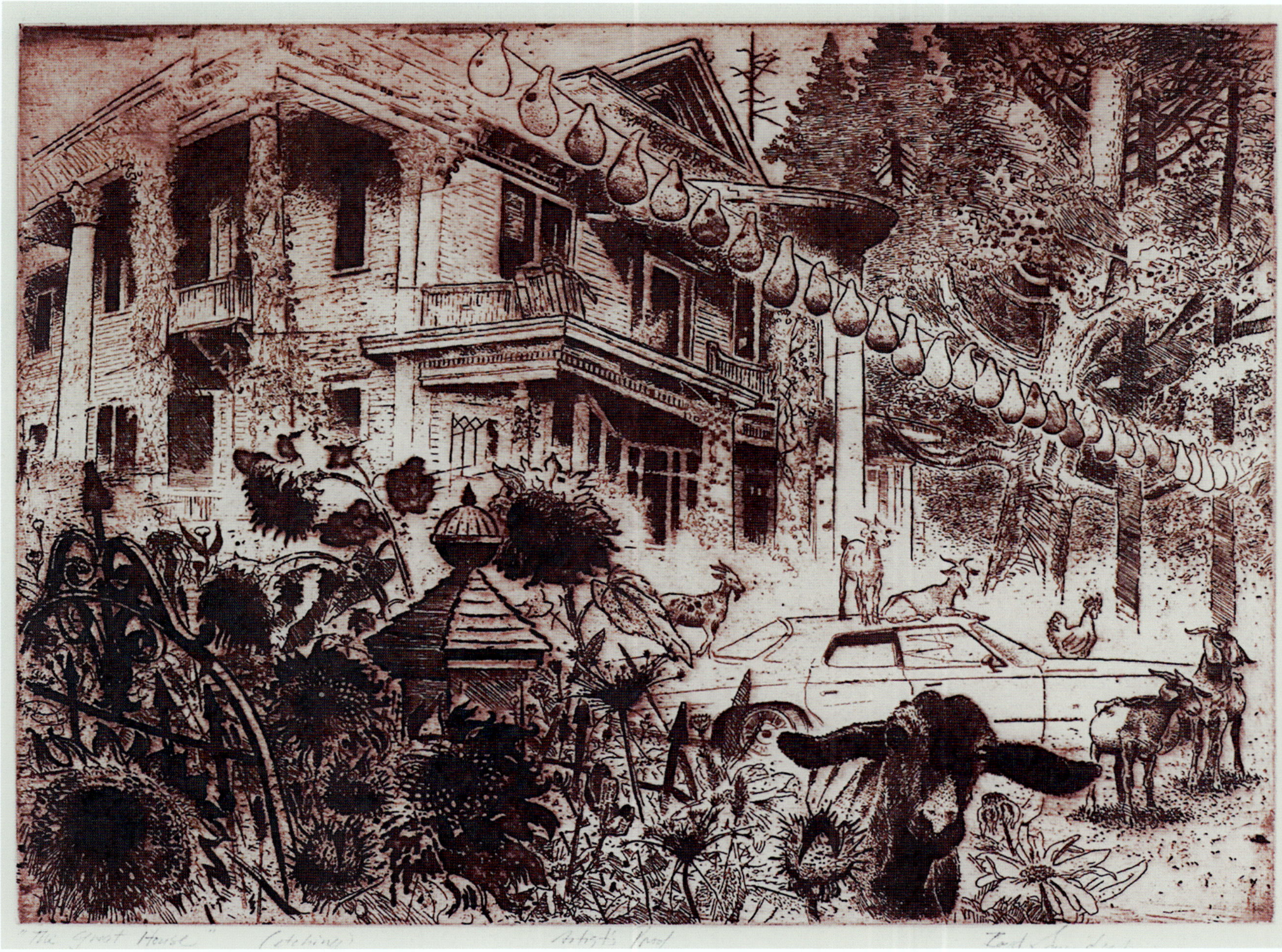

The Great House, etching

marking his retirement from teaching but not from producing art. Now compare the above statement to the one below from March 2010 as the above series has evolved nine more years: "Over the ensuing years (since *Southern Cross/A Trilogy*), I have pursued other artistic directions, but my attention has returned again and again to this theme. In this visual poem The Wanderer Returns to a small southern town once well known by himself. The location has taken on the name of 'St. James Crossing.' Various scenes which the wanderer encounters, evoke memories and reflections on the reality, poetic irony, and the passage of time. Anyone who has ever experienced lengthy separation and return, knows how places and people change over time, yet retain a degree of sameness. It may well be that the artist or writer needs to experience this separation and return in order to gain objectivity. It can, nonetheless be a somewhat disquieting experience."[2]

At the risk of being too tedious, notice that the theme wording of this series has evolved from *St. James Crossing* to *The Wanderer Returns* wherein a wanderer (possibly the artist) visits a community called St. James Crossing. Whatever the case, Saunders's current

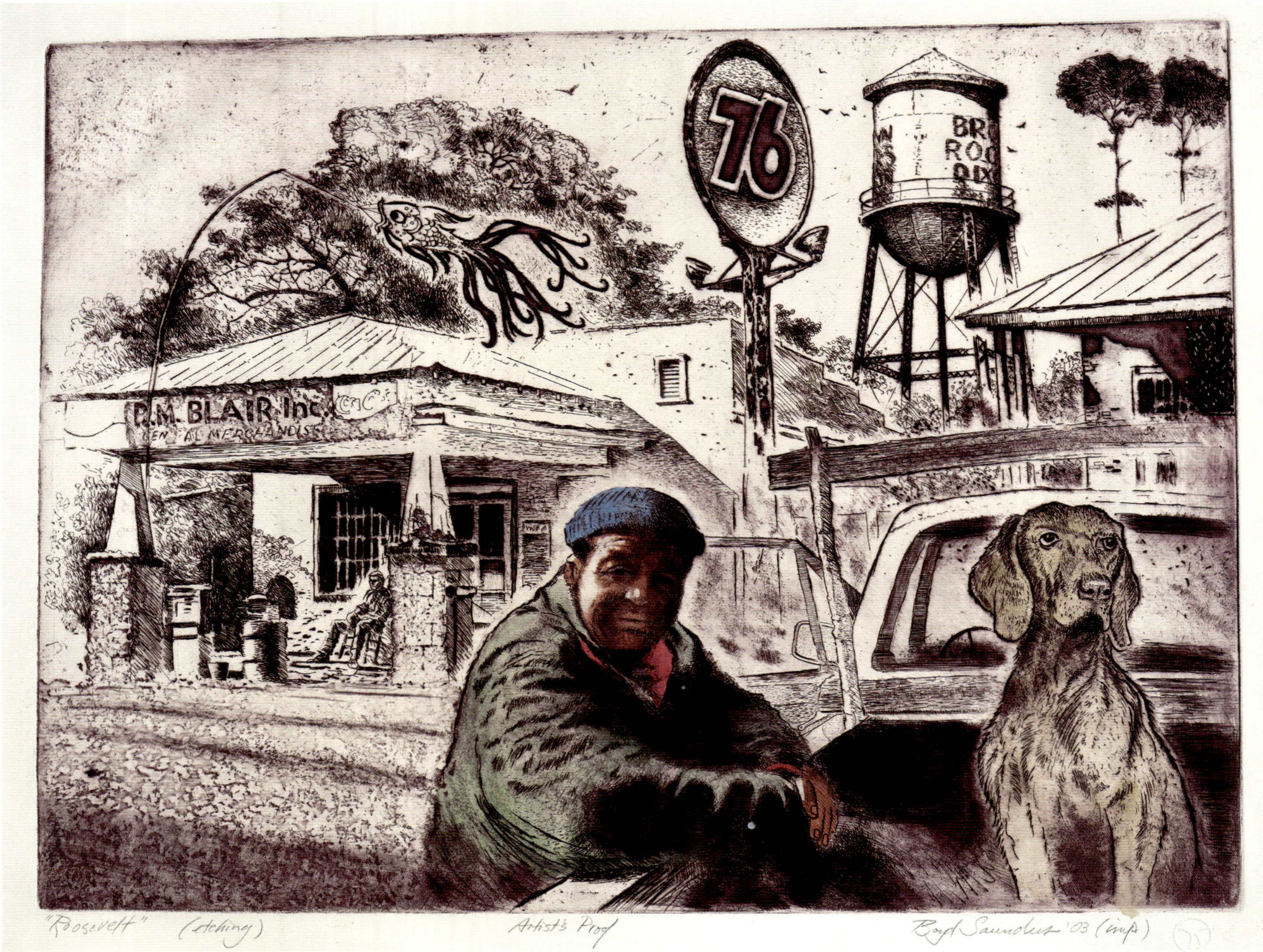

Roosevelt, etching, 18 × 24 in.

series *The Return of the Wanderer* offers viewers the most recent installments of visual poetry reflecting his decades-long southern journey: "The pictorial aspects of my work always deal with a point of view, an observation or commentary. Sometimes a bit of surrealism is employed. I have little interest in simply making a picture of what this or that looks like. It is my hope that viewers respond to my works in similar fashion; might experience visual beauty, and yet, see beyond what the piece is about; whether irony or humor or contradiction or mood or other conceptual responses."[3]

THE GREAT HOUSE

Saunders considers that *The Great House* exemplifies, in particular, his above stated goals: "This etching, goes beyond a mere architectural portrait and becomes a decaying romantic ruins with its own implied, yet unknown story of history and drama, and human habitation, and passion. The goats have gone from being mere farm animals to the role of proprietary inhabitants who challenge the viewer's right to be there.

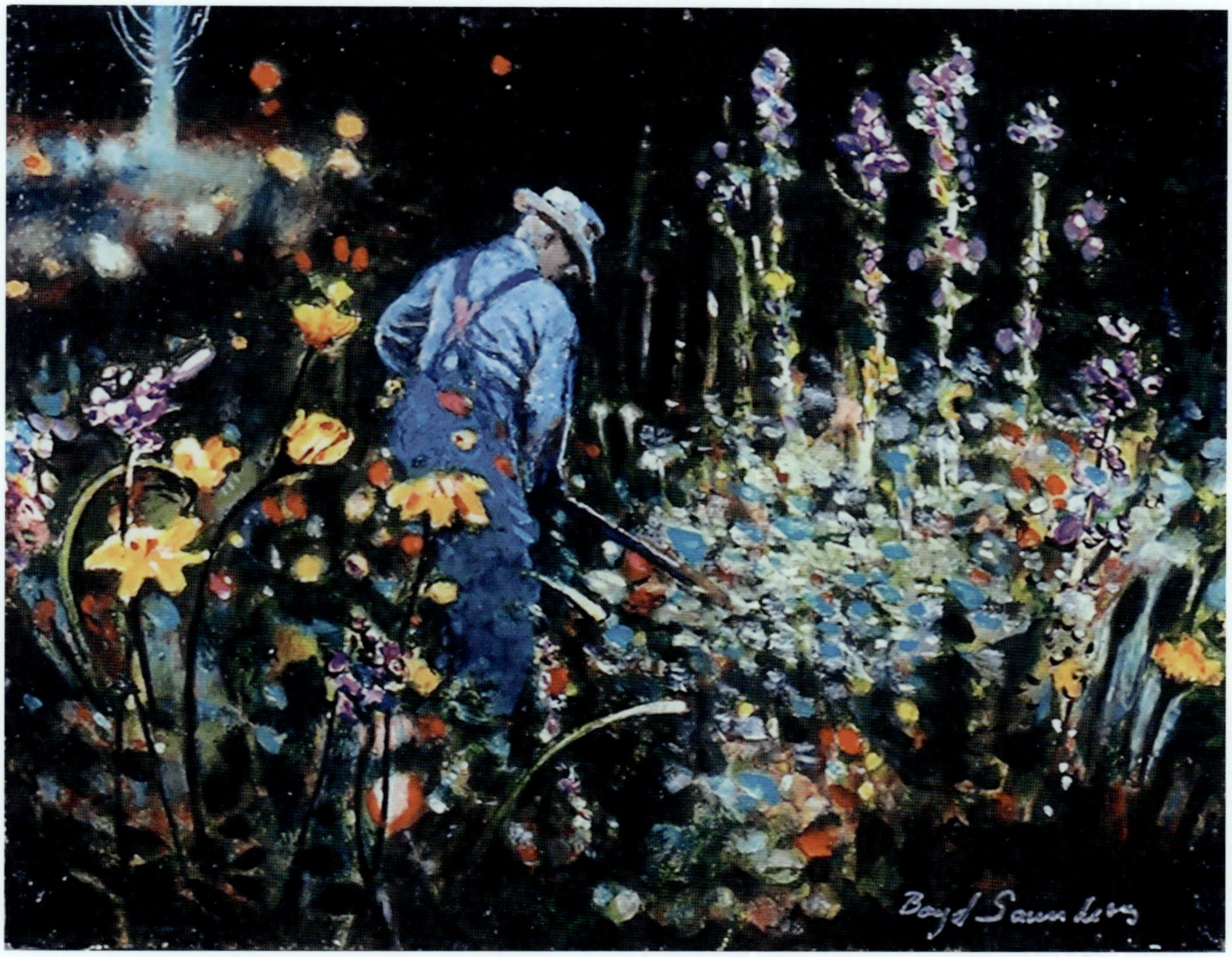

The Gardener, acrylic painting

The car, once ruler of the road, is now their immovable dwelling. The mixed tangle of flowers and weeds overtakes the ornate gate . . . and the row of hanging purple martin gourds; what are they all about?"[4]

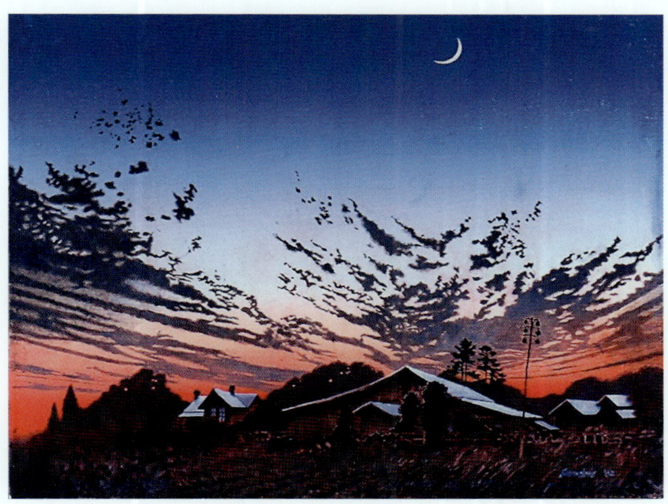

The Homestead, oil painting

Companion etchings to *The Great House* include but are not limited to *Roosevelt* and *Dutch Fork Gothic* and are part of the *St. James Crossing* group. Two works in color, *The Homestead* and *The Gardener,* would fit either the *St. James Crossing* works or those of *The Return of the Wanderer.*

The expression "the Dutch Fork" and its shorter or longer variations appear several times in this book. By chapter 5 ("*Southern Cross/A Trilogy*") a reference to the above can be found early on in *The Farm Suite.* Some of the images are based in general on barns, outbuildings, and farmhouses from the Dutch Fork

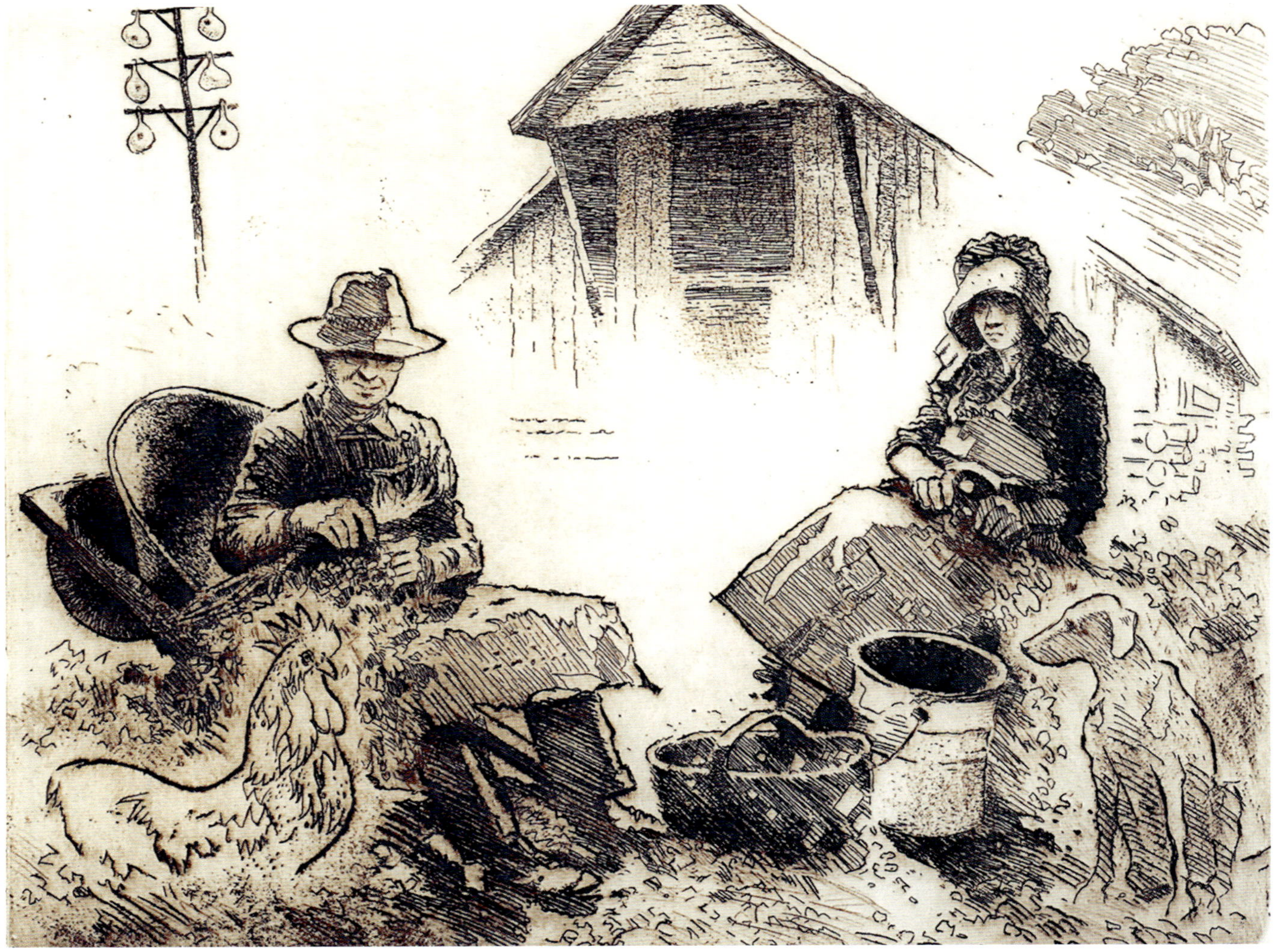

Dutch Fork Gothic, etching, 12 × 15 in.

community, which is a rural area around Saunders's home.

From the *St. James Crossing/Return of the Wanderer* overlapping sections, an etching with a rural couple tending to their chores with the suggestion of barn structure in the background is titled *Dutch Fork Gothic*. Then in the last chapter, "The Storyteller's Art," the words "the Dutch Fork," and "the Fork" appear twice in the stories—"Henry the Mule" and "The Return of Miss Dixie." All these uses serve invented, that is, fictional, circumstances.

However there is cartographical area in the South Carolina midlands that has been called the Dutch Fork by locals since the late 1770s to early 1800s. Art historian Dr. Jessie Poesch noted as much in her groundbreaking 1983 survey of southern art and decorative art.[5] "The settlers in the German-Swiss communities in South Carolina included both those who had come directly from Europe and those from Pennsylvania. They were concentrated in the area known as the 'Dutch Fork' (the term 'Dutch' a mispronunciation of 'Deutsch' that is, German), an area between the Broad and Saluda rivers, slightly north of the central area of the state."[6]

THE RETURN OF THE WANDERER: RAILROAD MUSES

Said Saunders, "In the *Return of the Wanderer: Railroad Muses* series there are, at present, seven images (Four of those which are included in this section.) which make reference to trains. Train imagery in general suggests power, speed, romance, mystery, mobility, escape to faraway places and a host of other

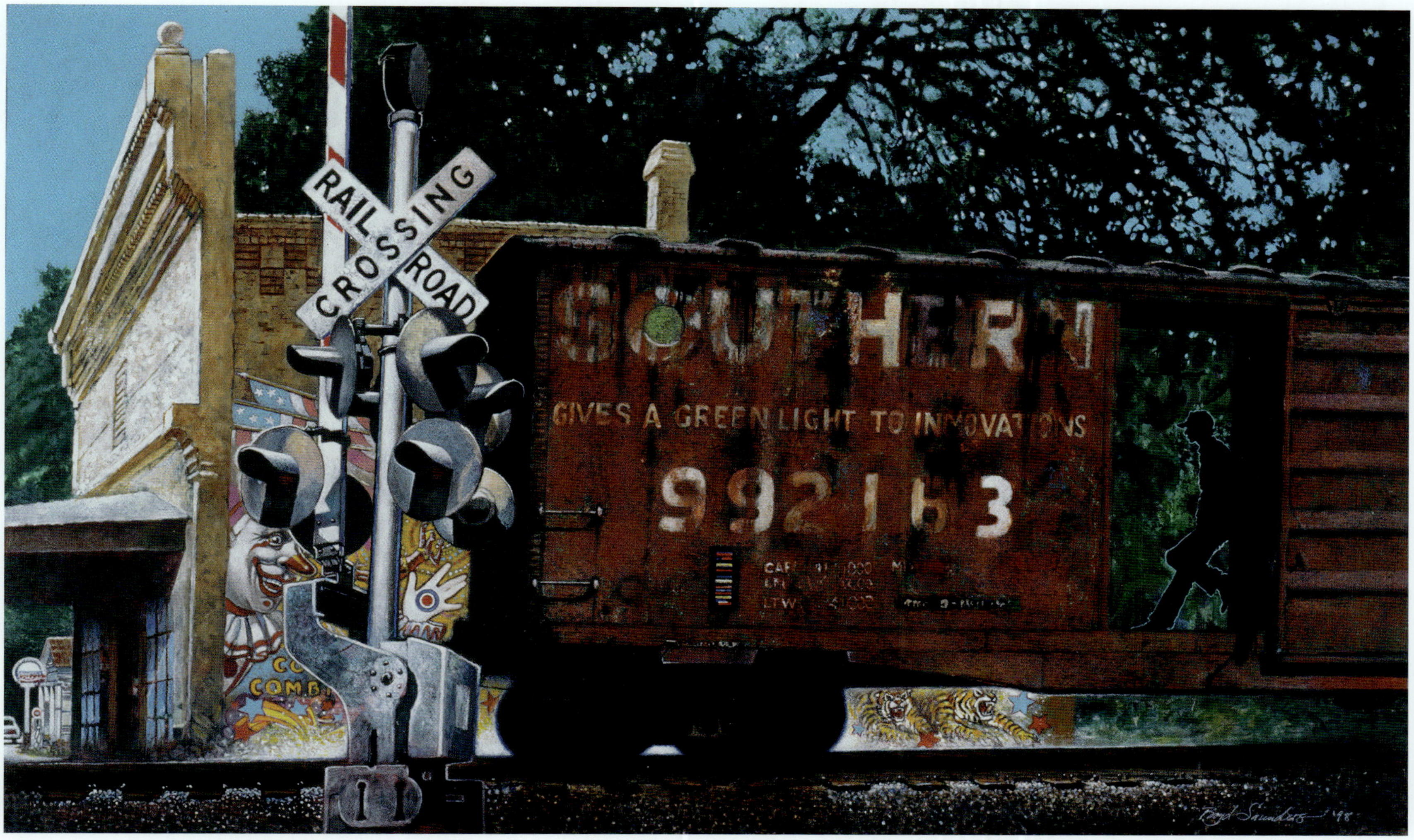

Wednesday Afternoon,
acrylic painting

responses. However, it may not suggest just power, speed, romance, and the like, but maybe a touch of loneliness. Some of the images seem to be shrouded in a mysterious fog or mist; others are quite the opposite."

> [Saunders] The acrylic painting *Wednesday Afternoon* is, to me, a study in complexity and contradiction. The color is meant to be rich and the composition features multiple images intersecting, fragmenting and overlapping each other, reminiscent of some musical compositions by American composer Charles Ives [1874–1954]. The title refers to an old small town custom of the stores closing up on summertime Wednesdays as a sort of payback for having been open on Saturdays for market days. On this hot summer afternoon the place is so quiet one can almost hear a cat walk.
>
> There is no sound quite as evocative as a train whistle or horn, far off in the distance late at night. During the Great Depression of the 1930s, thousands of men climbed on freight trains to seek salvation from their desperate poverty in far-off places. Perhaps "The Wanderer" departed in this fashion; or maybe it was the means of his return.[7]

Saunders's statement that "some of the [railroad car] images seem to be shrouded in a mysterious fog or mist" is an understatement to be sure. In the lithographs *The Siding* and *The Crossing,* each presents a monumental but mundane object that has been transformed into a stunning objet d'art. Both sidelined, dark tank cars are engulfed in a whitish-gray, almost impenetrable mist or rain shower. If a mist, it flutters around the contours of those black forms; if rain, the shower dances off the black giants in thousands of tiny particles. Whatever the atmospheric and light conditions, such elements both describe and dematerialize the tank cars. It's magic.

Saunders's railroad car images, regardless of medium, all appear on sidetracks and sometimes in the middle of nowhere . . . as if abandoned, alone, and forgotten. Is that the case here? Before diving into romanticism, it is worthwhile considering pragmatic circumstances. According to Howard Shepherd of

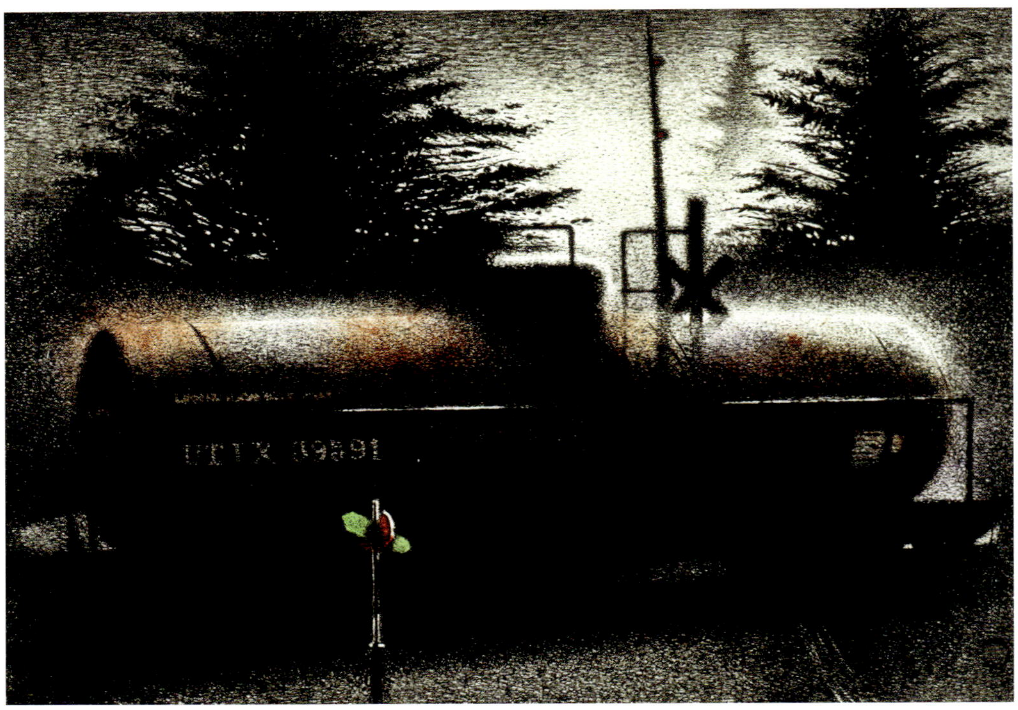

The Crossing, stone lithograph

the South Carolina Railroad Museum at Winnsboro, South Carolina, an individual car might be on a siding so that its freight may be unloaded over an extended period of time without delaying the rest of the train.[8] In addition the types of railroad cars depicted by Saunders (boxcar, tank car, flatcar, and caboose) may just be waiting for maintenance work or repairs of, for example, loose couplers, faulty trucks, bad wheel bearings, compromised airlines, or other problems.

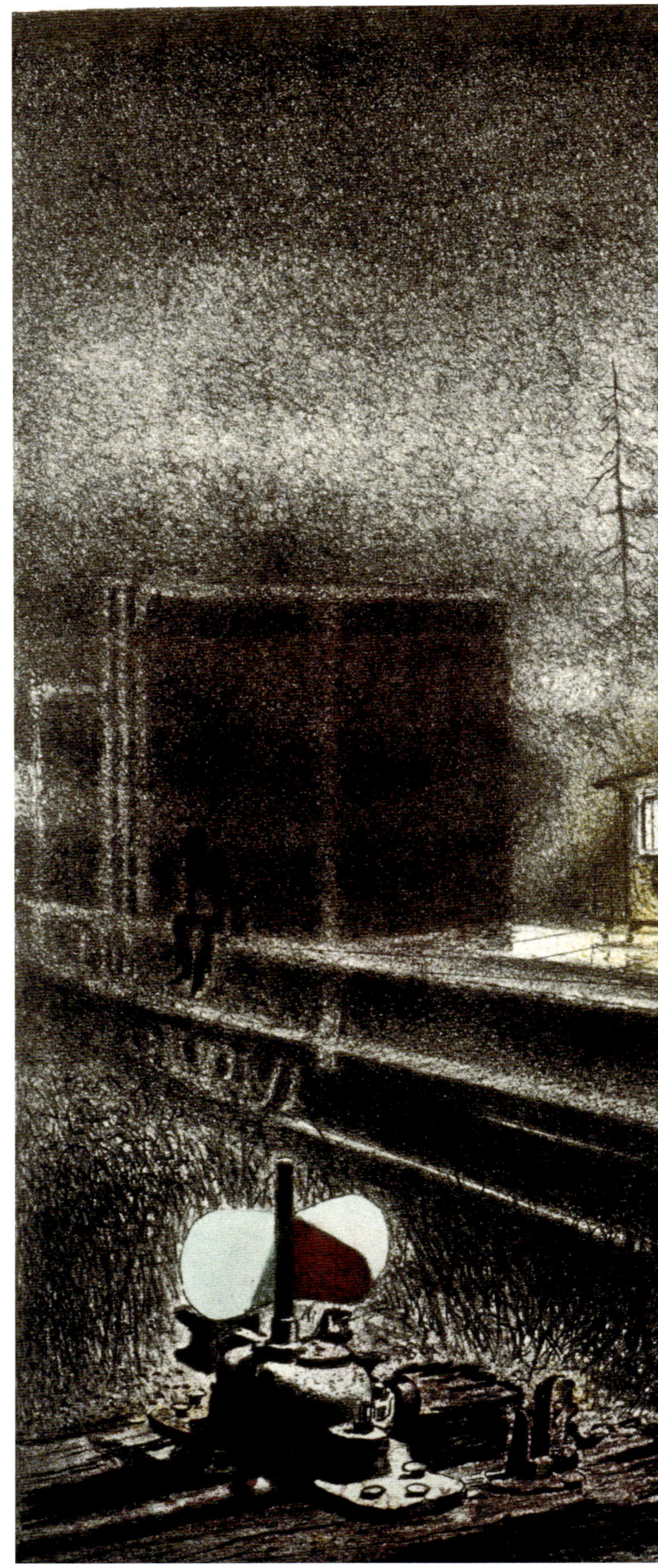

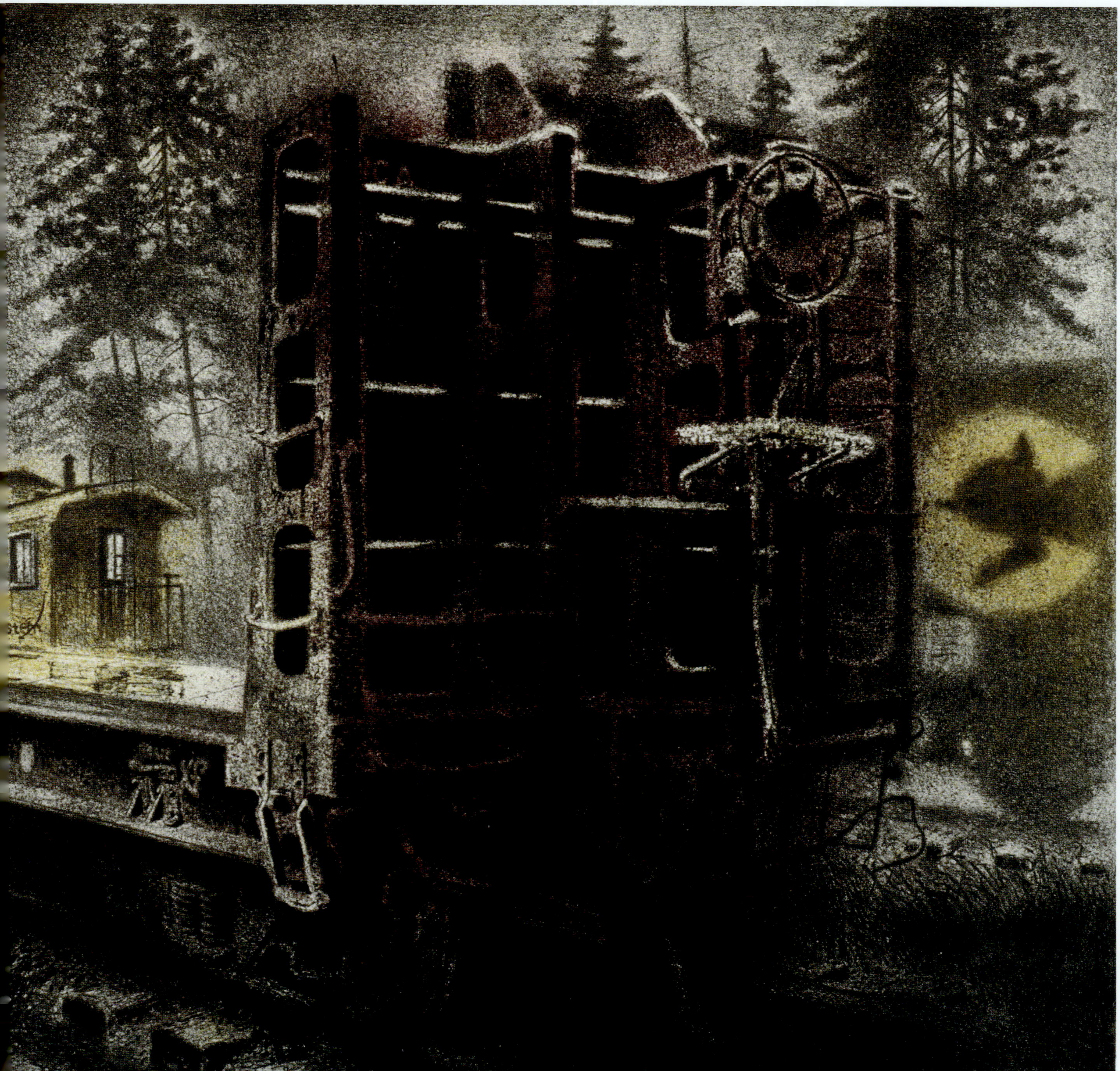

The Prodigal, stone lithograph

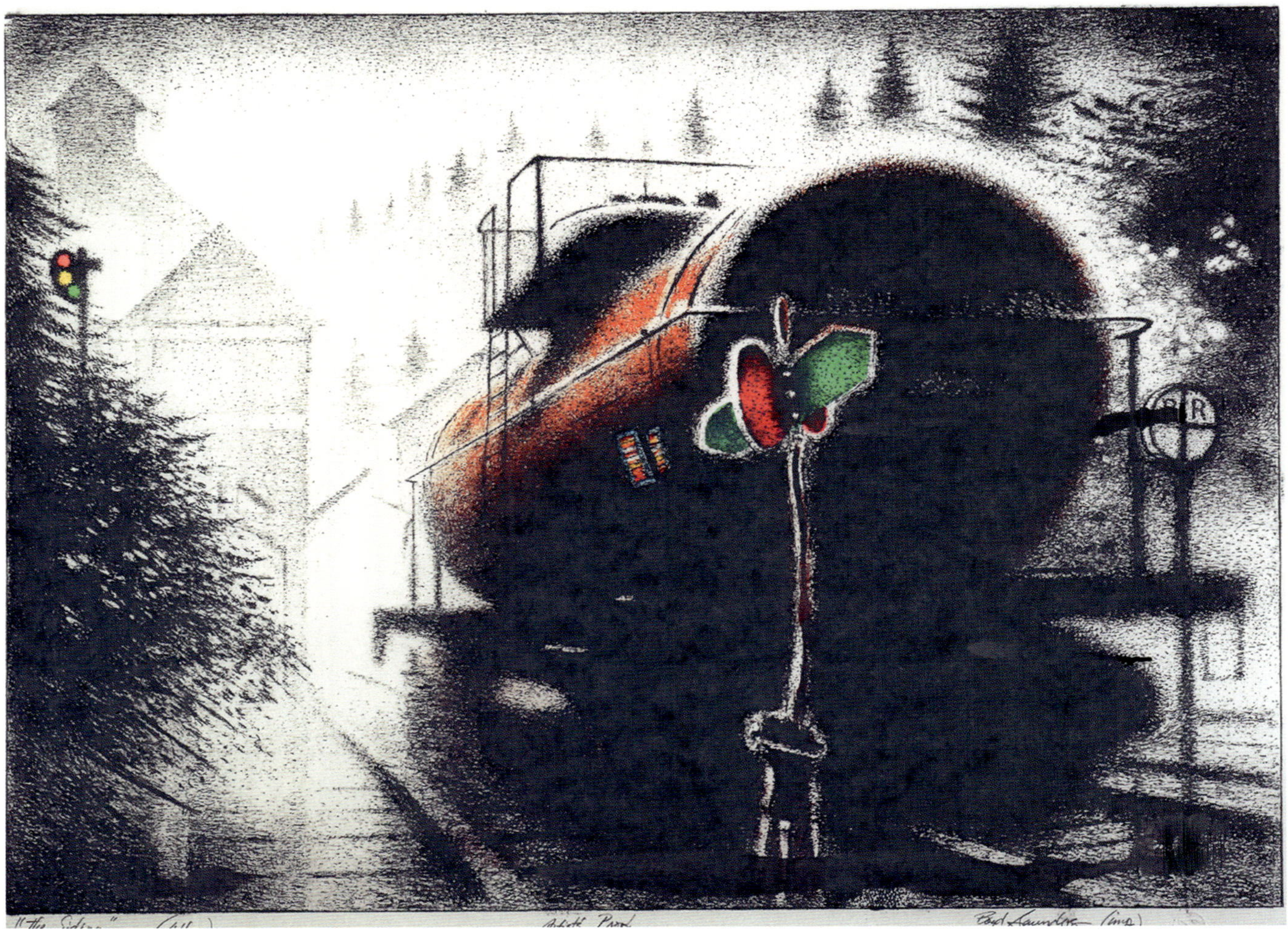

The Siding, stone lithograph

THE RETURN OF THE WANDERER: SEPTEMBER FOLLY

[Saunders] In the coastal states of the American Southland, the beach has long been a fundamental part of life and has shaped much of the lore and customs for generations of people. Students experience rites of passage at the beach; a whole genre of music celebrates this tradition; and even families of modest means find it necessary to own or rent vacation houses there. It is said that pre-Columbian Indians in the region made annual pilgrimages to the ocean to gorge themselves on seafood and visit relatives.

During the days before air conditioning the beach pilgrimage often became a matter of necessity just to escape the stifling heat of summers in the American South. Obviously, it also served as an opportunity for yearly gatherings of extended families.

Iconic beach houses were passed down from generation to generation or, if sold, they often retained the names of the original owners. Over the years some houses were added onto and modified until they evolved into rather unique forms; some became hotels. Sun, sand, and extreme weather also left their own signatures. Occasionally, the wandering shoreline has moved away and left some of these structures standing alone out in the water. It is easy to understand how many of these architectural monuments have taken on a surreal aura and personality of their own. Certainly there are few experiences more introspective than a long walk on a deserted Atlantic beach in mid-winter.

Several of the images in *The Return of the Wanderer* explore this Beach House theme. Collectively named *September Folly,* they share a quiet

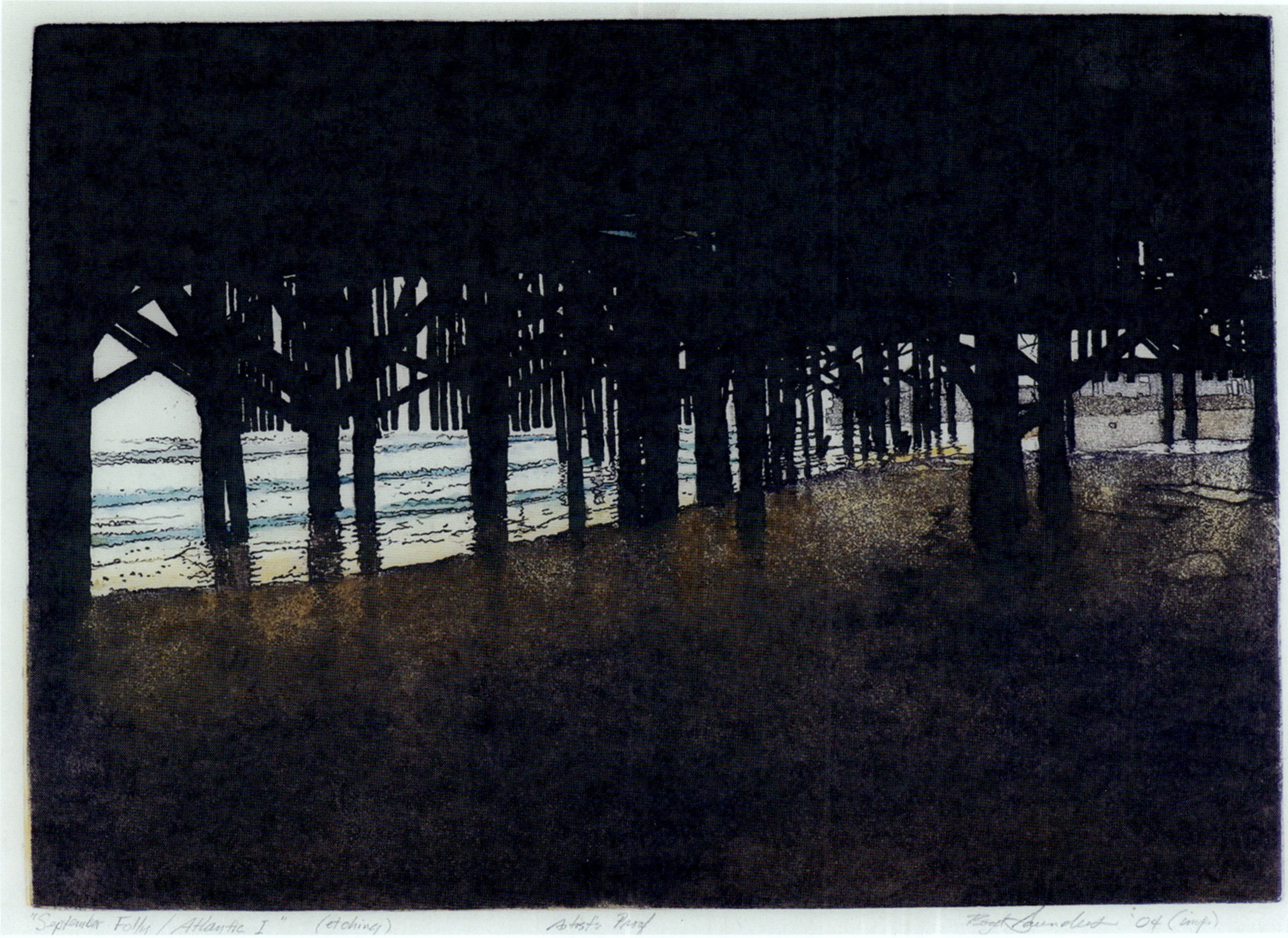

Atlantic I, etching

sense of isolation, starkness, and architectonic solidity. I hope they offer modes of examination; from the study of rhythm, pattern, and positive/negative reversal found in *September Folly/Atlantic I,* to overt surrealism in *September Folly/Atlantic III,* or the fog-shrouded film-noir sensibility of *September Folly/Evensong.* In this last image, there is a brief glimpse of The Wanderer himself.[9]

Saunders's *September Folly* beach house theme is not conceptually restricted to Folly Beach as he has stated. It easily refers to the attraction or allure of many other beaches and barrier islands of South Carolina's Atlantic coast, and to the rest of the enticing beaches in the Southeast from Virginia to Alabama. Granted many South Carolina beaches are much more commercialized than Folly Beach, for example Myrtle Beach considerably up the coast, or Hilton Head Island, a marquee resort destination south of Charleston near Savannah, Georgia. Likewise South Carolina's commercialized beaches were probably not as developed in the 1940s when Folly Island represented affordable, unpretentious vacations with simple pleasures for families and likeminded others. An aggressive desire for extensive or lavish attractions may have even been rejected by the island's residents,

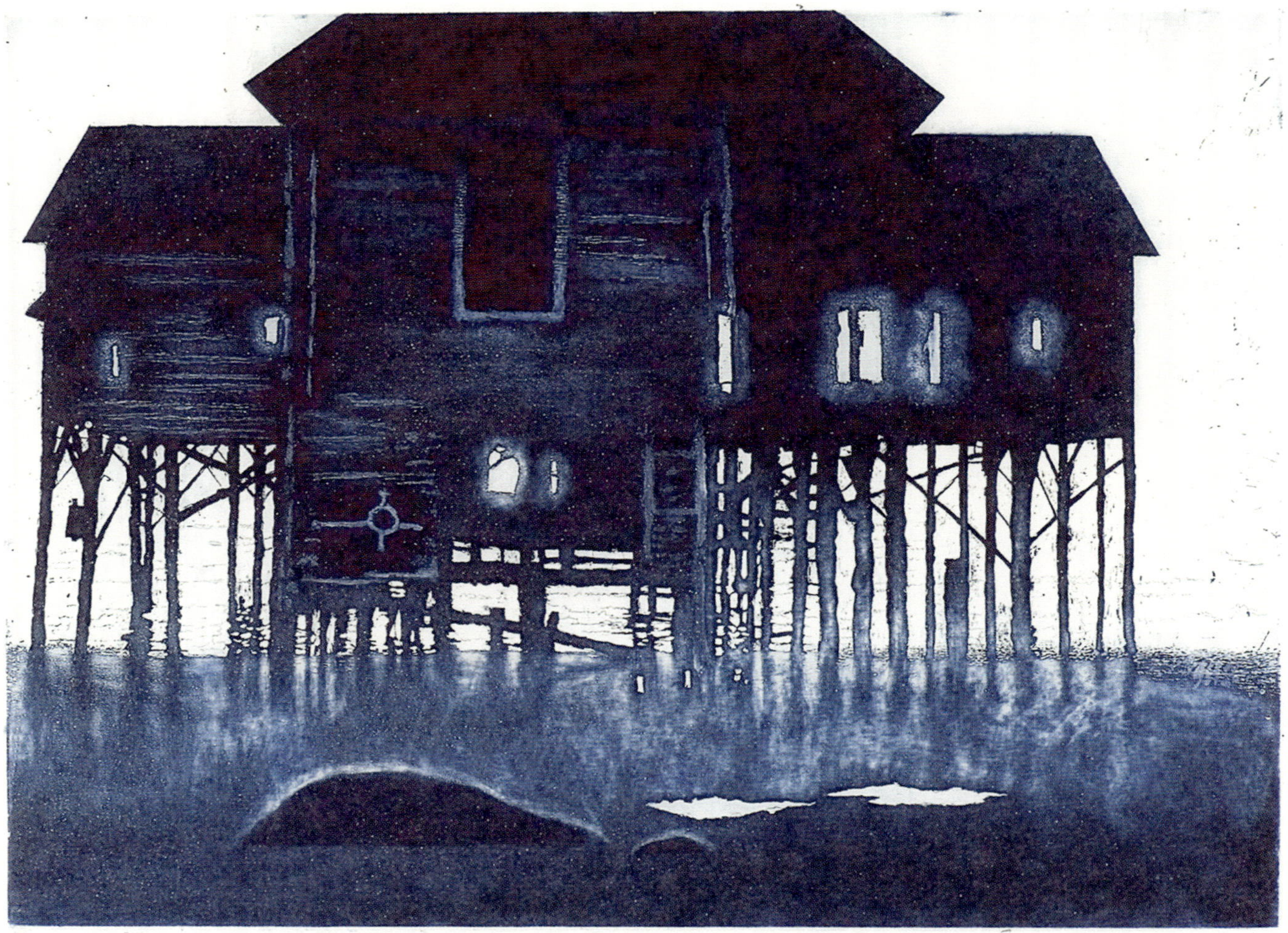

Atlantic II, etching

or such "progress" may have simply bypassed the island like an interstate highway bypasses small towns. Whatever the case Folly Island has not been forgotten by beach lovers or historians, and perhaps not even seriously marginalized. A website provides a rather spicy history and chronological evolution of the maverick little island, a summary of which follows:

> According to the Folly Island website, the word Folly comes from Old English usage as a reference to dense foliage or a thicket. When European settlers to North America began arriving in the 1600s, a Native American tribe, the Bohickets, was already living on the island. The first record of Folly Island, which is six and one half miles long and a half mile wide, appeared on September 9, 1696, when it was given to William Rivers as a royal grant. Presumably Rivers accepted it for future development but never lived there. Folly Island was passed down for a generation or two in the Rivers family, and then ownership changed hands frequently. Eventually, the Native Americans were forced off the island when waves of immigrants continued to arrive to the South Carolina colony.
>
> In the 1700s and early 1800s, Folly Island had a reputation as a sanctuary for pirates which may suggest minimal law enforcement during that era from Charleston. During the American Civil War, the island was occupied by thousands of Union Army troops who initially regarded the place as strange, jungle-like, and uninhabitable. Not much fighting happened there, but many of those soldiers died or became ill from exposure to the elements and from inadequate sanitation.
>
> A new century witnessed significant changes and challenges. A public pavilion was constructed

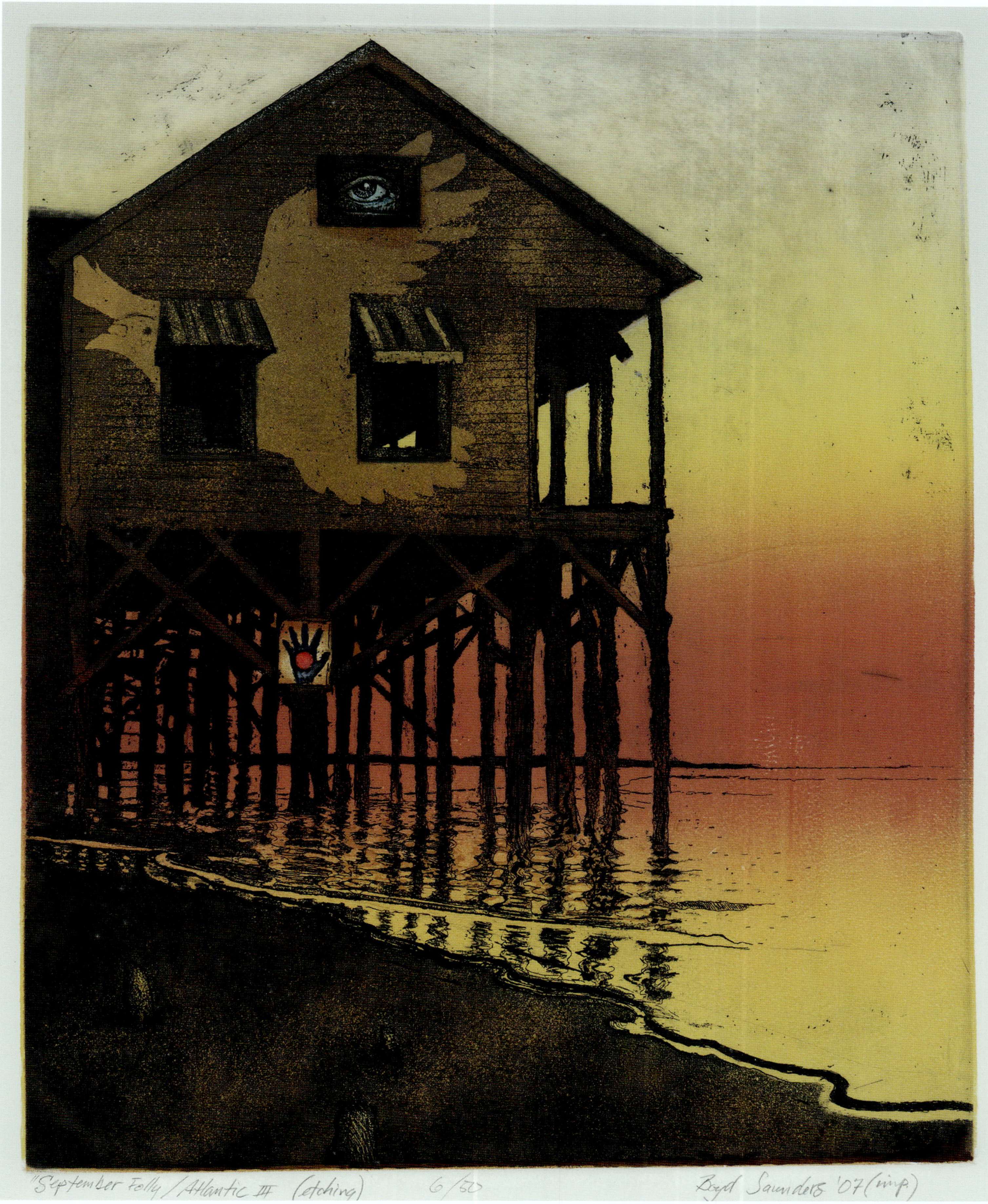

Atlantic III, etching

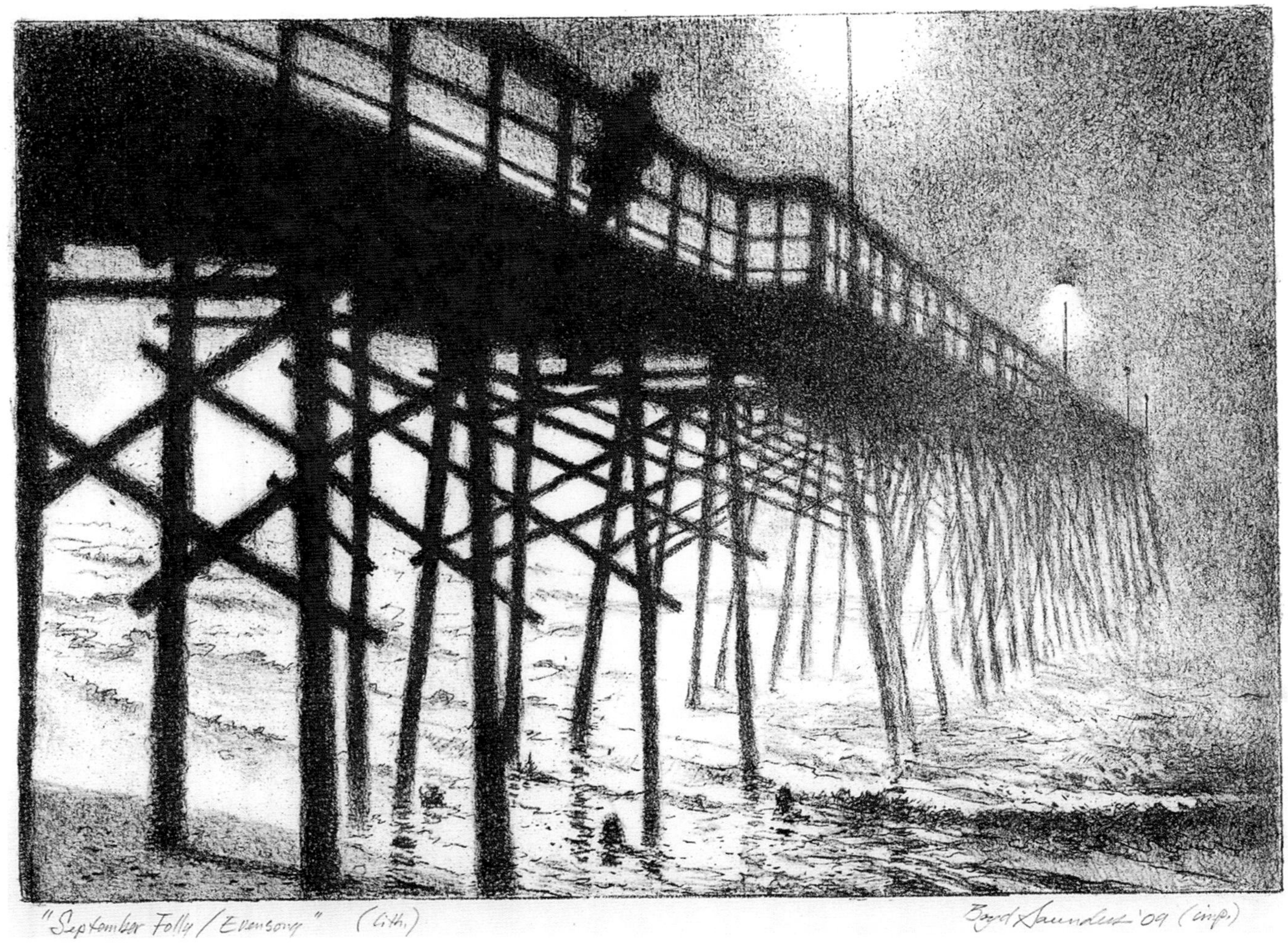

September Folly/Evensong, lithograph

on the island in the 1920s and was replaced in the 1930s with the new Atlantic Pavilion, The Boardwalk, and the Pier and Oceanfront Hotel. Several families began living on the island permanently about that time. In 1934 the gifted American composer George Gershwin lived on Folly Island for a while at 704 West Arctic. He collaborated with Charlestonian Dubose Heyward, author of the book *Porgy* (1926), to create the groundbreaking folk opera *Porgy and Bess* (1935). Heyward wrote the entire libretto with his wife Dorothy, and then they worked closely with George Gershwin and his brother Ira, who was already a well-established lyricist. The Fourth of July celebration at the Folly Island Pier in 1937 attracted over 15,000 people.

The 1940s saw much more island home construction and, with that, came road and utilities upgrades. In 1957, a fire destroyed the aforementioned 1930s hotel, pavilion, and restaurant, but during the 1960s a large lodging, entertainment, and tourist complex brought prosperity to Folly Island. Unfortunately, the next two decades amounted to a roller coaster ride experience for islanders as the Pier burned in 1977, a Holiday Inn was constructed in 1985, but in 1989 Hurricane Hugo wiped out many homes and wrecked the beaches. Though sometimes bad news for Folly Island dwellers and businesses, the island has performed its duties as a barrier island by partly protecting Charleston from the worst wind and waves associated with Atlantic storms. Despite Hurricane Hugo, by 1995 recovery was evident once more when, the present pier restaurant and tackle shop were built, and eventually the beaches were inviting again.[10]

Chapter 7

The Aikenhead Collection

After a brief introduction to the origination of this commission, this section evolves into an informal discussion of *The Aikenhead Collection* with again particular emphasis on probing the creative process. The discussions took place on August 13–14, 2006, at Saunders's home and studio near Chapin, South Carolina.

In 1986 Dr. Robert Alexander, then chancellor of the University of South Carolina–Aiken, was interested in sponsoring a project with the South Carolina National Bank that would recognize the importance of the harness horse industry in the Aiken community. The city was long known for its fine course, the Mile Track at Aiken, and the annual harness-racing training season (winter and early spring) there. Not incidentally the mascot for University of South Carolina–Aiken is a pacer, so the chancellor's gesture was, at the very least, an expression of gratitude to the community of Aiken for its support and of hope for cooperation for future projects with mutual benefits. Chancellor Alexander was a longtime friend of Saunders, and he asked the artist to consider producing a series of artworks that celebrated harness racing.

As the proposal moved forward, a general concept emerged of producing a number of prints and perhaps two small bronze sculptures celebrating harness-racing training at Aiken and offering them for sale with the revenues to be used in establishing the Boyd Saunders

Endowment for the Arts Fund at University of South Carolina–Aiken. The title of the project—*The Aikenhead Collection*—was derived from the name of one of the progenitors of the trotting horse breed in the modern era, Aikenhead, and the nifty coincidence that the city has part of that name, "Aiken," and is the center of harness horse-racing training in South Carolina. In its more specific agreed-on format, the project proposed eight original hand-printed color lithographs 29½ × 41½ inches (height preceding length) ranging in edition size from twenty-five to forty-two impressions. Two cast-bronze sculptures of the same theme about 9 × 15½ inches and 12¾ × 22 inches (height preceding length) respectively in editions of twenty-five each were projected to complete the project. According to *The Aikenhead Collection* exhibition catalogue, the works were to be marketed in the following ways. One could purchase the complete set of lithographs and sculptures or purchase the set of lithographs only or the sculptures only or any of those works individually, making it easy for almost every interested person to participate in the creation of the above-mentioned endowment.[1]

Yet despite the pragmatic and optimistic project proposal, Saunders was hesitant about accepting Chancellor Alexander's request.

The rest of the chapter, though irregular, appears as an interview or conversation with the goal of more spontaneity and experiment with chapter formats. Saunders said, "When I got into this project, I'd been a horseman all my life and was working on equestrian images for the *Spotted Horses* at the time my friend urged me to do this. I said, I'll see where it leads me . . . but I don't know anything about harness racing. Nevertheless, I proceeded to learn."

One of the areas Saunders looked into was the origin and general nature of harness racing in America. Some of his findings and observations follow.

"Harness racing began in middle America with buggy horses pulling the family buggy, going to church or to town. Farmers would come alongside one another, and one thing would lead to another, and you'd have a race going down a country road. Thoroughbred racing is an elite gentleman's sport. It is expensive, it is high class, it is aristocratic, and it is high stakes. Harness racing, on the other hand, is very middle class. Harness racing existed in areas of America where thoroughbred racing did not. The purses are not as high as they are in thoroughbred racing, nor are the raceways as grand. The Red Mile at Lexington, Kentucky, is a charming old racetrack, but it is not nearly as posh as its neighbor across town, Keeneland, where they race thoroughbreds. You just won't see the posh set in the grandstands. The whole thing is on a much lower keel."

Dewey: "What breed of horses are used in harness racing, maybe thoroughbreds projected to be unsuitable for racing longer distances?"

Saunders: "You don't drive thoroughbreds. You use American standard-bred horses. They're built differently and bred differently."

Dewey: "I think thoroughbred horses are raced as early as three years of age, and maybe younger, but then they may stop racing somewhat early as well. What's it like for an American standard-bred harness horse?"

Saunders: "It's not uncommon to see a trotting horse or a harness horse race for a long time. He might race until he's ten or twelve years old."

Dewey: "You stated that when you agreed to begin to develop *The Aikenhead Collection,* you lacked knowledge of harness racing but said you "proceeded to learn." How did you start to learn specific information that might end up in the lithographs? Was there a priority scale as to what you needed to learn?"

Saunders: In the first place I needed to learn my chops, so I went down to Aiken [during the off season] and started hanging out at the track. I found the trainers and the drivers all to be very kind, hospitable, and down-to-earth people. They welcomed me warmly, they showed me regularly what was going on, and, little by little I began to learn the ropes. One of the first things I thought I needed to know was harness, the tack [short for tackle or gear], and its function. At first glance it's a bunch of strange-looking stuff hanging there all around a racehorse. In point of fact, every piece of it on there has a function. It may not all be there at the same time, and the function may vary, but it all has a function, and I needed to know that. I helped them harness up and learned what every strap was all about and what it was supposed to do.

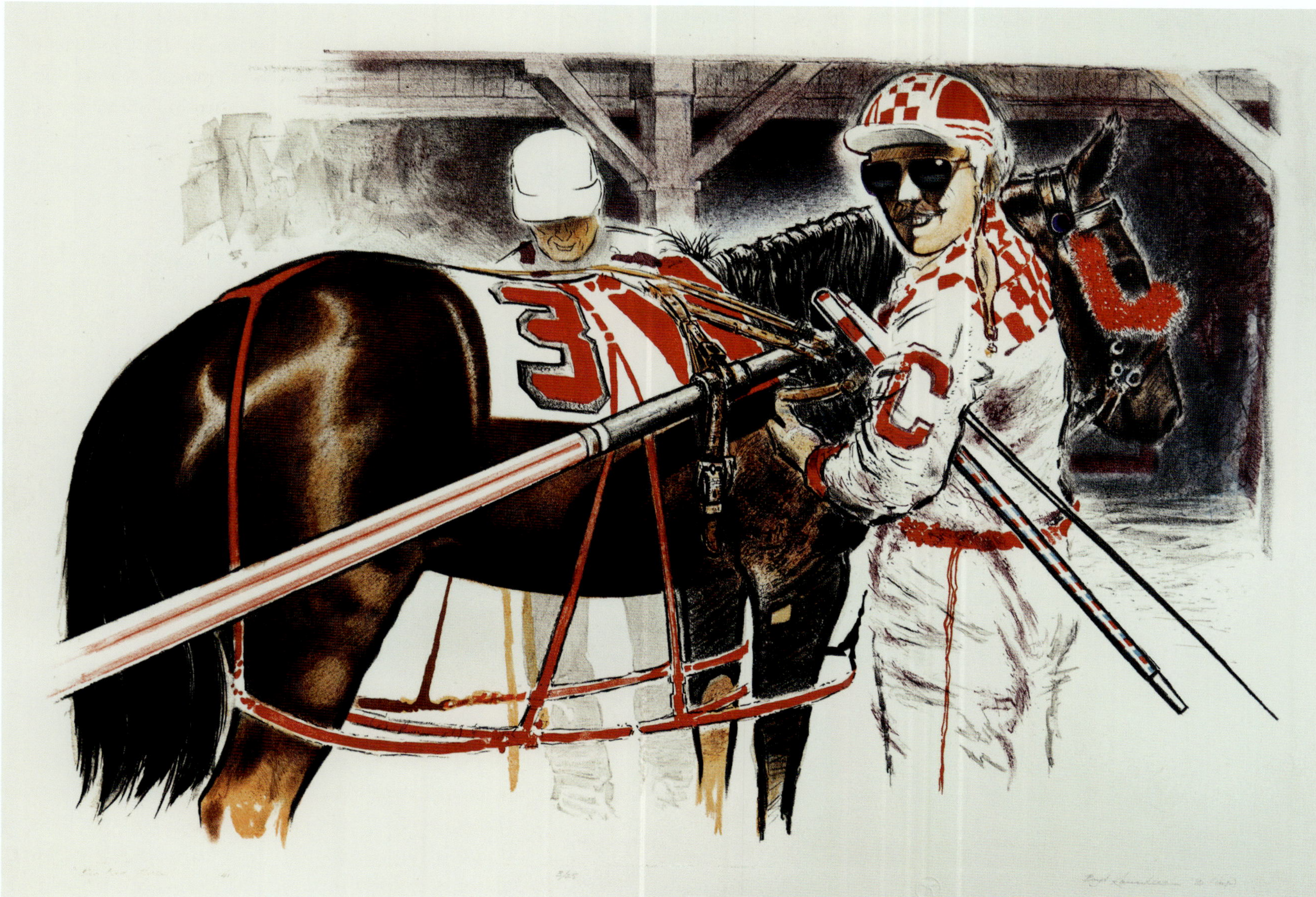

Big Red Three, 1986, stone lithograph in seven colors, 29½ × 41½ in.

BIG RED THREE

In *Big Red Three,* the first color lithograph in *The Aikenhead Collection,* the intricate harness is visible, and it is the focus at the moment of the driver and a handler. In addition to the right-side sulky shaft, its guides, various straps, and the long line reins, two other features are present.

Dewey: "What is the horse wearing on the sides of its head and over the bridge of its nose?"

Saunders: "They usually call that a shadow roll. It's a roll of fur or lamb's wool, something like that. Its primary purpose is to keep the horse from being distracted by seeing things off to the side or down on the track like shadows in front of him that would distract or frighten him."

Dewey: "The horse in the lithograph *Big Red Three* is wearing, or has been outfitted with, I think you said, hobbles. Could you explain the purpose for that?"

Saunders: "Yes, one of the reasons I like to use the term "harness racing" is (they used to call it the "trotting races") because the truth is, there are two designations with it at least. There are trotters, and there are pacers. The difference between a trotter and a pacer, as I understand it, is this. A trotting horse, when he is trotting, he's not galloping, he's surely not walking, he's at that middle stage between walking and running. When he's trotting, his front legs and his back legs move in opposition to each other. In other words, when his front left leg is extended [forward], his left back leg is back and vice versa.

On the other hand, with a pacer, both the front legs and the back legs move parallel to each other. When a front leg is extended forward, the back leg on the same side is also extended forward. To be sure that this stays that way and that they don't slip into another gait, they put hobbles on these horses which tend to guarantee that both legs on the same side of the horse move in the same direction. It is not a big deal. It's just a little series of straps that hang down there and, as long as the horse follows the gait that it's supposed to, then it doesn't impede him. If, on the other hand, he tries to slip into a trot and extend a front leg forward and a back leg backward on the same side at the same time, then the hobble will interfere with it." (If a pacer or a trotter slips out of the proper gait into a gallop or a canter, for example, its driver must bring the horse back to the correct gait soon or else face disqualification from the race.)[2]

Saunders: "I had several mentors in all this. The man in the foreground of this print [facing us] is Jim Crane. He was very kind to me, very charitable, and wound up in this piece."

Dewey: "The left sleeve of Jim Crane's driving suit bears a large red capital C, and a red-and-white checkered pattern decorates the upper part of his jacket (front and back) as well as his helmet. Unlike thoroughbred jockeys, who wear the colors or "silks" of the horse's owner/stable, a harness-racing driver wears his or her own colors regardless of the owner. The drivers have the option to create their own designs and choose the colors, but the final design must be approved by the USTA [United States Trotting Association], and the drivers must wear those colors every time they drive. Furthermore a harness-racing driver must obtain a license or permit to drive such horses and licenses vary based on the experience of the driver. Drivers are basically either so-called catch-drivers hired on a per-race basis, or they are trainer-drivers, that is, trainers who generally drive their own horses.[3]

In *Big Red Three,* the trainer-driver Jim Crane and his assistant double-check and adjust the harness to the shafts of the sulky, a lightweight, two-wheeled vehicle in which the driver sits and is used specifically for racing.

THE VETERAN

The Veteran is the second color lithograph in *The Aikenhead Collection,* and it features a stretch of X-braced wooden fence or stall railing over which are draped drivers' silks, which also partly block a racehorse in profile behind the fence. This haltered horse of advanced age was not sought out for any special reason; it was factored into the composition and may just exist there in an indefinite space as a monochromatic foil to the colorful silks. The composition was invented rather spontaneously.

Saunders: "I was trying to look for different sorts of images and the visual aspects of some of those images. I mean you can do just so many pictures of a group of horses coming across a finish line, and it gets pretty cliché after awhile. I found the patterning of silks and numbers to be visually exciting. I found the trappings on the clothing that people wore to be exciting. For instance in *The Veteran* you've got a bunch of silks thrown across a railing there. I just found that to be a beautiful abstract pattern . . . and playing that off the old horse behind the group of silks was an effective device."

Dewey: "Did you study this group of silks with your camera like previsualizing for compositional impact before you took the photograph, and do you remember at what race track you photographed them?"

Saunders: "I noticed it, and I took a photograph of it, but I saw that bunch of silks across there, and without analyzing I thought, that looks good! In this particular case I don't remember where it was, but that's the way it [the arrangement] was."

THE PROCESSION

The third print in succession presents glimpses of at least four horses harnessed to sulkies, being driven or led, and moving left to right in front of the gable end

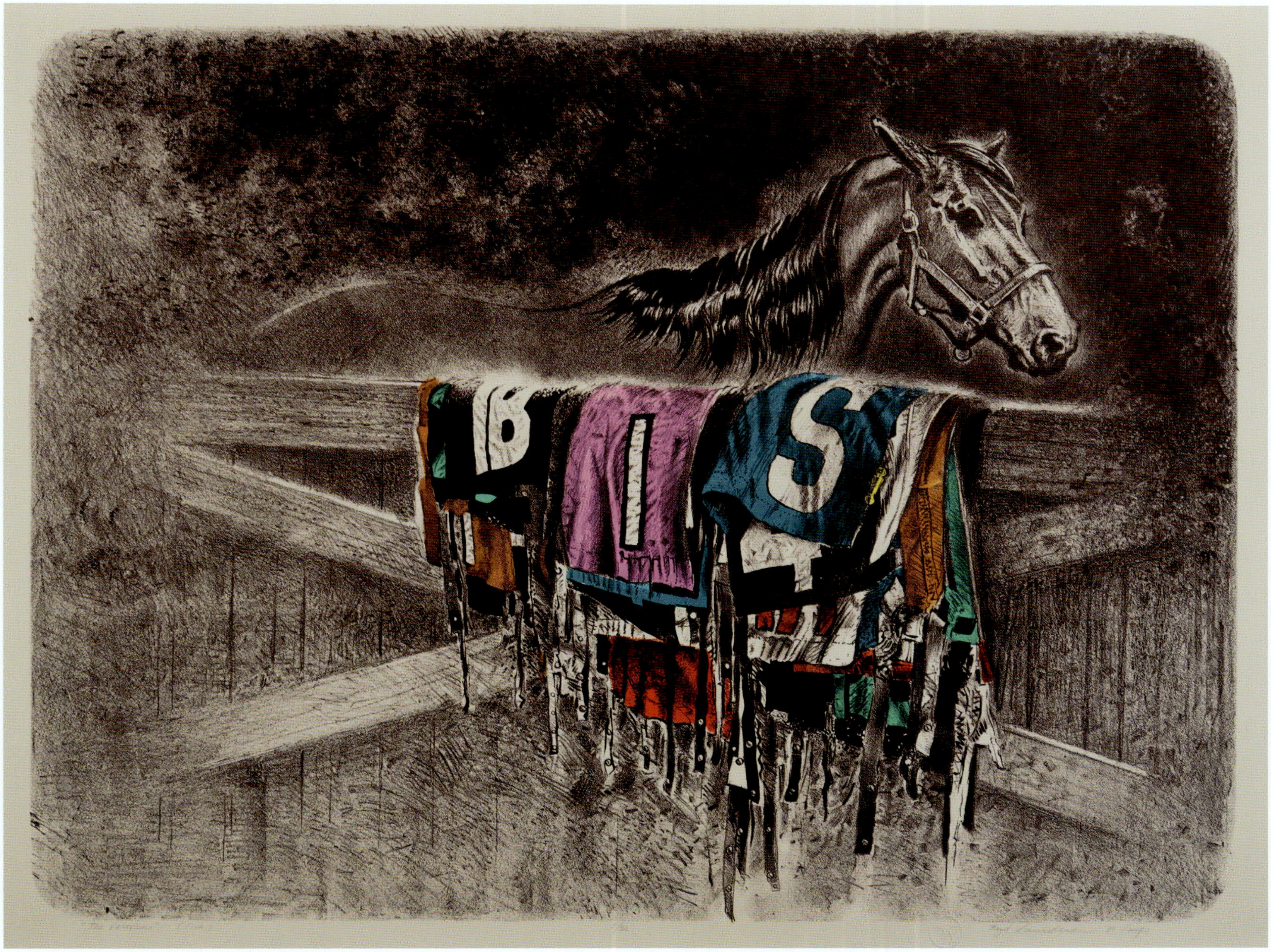

The Veteran, 1987,
stone lithograph in six colors,
21½ × 30 in.

of a barn. It's titled *The Procession,* which might ordinarily imply that the three or four harnessed horses are headed to a racetrack and the call to post. Yet they might be returning from a race heat to the racetrack barns.

Dewey: "What kind of thematic possibilities were you exploring in this lithograph?"

Saunders: "This is a staging area of many barns, and the spaces between them amounted to streets or avenues, and there was traffic of horses and sulkies and drivers passing up and down those streets but not necessarily all with the same purpose or intent at the same time. It's unglamorous, and it's down to earth. It kind of reminds me of Degas's paintings of ballet dancers backstage getting ready for a performance."

Dewey: "In adjusting their costumes, stretching, or practicing certain positions?"

Saunders: "Yes."

Dewey: "There is some interesting body language in some of the horses here. The one in the foreground

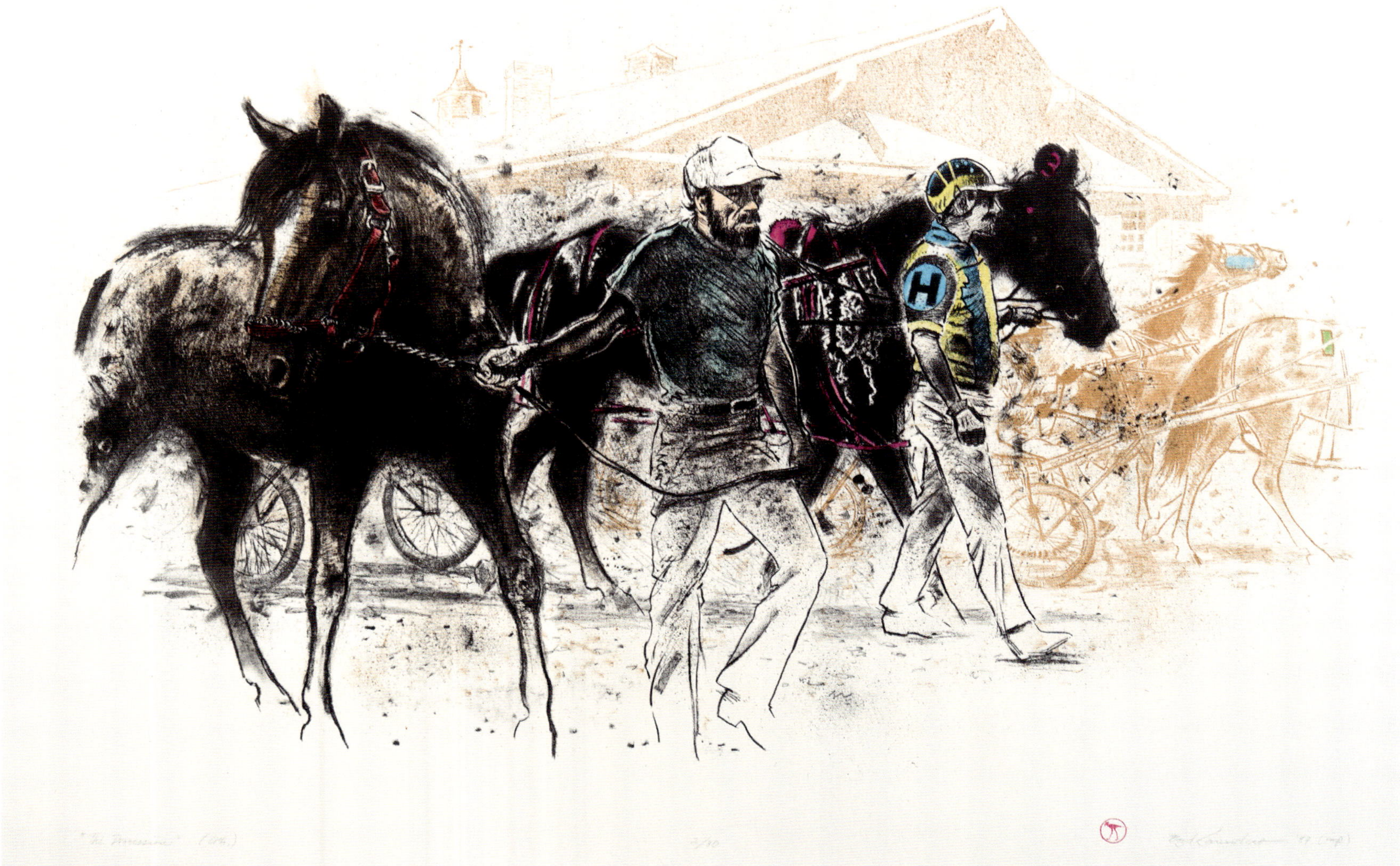

The Procession, 1987, stone lithograph with two stones and hand-applied color, 29½ × 41½

with a handler seems to have found something that has caught his eye to one side. Then there is a horse to the far right with its head up and stretched out maybe resisting a tight check rein?"

Saunders: "Tossing his head?"

Dewey: "Yes, tossing its head. Also I sense in this piece that you like asymmetrical compositions and like cropping imagery, which may go along with it. Maybe you do it unconsciously by now. Furthermore those devices are tied to a truth. When one sees life it's rarely composed symmetrically; instead it's usually random, even chaotic."

Saunders: "Well, I'm very involved with composition. If I'm working with a rectangular format, it is important to me that that rectangular format be completely engaged, that I utilize the space in it. . . . It's all of equal importance to me."

Dewey: "I sense something else at work in *Big Red Three, The Procession, Brandywine Sunset,* and *The Four Horsemen.* I'm referring to the device of overlapping compositional elements like whole figures, legs, or sequences of related strokes resulting in a sense of rhythm or meter, which leads one's eye across a composition. I've seen that in photographs of the Parthenon friezes and repeatedly in Degas's paintings and pastels of horses in meadows or steeplechases, and in his studies of ballet dancers practicing. He always provided an entry point into such compositions, say on the left, which created a visual flow all the way across to the other side. He never hit you over the head with it. He just provided an entry point."

Saunders: "Yes. Notice how in this piece [*The Procession*] the composition almost forms an arrowhead or a wedge going across, large and bold on the left, getting smaller and more compact to the far right. Also you have to remember that I am, in another life, an amateur musician. So line and melody mean a lot to me, as does rhythmic pattern. One of the things that this work is all about to me is the rhythmic repetition, the patterning of their legs, the repetition of heads and figures. The rhythmic similarity, for instance, of the moving legs of the men and the horses is important to me in place of what you said."

Dewey: "Did you draw these horses more or less from life?"

Saunders: "Yes."

Dewey: "Degas was trained in the conventions of his time regarding rendering landscape before there was plein-air painting and made sketches on the spot but then relied on memory for an approximation of the truth."

Saunders: "Well I do too. I'm not fast enough to sit there at the edge of the track, or wherever, and draw the whole thing out to its completeness . . . and I'll have to confess to you, I might rely on twenty-five slides for details too. In the cool of the evening I could set up a projector aimed at a wall [in my studio] and look across there and make that horse hold still for a minute, and I'd get the detail I wanted."

Dewey: "Later in Degas's life, when his eyesight was weakening, he began to experiment with photography and to appreciate its value for anatomical accuracy. But in my studies of his ballet and thoroughbred horse subjects, I've noted incorrect leg alignments among the ballet corps and in some of the thoroughbred horse-racing imagery. Yet in general the compositions are so compelling that the errors do not particularly detract. I expect, however, that the equine anatomy and implied movements in your works are correct since you are a lifelong horseman and your experience and sensibilities as a rider and a driver help to make your images true. Degas apparently was not an equestrian."

Saunders: "Well, for instance, I know that a horse's leg is in a certain position well enough that I don't have to belabor how big a knee ought to be or the turn of the ankle or the fetlock. I just know that."

Dewey: "Also, if you know where one or two legs are positioned, you probably know what's happening with the others."

Saunders: "Yes, I know the rest of it. I don't have to sit there and belabor it as if it were the first time. I worked that out while I was in grammar school . . . when I should have been working on my arithmetic notebook . . . and had to stay in the classroom during recess for it. [Laughter] I have great respect for technical accuracy in something. Yet something doesn't have to be anatomically perfect. Just like when you're drawing a figure, parts have to be where they're generally supposed to be."

CAROLINA MORNING WORKOUT

Dewey: "This next work *Carolina Morning Workout,* almost seems to occur in two different worlds simultaneously, one ordinary, drab, and repetitious, and the other world rarified, crisp, with a mantle of frost, fog, sunrise, and a stillness broken only by the sound of the trotting horse's hoofbeats and its pronounced breathing."

Saunders: "Well, to begin with . . . I need to describe for you the circumstances. I went down to the track at Aiken and hung around a lot, but I also did my share of mucking out and shoveling detritus and what have you. I was hanging around and talking to people. Then I got to know the trainers. I began to understand their world a little bit.

"One of my favorite trainers, other than Jim Crane, was a man named Jimmy Larente, who also shared generously with me of his knowledge. He was a Canadian from Montreal, and he had been doing this for many years. He'd buy a horse at auction. Actually he might buy a dozen horses. They were not necessarily

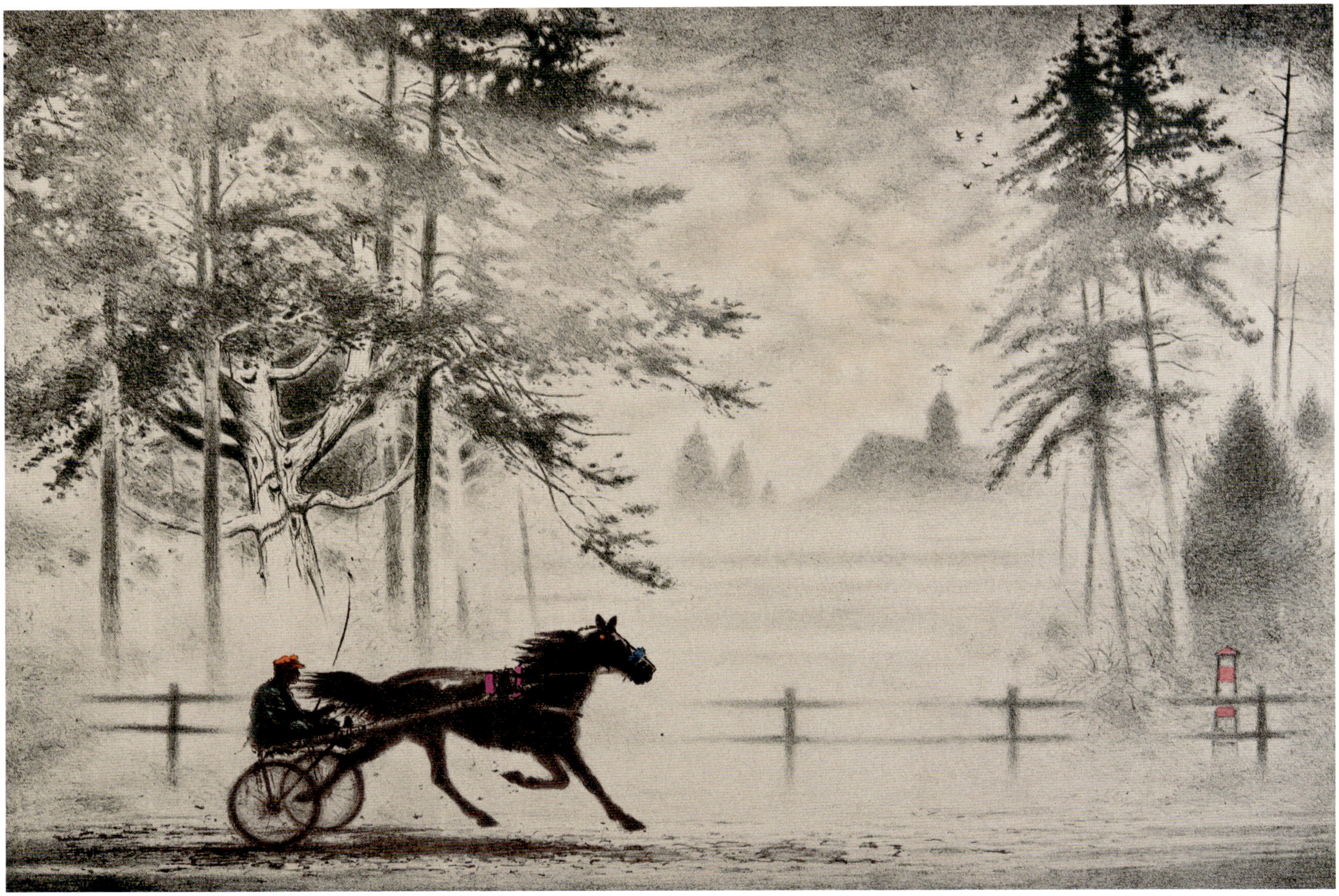

Carolina Morning Workout, 1989, stone lithograph with three stones and hand-applied color, 26 × 40 in.

his. He bought them under commission from an owner who might live in Philadelphia or Boston, et cetera, who would call Jimmy and say 'I want you to go to auction and buy me two colts [horses three years of age or less][4] and train them and race them.'

"Jimmy told me that in some cases he had been dealing with people for ten years and had never laid eyes on them, never met them in person. Also the owners had never laid eyes on even one of their own horses! That's absolutely amazing to me. It's a bad venture; it's a bad gamble. Nonetheless he would bring those yearlings [any horse between its first and second birthday—the birth date of all standard breds is January 1][5] just barely grown in the fall, after the racing season was over, and started working them; teaching them how to wear the harness and things like that . . . and work them all winter. Then by the next April or May they were ready to go on the circuit . . . which was also amazing to me.

Dewey: "What was a morning workout like?"

Saunders: "The morning started at daybreak. I'd be down there [to the barns and track] just as the sun came up. The handlers, grooms, and trainers would get in there with the horses and start rubbing them down, preparing them for the day."

Dewey: "Were the horses put in crossties?"

Saunders: "Put in crossties and handled. Each horse had a particular handler who was assigned to look after it. There was almost a symbiotic relationship between the handler and the horse. The handler might not be the driver of the horse on the track. Whatever his function, it was certainly to take care of the horse when it was in the stable.

"When his horse was ready to go to the track, a trainer or a driver drove the horse onto the track [in a jog cart, which is bigger, longer, and heavier than a sulky, used in races].[6] He'd take him out, and he'd jog him four or five times around this mile track every morning.

"As I said earlier, I was hanging around and talking with people, and the next thing you know I was allowed to drive some of those jog carts. An awful lot of time is spent in jogging the horses around the track just getting them used to pulling a jog cart, jogging like an athlete exercising. When I was out there driving one of the horses, the drivers (or trainers) enjoyed it because one of them didn't have to be out there.

Dewey: "You sort of spelled them?"

Saunders: "I'd spell them, and after a while they knew I knew what was going on and understood it."

Dewey: "Exercising horses early in the morning from autumn until spring about two to three days a week became a routine for you but never drudgery. Over that time the weather cooled considerably, the days shortened, and arriving at Aiken before sunrise meant leaving Chapin hours earlier, in the dead of night. By November the weather finally changes noticeably, but your winters are still mild compared to northern states, right?"

Saunders: "Yes, but by February when you are doing this thing seriously, it's season enough that it's slap wintertime. That's why they come south for it. I used a number of sketches that I had done for this [*Carolina Morning Workout*], and then I came to realize that, lo and behold, the driver with that cap and all . . . that's me! It just happened. It wasn't me before; it is now! It's me behind the horse out there jogging around that track! Now actually it was a quiet sort of time, almost Zen-like. If you can imagine a cold February morning, twenty-some degrees, if that, and there is a mist. The sun is beginning to come up. The horse is feeling frisky and cranky about being out there. In many cases there might be as many as a dozen horses out there, but the track was large enough that it seemed like you're all by yourself. It's a reflective time.

Dewey: "Was *Carolina Morning Workout* printed on gray-toned paper?"

Saunders: "Gray-toned paper, and the primary ink is Senefelder's Grey, which has a grayish-green cast about it, which just gently rose out of that paper. Then there are darker tones for the horse and the driver. But the heart of this whole thing is not what you draw but what you don't draw . . . and what you're leaving out judiciously, so that it appears that there is fog and mist moving all over the place. One of the secrets of this piece is that it's done on gray paper, like gray flannel."

Dewey: "Harness horses are taught to jog, and they are also taught which direction to jog, that is, clockwise. In actual races harness horses run counterclockwise as do thoroughbreds with jockeys. The instruction begins when the horse and its driver approach the track for the first time."

Saunders: "If you're planning to jog the horse, when you take him onto the track, you go clockwise around the track. On the other hand, if you are running (racing) the horse, you go counterclockwise. After awhile the horse knows the difference. If the driver turns onto the track in a counterclockwise direction, it's run for the money sweetheart. It's line up beside the other horses and haul it."

BRANDYWINE SUNSET

Saunders: "One weekend I went to the Brandywine Racetrack in Wilmington, Delaware. It was an old racetrack wonderfully still in operation all year long. I moved among the drivers and trainers, and I had a wonderful time. When I came back home I realized I had some burgundy-toned paper, and I used it for the *Brandywine Sunset* lithograph. It is at the end of the day; the sun is going down, and, as it turned out, I did this very complex print, which has at least nine colors."

Dewey: "Nine stencil and hand-applied colors?"

Saunders: "Yes, and not only that, but the paper expanded and contracted between each color printing so the registration was a beast on that print. That color blend in the sky back there is a silkscreen application. Some of the other colors are also silkscreen [applied]. I think it is a visually rich print, and I love that toned paper."

Dewey: "In terms of immediate thematic content, is it fair to suggest that the racing program is over for the day, coinciding with the sunset? On the other hand, two banks of lights on high poles are silhouetted in the distance, which could indicate night racing."

Saunders: "Well, they're [the horses and drivers] returning. But the sunset at Brandywine is symbolic in another way, and I didn't even have the sense to know it at the time. As it turned out, shortly after I was there, they closed down the old track and proceeded to tear it down to make way for a housing development. So this print becomes a very portentous image of the old Brandywine Racetrack."

Dewey: "They are walking back to the stables, back to the barns?"

Saunders: "Yes, they will be washed down and cooled out. See this white on the horse here [horse in foreground]? That's lather; that's foam where he's been sweating while he was out running. The driver is walking beside the horse talking to him, and the horse knows exactly where he is going, not necessarily being led by the driver, just walking along . . . I think it is such a wonderfully companionable pose."

Dewey: "Behind that pair to the left is another pair almost silhouetted in the evening light with an unharnessed horse being cooled out by a handler."

Saunders: "Yes, but I have to tell you this pair of figures is an absolute tribute to Degas, even the light casting its shadows on the fence . . . that's unabashedly paying tribute to Degas with that [the long shadows]. Also back up here [top-left area] you see just a corner of the grandstand. I reduced that whole corner of the grandstand to a zigzag line as a tribute to Toulouse-Lautrec."

The late nineteenth-century French expressionist painter and printmaker Henri de Toulouse-Lautrec (1864–1901) came to fame first as a graphic designer of large, multicolor lithographs advertising entertainers and cabarets in the Montmartre district of Paris. He is especially associated with the Moulin Rouge, its singers, and the behind-the-scenes lives of prostitutes who lived and worked there. His colorful posters, with their large simplified shapes, put him among those at the forefront of the color revolution in lithography of the 1880s and 1890s. Lautrec's lithographic posters were often five to six feet high and carried large type over the imagery. That imagery was summarized flat, meaning often without chiaroscuro, so a few individual lines had to suggest, convincingly, complete shapes and figures. Therefore the single zigzag line referred to in Saunders's lithograph *Brandywine Sunset* helps describe an entire grandstand area.

Both Lautrec and the older Degas frequently utilized long, slender shadows and silhouetted forms as summary information, which at times even appear casual but were always deftly executed and based on a life of drawing and relentless observing.

THE STAR

The Star is the sixth color lithograph in *The Aikenhead Collection* and presents an up-close view of a behind-the-scenes menial chore. Be that as it may, in the harness horse industry, attentiveness to equine hygiene is not a choice. It's an everyday necessity.

Saunders: "Those horses get washed more than you or I would ever think about. Why? Because, as they are running on the track, they are throwing sand up, and it has a way of imbedding itself in the skin of their legs. That's one of the reasons handlers wrap their legs as much as they do. The sand and dirt of the track are filled with bacteria from manure, etc. If you leave it there, you risk all kinds of infections. So after every race horses are washed daily with brushes, sponges, and soap and water. They are washed daily and sometimes three times a day to keep them clean."

Dewey: "These two handlers . . . that's a girl perhaps, to the right . . . ?"

Saunders: "Yes, you caught that right away."

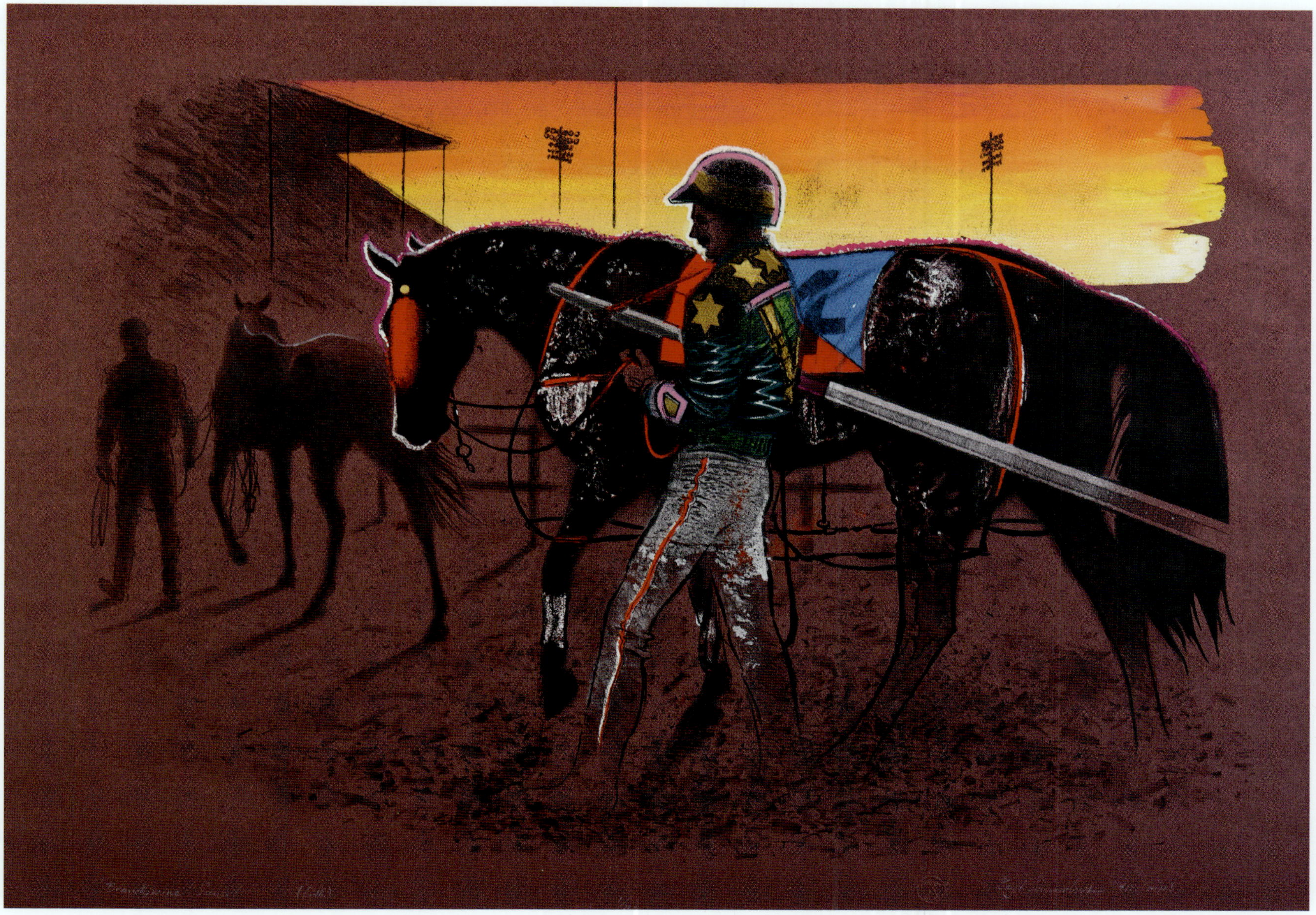

Dewey: "Since they are squatting down to wash the lower legs, et cetera, it's almost like they are pampering or giving special care."

Saunders: "I think this horse has taken on the sense of nobility with these handlers virtually kneeling at its feet, washing his feet."

Dewey: "That's pretty tame, pretty trusting. The horse is not in a cross-tie, not in a stall, not even in a barn."

Saunders: "It's the halter line for the horse. They get used to it. That's part of their life."

Dewey: "Some people might say, gee why didn't you depict this horse with its ears forward as they generally are in the photographs of champion horses in equine journals?"

Saunders: "Well, I was looking at the horse. I took a photograph of that horse in that situation, and I liked it. A horse lays his ears back for several reasons. It's a very expressive thing."

Dewey: "Not just for displeasure or fear?"

Saunders: "Not necessarily displeasure. Sometimes, if a breeze is blowing in his face, he lays his ears back.

Brandywine Sunset, 1990, stone lithograph with two stones, five stencils, hand-applied colors, 26 × 40 in.

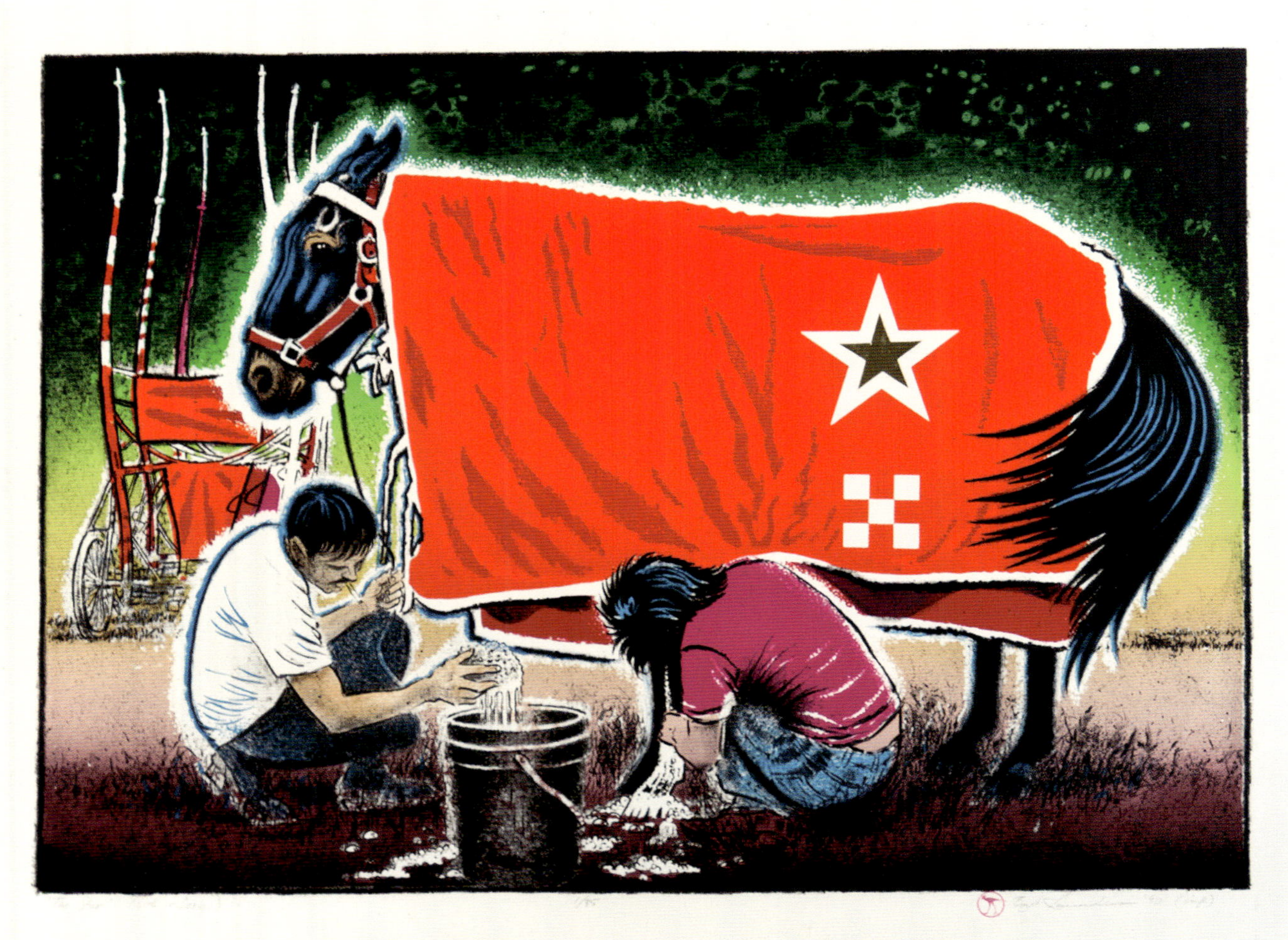

The Star, 1990, stone lithograph with two stones, five stencils, hand-applied colors and gold appliqué, 27 × 36 in.

What is going on with this horse is happening below and behind his ears. It's mostly out of his line of sight, so he's paying attention to what's going on down there, and he's happy with it."

Dewey: "The horse is wearing a cooler, I think."

Saunders: "Yes, that blanket is called a cooler."

Dewey: "Is that a Ralston-Purina emblem on it?"

Saunders: "Yes it is, and it's there mainly because I like it. I think it is a wonderful graphic image . . . along with the star . . . both against that very flat, large shape of bold color. This becomes almost minimal art [as in the 1960s]."

Dewey: "There's almost an aura or halo effect around the horse's head and all across the top of the horse including its tail, and the horse and handlers are backlit."

Saunders: "Sometimes I do that. I exaggerate color to bring out something that surrounds it. I learned that from looking at paintings by Charles Russell and Frederick Remington. If you think back to the *Spotted Horses* [illustrations], Henry Armstid might well have an aura around him like that. The rhythm of the sulky shafts turned up back there is a very graphic place also."

Dewey: "And the wire wheels and chassis as well. That's the traditional way to park sulkies, I think."

Saunders: "Yes, otherwise you could fall over them. Also they would take up a lot of space. You can back them up in a corner and stack six of them just so. They look so wonderful when they're stacked up like that."

Before introducing *The Four Horsemen* lithograph with its classic racing imagery, it is necessary to mention Saunders's race training for harness horses.

As already discussed, Saunders was first taught to give harness horses morning workouts involving jogging. But he was also taught how to "drive" harness horses in competition, and in that task he was especially instructed by one of his mentors, Jimmy Larente. A taste of Larente's instruction follows:

Saunders: "Jimmy would say: "Take him four miles around the one-mile track." Four trips, four miles, and then he'd say: 'We'll train him later on.' Training did not mean jogging. Training meant racing against one another, and after awhile it got to where they let me train. That's when you line up two horses against one another, and then three, and then four, and so on. Jimmy would say to me: 'Just hold him back until the half mile and then show him some daylight, and he'll do the rest.' My job was to keep the horse from running away too fast. The horses are bred for it. They want to run; they want to race!"

THE FOUR HORSEMEN

Dewey: "This is a race scene, and it's the seriously tense part of a race."

Saunders: "It's absolutely a race scene . . . coming into that last quarter mile, coming into the home stretch. The drivers are encouraging them. They are getting out the whip, encouraging them on. Their ears are laid back because they don't want to catch the wind in their ears. Sometimes the drivers put plugs in the horse's ears or little cups over them [though not to block any wind], so they don't hear the crowd yet and thus remain somewhat calm. But they [the drivers] also have a little string attached to those things, and when they come into the home stretch, the drivers pull those strings, and the plugs [come] out of the horses' ears. All of a sudden the horses could hear the roar of the crowd, get all excited, and run even faster."

Harness racing is a dangerous sport especially when the horses and drivers are bunched together as in *The Four Horsemen,* 1991. Sulkies bind driver and horse together during a race. They are lighter, narrower, shorter, and more streamlined than a jog cart, and the driver is placed up closer behind the horse with legs outstretched, all of which adds up to being extra dangerous.

Saunders: "Your legs are almost straddling his back feet. Delicacy prevents me from getting as graphic as I might about how dangerous it is. Veteran drivers like to tell tales of those ash wood shafts breaking during a pile-up in a race and becoming like spears, like a knight's lance, and impaling a horse or a driver."

Returning to Saunders's impassioned description of the home stretch run by the four front competitors in *The Four Horsemen,* the artist puts the viewers right into the race itself.

Saunders: "With the roar of the grandstand crowd in their ears, the horses run faster and start whinnying and screaming at one another!"

Dewey: "Are they suddenly panic stricken by the noise and the whips?"

Saunders: "No. I mean the horses love it! Man, they get so excited! It's the high point of their existence. They want to race, and they want to win!"

Fans of horse races, regardless of the type of horses racing, no doubt share Saunders's enthusiasm for watching races and loving horses in general. One last note regarding this print comes from Saunders's admiration and respect for the printmaking of Albrecht Dürer (1471–1528), the High Renaissance master from Nuremberg, Germany. His well-known woodcut from 1497–1498 *The Four Horsemen of the Apocalypse* inspired Saunders's lithograph with a similar title but quite different subject. However, Saunders's ability to earn the trust of the drivers, trainers, and handlers to the point that he was able to jog and to race horses during their training is quite remarkable, but that did not prepare him for the following surprises.

Saunders: "After awhile the trainer-drivers all knew each other, and some of the drivers had known one another for years and were friends. Well one of the last great revelations of being out there on the track was something I never would have guessed. During training races when the horses are coming down the backstretch and nearing the final turn, trainer-drivers sometimes have conversations not related to the business of the moment. The drivers had short exchanges, for example, Joe: 'How's your wife getting along?' Other driver: 'Well, she had an operation' . . . and so on. Or a comment might be: 'How's that old car of

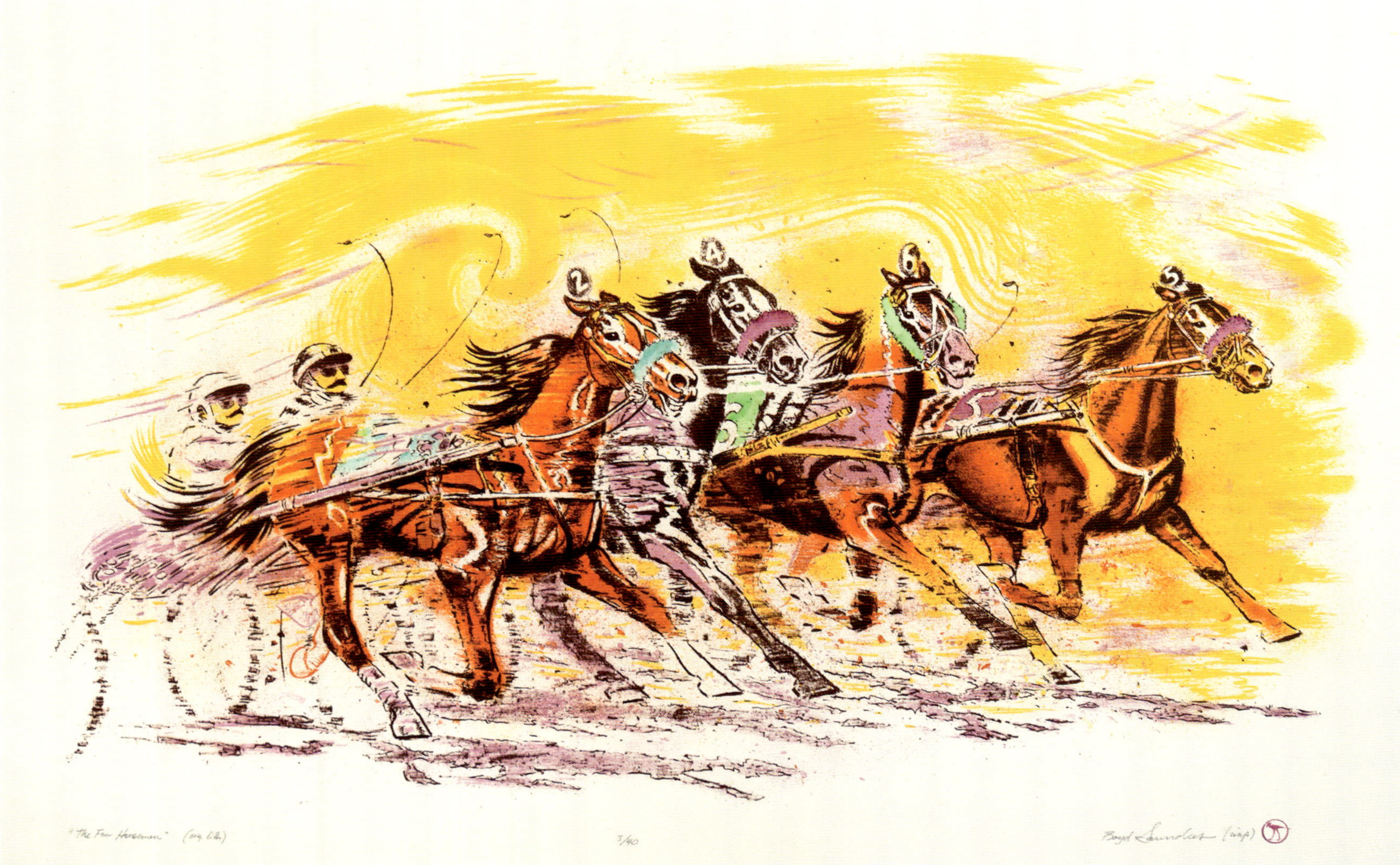

The Four Horsemen, 1991, stone lithograph in four colors with hand-applied accent colors, 28 × 40½ in.

yours doing?' It was so casual you'd think they were having a beer down at the pool room or something. Of course when they would get into the home stretch sometimes it would get tense especially when they were working around [when drivers were trying to pass one another]: 'I'm coming over' or 'All right get out of the way, here I come!"

"By contrast, during the daily jogging workouts, casual conversations, banter, and teasing were often the norm."

AT THE FARRIER'S

Among the specialists in the life of a domesticated horse, particularly for a racing horse, the veterinarian and the farrier (or horseshoer) may be the most important. At the Aiken track there was a farrier's shop on the grounds, which stayed busy most of the year. Saunders was impressed with its forge as well as with the farrier who worked there. Eager to create imagery acknowledging the importance of this service to the horses and trainers, Saunders befriended the farrier and spent much time observing the process of horse shoeing and the efficient manner of the farrier's procedures. In the lithograph *At the Farrier's,* a hot shoe hangs over an anvil possibly waiting to be further shaped and then matched to a hoof on the horse there in the shop.

Saunders: "Horses were coming in there constantly; the farrier was always at it. In addition to horses throwing shoes, new shoes were shaped to help a horse with its gait or to make the horse's hoof grow like the trainers wanted it. They would also use shoes for orthopedic reasons; for example if a horse was turning his toe in, the farrier shaped a shoe to correct that. Some horses would be brought in after having been shod only a couple of days before for a redo [to try another strategy]."

Dewey: "What is the whole makeup or constitution of a horse's hoof?"

Saunders: "Well, the hoof is similar to the makeup of finger nails, and basically it has no feeling except at the back, and underneath."

Dewey: "In the quick?"

Saunders: "Inside the hoof, in the quick of the frog [a wedge-shaped horny prominence in the sole of a horse's hoof],[6] can be very sensitive. Let a horse get a pebble under that frog, and you've got real problems. The area out around the edges of the hoof grows all the time. If they aren't kept trimmed and the horse stays in a stall, they will grow longer and longer and turn and curl up and throw the horse back on its pasterns [the part of a horse's foot between the fetlock and the hoof][7] and cripple the horse."

Dewey: "In the lithograph, it looks like that farrier has a file in his right hand and is using it on the horse's left front hoof."

Saunders: "It's a rasp. They're heavy and have big teeth. You put the shoe on and then rasp off around it so the hoof comes in at a nice union with the shoe. It [shoeing horses] seemed easy enough when I watched him do it, but you have to realize that if he angled a nail or two wrong, it could cripple a horse."

Dewey: "What is the horse wearing under its halter? Did it rub itself raw?"

Saunders: "One of the reasons this horse's image is in this composition is because I liked the hood on that horse's head. I just liked the visual aspects of it. I thought the hood looked dramatic, much like something worn by a knight's horse. The truth is that hood was there for a medical reason. This horse developed an abscess in its jaw in one of its teeth, and then the horse was transported to the University of Georgia, where the abscess was lanced and an operation was performed. By the time the horse was trailored back to Aiken it was wearing this cloth hood over its head to protect the dressing during recuperation."

Since the print being discussed is dated 1991, the infection, surgery, recuperation, and appearance of the horse in the farrier's shop for needed attention all occurred by that date or before. Said Saunders: "However, the horse eventually failed to recover from that infection and died."

When the specified number of editions of *The Aikenhead Collection* of eight color lithographs was printed, an exhibition was planned to open at the Etherredge Center, USC-Aiken, March 7, 1991. Yet before *The Aikenhead Collection* exhibition opened, June Murff, described by Saunders as being quite active in the Aiken chamber of commerce, proposed borrowing the racing silks and related memorabilia from the barns at the Aiken track for a tandem exhibition titled *The Silks of Aiken.* That gesture of widening the scope of the original exhibit, and of involving other segments of the community at the heart of the harness racing business in South Carolina, proved to be fortuitous to say the least.

Said Saunders: "Well, all the track people got so excited by *The Silks of Aiken,* they gave her [June Murff] everything in the world. They gave her harness[es] and all kinds of racing memorabilia of harness racing. [At the opening] all the track people were there, and I made it a point to invite all the horse handlers from around the track to come to the opening. Many of them had never been to an event like this before. Cleaning out stalls is not exactly one of your glamorous occupations, you know. They dressed up nicely, and they came to the opening. Also there was lots of food and there were lots of beverages, etc."

When a person creates a piece of art there may be basic expectations as to the reactions of viewers once it is exhibited, as mentioned in chapter 1. But in actuality it is nearly impossible to predict certainly, which is good because it allows freedom of response and interpretation. That said, Saunders definitely did not expect what happened when one particular person encountered the lithograph *At the Farrier's* at the opening reception.

Said Saunders: "When the farrier came up to this piece he got tears in his eyes and he said, 'That's my shop, that's me!' I said yes. He then searched for a chair, brought one back, sat down in front of this print and spent the rest of the evening sitting in that chair with tears streaming down his face. He not only realized that he was looking at an approximation of his workplace, he recognized the horse . . . and he said to me, 'That's Bonnie, isn't it and . . . she died.'"

The horseshoer's response was amazing and tender. It was understandably emotional and sincere, yet this work is neither sentimental nor heroic. Saunders observed a horseshoer at work, respected his high level of craft and professionalism, and was grateful for the knowledge the farrier shared. It is about work, dailiness, understatement, right in line with the demeanor of most of the other works in *The Aikenhead Collection;* that is, faithfulness to the behind-the-scenes life of harness horse-racing training day to day.

The Aikenhead Collection was on exhibit at USC-Aiken March 7–30, 1991, and then traveled to the following cities in South Carolina: Myrtle Beach, Orangeburg, Beaufort, and Camden, ending at Spartanburg in April 1992.

The above section was compiled from a taped discussion between Saunders and Dewey which occurred while they viewed artwork in The Aikenhead Collection, *in the artist's studio and home near Chapin, South Carolina, August 13–15, 2006.*

The following stories are from Saunders's direct experiences while gathering ideas for The Aikenhead Collection, *1986–91.*

OF HORSE'S IDIOSYNCRASIES: PAINFUL PERCEPTIONS

I was standing one day in the hallway of an Aiken Track horse barn next to one of the women handlers. Then, as she was talking, a horse in a stall behind her came up, stuck its head out over the stall door, and put it across her shoulder and rooted against her. She turned around and said: "What's the matter, big boy?" Then the horse stuck out its face, and she said: "Oh, he has a piece of sawdust or wood shavings in his eye," which he had picked up from the floor of his stall. She took the wood shavings out of his eye, and the horse when on about his business.

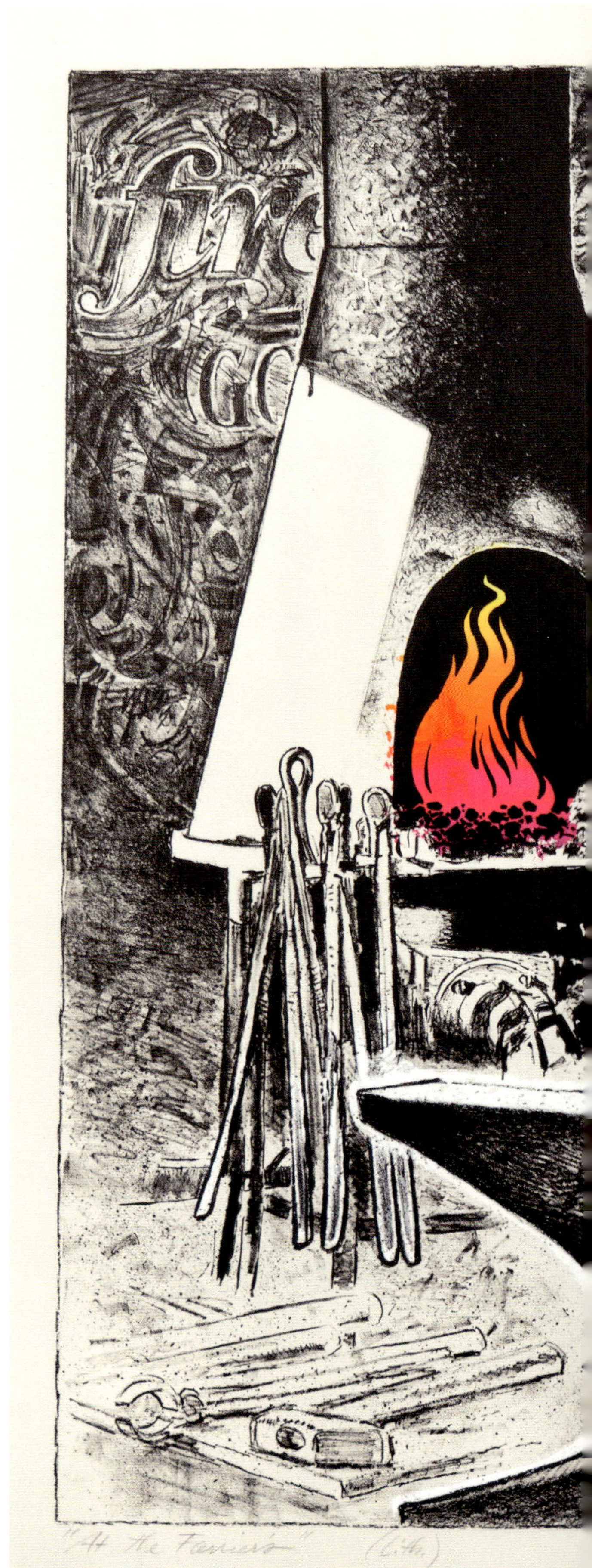

At the Farrier's, 1991, stone lithograph with stencil color and printed appliqué, 27 × 36 in.

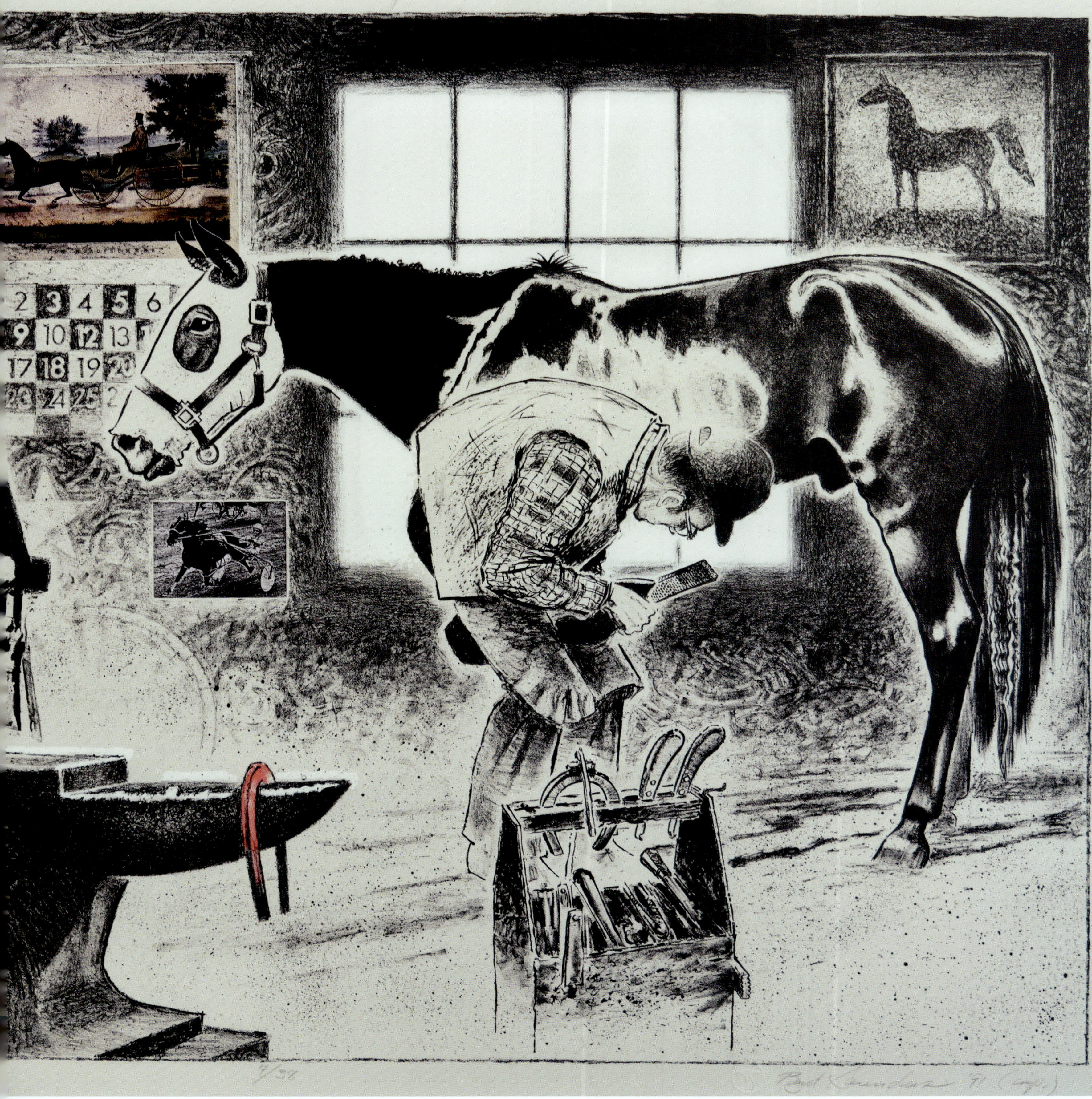
2 3 4 5 6
9 10 12 13
17 18 19 20
23 24 25

STABLE COMPANIONS

Down the hallway was a horse who shared its stall with a nanny goat, a particular nanny goat. They [the trainers or handlers] said the horse would get lonesome, and it would be fractious and unhappy if that nanny goat wasn't there, and so that nanny goat was always there. When they [trainers, drivers, handlers, and racehorses] went on the road, that horse and that nanny goat always went together.

THE PLASTIC MILK JUG

Another horse in the same barn had a toy to play with . . . a gallon plastic milk jug, which he had long since beat into submission. It was collapsed and crumpled down, but it was his toy and was always in his stall with him. Well there was a little Jack Russell terrier that was also the mascot of one of the stables. They're smart little devils, and of course he liked to dally with that horse. In the daytime when handlers and trainers are working with these harness horses, they just have a chain across the entrance to their stalls. Well, that Jack Russell terrier would look around and wait until nobody was watching, and then he would dart into that horse's stall, grab that mashed milk jug, and take it out right into the hallway of the barn. He wouldn't run away with it; he'd just run out into the middle of the hall and set it down and then sit there and watch until the horse pitched a fit over the absence of his toy. Sooner or later one of the handlers would come along, grab up the jug, and throw it back in the stall with the horse, scold the dog, which would run away, and then the horse would be happy he had his jug back. Half an hour later the dog would come back, look all around, and go into the stall and steal that jug again. He didn't have any use for the jug whatsoever. All he wanted to do was amuse himself by tormenting the horse about it.

NATURE CALLS

I've seen Chinese mothers potty train their children by making *swiyr, swiyr, swiyr* sounds when a child urinated, and after a while, when the mother wanted her child to tinkle, she whispered *swiyr, swiyr, swiyr* to her child, and it worked.

The horse handlers at the Aiken track did the same thing, and after a while, they were able to train racehorses to relieve themselves before they went onto the track by saying *swiyr swiyr, swiyr* near their ears, and the horses would respond appropriately.

QUESTIONABLE JUDGMENT

A circuit court judge, who was also a harness-racing enthusiast, frequently visited the horse barns at the Aiken racetrack. He befriended the trainers and handlers, and during the off-season he sometimes cooked breakfast for them at daybreak, something definitely appreciated on cold February mornings during workouts for the horses.

One day the judge brought a court stenographer with him . . . young and pretty. He would say "Aw honey, you gonna like this," chuckling. Next thing you know they had her dressed out in some overalls, and it was "Aw no problem, just take him [a horse hitched to a jog cart], and hold him like this, and go around the track you know." Many people at the track were skeptical about it, but this judge was special, so they all kind of deferred to him, and besides, he was a lot of fun.

So that young lady started to drive out of that barn toward the track a short distance away. But before she was even well out of the barn the horse realized that somebody at the other end of those reins didn't know what he or she was doing. It frightened the horse. He panicked and pitched the damnedest fit you ever saw in your life. He went berserk! He peeled that gal off that jog cart, went charging around there, and jumped through two or three fences tearing that $2,000 cart all to pieces. He wiped out at least one other fence before we could finally hem him up in a corner and calm him down . . . all because somebody on the other end of those reins didn't have the right touch . . . or who exuded something that said to the horse, I don't have confidence.

Chapter 8

The Shanghai Etchers Workshop, 1995

On May 20, 1995, Professor Saunders flew to China at the invitation of the East China Normal University in Shanghai (city population about fourteen million) to host an exhibition of his prints and to conduct a workshop in etching. He was accompanied on the trip by a former University of South Carolina graduate student and friend B.J. Zhiang, who in turn became Saunders's guide and translator throughout his stay. Upon arrival Saunders was met by his official hosts, the Lu brothers—Zhiang and Zhaohong—both of whom were artists and teachers, plus Mr. S. J. Xu.[1]

On May 22 Saunders was escorted to the Shanghai Eastern Culture Institute (formerly a private estate), which had the distinction of being the first private art school in China's long history. At that freshly renovated facility, Saunders presented an illustrated lecture on the printmaking program at the University of South Carolina. By the next day Saunders's show was installed at the East China Normal University Exhibition Hall. The opening attracted dignitaries and a large crowd and was covered by the *Wen Hui Daily,* Shanghai's largest newspaper, as well as by a local paper whose name in English means "The Labor Daily." The exhibition consisted of etchings from *Southern Cross/A Trilogy* and lithographs from *Spotted Horses.*[2]

May 24 found Saunders beginning to teach the fundamentals of etching to twelve local artists. According to the report on the trip, "Shanghai, now has a vibrant art community but [in 1995] almost no one there had the skills or equipment to produce etchings. The print workshop was a tiny, cramped, makeshift studio dominated by a large, antique, ornate, oval conference table and chairs to match, plus a rust and dust encrusted etching press. Zhi-Ping Lu, Saunders's host, had provided each of the twelve participating Shanghai artists with individual packets of tools, materials, gloves, aprons and other items deemed reasonably necessary."[3]

The receptive artists were not green undergraduate students; they were mature professionals with considerable reputations as painters. The first session of instruction began with a round of formal introductions that included the reading of long pedigrees or résumés. When instruction commenced the painters were enthusiastically engaged amid good-natured joking, laughter, and sign language . . . and all that despite a room too small and poorly ventilated. In fact the acid and water trays were hung outside the windows.[4] Every part of Saunders's workshop instruction was faithfully related by his interpreter B. J. Zhiang to the eager artists.[5]

Said Saunders, "B. J. was at my side constantly for translation as needed, and having made etchings himself under my tutelage, he could bring his own level of artistic competence to bear. In point of fact, I was never quite sure just how faithfully he was translating what I said. I could offer up a short, cryptic sentence and he could take three minutes of talk to translate it; or I could offer a paragraph of talk which he could toss off in a few words. Maybe it was just as well that I didn't know."[6]

Teaching, productivity, and interest continued for the several-days-long workshop. In hindsight Saunders proclaimed it the best workshop of its kind that he had ever led: "The participants, all accomplished artists, turned to the etching process with dispatch, initiative and enthusiasm. They assumed responsibility for their own imagery rather than looking to me to make something happen. They quickly grasped the technical processes and made them their own; they did more than was asked, and they produced some dynamite images on small plates."[7]

At the end of the last workshop session the studio space was cleaned. Then Saunders and his new printmakers sat at a table, made tea, and made speeches to one another. Each of the participants gave Saunders prints from their editions as gifts followed by picture taking.[8]

While in Shanghai, Saunders also visited the Shanghai Oil Painters and Sculptors Institute, about which he later remarked: "The artists we met were very talented and dedicated individuals, and their art was quite sophisticated and showed great technical mastery of medium. Stylistic approaches were varied and cosmopolitan, but blissfully unstained by New York."[9]

On another occasion Saunders was taken to downtown Shanghai for an evening by his hosts to experience "the spectacular lights on the famous Nanjin Road, a waterfront promenade overlooking the Hwangpo River . . . which is part of an old financial district called 'The Bund.'"[10]

Among other particularly memorable activities for Saunders was a tour through the Yu Gardens, formerly part of a nobleman's estate. The Yu Gardens possess the following picturesque features: "Covered walkways, bridges over pools of water containing water lilies, lotus flowers and schools of carp, limestone grottos, moon gates, and serpentine stone walls topped with carved dragons."[11]

On May 29, 1995, Saunders and B. J. Zhang, his translator and traveling companion, went by train to the ancient city of Suchou, about a one-hour journey from Shanghai. There Saunders got to experience more unforgettable gardens. The last one they visited was located in perhaps the oldest part of Suchou and boasts canals, barges, and arched bridges, and it is known as "the Venice of the East."[12] Picturesque, as its nickname suggests, it long ago became a destination for Chinese artists.

Upon returning to Shanghai later in the day, Saunders was treated to a farewell dinner and ceremony complete with toasts and speeches. The memorable meal featured entrees that impressed the eye as well as the taste buds, for example aesthetically created fish dishes and a wedge-shaped dessert in the form of a dragon ship complete with a miniature American flag on the prow. Additional watermelon slices resembled sails. Saunders was told that the ship under

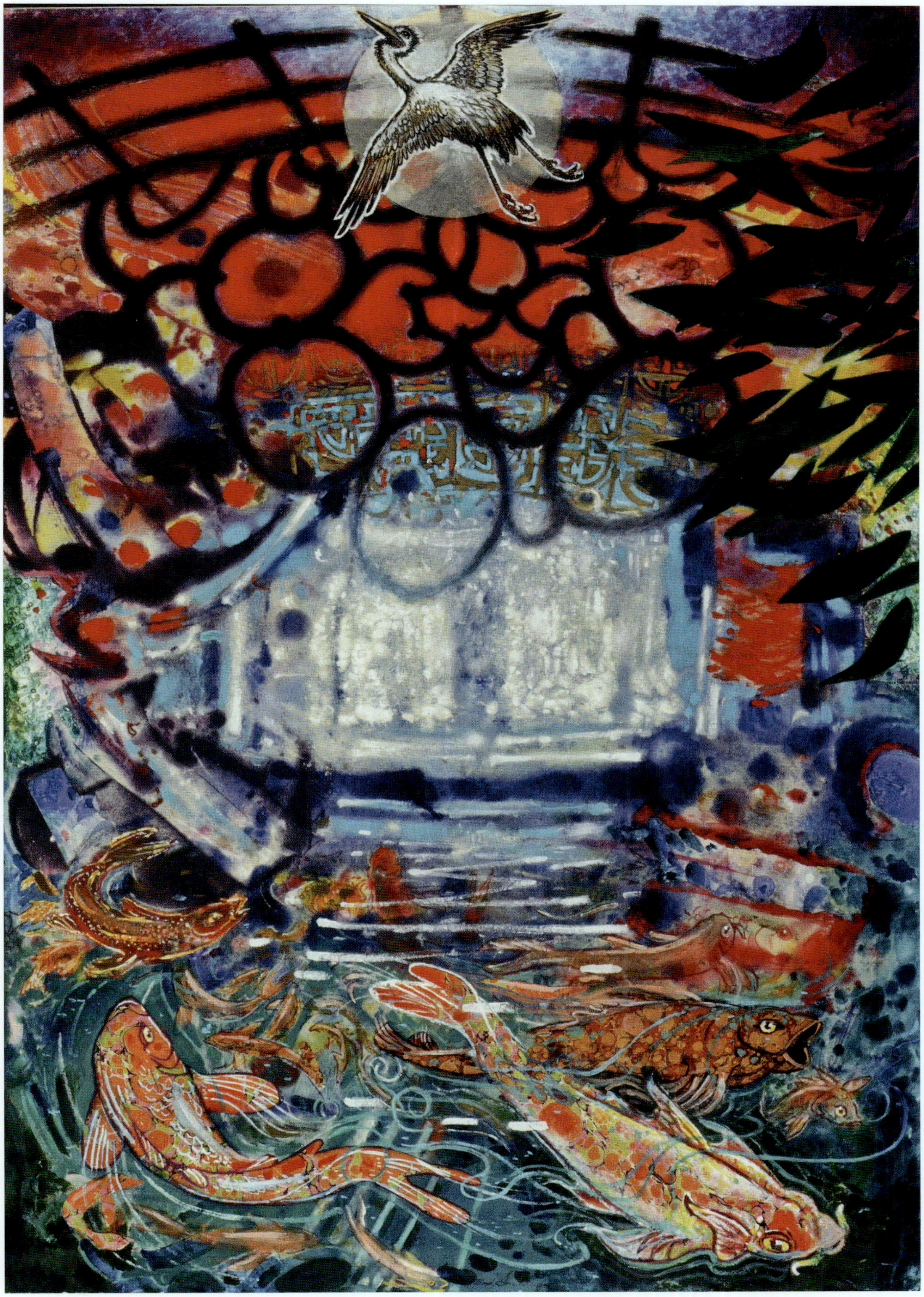

Suchou Gardens, 1995, acrylic on paper

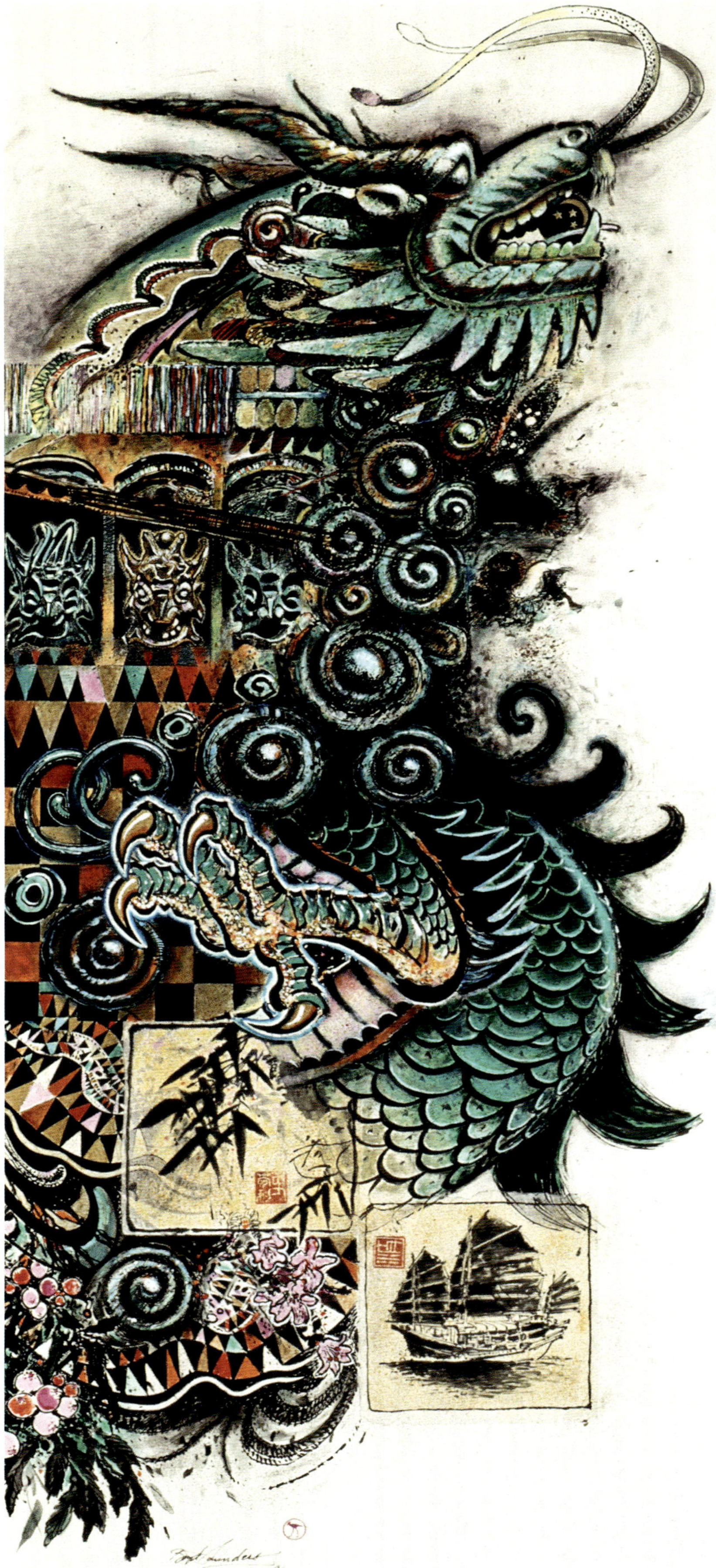

Gate Guardian, 1995, ink and watercolor on paper

discussion was, metaphorically speaking, not to carry him away, but to bring him back again.[13]

Saunders later declared his China trip wonderful: "I disseminated a little of the gospel of prints, made some lasting friendships, saw some glorious sights and am now waiting for that watermelon ship to come and take me back there."[14]

When Saunders returned to America, he was eager to plunge into projects inspired by his Asian trip. He was primed with mental images and by more in his sketchbooks. However, some projected paintings and works in other media were bluntly interrupted by a personal health crisis. Some physical irregularities had surfaced before going on the China trip and resurfaced while there. "I renewed my search to find the reason for some of the physical problems I'd been having and discovered that I had a brain tumor for which I subsequently had to undergo surgery. It was an ordeal, to put it mildly, as I was laced up with all kinds of drugs, half paralyzed and half blind."[15]

Whether due to misdiagnosis, incorrect surgical procedures, incorrect prescriptions, unforeseen serious side effects to the prescribed pharmaceuticals, or all the above, Saunders lost partial sight in his left eye and lost significant hearing in his left ear. Such developments could have ended or seriously compromised his teaching career, his career as a productive visual artist, or both. Saunders's health crisis did not noticeably compromise his abilities to make drawings, paintings, or prints: "I was very sick but my way of dealing with therapy was to get off my behind as quick as I could, get moving and get out into the studio and start working. That was no small task because I could not see what I was doing."[16]

SUCHOU GARDENS

Saunders began a series of mostly abstract paintings based on his fresh memories and his China sketchbooks. The painting series became known as *Suchou Gardens.* Those famous gardens in the ancient city of Suchou amount to a vast, complex maze of pools, covered walkways, and pavilions, all expressed in organic configurations. Presently a public park, the Suchou Gardens was originally part of a private estate. Saunders and his enthusiastic guide, B. J. Zhiang, had indulged in photographing the Suchou Gardens and discussed their aesthetic characteristics.[17]

GATE GUARDIAN

The 1995 China experience was also responsible for additional exotic imagery in Saunders's art, for instance, weird and aggressive spirits.

"It was a strange thing, i.e., because of my delirium, I was often fighting things: dragons, monsters and things like that—trying to survive. But there was one dragon that kept showing up over and over again. I wasn't sure what it meant, but he ended up being painted. Strangely, I am now aware, however curious, that the dragon is not an evil monster in Chinese culture, but a benevolent being that brings good fortune, etc."[18]

Chapter 9

The Battle of Hanging Rock, South Carolina, 1780

In the later 1990s Professor Boyd Saunders was approached by a staff member of the Office of University Development at the University of South Carolina who informed Saunders of a possible painting commission. The inquiry came from a person who had been a patron or donor to the University of South Carolina for a number of years who was seeking someone to produce a large painting of the Battle of Hanging Rock, South Carolina, for a room in his home. The battle was a significant skirmish in the backcountry of the South Carolina colony during the American Revolution. It was also a partisan victory. The engagement began to turn the tide of control in favor of those seeking independence from England in all sections of the South Carolina backcountry. That area represented more than two-thirds of the colony.

Saunders's initial reaction was mixed; he was excited about the prospect of an ambitious project, but he was not familiar with the painting's subject. Indeed the resistance of the partisans in the backcountry of South Carolina during the American Revolution seemed to have been largely forgotten until recently.

True to form Saunders began background studies before committing any marks onto a canvas, and his studies started with the element of land. His desire to locate, if possible, the original battle site was to study the lay of land. His search led him to the extreme north central part of the state in Lancaster County, near the tiny community of Heath Springs, which in turn is about midway and a little north of Kershaw to the east and Great Falls to the west. That also makes Heath Springs and the battle site about fifteen to twenty miles south of Lancaster or about ten miles from the North Carolina border. It might seem odd that any important engagements happened in the backcountry or as far as North Carolina. However there were twenty-seven engagements between partisans and redcoats in the backcountry from July 1780 to January 1781, and of that number eighteen occurred within forty miles or so of the North Carolina border.

As if by providence Saunders was introduced to Kip Carter, an amateur historian and Revolutionary War reenactor who lived in an antebellum farmhouse near the Hanging Rock site. Carter guided and assisted Saunders in his survey of the site. Saunders had this to say about the guided tour: "The battle took place a few miles south of Heath Springs on gently rolling terrain near a rocky prominence known as 'Hanging Rock,' which juts out of the top of a wooded ravine formed by Hanging Rock Creek. The rock is shaped rather like a parrot's beak. Nearby are intermittent woods and open fields which have been farmed since colonial times."[1]

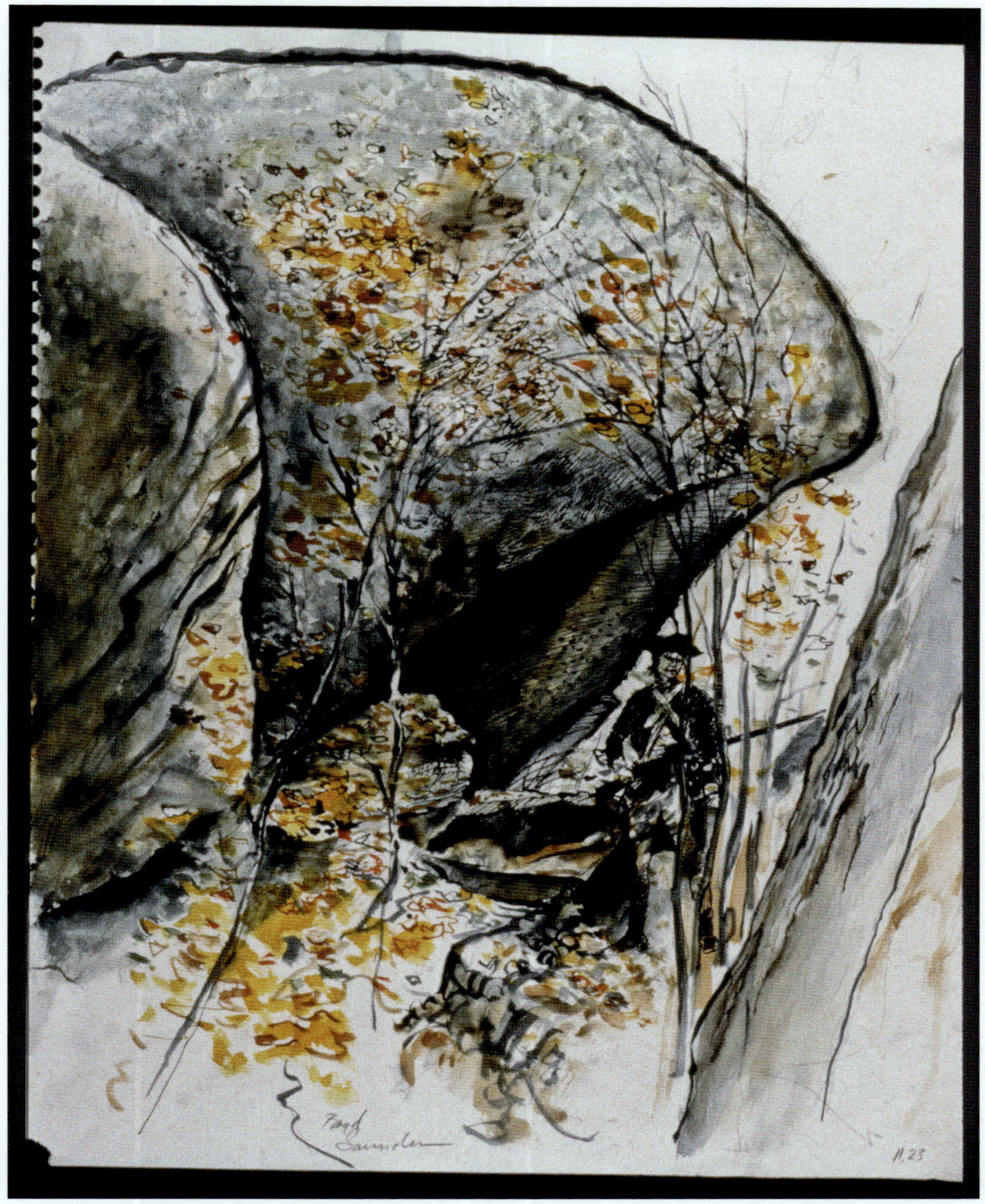

Hanging Rock, SC, 2000, preliminary sketch, watercolor

At or about the same time and place, Saunders met another local historian, Andy Steen, and her husband, Frank. The artist and the Steens walked over the battle site together discussing possible troop movements and tried to locate the earthworks made by the British forces. Next Saunders turned his attention to the battle itself and to South Carolina's role in the American Revolution. A voracious reader, the artist delved into early American history: "I went to many historical sources, including Walter Edgar's just published *South Carolina: A History,* Henry Lumpkin's *From Savannah to Yorktown: The American Revolution in the South* [1981], and the source which I relied upon most heavily, Andrea Deborah Van Landingham's *Stoneboro: An Historical Sketch of a Historical South Carolina Community* [1993–2002] which describes the Battle of Hanging Rock in careful detail and patient completeness."[2]

Saunders then wrote a respectable summary of the onset of the American Revolution in South Carolina and the Battle of Hanging Rock. His recounting of the involvement follows:

> The American Revolution in South Carolina was somewhat sporadic. The first military engagement to draw blood was a skirmish between loyalist and patriot militia units at [a place called] Ninety Six in November of 1775. This was a highly symbolic event. King George announced early on that he intended to fight this American war with Americans, and to a large extent, that is what he did. To a larger degree than most laymen realize, the

American Revolution [also] was a civil war, with Americans fighting Americans. In many cases, it was neighbors going raiding against neighbors, ostensibly over loyalty to the English crown [or the absence of it].

Several rather famous guerilla-type militia units were formed, often financed by the personal fortunes of their commanding officers. One of the most famous leaders was Francis Marion, *The Swamp Fox.* But even before Marion was at his strongest, there was Thomas Sumter. When the British burned his home down, he took it personally and proceeded to raise his own independent backcountry militia. Mostly he and his men fought the British with hit-and-run tactics, hitting supply lines and weak points, then falling back, using their knowledge of the land to great advantage. Perhaps his largest contribution, though, was more psychological than military. In the summer of 1780, he and his men were virtually the only organized resistance, and they became a rallying point for the patriot cause throughout the colony.

In late July and early August of 1780, at Hanging Rock, his men attacked a Loyalist militia unit in two battles, several days apart, and defeated them in both engagements. The first was a brief skirmish, the second, a full-fledged battle. The battle (or battles) of Hanging Rock, while relatively unsung, may well be seen as the turning point of the Revolutionary War in South Carolina.

It is true that, a week later, General Horatio Gates led an army of Continental Regulars against the British at Camden, South Carolina, and was defeated, and two days thereafter, Banastre Tarleton's Legion badly beat Thomas Sumter's forces at Fishing Creek, but from August of 1780 onward, the war in South Carolina took on a different character.

Emboldened by Sumter, other leaders emerged to conduct guerilla warfare; Marion in the Pee Dee, Pickens in the upstate, and Harden in the Beaufort area. Soon, inspired by these groups of patriots and, angered by the tactics of the loyalists, the whole colony was up in arms at the British. That winter [1780–81] saw the famous battles at Kings Mountain and Cowpens, the further deterioration of the Loyalist cause in South Carolina and, the gathering strength of the Patriot movement which was to culminate with the British surrender at Yorktown, October 19, 1781. Maybe that whole change of fortunes began at Hanging Rock.[3]

South Carolina historian Dr. Walter Edgar has described background information and the Battle of Hanging Rock, which occurred in two stages, in the following concise manner: "At the end of July 1780 and after several surprising partisan victories, a council of war was held to plan future operations. Partisan commanders Thomas Sumter, William Richardson Davie and others agreed that the two primary British strongholds in the Catawba River Valley, Rocky Mount and Hanging Rock, should be attacked and, that Sumter et al. would attack Rocky Mount while simultaneously Davie's forces, which also included a detachment of North Carolinians, would march on Hanging Rock."[4]

Initially Davie's plan was to raid the five-hundred-man garrison as a feint so that the large force of Tories would continue on, instead of sending a lot of reinforcements to Rocky Mount.

> [Edgar] Shortly after noon on 30 July, Davie's small band of about eighty mounted men approached Hanging Rock. From a local patriot informer they learned that three companies of North Carolina Tories had recently arrived and were in [and around] a farmhouse just outside the British lines. Sizing up the situation, Davie divided his troops. He boldly marched half of his men down a road past the farmhouse [without arousing suspicion]. Since militia on both sides wore their everyday clothes, not uniforms, it appeared that Davie's men were just more Tory militia heading toward Hanging Rock. However, once these men were in place, Davie stationed twenty dragoons [cavalrymen] in the road below the house and sent another twenty into an open field beside it.
>
> When the firing started, there was chaos. The astonished Loyalists fled instantly the other way,

> and were immediately charged by the dragoons in a full gallop and driven back in great confusion. They were surrounded . . . and literally cut to pieces; as this was done under the eye of the whole British camp, no prisoners could be taken. It was a veritable slaughter. While the British were attempting to form a counter attack from the garrison, Davie's men made off with sixty valuable horses with their furniture and one hundred muskets and rifles. There were no Whig casualties! As one modern historian has noted, Davie's action at Hanging Rock was a textbook model of a partisan operation.[5]

On August 5, 1780, Davie and Sumter met again, this time with their combined forces in excess of eight hundred men, to discuss strategy once more concerning Rocky Mount and Hanging Rock. A decision between the two commanders and the entire fighting force of partisans or Whigs was made. That decision was to assault Hanging Rock only instead of Rocky Mount, because that garrison had better defenses but fewer combatants. By comparison Hanging Rock had more British and Tories than Rocky Mount, but they camped in an open field near a crude earthen berm.

On August 6, 1780, the eight hundred plus Patriots arrived in the vicinity of their enemy after marching all night, a distance of sixteen miles. After another strategy session between Sumter and Davie, the partisans split into three large columns, each assigned a different sector to attack. All the columns had to cross Hanging Rock Creek and then climb a steep ravine to get to their sectors. Somehow the three columns of Patriots ended up attacking the same sector, but it worked. Perhaps it was successful because it was the weak part of the British defenses. Tory militia units defending that part of the ravine were reportedly caught totally off guard.

> [Saunders] The partisans fought as if possessed. A detachment of the British Legion mounted a bayonet charge, but they were cut down. Those who survived joined the Tory militia in fleeing the field. At the height of the battle, a Tory regiment slipped into some woods adjacent to the field and began to fire into the Whig lines. The partisans took instinctively to the trees and bush heaps

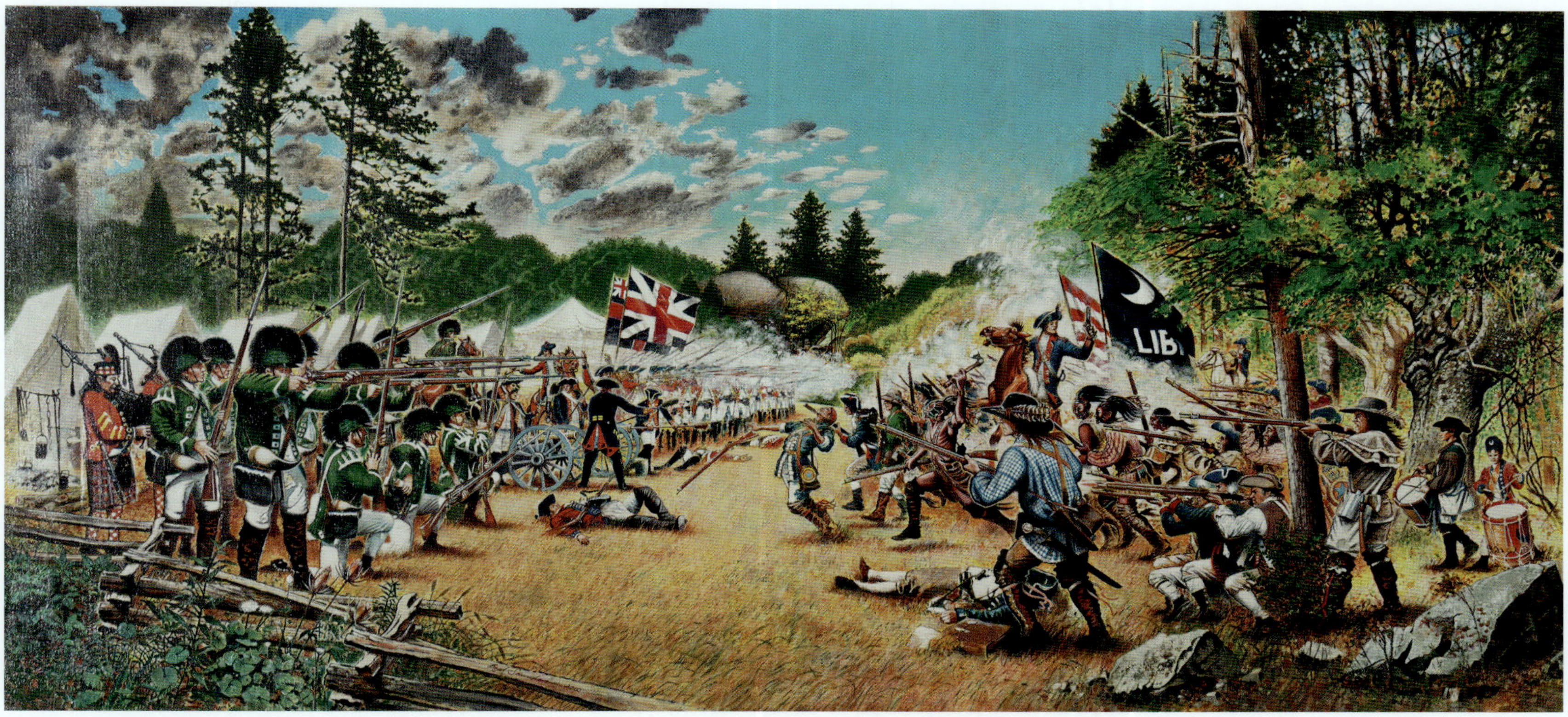

The Battle of Hanging Rock, 2000, acrylic on canvas, 4 × 8 ft. Courtesy of the South Carolina State Museum

> and returned fire with deadly effect, and in a few minutes there was not a British officer standing because one half of the regiment had fallen.
>
> When scouts reported that a British relief force from Rocky Mount was en route, Sumter and Davie managed to get their men to assemble and then withdrew. They left more than two hundred British and Tory killed and wounded. The Prince of Wales Regiment, a regular Tory unit, was almost annihilated. Of the eight hundred Whigs who entered battle, twelve were killed and forty-one were wounded. Incidentally, it was at Hanging Rock, as a messenger for Davie, that Andrew Jackson [age thirteen] gained his first military experience.[6]

Preliminary preparation by Saunders for specific elements in the planned painting began only after studying many additional historical sources regarding the battle in question. The elements and objects included: "Battlefield movements and tactics, weapons and equipment, costumes and uniforms, battlefield paintings from the eighteenth century, and more."[7]

Saunders visited Revolutionary War battlefields throughout South Carolina, especially at Kings Mountain, Cowpens, Brattonsville, and Camden. He also attended Revolutionary War reenactments, where he made hundreds of photographs and numerous drawings, and conducted interviews with reenactors. Two persons of note were especially helpful throughout the technical information-gathering phase for this painting; Darby Erd and Kip Carter. By the time the project began Darby Erd, a former student of Saunders and a longtime friend, had become an artist-illustrator and staff member at the South Carolina State History Museum, Columbia. He was also regarded as an expert on military weapons and uniforms and produced illustrations for the book *The United States Infantry: An illustrated History, 1775–1918* by Gregory Urwin (University of Oklahoma Press, 2000). However, Kip Carter became Saunders's primary source for military uniforms and weapons of the eighteenth century and certainly for the workings of the English Brown Bess musket and the American long rifle. Carter lent Saunders a Brown Bess musket to take home and become familiar with it. He also lent Saunders a Pennsylvania long rifle (or a Kentucky long rifle), whereupon Saunders not only drew such weapons, but he learned to load and fire some of them with a flint spark, and so on.

Carter, who lived practically next to the Hanging Rock Battlefield, was already a devoted Revolutionary War reenactor, an amateur historian of that period, and an avid collector of Revolutionary War memorabilia. His collection at the time contained items that became particularly useful for Saunders's painting project such as: weapons of many types, replicated uniforms, apparel worn by combatants, saddles, and other artifacts. Saunders, as mentioned earlier, met Carter during his first trip to the Hanging Rock Battlefield site. Carter became Saunders's friend, teacher, and mentor. Carter definitely introduced the artist to the world of Revolutionary War reenactments. Said Saunders, "The re-enactments and their participants were a wonderful source of information and inspiration to me. The individuals were, without exception, very approachable and helpful. They were patient with my interviews and happy to pose for photographs and drawings. They had all outfitted themselves at considerable expense and were eager to share and talk about it. You know, we'd be standing around a campfire while I was taking photographs and I'd say talk to me about your rig [uniform, weapon, equipment, and so on] and an hour later they were still telling me about it. Honey, they'll eat you alive."[8]

The reenactors represented authenticity in their uniforms, marching drills, and maneuvers which became quite apparent to Saunders after he had photographed several reenactments and interviewed many reenactors. Then . . . he experienced a kind of revelation; that is, he had imagined early on in this commission that he would probably need to hire models. But after taking hundreds of photographs, he decided maybe not. "I'd go to these things and Kip was good help in pointing out things to look for. The re-enactors were very accessible and all of a sudden, I didn't need models. I had thought I was going to hire models for all of this and do heavy research yet, a lot of it was right there. Frankly, I must confess that many did not know they were being recorded by my camera and sketchbook. . . . Don't ask, don't tell. It is easier to obtain forgiveness than permission."[9]

One reenactment turned out to be particularly important to Saunders's project, one he could have only dreamed about. "At the Camden rally, I had one of the most exciting and affirming moments of this whole project. On the second day of the rally, it was announced that at 3:00 P.M. there would be a re-enactment of *The Battle of Hanging Rock.* I was both surprised and delighted! Then, as the players arrayed themselves before me and acted out the battle, they fell, almost perfectly into the compositional arrangement that I had already laid out for the painting; and my position and point of view, as spectator, corresponded almost exactly with the point of the viewer of my composition. It was a special and transcendent moment. I think I broke out in chill bumps."[10]

Saunders's photographs and sketches of battlefields, reenacted battles, reenactors, gear, weapons, and the like began to evolve into sketches and drawings as studies. Then, with a partial composition in mind, Saunders made sketches on tracing paper to scale, which were then shifted around many times. In so doing the artist started the actual composition with the British and Tory forces first, perhaps because their uniforms, weapons, and disciplined formations were better known.

THE PAINTING BEGINS

Said Saunders, "Now it was time to start constructing the battle and the battleground. Since there were about two thousand troops involved, it was clearly impossible and redundant anyway, to try to show them all. I chose, instead, to focus on a relatively small group at a selected moment of contact. With some rough sketches of the overall design in mind, I started building the Tory army, one soldier at a time. For reasons that were mostly visual, I decided to concentrate primarily on two units; a detachment of Tarleton's Legion, and part of the Prince of Wales Regiment."

> [Saunders] Compositionally speaking, I have found that I work best if I start at a reasonably critical point somewhere near the center and work myself out, slowly creating an increasingly believable three dimensional space as I go with boundaries established last. The more tangible that space becomes, the easier it is to compose it. In short, I find I generally work better from the specific to the general than from the general to the specific.
>
> A dismounted, kneeling Dragoon [heavily armed trooper] from Tarleton's Legion was one of the first complete figures to be realized. An image like this one might well have gone through half a dozen stages of development on as many sheets of tracing paper. Once this first figure started working for me, he became part of a small group. Each successive figure was developed with the same care as the first and needed to be psychologically and spatially related to each other (e.g., the kneeling bugle boy) and form a cohesive visual unit. Then that small unit became part of a yet larger group, and so on.
>
> One of the constant challenges facing the designer of this sort of illusionism is the fact that as the figures and objects move in imaginary space away from the viewer, they need to diminish in size at a very specific and constant ratio. It is especially challenging with a mass of figures of differing sizes and configurations swirling around each other in combat on uneven terrain and still has the same rules of perspective apply and create the same illusion of depth.[11]

In the midst of the disciplined ranks of Tarleton's Legion and the Prince of Wales Regiment can be seen two cannons being readied to fire. Because of their modest size, weight, and particular structural features, they were nicknamed grasshopper cannons.

> [Saunders] I must confess that I had never even heard of a grasshopper cannon, but several sources mentioned that at least two grasshopper cannons were attached to this Tory army. I learned that a grasshopper cannon was a small reasonably portable three pound cannon that could be disassembled and carried by infantry troops into rough terrain without roads where larger ordinance could not go. The term 'three pound cannon' does not mean that it weighs three pounds, but rather that it fired a three pound ball. It could be assembled in five minutes and could be manipulated about a battlefield by a pair of poles projecting backwards from the trails. These made it resemble a grasshopper, hence its name. It was designed to be used at a reasonably short range, usually against massed infantry.

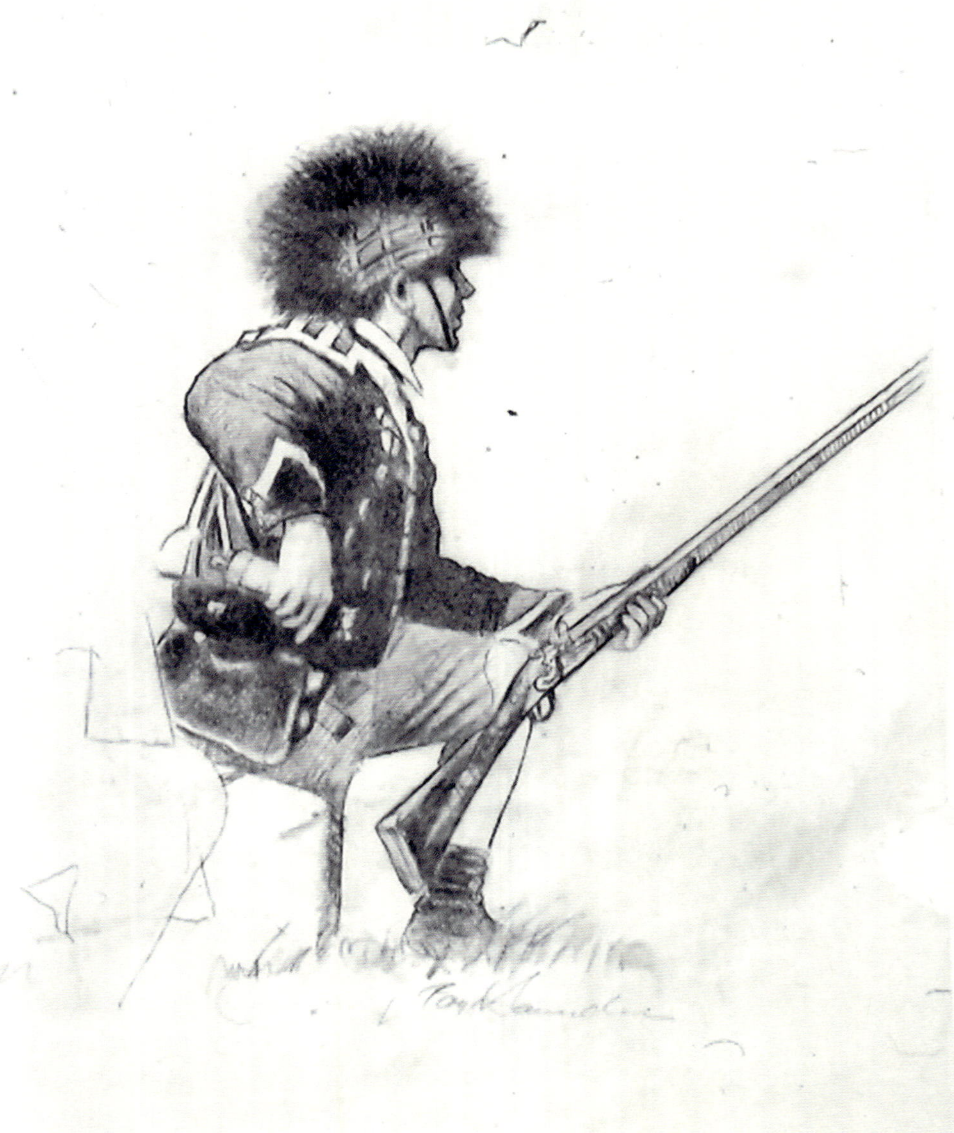

A Redcoat Musketeer, 2000, pencil

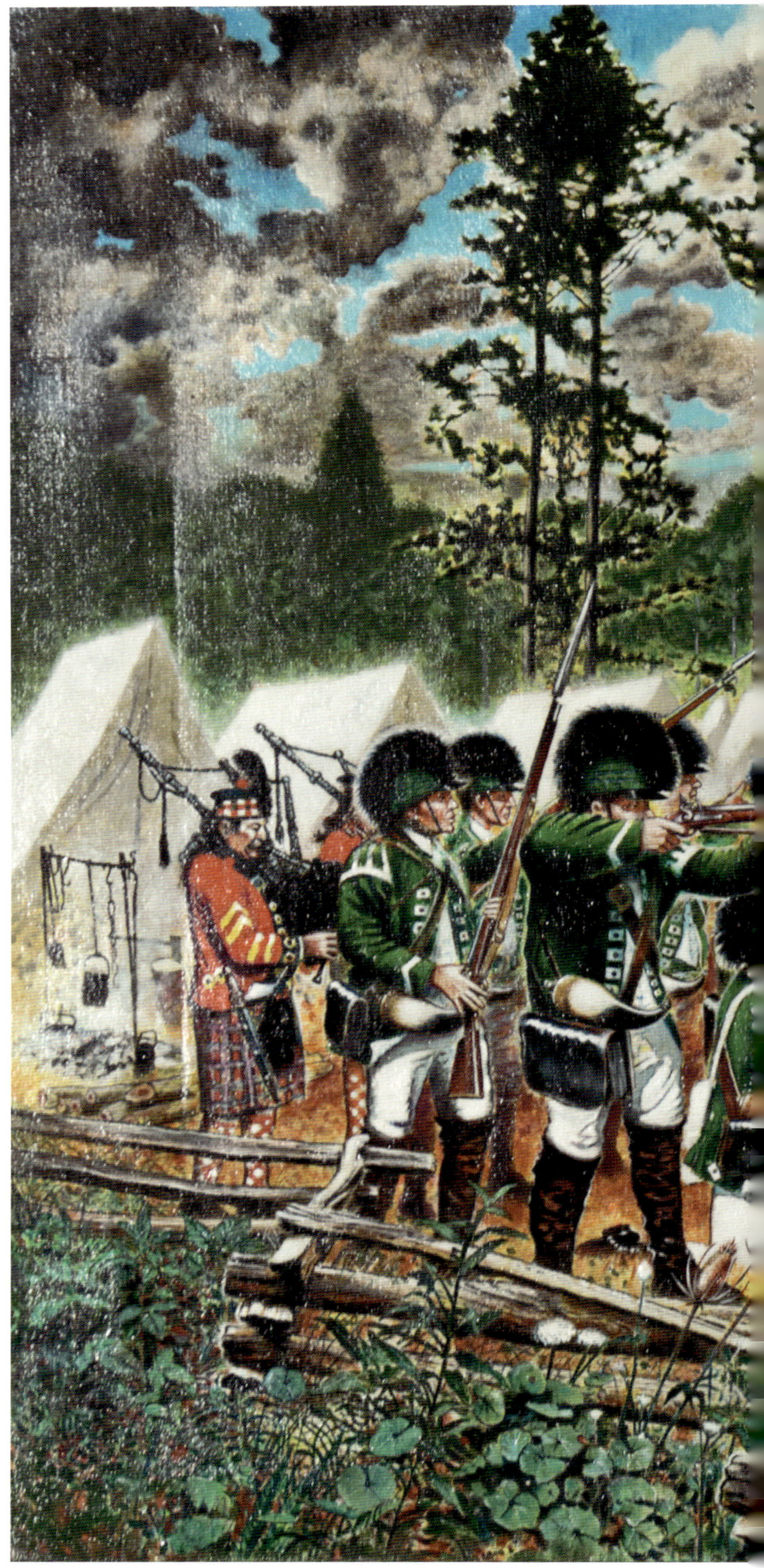

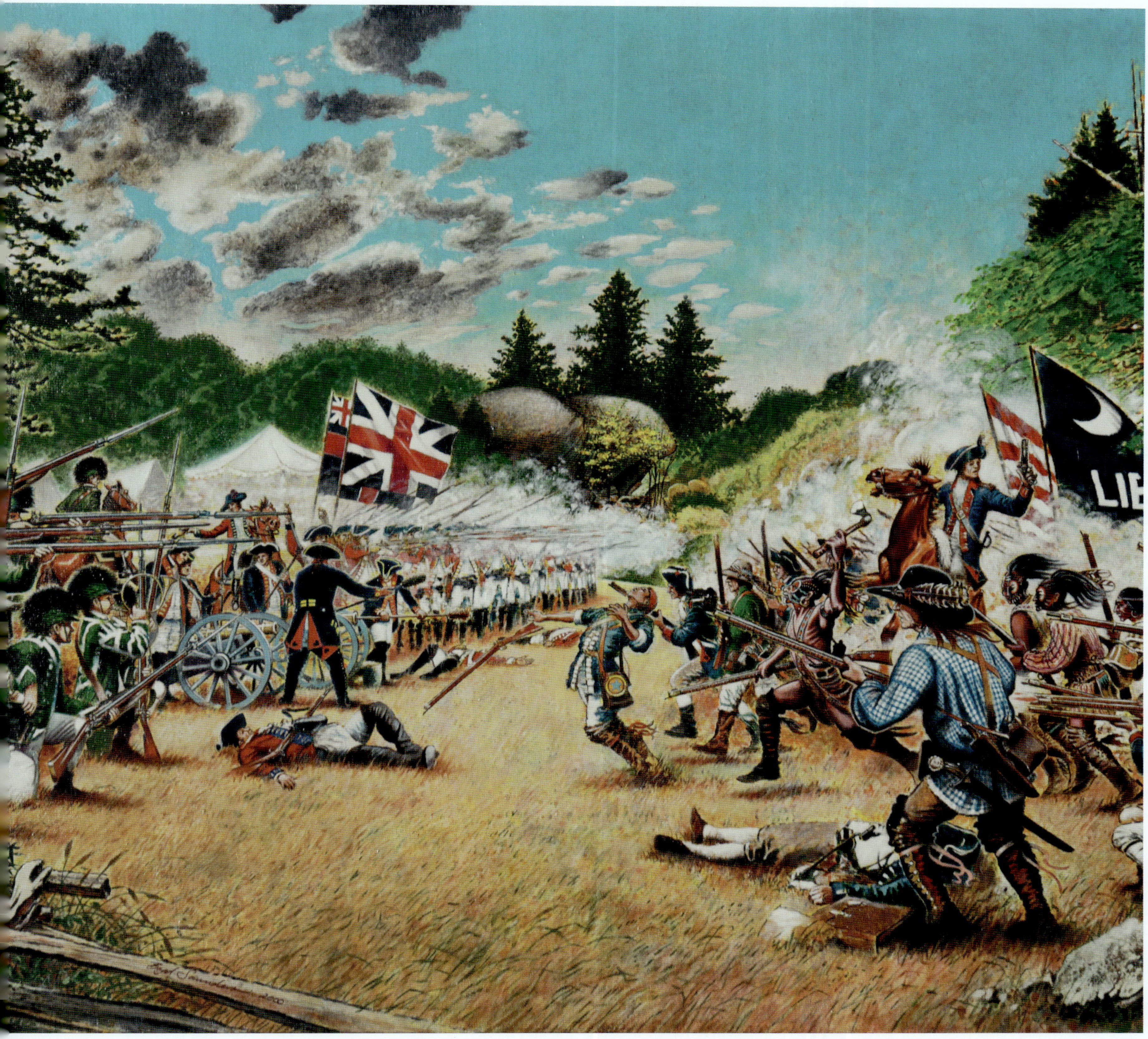

The Battle of Hanging Rock, British Legion and the Prince of Wales Regiment, left side, 2000, acrylic on canvas. Courtesy of the South Carolina State Museum

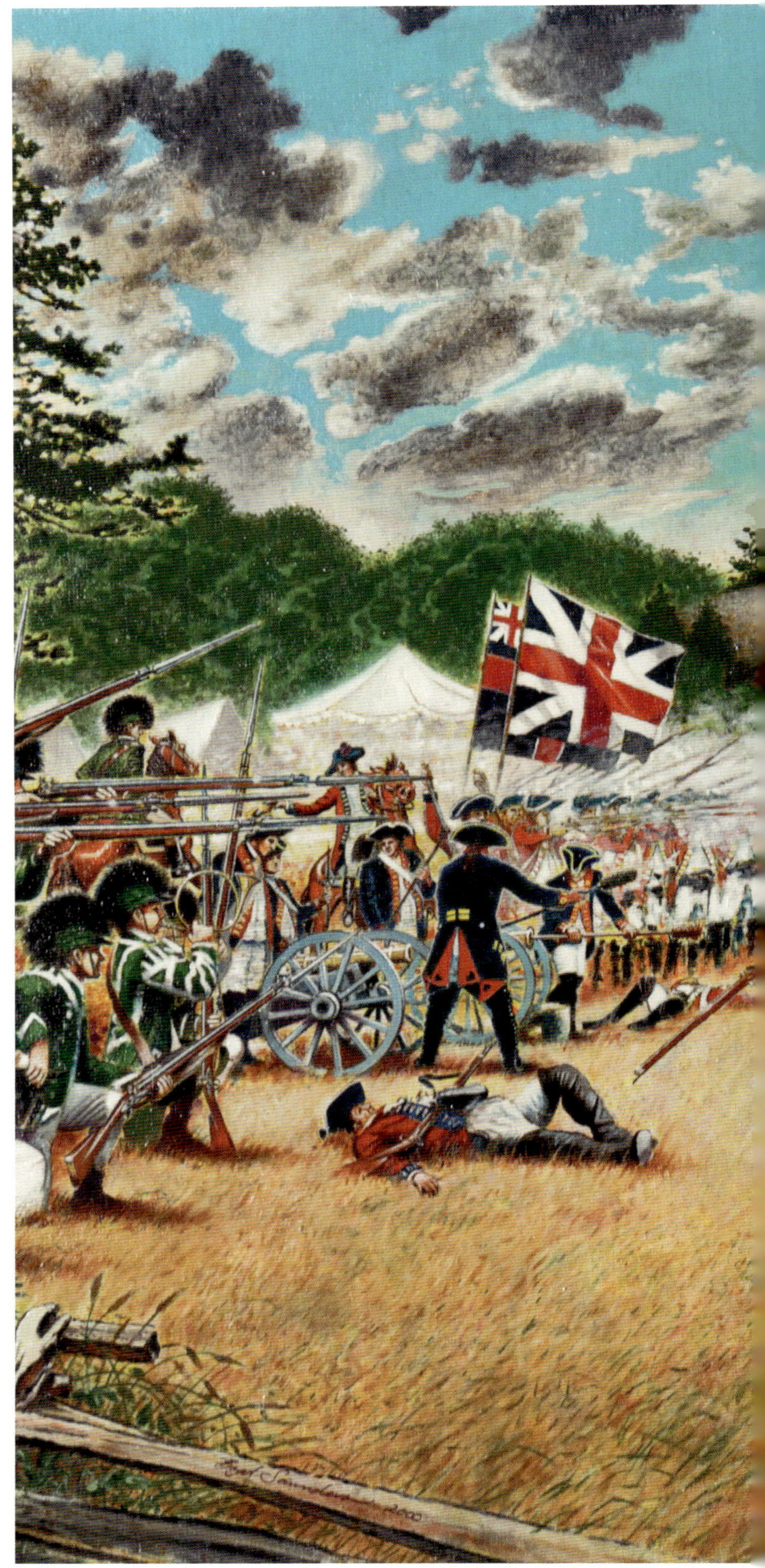

At a Camden rally and re-enactment there were a few such pieces. Kip and I persuaded the crew of one of them to pose for photographs and even to run a few firing drills. They were very accommodating and helpful. I got a wealth of visual information which quickly found its way into the composition.[12]

As the artist stated earlier, he began the composition with the figures in the army of occupation in part because their uniforms and so forth were better known and consistent and their strategies and alignments were more disciplined or classic in the European sense. By contrast the guerilla rebel units in the South Carolina backcountry tended to wear whatever was at hand to provide protection and be reasonably durable. Somewhat surprising for the artist was the personnel makeup of the backcountry fighters at Hanging Rock, South Carolina. The contrasts between the two opposing forces became one of the most dynamic elements of the painting.

[Saunders] The Patriot army proved to be a more demanding compositional challenge than the Loyalist group. From the beginning the foundation of the composition had been the contrast between the order and discipline of traditional British infantry tactics and the relative disorder, noise and confusion of the attacking Patriot forces. The chaos part is easy. Bringing to that chaos the order necessary to convey the desired visual information is not. Many figures came and went from this group or got moved around in it. However, the central anchoring figure of General Sumter remained somewhat constant.[13]

Visualizing the Patriot army brought with it the importance of getting its apparel and, the wide variety of it, correct. Unlike the Tory forces with standardized uniforms, it was pretty much every man for himself; certainly as far as the enlisted men were concerned. The officers were a bit more standardized.

For the infantry troops, the hunting frocks or fatigue shirts were a form unto themselves, with a number of variations. Perhaps the most interesting clothing feature of all was the leather leggings which most infantry troops wore to protect their

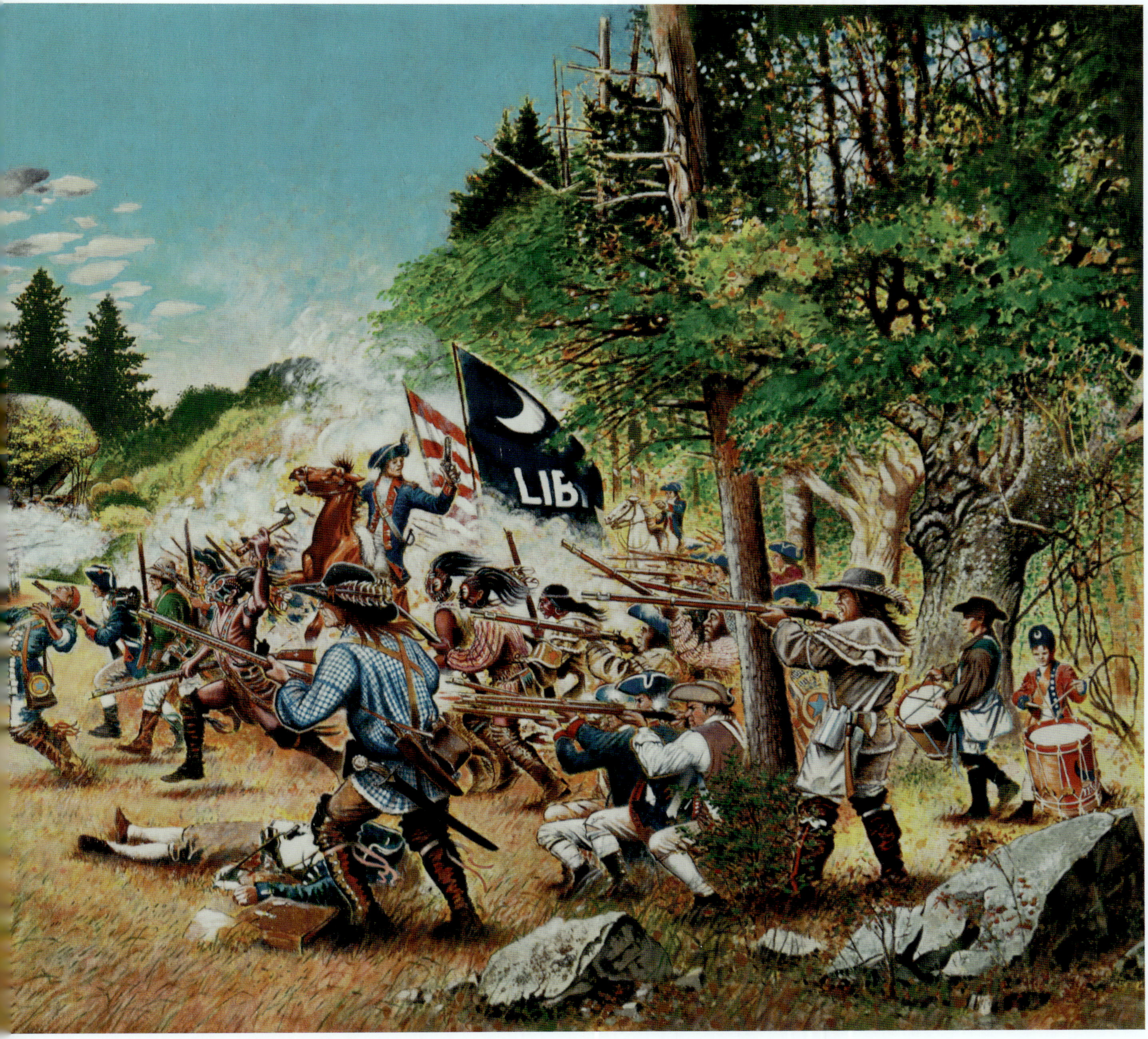

The Battle of Hanging Rock, Patriots Army, right side, 2000, acrylic on canvas.
Courtesy of the South Carolina State Museum

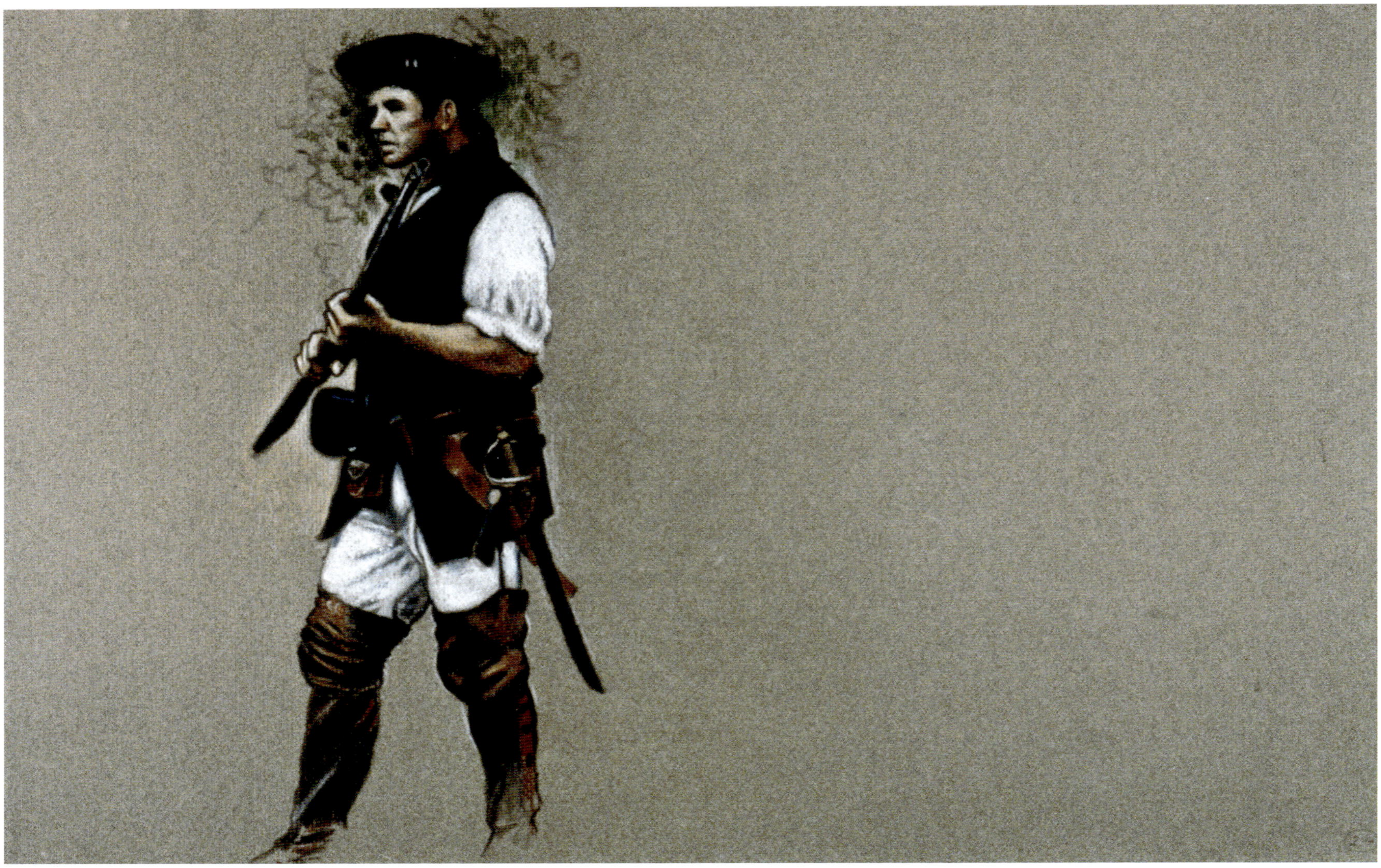

Patriot Militiaman, 2000, pastel

legs and clothing from brambles and undergrowth; rather like cowboys' chaps. Regarding headgear, when not folded into its signature shape, the famous tricorn hat was simply a felt hat with a round crown and a wide brim which could and often did take on a wide variety of creative shapes. They would have also been carrying personal gear such as haversacks, bedrolls and canteens, as well as containers of powder and shot for their firearms.

Their side weapons would have been a wide assortment of pistols, knives, swords, hatchets, tomahawks, or clubs. Their long guns might have been French or English muskets or American long rifles. Above all, it was the American long rifle which captured my imagination. That uniquely American invention, handmade with crude tools in small village shops, was technically superior to any similar weapon ever produced by any European kingdom. Those rifles, in the hands of their backwoods, hunter/fighter owners, literally changed the nature of warfare forever.[14]

When consulting various historical sources about the makeup of the Patriot guerilla units in the South Carolina backcountry, Saunders found that Native Americans participated in the American Revolution more than he had realized. Likewise several reputable sources, including Andrea Van Landingham Steen, recorded that a number of Catawba Indian fighters were among Patriot forces. The artist wanted to include them in this painting but was soon frustrated

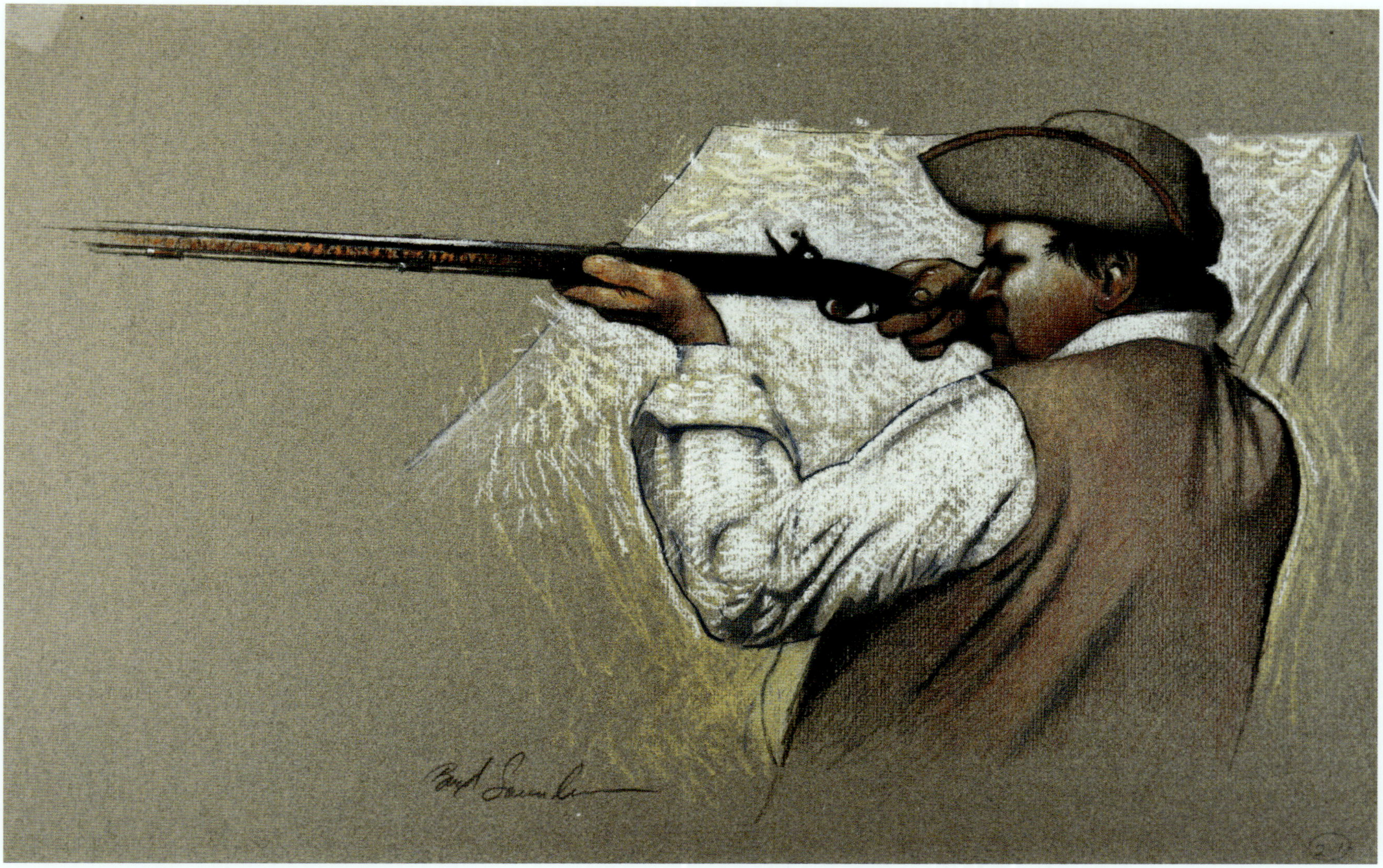

Patriot Rifleman, 2000, pastel

in his search for accurate descriptions of their regional territories, their physical appearance, weaponry, tactics, and so forth. Finding out that the Catawbas were small in number as a tribe but among the most Europeanized of the Native Americans in the region caused him puzzlement. He then decided on a field trip to the ancestral lands of the Catawbas, that is, around Rock Hill, South Carolina, in the extreme north central part of the state. There Saunders visited the Museum of York County and went to the Catawba Reservation for a powwow, but that trip was not much help. The artist then speculated that the Catawbas might have imitated the more dominant tribes in the southeastern colonies like the Cherokees. Gradually his hunches and searches began to bear favorable results. For example he learned that Native American tribes, living in the eastern woodlands, dressed and were armed similarly. In 1764 an eyewitness recorded that "their dress consists of the skins of some wild beast or a blanket, a breach cloth, leggings reaching halfway up the thigh, and fastened to the belt, and with moccasins on their feet. . . . They shave their heads reserving only a small tuft of hair on the top and paint their faces with various colors. When they prepare for an engagement, they paint themselves black and fight naked."[15]

Thanks to a number of Saunders's friends, who shared his interests and who expanded his searches via the Internet, a key description follows: "Catawba warriors had a fearsome reputation and an appearance to match: a Ponytail or Mohawk hairstyle with a distinctive war paint pattern of one eye in a black

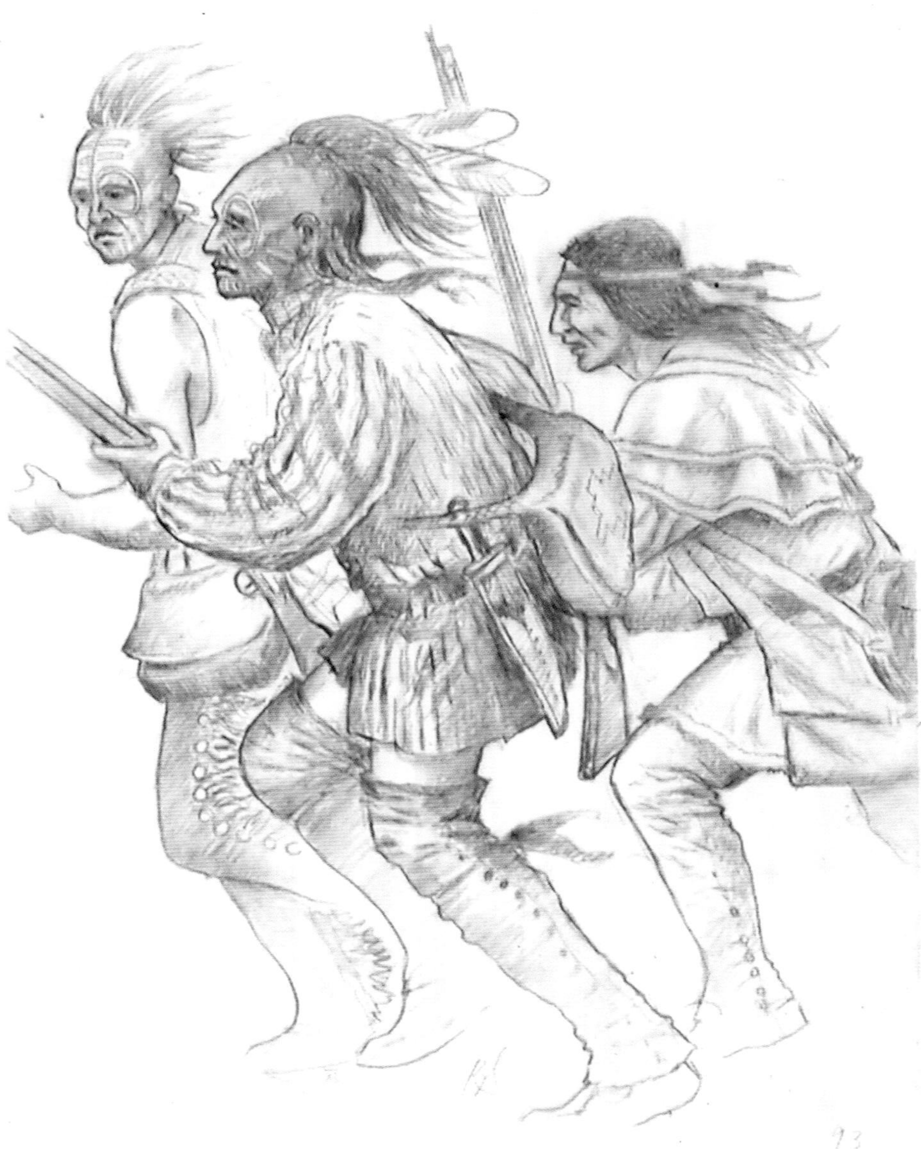

Catawba Warriors, 2000, pencil

circle, the other in a white circle and the remainder of the face painted black. Coupled with their flattened foreheads, some of their enemies must have died from sheer fright."[16]

Not yet finished with his inquiry into the physical appearance of Catawba warriors, Saunders benefited from two more sources, the latter closer to the artist's home. He located a sketch of a Catawba warrior dated 1771 by an anonymous artist published in the book *The Indians' New World: Catawbas and Their Neighbors from European Contact through the Era of Removal* by James Merrell (Norton 1991), which somewhat reinforced several descriptions in hand. The other source had a much more dramatic impact. Said Saunders, "Some of my most pointed help came from an archaeology seminar and field day at the Sesquicentennial State Park [located at the north edge of Columbia, South Carolina]. One of the exhibitors was a Catawba Indian who spent the day carefully and methodically applying war paint and battle paraphernalia, layer by layer. He was a treasure! I got a wealth of sketches and photographs of him. Out of all that came these images [of at least three Catawba Indians] to add into the Patriot army."[17]

From the 1764 eyewitness account, regarding the appearance of most eastern woodlands Indians, Saunders also learned how, in general, they armed themselves and how the Catawba Indians may have been armed. Said Saunders, "Their arms are a rifle, a powder horn, a shot pouch, a tomahawk, and a scalping knife hanging to their neck. When they are in want of fire arms, they supply them with a bow, a spear, or a death hammer, which is a short club made of hard wood."[18]

Then, regarding the presence of African American fighters among the Patriot forces at the Battle of Hanging Rock, Saunders had this to say: "Some of the African-American fighters were free-men; some were slaves, serving by command of their masters. I assumed that their clothing and equipment would be essentially the same as their Caucasian comrades. That idea was also supported by the William Ranney painting *Washington and Tarleton Duel at Cowpens.* In it the African-American fighter is dressed and outfitted essentially the same as the other protagonists in the scene."[19]

After Saunders's substantial historical background preparation regarding subject matter, he seemed to reach a critical mass of knowledge, sketches, and fully drawn imagery. Then he transferred a multitude of sketches onto a large roll of tracing paper and carefully established a composition that was faithful to the *Battle of Hanging Rock, August 6, 1780.* Completing that phase the artist was finally ready to transfer the finished composition to a large canvas.

> [Saunders] At this point, not a single stroke of paint had been applied to canvas, but I felt that the hardest part was over. I laid out the unstretched oversized canvas [in this case longer than

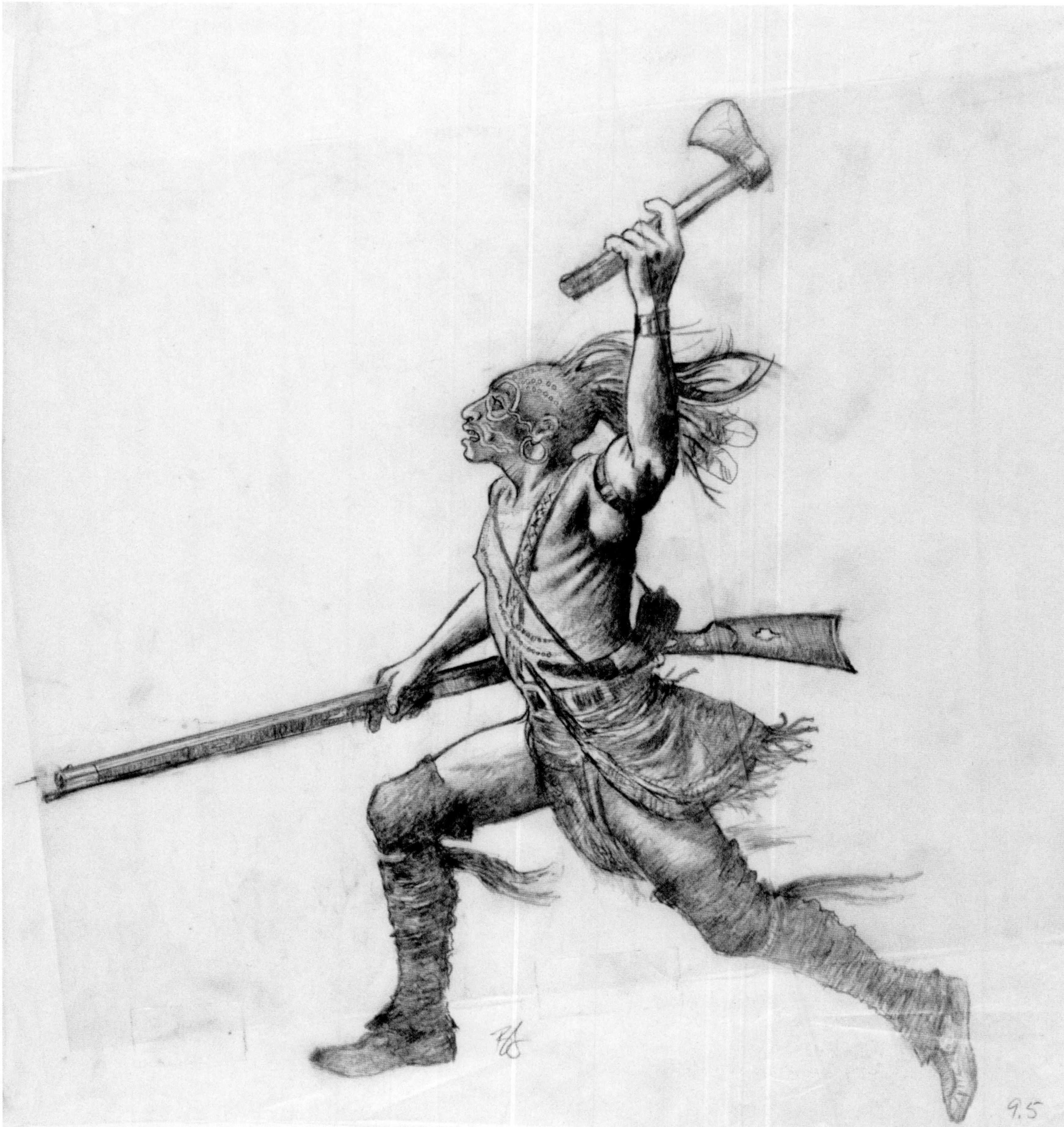

Catawba Warrior, 2000, pencil

4' × 8'] on a table on my front porch and started in. Without regard for design or boundaries, I covered the canvas with an irregularly patterned acrylic under-painting of yellow ochre and raw umber with flecks of rose madder. Onto this I transferred the imagery from the tracing paper maquette then started painting. I prefer to work from the center out, and don't like boundaries or fences. The golden under-painting established a warm, unified tonality for the whole painting, thus it acted as a default color, and tended to infuse all overlying colors with a sort of golden glow. Acrylic paint was used from start to finish. The good thing about acrylic is that it dries fast and turns to plastic on the canvas. The bad thing about acrylic paint is that it dries fast and turns to plastic on the palette. This produces a rather worrisome attention to the clock, and a lot of wasted paint. Still, I spent every available minute of the summer, fall, and winter months on the porch draped over that table, moving round it to reach different portions, sometimes painting the composition upside down.

While the terrain and landscape had been laid out from the start, the details were not worked out until last, then they were used to complete the compositional structures established by the figure groups. It was also important to me that the botanical forms be appropriate to the location and season.

When the painting was finished a stretcher frame was built. Then the canvas was stretched onto it and trimmed. Subsequently it was covered with four layers of clear acrylic varnish.[20]

Finally Saunders and his cabinetmaker friend Doug Williams designed an appropriate frame for the sizeable painting.

"It should be mentioned that somewhere, reasonably early in this process, my patron grew unhappy with me and fired me. I am not sure yet exactly why; it couldn't have been the painting, he hadn't even seen it yet, so it had to be me. But no matter, the original agreement provided me with one-third of the commission amount upfront. I kept on working; I was too committed to the project and I was having too much fun to turn back. Anyway, I was confident that I could find a home for the painting. And, if I didn't, well, unsold paintings are not exactly a novelty to me. One more would not be a big deal. In fact, it proved to be a rather liberating experience; I no longer had to be subservient to the calendar or someone else's whims."[21]

The South Carolina State Museum purchased the painting and a collection of all the preliminary drawings and sketches that went into its design (for $50,000). A permanent educational exhibit was produced for all these pieces, which feature both historical and artistic aspects of this project. The painting, as an image, was chosen to appear on the cover of Walter Edgar's book *Partisans and Redcoats* in 2001.[22]

Chapter 10

Service to the Field

Background, Birth, and Early Years of What Became Southern Graphics Council International—a Personal History by Boyd Saunders

World War II was the great defining event of the current era. It changed the world in many ways. It also transformed American higher education. After the war tens of thousands of military veterans brought with them a level of intensity, discipline, and maturity that academe had never before experienced. And there were so many of them! The dominant sound on college campuses in those days was the noise of construction, as these institutions went into a building boom to try to accommodate the explosively growing student body. Incidentally this boom was repeated (or maybe just continued) years later when those veterans' children, also known as baby boomers, entered college.

The famous ancient Greek orator Demosthenes is said to have trained himself to speak clearly and forcefully by practicing with his mouth full of pebbles. My own speaking style was probably shaped in some way in those "baby boomer building" days by having to lecture above the sound of jackhammers and heavy construction equipment outside college classroom windows. If there was any benefit in all this, it was the fact that it was very difficult for students to sleep in class with that racket going on.

As colleges and universities expanded rapidly, so did their art departments. Likewise their printmaking courses and studios, many of which had not even existed before, expanded rapidly. Surely there is a certain expense involved in making paintings (paint, canvas, paper, brushes, and so on), but it is pitifully small in comparison to the cost of the equipment required for a print studio. This cost also is usually prohibitive to most individual artists. However, with the proliferation of college and university print studios, in which the communal equipment and labor had to be shared, many talented individuals had opportunities to become artist-printmakers:

They learned the benefits and necessity of working together as well as the wide range of technical skills necessary to being a printmaker.

They learned the honesty of hard physical labor.

They learned the humility of respect for a highly complicated medium.

Most of all, though, they learned that *we need each other.*

Many of these artist-printmakers wound up teaching at colleges and universities across the American southland, where they were often the only printmaker in the art department, or the college, or the town, or anywhere around. They operated on meager salaries, shoestring budgets, and makeshift equipment. There were few supply sources nearby and no real market for their editions. The closest thing to an art gallery in town would often be the local frame shop. I remember chatting with Vern Clark, the founder of Graphic Chemical and Ink Company of Chicago some years ago. He told how when they began selling printmaking supplies back in 1947, there were, according to a government survey, fewer than three hundred printmakers in the entire country.

Two of our pioneers were Richard Zoellner and Maltby Sykes, who taught printmaking at the University of Alabama and Auburn University, respectively. I remember hearing them tell how, back in the day, their lithography students would draw on litho stones, which would then be crated and shipped to the George Miller studios in New York City, where the stones would be printed and regrained, then shipped back to Alabama for the process to begin all over again. That story reminded me of the ancient Greek legend of Sisyphus, who, as punishment for his arrogance and ambition, was condemned by the gods to forever push a large stone up a hill, only to have it roll back down the hill again, over and over. Many of us have faced similar frustration.

In 1965 I was invited to join the faculty of the University of South Carolina–Columbia with a mandate to establish a printmaking program, as none had existed there before. When I asked where the new print studio was to be located, the department chairman proudly showed me a small room on the ground floor of a building, called McMaster College, which the art department shared with the music department. The only problem was that "the small room" was the men's bathroom. When I pointed this out to him, he replied, "Well, yes, but it has plenty of water." When I suggested to the dean that I would need some money to buy equipment and supplies, he very generously bestowed $1,200 on me.

Well, dear hearts, I am here to tell you, I DID IT. I made it work, and in the process I utilized mechanical and financial skills that surprised even me.

The room was maybe 18 × 24 feet in size, and we did woodcut, etching, lithography, and silkscreen in there. Believe you me we got to know each other very well. We knew what each other looked like, sounded like, and smelled like. Of course some of the other male students in the building took a while to get used to the idea that the studio was not a men's bathroom anymore. For example we would be sitting around a big table in a critique, and some Joe College would absentmindedly blunder in and be halfway across the room toward where "that certain plumbing fixture" used to be, undoing himself, before it would dawn on him that something was wrong, and he would retreat in a state of embarrassed confusion.

In most locations like that, there was not much awareness of, or appreciation for, original prints. Most people did not know what an original print was, and to those who did, it was still relegated to the bottom rung of the hierarchical ladder. No matter how conceptually powerful or skillfully executed a print might be, it was still, after all, "just a print." I cannot begin to count how many presentations and demonstrations I gave to local Rotary Clubs and other civic groups explaining what an original part was. While they were always kind and gracious, the looks on their faces often told me I might as well have been speaking in Latin or Farsi or Erdu.

In 1972 I sent letters to every printmaker in the Southeast that I knew of and asked them to meet me in New Orleans at the upcoming Southeastern College Art Conference (also known as SECAC) to try to form some sort of a professional organization of southern printmakers. There a handful of us abandoned the fleshpots of Bourbon Street long enough to meet up in my room at the old St. Charles Hotel and, guided by a bottle of Jack Daniels and a blinking red neon light outside the window, agreed to form a printmakers' support organization.

I remember vividly introducing Bernard Solomon, from Georgia Southern College–Statesboro, to John O'Neil of the University of South Carolina–Columbia in that room on that occasion. John had arrived late because he had been suffering the agonies of Hell within his right big toe. Bernie was built wide, solid, and low to the ground, and physical grace was not one of his many charms. Well, upon being introduced to John, he stepped forward to shake John's hand and, in the same movement, accidentally stepped down with all his considerable weight on John's gout-inflamed right foot. John's involuntary response was loud, passionate, and profane and could be heard the full length of Bourbon Street. Little did I realize how portentous that event was. It sort of established the way things would go for us in the years that followed. However, the small group of printmakers in attendance agreed to form the Southeastern Graphics Council (SGC). Bernie Solomon, John O'Neil, and I wound up as the ruling triumvirate of the ragtag group. There will be more about Bernie later. A set of bylaws was written and approved, and the following year we were officially chartered by the state of South Carolina as a nonprofit organization. Boy, did we ever have that part right! A young South Carolina lawyer named John Taylor helped me draft the necessary papers to get us chartered. Somehow, because of that encounter, he became a hopeless and lifelong devotee of prints and printmaking. Even though I am now retired from teaching, from time to time I have dropped by the University of South Carolina Art Department and found John Taylor in the print studio, still taking print classes . . . and he is almost as old as I am. Poor thing.

Returning to those early, challenging years, we teetered constantly between the exhilaration of what we were doing and the abyss of total collapse and financial ruin. It certainly would be interesting to see an accounting of personal out-of-pocket money expended by charter officers and slightly later officers on behalf of the organization. It would also be informative to realize what our various home institutions unwittingly contributed in the form of postage, printing, phone calls, travel, and related expenses. Whatever it took we were determined to hold down the cost of membership and make sure that the members got more than just a membership card and dues notices for their trouble. For example: We held annual conferences and workshops. Our first annual workshop conference was hosted by Bernie in 1974 at his home institution, Georgia Southern College, and lasted . . . all afternoon. All presenters were member volunteers, and student registration was five dollars.

We organized traveling print shows of members' work. We arranged international exchanges complete with exhibition catalogues. We lobbied for protective legislation. We published a quarterly newsletter, which in time became an excellent publication titled *Graphic Impressions: The Journal of the Southern Graphics Council.*

But best of all we had each other. We were not alone anymore. We became like a family and got to know and love each other. As new members joined this family they would often say, "What can I do to help?" and we would give them a job. Dr. Thomas Dewey joined our ranks in 1977 and soon became our official archivist, historian, and print collection developer. Starting with about forty prints in 1978, he built the SGC collection to between six and seven thousand prints by 2013, which he has also had digitally photographed and catalogued for the SGC, for whose creation he consulted an outstanding Ole Miss student, Mary Warner, and visiting professor Dr. Esther Sparks, expert regarding American works on paper.

Ed O'Neal took on the product vendors' fair and turned it into what it is today. In our early days, Graphic Chemical and Ink Company was the only product vendor who regularly came to our conferences. One other vendor, who shall remain unnamed, said his firm would be represented only if we paid them to attend and set up. Now look at our product fair.

After a few years, in 1978 we were approached by printmakers from states west of the Mississippi River and were asked to expand our territory out their way. At first I was opposed. We were a small, close-knit organization, and I thought we could best serve our members by staying that way. Fortunately I was overruled, and like that ever-westward course of the American Republic, we expanded westward and changed our name to the Southern Graphics Council (SGC). Then our thin gray line was soon joined by many new and wonderful friends from the Southwest who brought high energy, fresh ideas, and their rich visual talents to the organization.

But we were still like a family, maybe a little larger, but still wonderfully close and supportive. I fondly remember the small children of Marge and Zdzislaw Sikora playing up and down the aisles during conference sessions. In a short time our family came to include printmakers from all over the country and, indeed, all over the world.

Over the years we have been graced by the leadership and vision of many talented and inspired individuals. The mind boggles as I think back over them. Each brought his or her own unique personality to the organization and left us richer. However few, if any, have made a more profound mark than Beauvais Lyons of the University of Tennessee–Knoxville. His energy, vision, and organizational skills have enriched us beyond measure. We all owe him a huge debt of gratitude. Bill Walmsley, also known as "Ding Dong Daddy," was our third president and, ever thereafter, a guiding force. He was a gentle, soft-spoken, charming man with a perpetual twinkle in his eye, who taught printmaking at Florida State University–Tallahassee and made audacious, irreverent lithograph prints that glowed in the dark and often scandalized the uptight. He was also an avid collector of prints and loved to talk about prints and printmakers.

During World War II, he served in the U.S. Army artillery. The great noise of the guns damaged his ears and left him with impaired hearing, which sort of wrote its own rules. As a result conversations with him were often filled with strange non sequiturs and wonderful surprises. Over the years he sort of designated himself as our unofficial photographer. At each annual conference he took copious photographs, which he then had developed and passed out at the next year's gathering. Ironically the last conference he was able to attend was our thirtieth anniversary conference held in New Orleans in 2002 to celebrate our beginnings there.

Many other wonderful individuals have passed our way as well. However none has been more influential or memorable than Bernard Solomon. Bernie grew up in a Jewish community in Chicago and had moved to Statesboro, Georgia, to teach at Georgia Southern College, just two years before we held that first informal meeting in New Orleans. He was on board from the very beginning and worked tirelessly on the organization's behalf. He was a colorful and truly unforgettable character. His imposing physiognomy, mentioned earlier, was topped by a luxurious black beard, bushy eyebrows, and mop of unruly black hair. His physical and intellectual energy were boundless. He was generous, cantankerous, charming, and totally devoted to his family and his faith. He was also unpredictable and argumentative and occasionally kept many of our early officers and members in a state of hand-wringing frustration and despair. I still remember the time he was helping to hang a juried show of members' work that was to open at one of our conferences. As he took one painting out of its crate, he decided the back of the framed painting looked better than the front, so he hung it backward with its face to the wall. Bernie never could understand why the artist who created this work became highly agitated at the show opening and wanted to kill him.

He often said that I was the father of the Southern Graphics Council, and he was the mother, a concept that to me still conjures bizarre and terrifying images. Yet he and I had a standing date for dinner together at each annual conference. Conversations between these two old friends, the Chicago-raised Jew and this unreconstructed southerner, usually were about family and whose kids had wrecked the family car the worst. I still remember clearly that day of June 10, 1995, when I had just received the grim news from my doctor that I had the dubious honor of playing host to a large brain tumor. I returned to my office and was reaching for the phone to call my wife with this news when the phone rang. It was Roger Steele from Beaufort, South Carolina, another SGC member of long tenure and faithful service to the organization, calling to tell me that Bernie had just died and under strange circumstances. When I called "Ding Dong Daddy" Walmsley in Tallahassee to tell him the news, he told me that he had just suffered a major blood clot in his leg, which had seriously endangered his heart. I still can hear Bill saying, "Damn, Boyd. Somebody out there is trying to kill us!" I guess I knew that day that we had all entered a new era and there was no turning back. By now many of our original members are no longer with us. However, they have been replaced by talented and energetic younger artists, most of whom were not even born when we began.

Perhaps some of the wisdom and stability we seek as printmakers might well be found in the pioneers of our own craft who have paved the way for us; I have always admired the Chinese tradition of respect for the senior members of their society and their willingness to learn from them. The Japanese government even designates certain highly skilled senior artisans as "National Treasures," provides them with financial support, and encourages students to study with them in order to protect and pass along their craft.

Early on it seemed to me to me that it would be fitting for our organization to find a way to pay respect to our senior printmakers and learn as much as possible from them. So in 1978 the Southern Graphics Council (then known as the Southeastern Graphics Council) instituted the practice of annually awarding, to a senior printmaker, the honorary title of "Printmaker Emeritus." Again it was agreed that the Printmaker Emeritus be a senior printmaker, one whose career was an established fact rather than a promise. However no specific age has ever been fixed. It was further agreed that the candidate's primary area of artistic endeavor needed to be in the field of printmaking, papermaking, or artist's books whether as a practitioner, educator, or administrator.

We then proceeded to collect nominations for the award and screen them, and a selection committee voted to decide the honoree. This person was invited to speak about his or her life and work at our annual conference and would be featured in an exhibition there. We also gathered as much data as possible about the recipient to add to our archives at Ole Miss and presented the recipient with an award to honor the occasion. The Printmakers Emeriti have also been made honorary lifetime members. In part it was also a way of giving roses to people who could still smell them, hearing their words while they could still speak them, and to let them know that they are not alone.

Of course the early Printmaker Emeritus Awards went to persons from the geographic region we served, namely the American South. For practical reasons we tried to match the candidates to a conference site that was reasonably close to where they lived. This made it easier to transport them and their work to the conference. I still remember with great pleasure the 1983 conference in Rockville, Maryland, organized by Zdzislaw Sikora, at which James L. Wells was the first African American named to the honor. He was a resident of Washington, D.C., and was accompanied to the awards ceremony by a large contingent of family and friends. Both he and they were very pleased by the award, and picture taking went on long after the awards ceremony had ended.

Now as we have grown into a truly international organization, renamed Southern Graphics Council International (SGCI), our laureates are increasingly drawn from a much larger base, and many of them have enjoyed much more hospitable circumstances thanks to the belated appreciation of prints.

In an attempt to give a tangible, physical presence to this honor, we have designed a plaque, which is cast in bronze each year by John Ward of Atlanta, to be presented to the honoree. This plaque is mounted on a mahogany base and features the engraver's burin, which we use as a logo, with the words "Printmaker Emeritus, Southern Graphics Council International" in high relief, as well as the recipient's name. Like a few other individuals, Michael Mazur, the 2003 honoree, took exception to the title, thinking that it suggested being old or finished or put out to pasture, as it were. We had no such thing in mind. When I asked him what he preferred, he said he rather liked the title "Supreme and living God."

Well as Shakespeare said, "What's in a name?" When we were creating the award in 1978 we had several choices of what to call it. Obviously some of us liked the designation or title "Printmaker Emeritus," feeling that it suggested meritorious accomplishment. A sampling of other choices included "Geezer and Old Fart." My personal favorite comes from my other life as a horseman. When a great racehorse is considered to have reached the peak of perfection he is . . . "retired to stud." I had rather thought that when I retired from teaching at the University of South Carolina–Columbia in 2001, my new title might be "Retired to Stud." Maybe I will still have some new cards made up. But maybe the best solution came from a rather taciturn southern farmer. When a Yankee tourist asked if he had lived on his farm all his life, he said, "Well, no, not yet."

Most certainly being an artist is not something one retires from. There are many professions from which one can retire and often quite joyously. Being an artist is not one of them. Being an artist is a philosophical commitment and maybe a spiritual calling. One does not retire from it. Throughout the ensuing years, some of the finest artists in the world have received this award and in so doing have honored and enriched the SGCI far beyond measure. We offer our sincere and heartfelt thanks to each of them.

Finally, to each of you, I extend the warmest welcome and the best wishes. I encourage you to make this wonderful organization your own and remember *We Have Each Other; We Are Not Alone!*[1]

The preceding informal, personal history of what became Southern Graphics Council International contains a taste of the many colorful excerpts from Printmaker Emeritus Award presentations at the annual conferences. All such presentation introductions, over the past three-plus decades, have included to some degree, Saunders's honesty, humility, respect, and irrepressible humor. However, the Printmaker Emeritus Award presentation remarks delivered by Saunders at the 2001 SGC Conference were decidedly sober. In fact, it was a formal, serious address constructed around heartfelt concerns about "false voices" especially relevant to the increasingly electronic age of "Information Exchanges."

"INFORMATION EXCHANGES AND FALSE VOICES"

SGC Annual Conference, University of Texas, Austin, March 7–11, 2001

[Saunders] Well, it seems that Y2K has come and gone, and we are safely embarked on a new millennium with very few problems. The world did not end in an apocalyptic calamity, and civilization did not grind to a halt due to massive computer failure; much to the disappointment, I am sure, of the doomsayers who were so determined that it would. Like any normal New Year's Day, however, the occasion does provide an opportunity for looking back and reflecting on time gone by. I find myself looking back to the middle of the century just past and remembering some of the ways we anticipated the half century then in front of us.

In 1950 America was what Charles Dickens might have called "the best of times and the worst of times." Optimism was very high. We had just overcome the Great Depression and had come out on the winning side of the most horrific and destructive war the world had ever known. America had renewed her love affair with the automobile, bread was five cents a loaf, Harry Truman was president, Joe DiMaggio was king, and calendar images of a nubile Marilyn Monroe wearing nothing but a smile convinced every pubescent American male that heaven really and truly did exist somewhere. Soothsayers looked into the upcoming half of the century and predicted a high-tech utopian tomorrow which looked like a cross between a Buck Rogers space movie and an evangelist's description of Heaven. Yet even as we reveled in this new day, we had to look ahead to the next big war which would probably be even more horrible than the last, and which might ultimately mean the end of life on the planet. Many of us were convinced that it would most certainly happen; we just weren't sure exactly when. Incidentally we weren't as crazy as you might think. A couple of times it very nearly did happen. Even in 1950 a new conflict was beginning on an unheard-of faraway peninsula called Korea.

One of the prophets of the day was George Orwell. In his book *1984* (published in 1949) he predicted a society in which all thought and speech of the citizens were completely controlled by the government. Of course, his "Newspeak" never did really occur, did it? Certainly it did! We just call it "political correctness" instead. And the punishment for wrongful thought or improper speech is called "sensitivity training."

Indeed there were many ways in which the new utopia did not materialize. Somewhere along the way, our national character seemed to change. What had once been a can-do nation of heroes and dreamers became an unruly crowd of whiners, crybabies, and finger-pointers. Victimhood now seems to be the ultimate form of status, and crying on television has been elevated to an art form.

Somewhere back during those earlier days, two bits of insight occurred to me which I have never quite managed to get out of my mind. One happened while I was serving as best man at the wedding of a good friend. At one of the prewedding parties, the father of the bride, in a moment reminiscent of a similar scene in the movie *The Graduate,* was offering advice to any young males who cared to listen. "Information Exchange," he would say, "Communication! It is the industry of the future. It will dominate the last half of the century. If you want to assure your future, go into the information exchange business." At the time I had no idea how perceptive that observation would prove to be.

During the fifteenth century Johannes Gutenberg began printing books from movable type on a converted winepress and changed the world forever. Many consider that occurrence to have been the most significant event of the past thousand years. However, the last half of this twentieth century with its exponential advances in electronic technology has seen an explosion of communication and information exchange which no one could have ever imagined, even in 1950. But it has not produced Utopia.

In 1928 an Austrian named Felix Salten published a book titled *Bambi.* The story was about a deer and the animals around him, and perhaps because the animals could speak, it was treated as a children's book. Whether it was intended as such or not, it was certainly a much darker story of violence and elemental struggle for survival than the piece of fluff that Walt Disney turned it into. At one point in the story the adolescent male Bambi has fallen in love or lust or something with the young doe Faline. One afternoon he hears her calling to him from across a clearing. The voice is plaintive and compelling, and he experiences an irresistible urge to go to her. Before he can, however, he is blocked by the old stag who has acted as his guide and mentor. "Don't go," says the old stag, "It is not what you think." "Of course it is," says Bambi. "Listen to her voice. It is Faline and she needs me. I must go to her." "No," says the old stag. "The voice is false." After a period of argument and confrontation, the old stag finally leads Bambi stealthily around and back to the other side of the clearing from downwind and shows him that the call of Faline was actually being made by a clever hunter with a gun who was prepared to kill Bambi the moment he stepped into the clearing. It is a subtle yet chilling lesson on the dangers of being misled and destroyed by listening to false voices.

I was too young to read for myself when that story was read to me, but it has remained with me ever since. Certainly it is not the only place in literature where we can find that lesson about the danger of false messages in one form or another. The ancient Greek poet Homer told of how the hero Odysseus encountered the Sirens during his voyage home. The Sirens, part bird and part woman, lured seamen to their death with beautiful singing. Odysseus filled his sailors' ears with wax but had himself tied to the mast so he could safely enjoy the singing.

Of course we all know the story from the Gospel of Luke of Jesus going on his forty-day retreat into the wilderness to discover the meaning of his mission only to have the Tempter try to beguile him with lies and false messages. And who among us has not watched Dorothy and her friends the Scarecrow, the Tin Man, and the Cowardly Lion travel across the Land of Oz in hopes of gaining enlightenment and transformation from the Great Wizard only to confront a travesty of smoke and noise in the deception?

Certainly the current era with its explosion of information technology has provided an avalanche of false voices. As I said, Gutenberg triggered the information explosion at the midpoint of the last millennium, and five hundred years later, what do we have? *Talking robots!!* My God! Talk about false voices! Whatever happened to the simple luxury of speaking with a real live person? The clowns who have visited such abominations on us should break out in a rash, and be afflicted with itching where they cannot scratch!

Like that Buck Rogers fantasy utopia I mentioned, we now have electronic machines doing things for us which would have been unimaginable a few short years ago. Indeed we have now set the one-eyed monsters to raise our children; then we tear our hair and wonder what went wrong when they go to school and kill their classmates, teachers, and themselves. Talk about false voices . . . Boy! It may well be that our supreme challenge in the current era is to cut through the cacophony of messages and try to figure out which voices are worth hearing and believing, and which are not. In many ways we printmakers have it easier than most. We have among us voices that we can believe in and prime examples that we can look up to. From them we can learn the rich tradition of our craft, and from them we are challenged to seek believable realities and other truths in life.[2]

SOUTHERN GRAPHICS COUNCIL INTERNATIONAL

Host sites and Printmaker Emeritus Award recipients
(beginning with the 1978 conference)

1974 Georgia Southern College–Statesboro
1975 University of Georgia–Athens
1976 Greenville County Museum of Art, Greenville, South Carolina
1977 Florida State University–Tallahassee
1978 University of Alabama–Birmingham and the Birmingham Museum of Art
  Elizabeth O'Neill Verner (Charleston, South Carolina)
1979 University of Mississippi–Oxford
  Richard Zoellner (University of Alabama–Tuscaloosa)
1980 Auburn University, Auburn, Alabama
  Caroline Durieux (Louisiana State University–Baton Rouge)
1981 University of South Carolina, the McKissick Museum, and the Columbia Museum
  Maltby Sykes (Auburn University, Alabama)
1982 Tulsa Junior College, Oklahoma
  Alexandre Hogue (University of Tulsa–Oklahoma)
  Mauricio Lasansky (University of Iowa–Iowa City)
  Doel Reed (Oklahoma State University, Stillwater, Oklahoma)
1983 Montgomery College, Rockville, Maryland
  Jacob Kainen (curator, Division of Graphic Arts, Smithsonian Institution, Washington, D.C.)
  Prentiss Taylor (American University, Washington, D.C.)
  James Lesesne Wells (founder of Graphic Arts Department, Howard University, Washington, D.C.)
1984 University of North Carolina–Charlotte
  Corrie Parker McCallum (founder of Charleston School of Art, Curator, Gibbes Museum of Art, South Carolina)
  Sally Frost Knerr (instructor, Gibbes Museum, Charleston, South Carolina, lithography demonstrator, Winterthur Museum, Winterthur, Delaware, and assistant professor of art, Baptist College of Charleston, South Carolina)
1985 Rice University, Houston, Texas
  Constance Forsythe (University of Texas–Austin)
1986 Atlanta College of Art and High Museum, Georgia
  William Walmsley (Florida State University–Tallahassee)
1987 University of Florida with Santa Fe Community College, Gainesville
  Gabor Peterdi (Yale University, New Haven, Connecticut)
1988 Furman University, Greenville, South Carolina
  Leonard Baskin (Smith College, North Hampton, Massachusetts)
1989 University of Texas–Austin
  Rudy Pozzatti (Indiana University–Bloomington)
1990 University of Alabama–Birmingham
  James Steg (Newcomb College of Tulane University, New Orleans, Louisiana)
1991 Kansas City Art Institute, Missouri
  Warrington Colescott (University of Wisconsin–Madison)
1992 University of Tennessee–Knoxville
  Lee R. Chesney Jr. (University of Texas–Austin)
1993 Maryland Printmakers, Maryland Institute College of Art, Baltimore
  Robert Hamilton Blackburn (Printmaking Workshop, New York City)
1994 Texas Christian University–Forth Worth
  Garo Antreasian (University of New Mexico–Albuquerque)
1995 University of Tennessee–Knoxville
  June Wayne (founder, Tamarind Lithography Workshop, Los Angeles, California)
1996 University of West Virginia–Morgantown
  Nancy Spero (independent printmaker and writer, Chicago, New York City, Paris, and Florence)
1997 University of South Florida–Tampa
  Donald Saff (Graphic Studio, University of South Florida–Tampa)
1998 Ohio University, Athens
  Clinton Adams (Tamarind Institute, University of New Mexico–Albuquerque)
  Ken Tyler (Tyler Graphics, Mount Kisco, New York)

1999 Arizona State University–Tempe
Jules Heller (Arizona State University–Tempe)

2000 University of Miami, Florida
Krishna Reddy (New York University and its Print Atelier, New York City)

2001 University of Texas at Austin
Antonio Frasconi (State University of New York–Purchase)

2002 New Orleans, Louisiana
Boyd Saunders (University of South Carolina–Columbia)

2003 Boston Massachusetts, Boston Printmakers Association
Michael Mazur (independent artist, Cambridge and Provincetown, Massachusetts)

2004 Rutgers University, New Brunswick, New Jersey
Judith K. Brodsky (Center for Innovative Editions, Rutgers, State University of New Jersey)

2005 Washington, D.C., Susan Goldman, assistants and many area entities and sponsors
Elizabeth Catlett (Universidad Nacional Autonoma de Mexico, Mexico City)

2006 University of Wisconsin–Madison
Susan Gosin (Hand Printmaking Incorporated and Center for the Book Arts, Beltsville, Maryland)

2007 Kansas City Art Institute, Kansas City, Missouri
Karen Kunc (University of Nebraska–Lincoln)

2008 Virginia Commonwealth University–Richmond
Helen Frederick (George Mason University, Fairfax, Virginia; and Navigation Press)

2009 Columbia College, Chicago, Illinois
Ray Martin (School of the Art Institute of Chicago)

2010 Philadelphia, Pennsylvania, University of the Arts, Moore College of Art and Design University of Pennsylvania, Pennsylvania Academy of Fine Arts and the Tyler School of Art of Temple University, Philadelphia
Rochelle Turner (Tyler School of Art of Temple University)

2011 Sam Fox School of Design and Visual Arts, Washington University, St. Louis, Missouri

2012 Southern Graphics Council International
Sue Cole (Tulane University, New Orleans, Louisiana)

2012 New Orleans, Louisiana
David Driesbach

2013 Milwaukee, Wisconsin
Margo Humphrey, Judith Solodkin

2014 San Francisco, California
Wayne Thiebaud

2015 Knoxville, Tennessee
Ruth Weisberg

2016 Portland, Oregon
John Risseeuw

2017 Atlanta, Georgia
Sydney Cross

2018 Las Vegas, Nevada
to be determined

SOUTHERN GRAPHICS COUNCIL PRESIDENTS

1972–74 Boyd Saunders (University of South Carolina–Columbia)
1974–76 Tom Hammond (University of Georgia–Athens)
1976–78 William Walmsley (Florida State University–Tallahassee)
1978–80 Thomas Dewey II (University of Mississippi–Oxford)
1980–82 John O'Neil (University of South Carolina–Columbia)
1982–84 Zdzislaw Sikora (Montgomery College, Rockville, Maryland)
1984–86 Karin Broker (Rice University, Houston, Texas)
1986–88 Donald Byrum (University of Tennessee–Chattanooga)
1988–90 Stephen Cook (Mississippi College–Clinton)
1990–92 Ken Kerslake (University of Florida–Gainesville)
1992–94 Hugh Merrill (Kansas City Art Institute, Kansas City, Missouri)
1994–96 Beauvais Lyons (University of Tennessee–Knoxville)
1996–98 Sergio Soave (West Virginia University–Morgantown)
1998–2000 Sydney Cross (Clemson University, Clemson, South Carolina)
2000–02 Joe Sanders (University of Georgia–Athens)
2002–04 Greg Carter (Georgia Southern University–Statesboro)
2004–06 April Katz (Iowa State University–Ames)
2006–08 Anita Jung (Kansas City Art Institute, Kansas City, Missouri)
2008–10 Joseph Lupo (West Virginia University–Morgantown)
2010–12 Eun Lee (Savannah College of Art, Georgia)
2012–14 Beth Grabowski (University of North Carolina–Chapel Hill)
2014–16 David Jones, Columbia College Chicago, Chicago, Illinois
2016–18 Nicole Pietrantoni, Whitman College, Walla Walla, Washington[3]

Chapter 11

More Service to the Field

James Fowler Cooper and Alfred Hutty

As mentioned in chapter 1, Saunders's commitment to printmaking has gone beyond being a prolific printmaker and teaching printmaking at the university level for essentially forty years. He simultaneously created and shepherded an organization devoted to print connoisseurship and education (since 1972), which has now become the largest such organization in the world. That's impressive without going any further, but his service to the field has not stopped there. Saunders collaborated first with his multitalented wife, Stephanie, and later with author Ann McAden to produce catalogues documenting the lives and graphic art of two South Carolina artists who were active mostly in the first half of the twentieth century.

THE ETCHINGS OF JAMES FOWLER COOPER

The first effort was devoted to James Fowler Cooper in 1982 and the second to Alfred Hutty in 1990. Those two artists shared numerous similarities as longtime residents of South Carolina, for example working in black and white in both drawing and printmaking media. They also had direct and indirect ties respectively to farming and a special affinity or sensitivity for recording South Carolina lowcountry topography, the Atlantic coastline, and various subsistence occupations of people residing there. Both artists faithfully recorded Charleston-area architectural landmarks when the architectural preservation movement began in the 1930s. However in the twenty-first century Cooper and Hutty may be best remembered for their recording of the everyday lives of ordinary citizens and usually ordinary places.

Like Saunders, J. F. Cooper was reared on a farm less than ten miles east of Kingstree, South Carolina. Kingstree is the county seat of Williamsburg County and located about sixty miles north of Charleston, South Carolina, and about the same distance east of Myrtle Beach. Unlike Saunders, Cooper is said to have been shy and introverted but, unlike Saunders, was not interested in riding horses, hunting, or fishing. However, like Saunders, Cooper learned to read early and became a voracious reader despite living with astigmatism well into manhood.[1]

He entered the University of South Carolina at age seventeen, selected a double major in English and Latin, studied art, and was one of the first students to earn a certificate in art in that young program at USC. After graduating with honors in 1928, he traveled to New York, where he entered the Art Students' League. He took instruction from several teachers, but Boardman Robinson was likely his most important influence.[2] (Robinson is remembered for his 1932 mural *Man and His Toys* in the Radio City Music Hall at Rockefeller Center, New York City, and for his illustrations in new editions of *The Brothers Karamazov, The Idiot, King Lear, Moby Dick, Spoon River Anthology*, and *Leaves of Grass*.)[3] In the 1940s Cooper reflected on his Art Students' League instruction with the following comments: "I studied with Boardman Robinson and it was probably his emphasis on draftsmanship that induced me to try etching, a medium that demands drawing more than any other. It is probably the preoccupation with draftsmanship that explains my preference for black and white."[4]

James F. Cooper returned to his home in 1930 at his semi-invalid mother's request to help manage the family's farming interests. When that position failed to materialize, Cooper found employment in a Kingstree bank.[5] Concurrently Cooper resumed an active sketching regimen followed by a desire to learn etching, which coincided with a chance meeting with Alfred Hutty. The latter taught etching in Charleston during the winters, and Cooper sought at least some advice from him.[6] In addition Cooper faithfully consulted printed resources, in particular, one regarded as a kind of printmaker's bible at the time, that is, E. S. Lumsden's *The Art of Etching*.[7]

Though initially a novice technician of the craft, Cooper was not ignorant of the monumental figures in the history of printmaking. According to Saunders, Cooper, like many other printmakers before him, was strongly attracted to certain master printmakers from the past and especially Rembrandt and Goya.[8] In their works he seems to have been smitten by lighting effects featuring both strong lights and darks, and often with dark tonalities dominating a composition.[9] Such effects were rooted in paintings by Michelangelo Merisi (known as Caravaggio [1573–1610]) in Italy mostly during the first decade of the 1600s. The dark values dominating his compositions just as often included a dramatic shaft of light from an unknown source. Art historians later termed that treatment *tenebrism* or the dark manner. Many later artists mastered it in paintings and prints particularly when using aquatint or mezzotint approaches. Tenebrism can readily be seen in two of Cooper's etchings reproduced in the Cooper book: *Woods Fire* and *Sausage Tomorrow*.[10] These two pieces reflect Cooper's mastery of etching and exploration of the supplemental techniques of soft ground and aquatint.

In 1932 Cooper's mother, Mary, died following a major heart attack. Seven years earlier a weakened heart had already rendered her a semi-invalid. Cooper grieved practically to the point of being inconsolable.[11] When he recovered, he was a changed person. For most of his youth and young manhood, Cooper had not been interested in farming. His mother had requested that he return home in 1930 to manage her part of the family's land holdings, but when he arrived she informed him that he was essentially ill prepared to do so.[12] Now resolute, Cooper decided to make his family's farm once again viable. He read extensively, became informed of the latest agribusiness techniques, methodically embraced them, and completely turned around the fortunes of the farm by efficiently and wisely growing cotton and tobacco without depleting the soil.[13]

Somehow Cooper found time to also create prints and was just as thorough and focused as he was when managing his new agricultural interests. Saunders described it this way: "Cooper's approach to etching was scholarly, intellectual, and traditional. He did not seem to be compelled to try to stretch the technical boundaries of the medium to new limits nor to define new directions of stylistic evolution. In fact, he was not greatly taken by the new directions coming into vogue. He seemed to feel, rather, that the art form was, just as he had inherited it, quite adequate to his needs. His work on his plates was painstaking and exacting and, as with music [he played the violin and was a choir director], he belabored much over subtleties and nuances that another [etcher] would have scarcely noticed. Each image was always worked out in one or more complete sketches before being committed to the copper [plate] and if, in retrospect, it was not completely to his liking, the image might be rethought, redrawn, and reprinted from another plate."[14]

One might think that from such professionalism and self-imposed high standards of technique Cooper would have been eager to seek one or several dealers and to regularly to send his prints to competitive exhibitions in major cities. After studying Cooper's life and visual work, Saunders sensed that the answers rather may lie in the artist's character, notably the traits of modesty and honesty: "Cooper grew up in a culture that put a very high value on modesty, and the reticence that was natural to him, was intensified by the social values he was accustomed to. He simply could not openly and actively promote and publicize an aspect of himself as personal and intimate as his art."[15] "He chose instead to attempt to give visual form to a way of life that he knew and loved best. All of his work speaks eloquently with the authority of first-hand experience, profound knowledge of the subject, and deeply felt conviction. There is no doubt that his work is a faithful chronicle of a particular time and place, but close examination shows it to be also a poetic and sensitive visualization of his response to that subject. The key factor seems to be honesty. There is no pandering to popular preconceptions or clichés, no manipulation of dramatic effect for its own sake. All of his work is informed by an unsentimental love of the land, a love that humbly accepts and rejoices in reality. His African-American neighbors are known and respected, without condescension; his white neighbors and kin are presented honestly and sensitively, with no attempt either to sanctify them or to mock them. His work became less a matter of public declaration and more and more a matter of private reflection."[16]

The catalog represents the body of the Cooper book and is composed of black-and-white reproductions of ninety-two of the artist's etchings. The text of the introduction is interspersed with reproductions of eleven Cooper drawings. Boyd Saunders and his artisan friends at Hubris Press cleaned and restored the copper etching plates and printed a small number of restrikes from them. For identification purposes the impressions were stamped with an estate signature and title appropriately.[17] Said Saunders, "It may never be possible to establish a chronology of Cooper's works. He did not date his prints, and he very rarely numbered them. It sometimes took him several years to complete a plate, [while] others [were] started and finished in the interim, and he usually printed only a few proofs at a time as the need arose. Exhibit records give us some approximate guidelines, of course, but we do not have complete information about which prints were shown to the public or when they were shown. We have included in this book all the prints we have been able to find that Cooper indicated his approval by signing them or that he is known to have shown in public exhibitions. We included some prints simply because we found them irresistible, but with a few exceptions, we have excluded those that Cooper seems to have regarded as unsuccessful or incomplete experiments."[18]

The cataloged prints have been arranged into sections of general relatedness in subject and points of Cooper's career. A selection of those works and Saunders's comments for them follow next.

AROUND HOME

"Twenty-four prints in this section reflect what Cooper saw around him on his family's farm, on the road and in the fields of Williamsburg County. They seem to have been etched in the 1930s."[19]

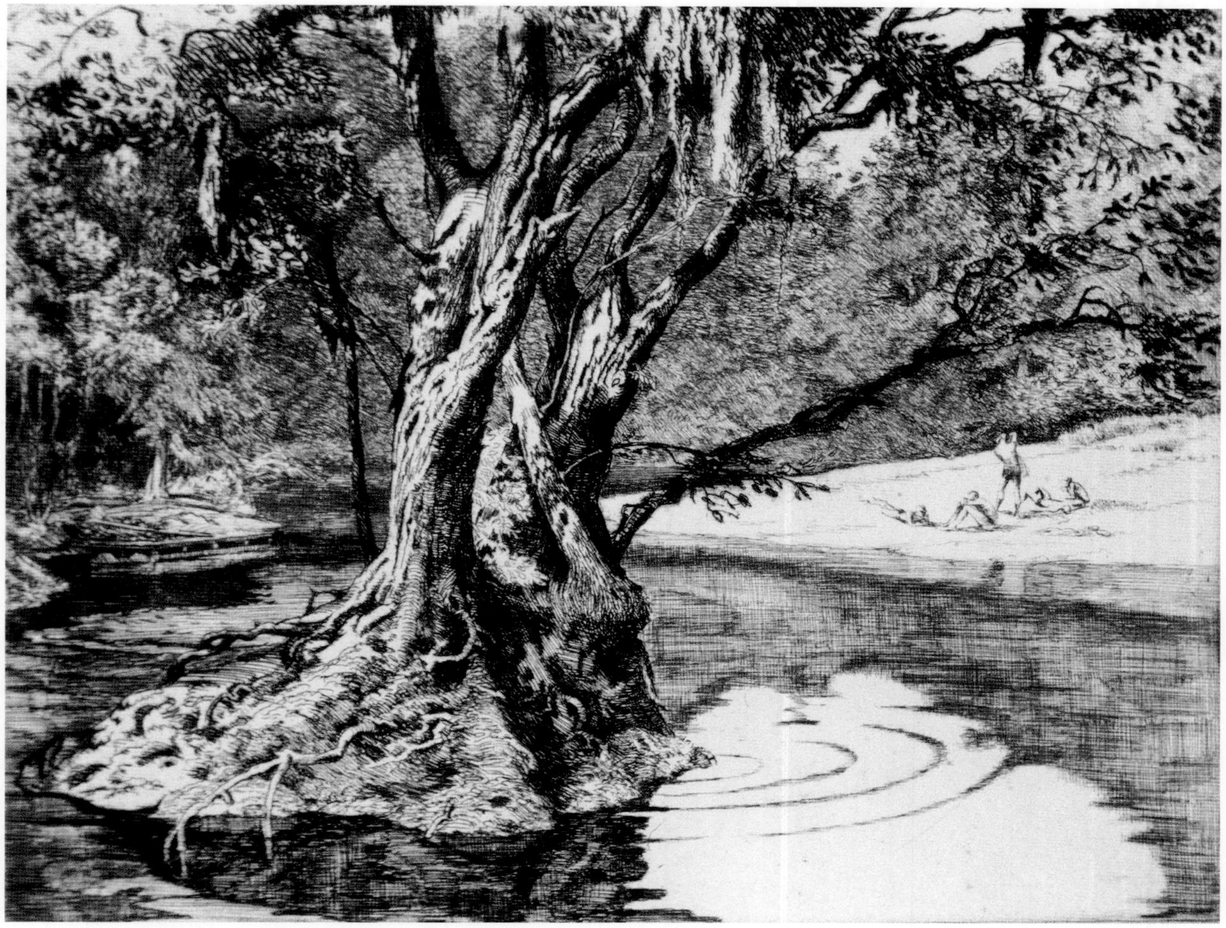

James Fowler Cooper, *Swimming Hole at Scout Cabin,* etching

Swimming Hole at Scout Cabin "This swimming hole was on the Black River, just outside Kingstree, and was where young people learned to swim."[20]

Princess Anne of the House of Flatter "This is Ann Preston, the quiet introspective daughter of a neighboring family. She invented many fantasies and sometimes acted them out, referring to herself as 'Princess Ann of the House of Flatter.' Having been a quiet, introspective, book-reading child himself, Cooper clearly liked and understood her."[21]

Woods Fire "This is one of Cooper's most ambitious and crowded prints. His notebooks contain many preliminary sketches not only for this scene but also for minute details of it (such as the fleeing rabbit). It is one of many in which he exploited the etching process to depict light in highly theatrical ways."[22]

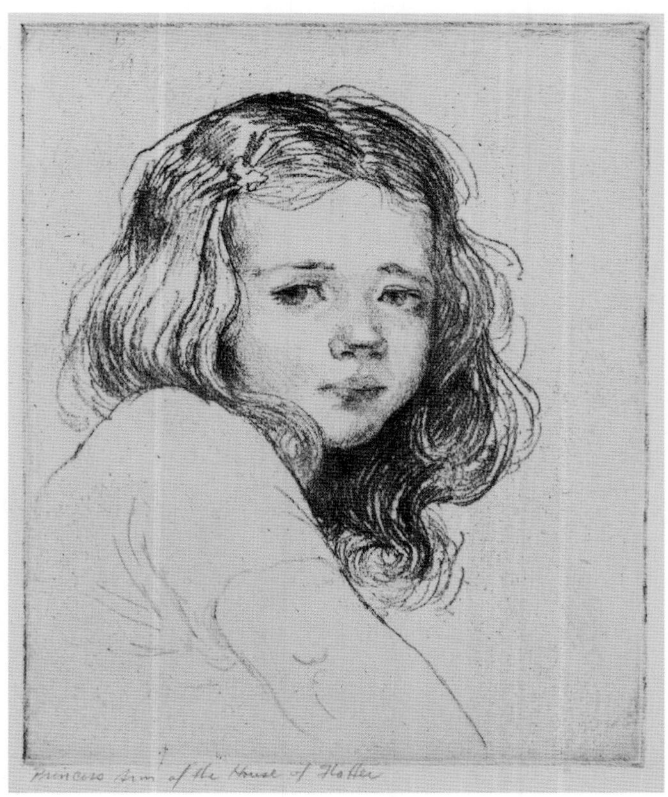

James Fowler Cooper, *Princess Anne of the House of Flatter,* etching

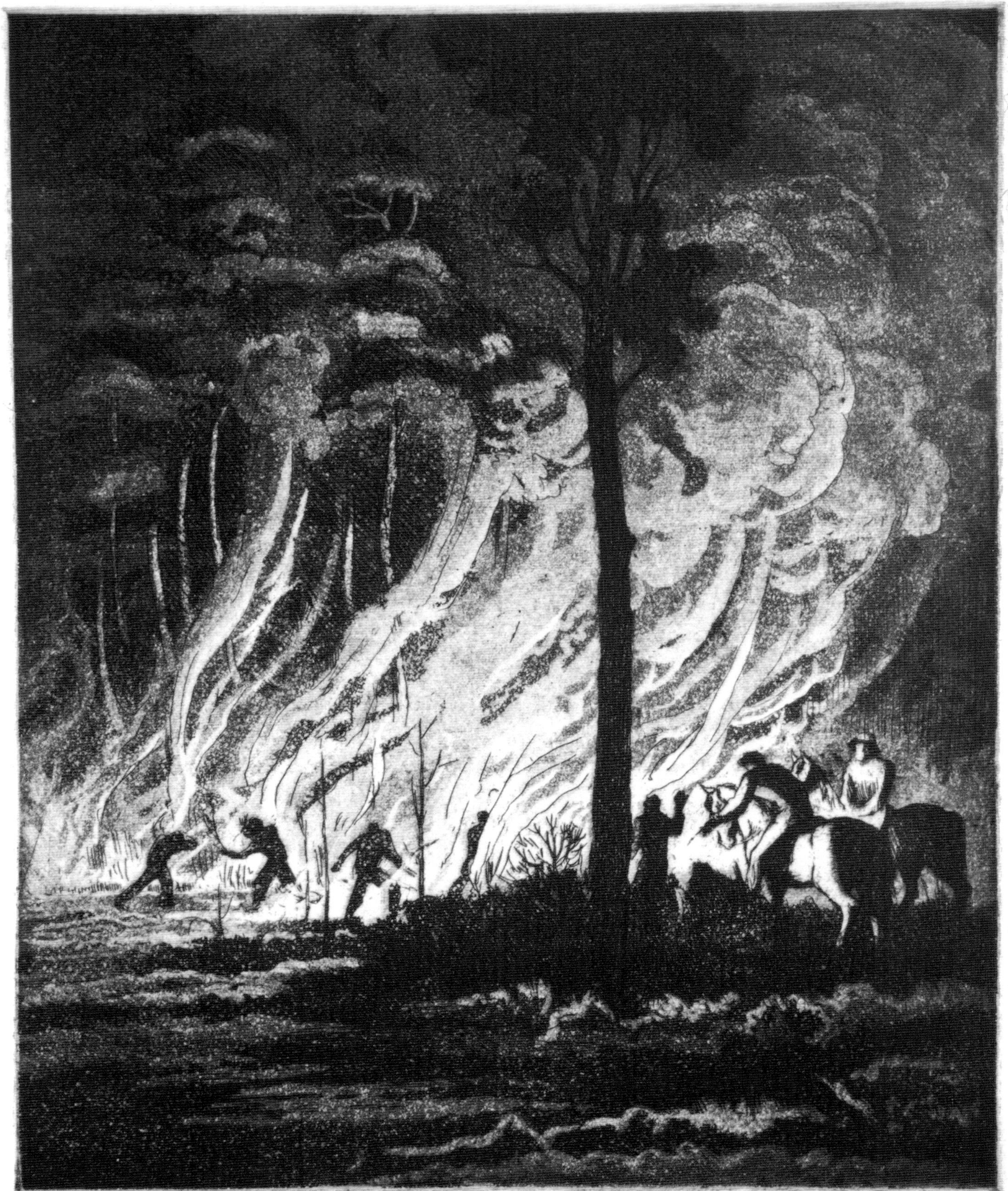

James Fowler Cooper, *Woods Fire*, etching

Waiting "The waiting is for death. John Cooper had cancer of the colon and had undergone a colostomy. Feeling himself to be socially unacceptable, he had withdrawn to his house to wait for death with a dignity the artist found impressive. *Waiting* was the artist's title but this print is frequently and affectionately referred to locally as Daddy John."[23]

Daddy John's Place "John Cooper, known as 'Daddy John' is said to have spent his entire life residing on and working for the farms of Tom M. Cooper, near the community of Fowler in Williamsburg County. When a good crop made additional storage space necessary, another corncrib was constructed, with the result that we can hardly see the house for the outbuildings. The artist [James Fowler Cooper] said

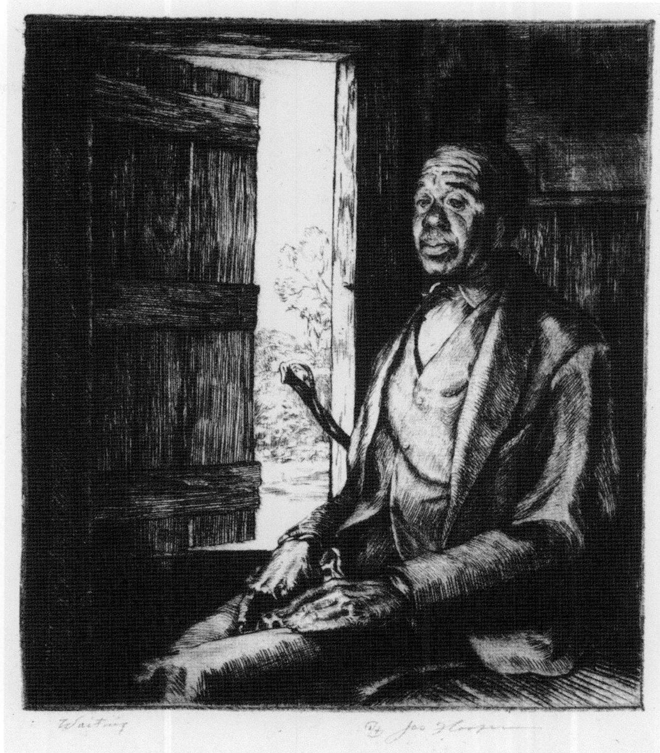

James Fowler Cooper, *Waiting*, etching

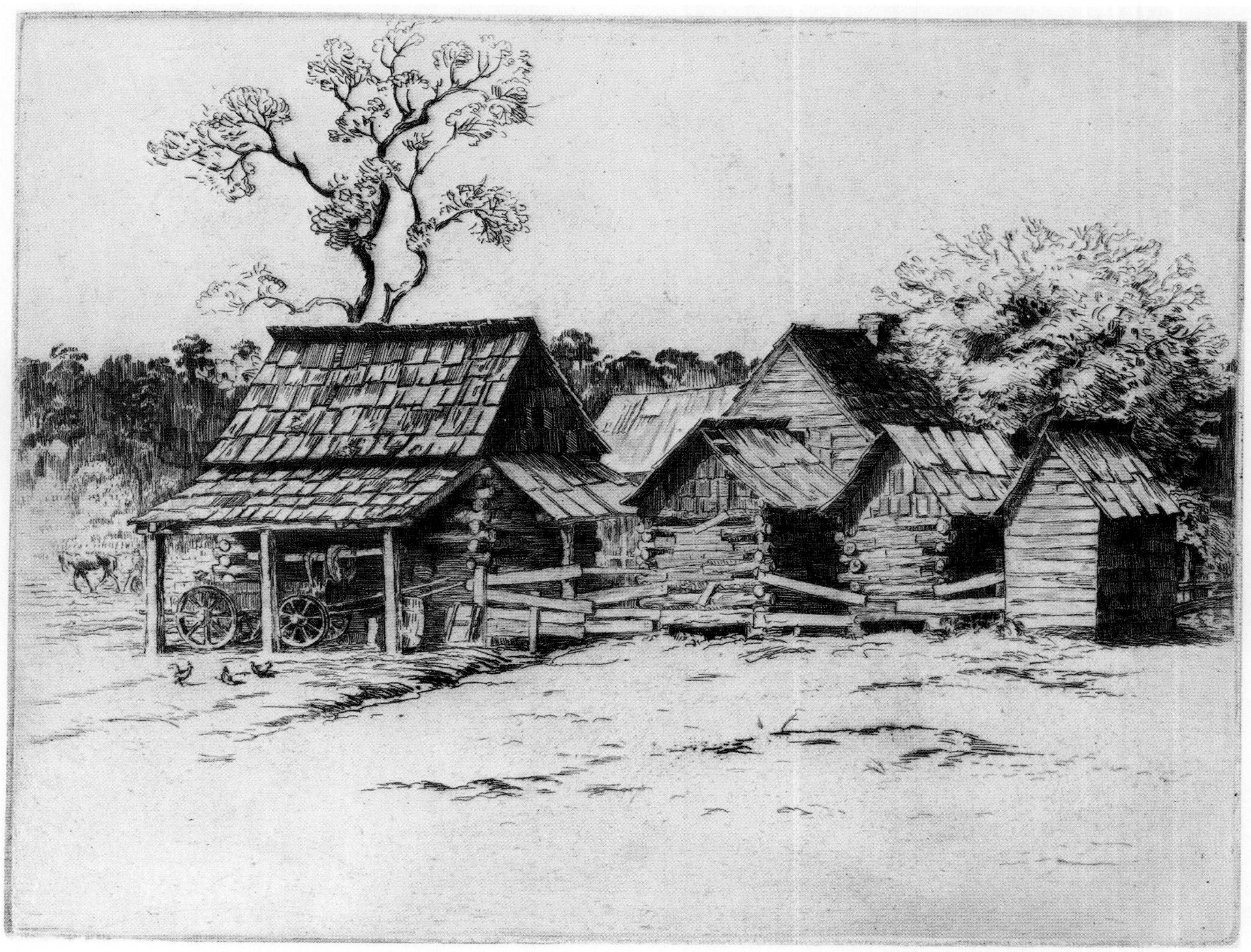

James Fowler Cooper, *Daddy John's Place*, etching

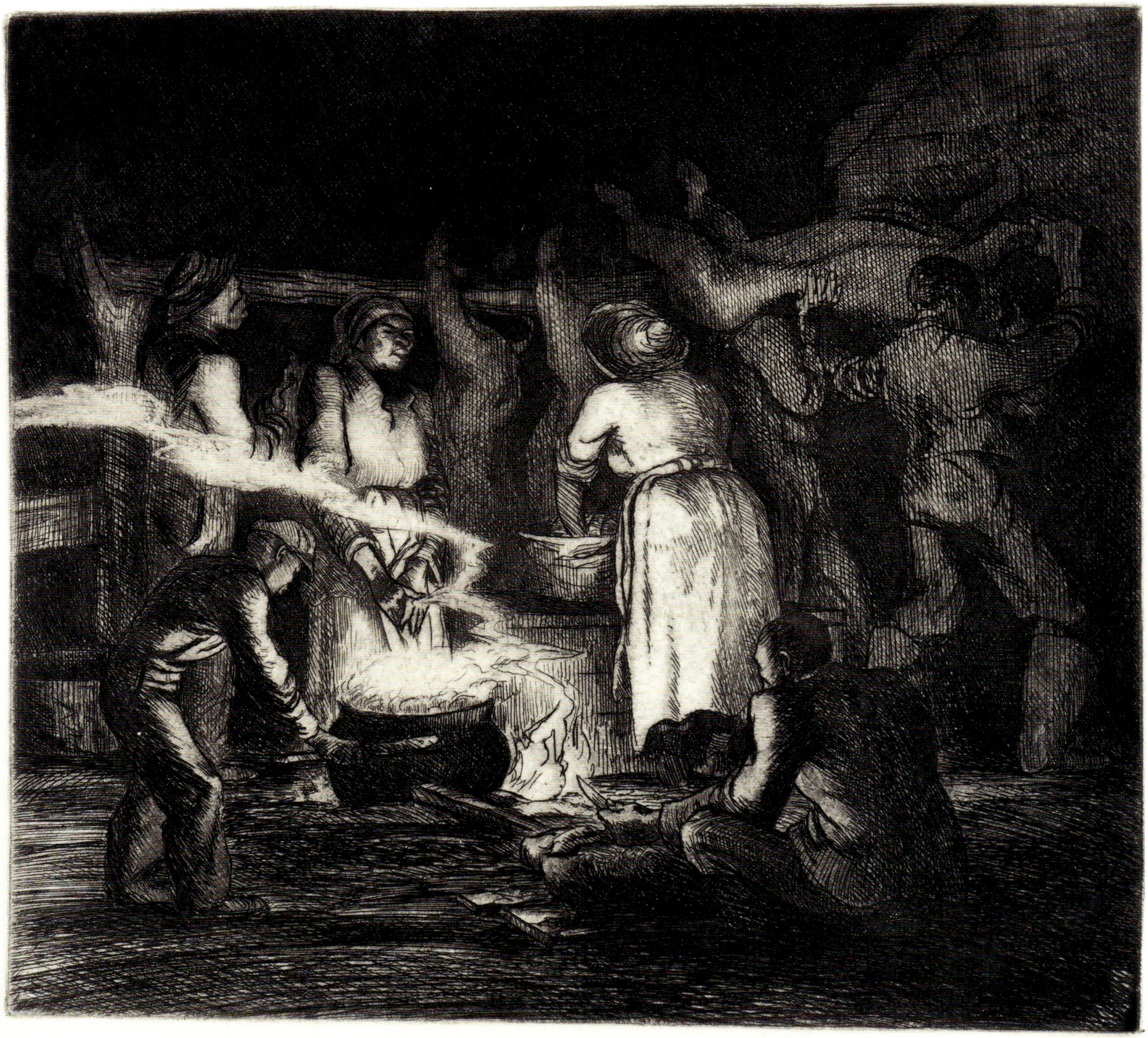

James Fowler Cooper, *Sausage Tomorrow,* etching

that Daddy John's place reminded him of the old hymn, *Build Me More Stately Mansions, Oh, My Soul.* Notice the man plowing with a mule in the field behind and to the left of the house. Daddy John's home is surrounded by work."[24]

Sausage Tomorrow The butchering of hogs was an immensely important event on the southern farm, producing lard and several kinds of meat.[25] Hog killing in the rural South takes on many aspects of both a pageant and a festival. It is an annual group activity involving many people, much preparation, and unusual types of work, and it frequently runs well into the night. With the chill snap of autumn air and the cooking fires, it becomes a very dramatic occasion.[26] The fact that the process could be observed at night gave the artist a wonderful opportunity to exploit the light of the fire for dramatic effect. The artist-farmer was very impressed with the ceremonial aspects of hog butchering, and his preparatory sketches for this etching are of considerable interest.

"It [this work] seems to have been his most frequently exhibited print, having been shown in 1939 at the National Arts Club in New York (24th Annual Exhibition of the Society of American Etchers, Inc.), at the University of South Carolina, in 1940, in New York again, in the (One Hundred Prints and 25 Miniature Prints from the 25th Annual Exhibition of the Society of American Etchers), in 1941 in Shreveport, Louisiana (21st Annual Exhibition of the Southern States League), in the Ferargil Gallery, New York, and in 1942 at the Metropolitan Museum of Art in New York (*Artists for Victory: An Exhibition of Contemporary American Art*).[27]

Maum Nellie "She is unfathomably old and majestic and African American. The rich articulation of her gnarled hands and wrinkled face contrast strikingly with the shapeless mass of clothing that covers her body. Her name is Nellie Myers, but she was called Maum Nellie for longer than anyone can remember. Among her talents she was a midwife, and for years she raised any child who was unwanted by its parents.[28] She is said to have raised fifteen such children.[29]

"The entire etching is no more than 4 × 5 inches and very unassuming in its presentation, but by its drama, simplicity of statement, and refinement of line, it achieves a sense of monumentality that is rare even in works many times its size. She is one of the characters who peopled the gentle world of James Fowler Cooper."[30]

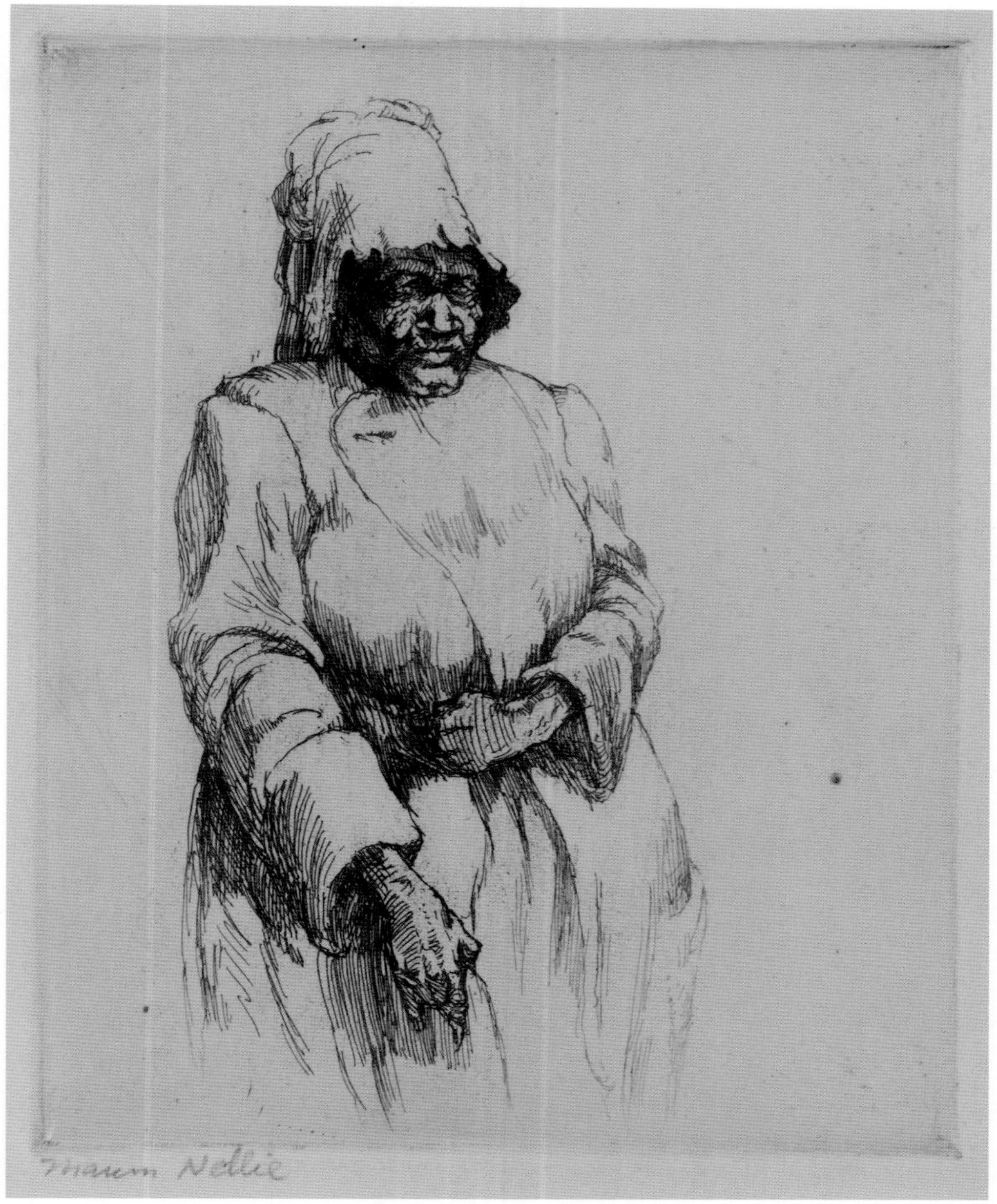

James Fowler Cooper, *Maum Nellie,* etching

THE LOWCOUNTRY

"There are fifteen prints in this group in which Cooper extended his gaze to the South Carolina coastline, especially the area around Murrells Inlet, and to the general atmosphere of the Lowcountry, which may

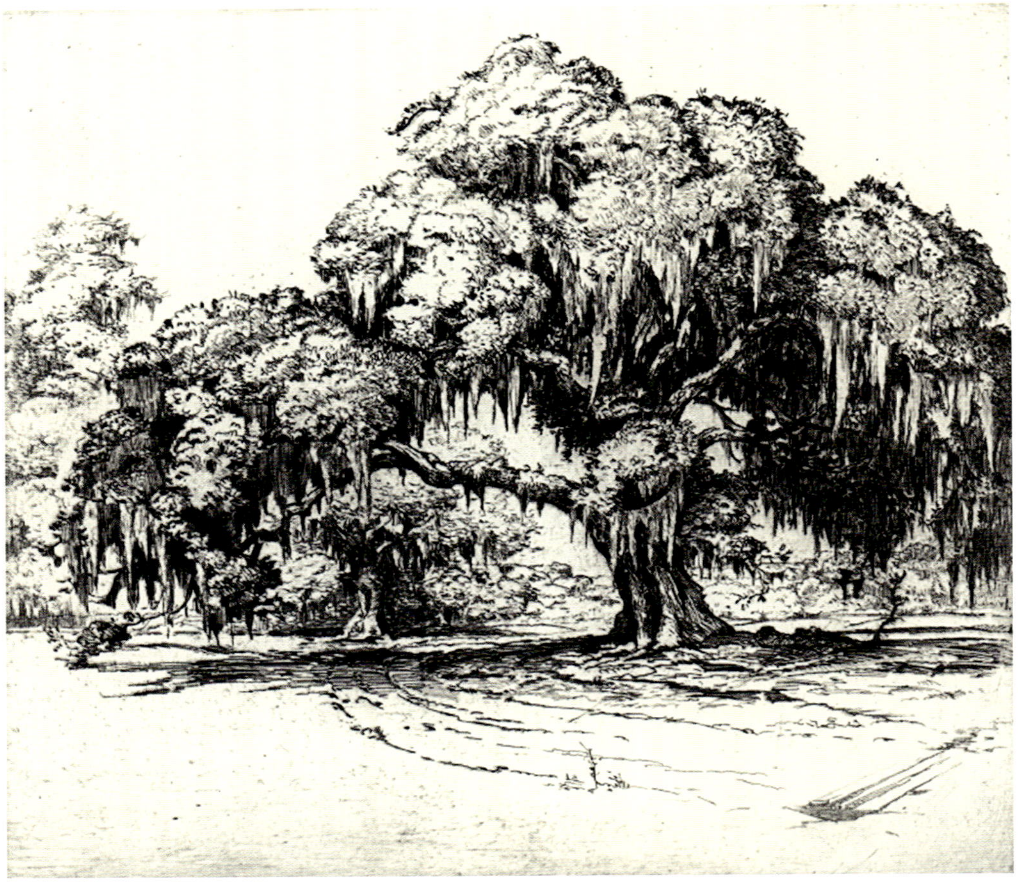

be regarded as a sort of boundary. No South Carolinian would apply the term 'Lowcountry' to any place north or west of Stateburg. The prints seem to date from the 1930s."[31]

Live Oak "A magisterial portrait of a magisterial tree. The live oaks of the South Carolina Lowcountry provided the extraordinarily tough timbers, exported through Charleston, of which the ship hulls of the British Navy were built in the Eighteenth Century."[32]

Murrells Inlet #2 "This is a glimpse of the quiet fishing port that is Murrells Inlet. Of all his Lowcountry landscapes this is the most complex and the most ambitious spatially."[33]

Still Waters "This impression was reproduced from a posthumous print. On the log there are two turtles, of the kind called 'cooters' in South Carolina, and a snake."[34]

James Fowler Cooper, *Live Oak,* etching

James Fowler Cooper, *Murrells Inlet #2,* etching

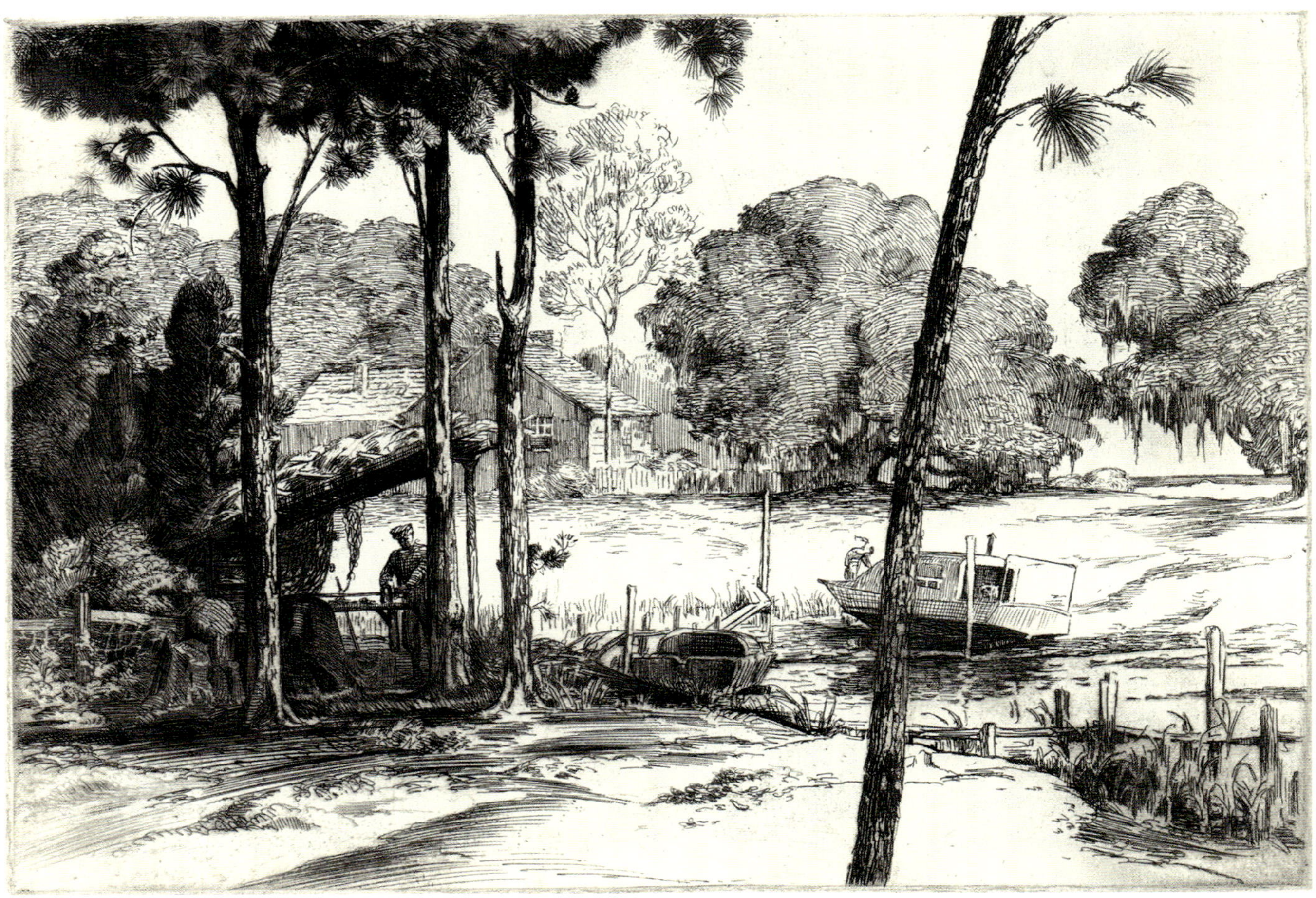

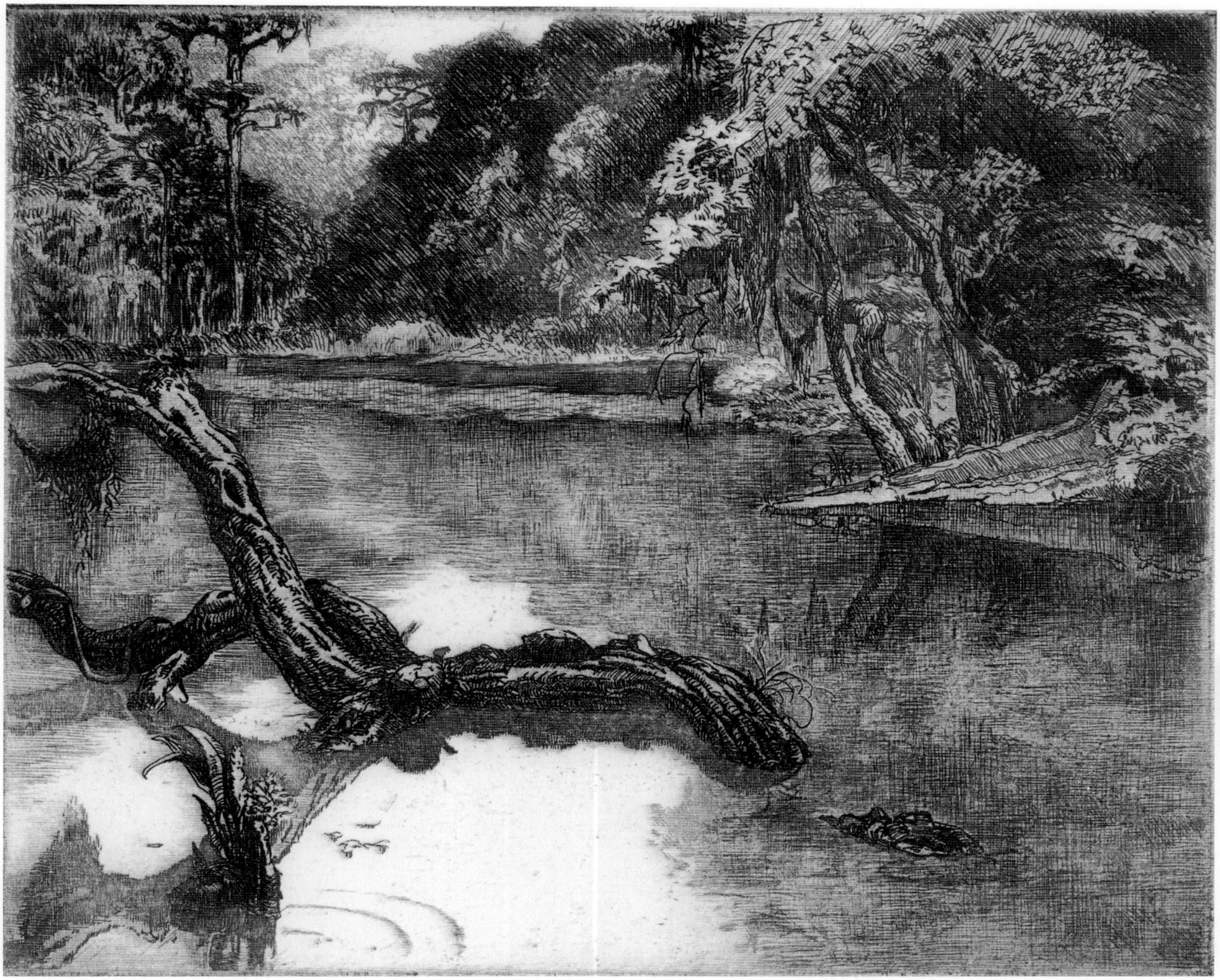

James Fowler Cooper, *Still Waters,* etching

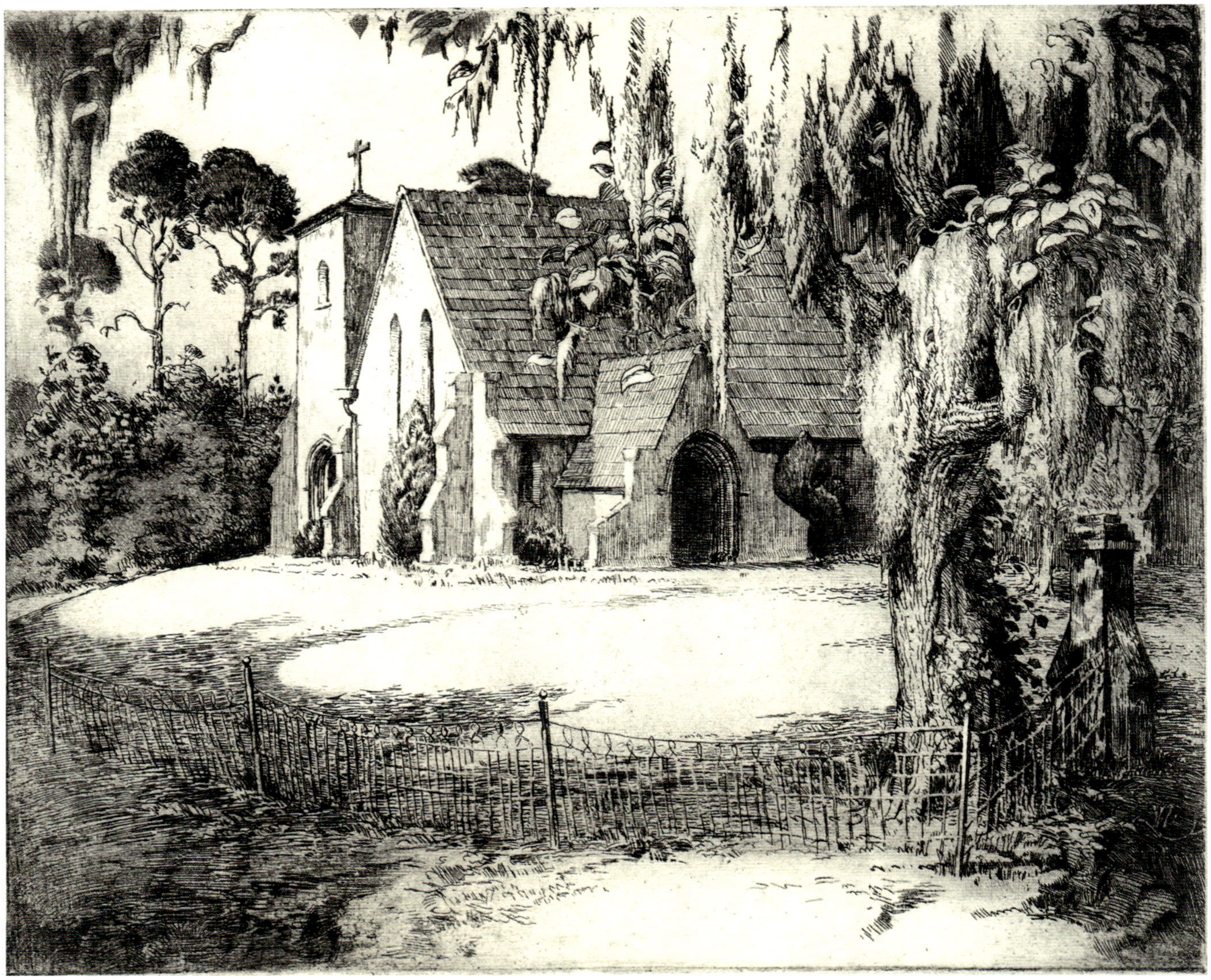

James Fowler Cooper, *The Church of the Holy Cross,* etching

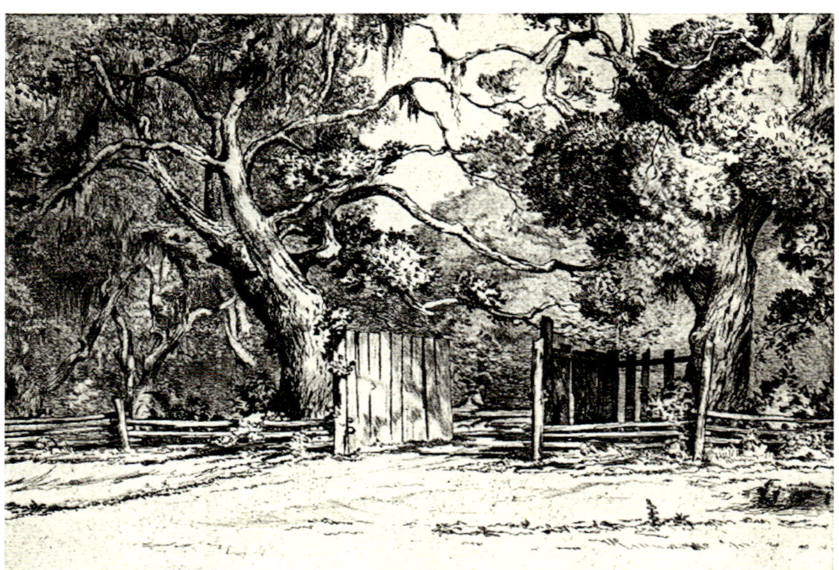

James Fowler Cooper, *Andante,* etching

The Church of the Holy Cross "This is the Episcopal Church at Stateburg in Sumter County. Restored in the 1970s, it now looks different from Cooper's view of it. It is built of rammed earth ('pise de terre') and is the westernmost site Cooper ever etched. He would have passed close to it when he traveled between Kingtree and Columbia."[35]

GEORGETOWN, BROOKGREEN GARDENS, AND THE BANKS OF THE WACCAMAW

"The Waccamaw is a Lowcountry river that drains the swamplands of Southeastern North Carolina, flowing slowly south until it joins the PeeDee and the Black

River in forming Winyah Bay, on which sits the old picturesque port of Georgetown. Brookgreen Gardens is an extraordinary outdoor museum for the exhibition of sculpture, established by Archer M. Huntington and his wife, Anna Hyatt. It opened to the public in 1931."[36]

Andante "It is said that this scene was in the neighborhood of an old rice plantation on the banks of the Waccamaw, although with its sweeping breadth of vision, it resembles many places in the Lowcountry. Monumental and lyric, this print is one of Cooper's most complete statements and may be regarded as a landmark in his career. 'Andante' is the musical direction meaning 'moderately slow,' the literal meaning of the Italian word being "walking."[37]

Prince George Winyah "This Episcopal Church in Georgetown opened August 16, 1747. There are four different views of this church by Cooper in this catalog, pages 50–53. The subject evidently intrigued him [Cooper] and this image is 'a strong and direct portrait' of the church."[38]

CHARLESTON AND MIDDLETON PLACE

"Williamsburg County looked to Charleston when it sought a metropolis. These scenes from the proud and colorful city are not his only Charleston studies. There is an impressive sketch of the facade of the Huguenot Church in his notebooks, for instance. The artist may have deliberately avoided Charleston subjects that other etchers had already treated."[39]

The Battery "The Battery is the name now given to the famous seawall at the southern tip of the peninsula. It literally protects a small park by the same name which is surrounded on at least two sides by some of Charleston's most elegant 'single' and 'double houses' from the 1700s and 1800s. It offers magnificent views of the harbor which the artist [Cooper] idiosyncratically ignores, preferring to contrast the concrete regularity of the stonework to the almost transparent ethereality of the ship in the background. That four-masted schooner was about to be superseded by the technology of the twentieth century."[40]

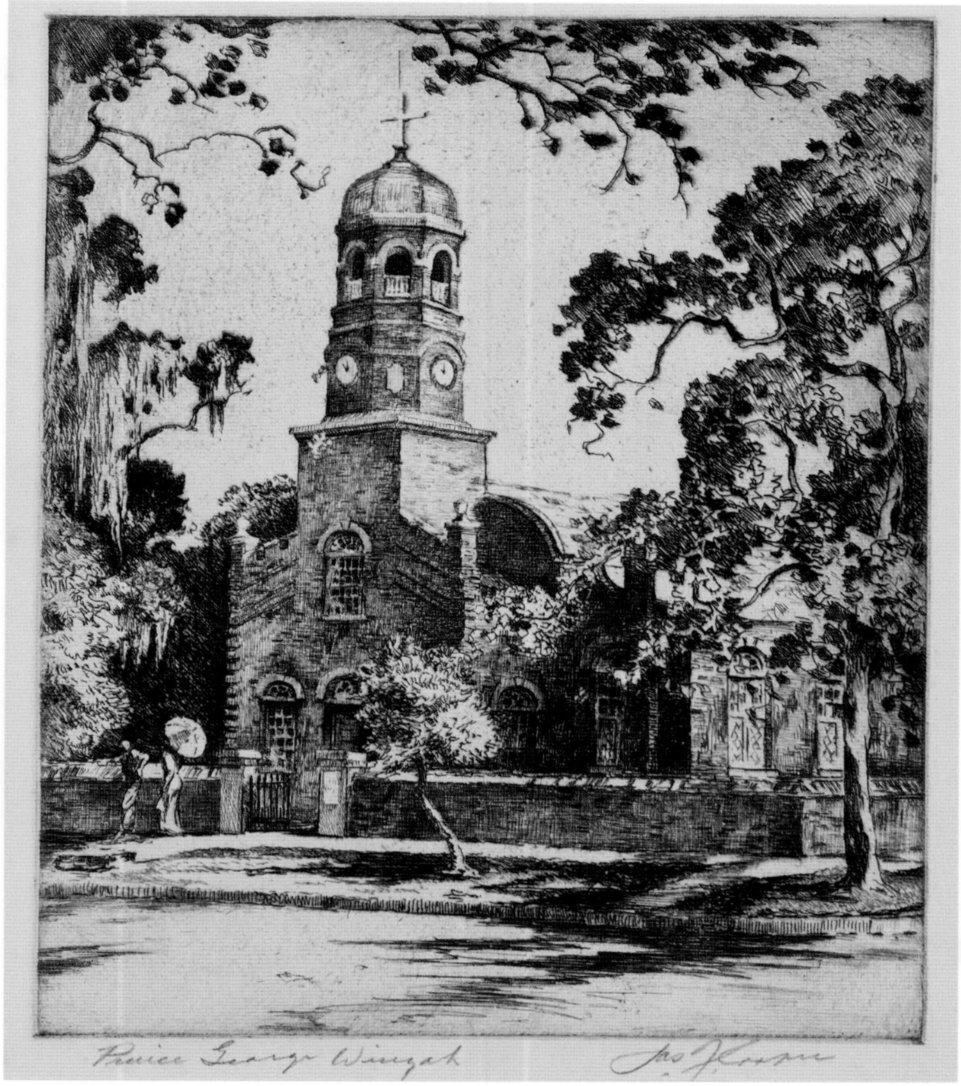

James Fowler Cooper, *Prince George Winyah,* etching

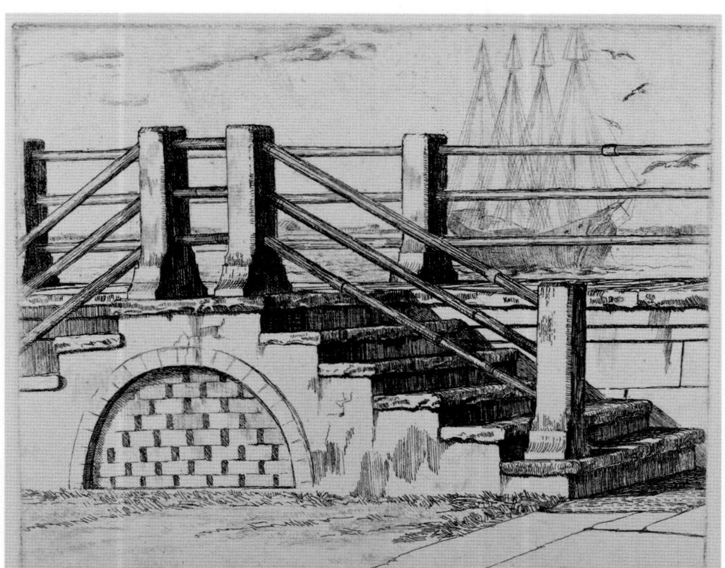

James Fowler Cooper, *The Battery,* etching. Collection of McKissick Museum, University of South Carolina, Columbia

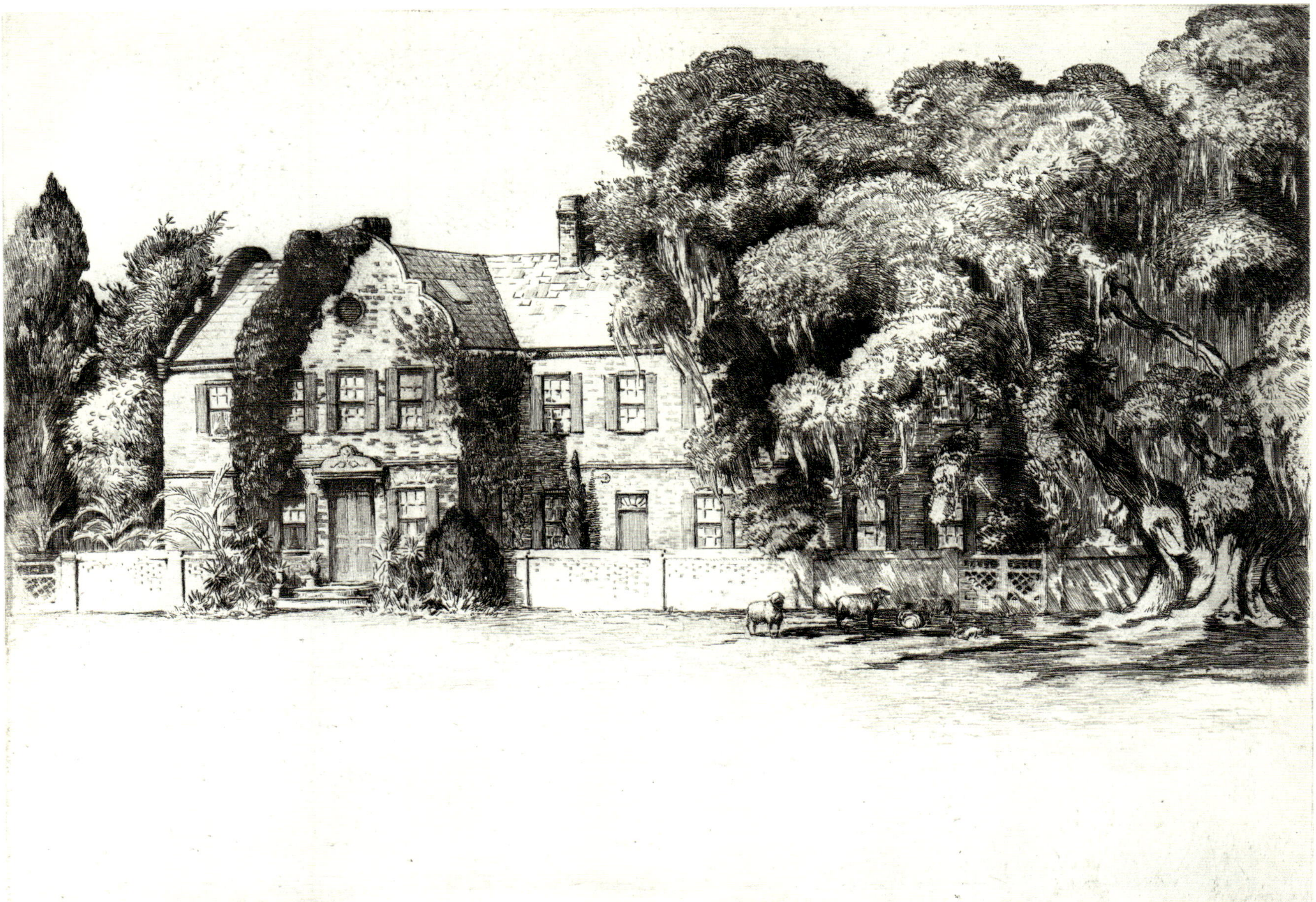

James Fowler Cooper,
Middleton Place (Entrance),
etching

MIDDLETON PLACE

"The home at Middleton Place was built about 1741 on the right bank of the Ashley River a few miles northwest of Charleston. The north and south wings were added in 1755. Its famous garden is said to be the first landscaped garden in the United States. Cooper was apparently fond of visiting the garden and the reconstructed south wing, the rest of the house having been destroyed by Union Troops and by the earthquake of 1886."[41]

Middleton Place (Entrance) "This was the largest plate the artist ever printed and one of only three it was necessary to reduce for reproduction in this book."[42]

PAWLEYS (ISLAND) AND PEOPLE

Nineteen prints make up a miscellany of both early and relatively late work. Pawleys Island is a very casual, sociable but uncrowded place where most people have known each other for a long time. Most of the unpretentious houses on the beach are owned by people who live and work inland and come to the island in the summer.[43] In 1936 Cooper bought land on the ocean side of Pawleys Island. The Coopers were

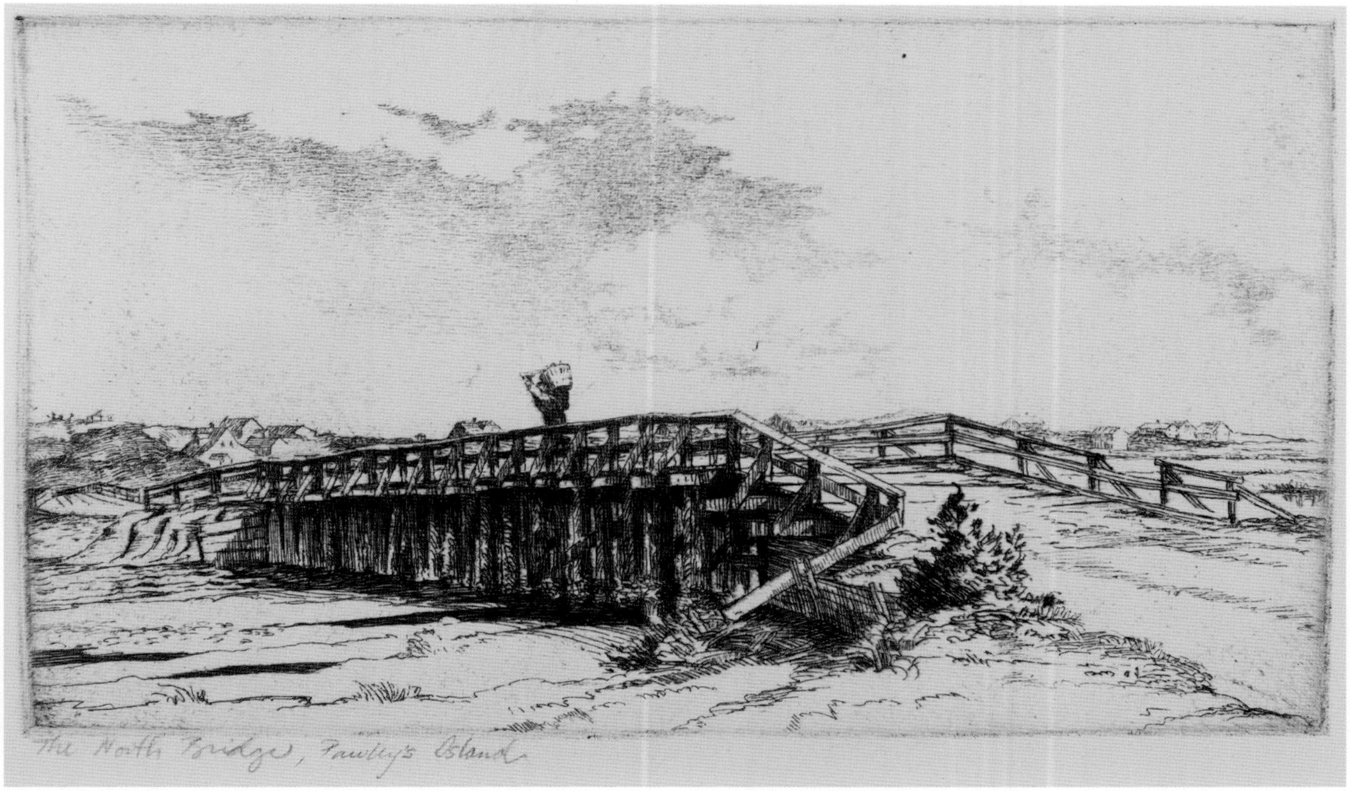

James Fowler Cooper, *The North Bridge, Pawleys Island*, etching

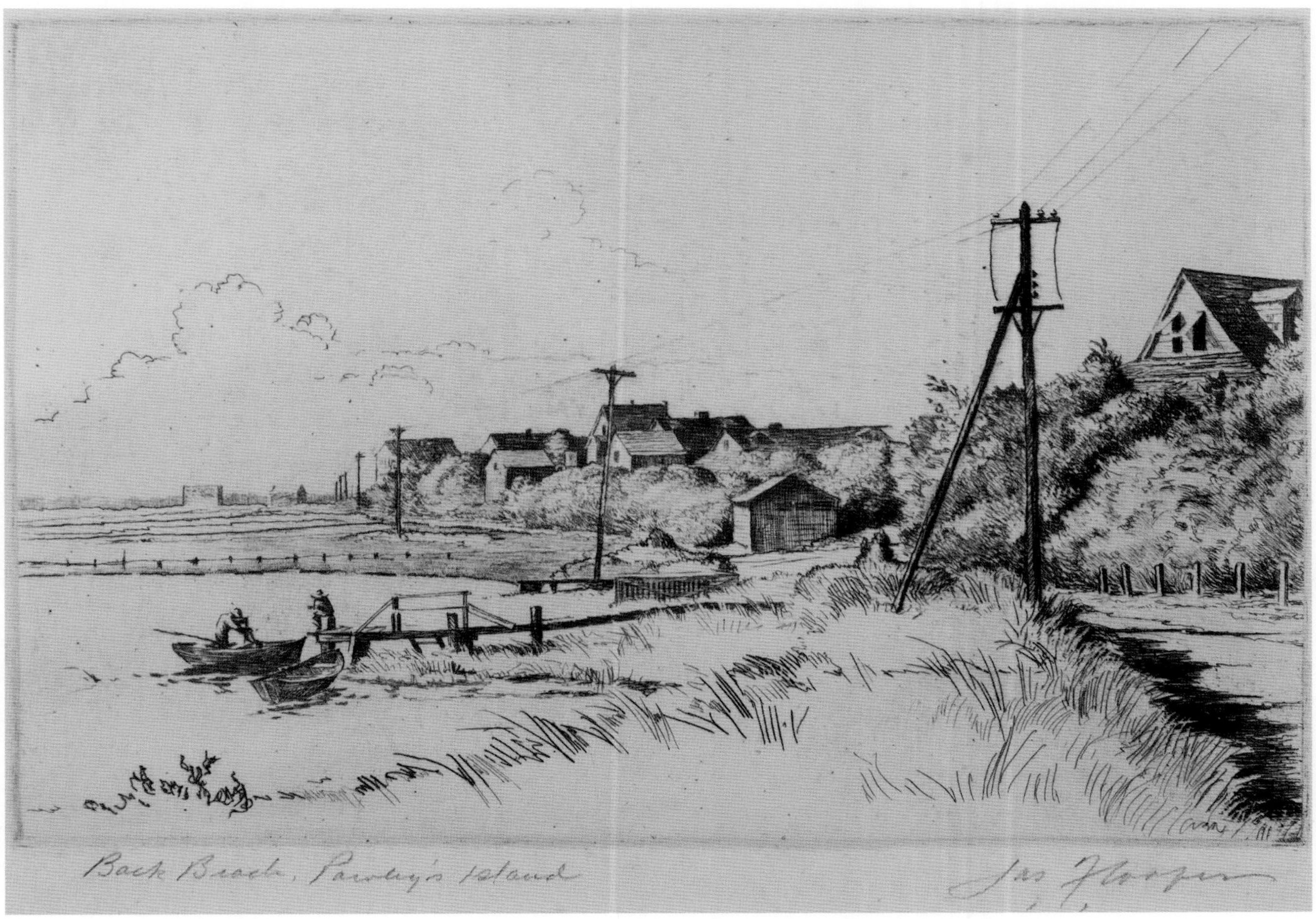

James Fowler Cooper, *Back Beach, Pawleys Island*, etching

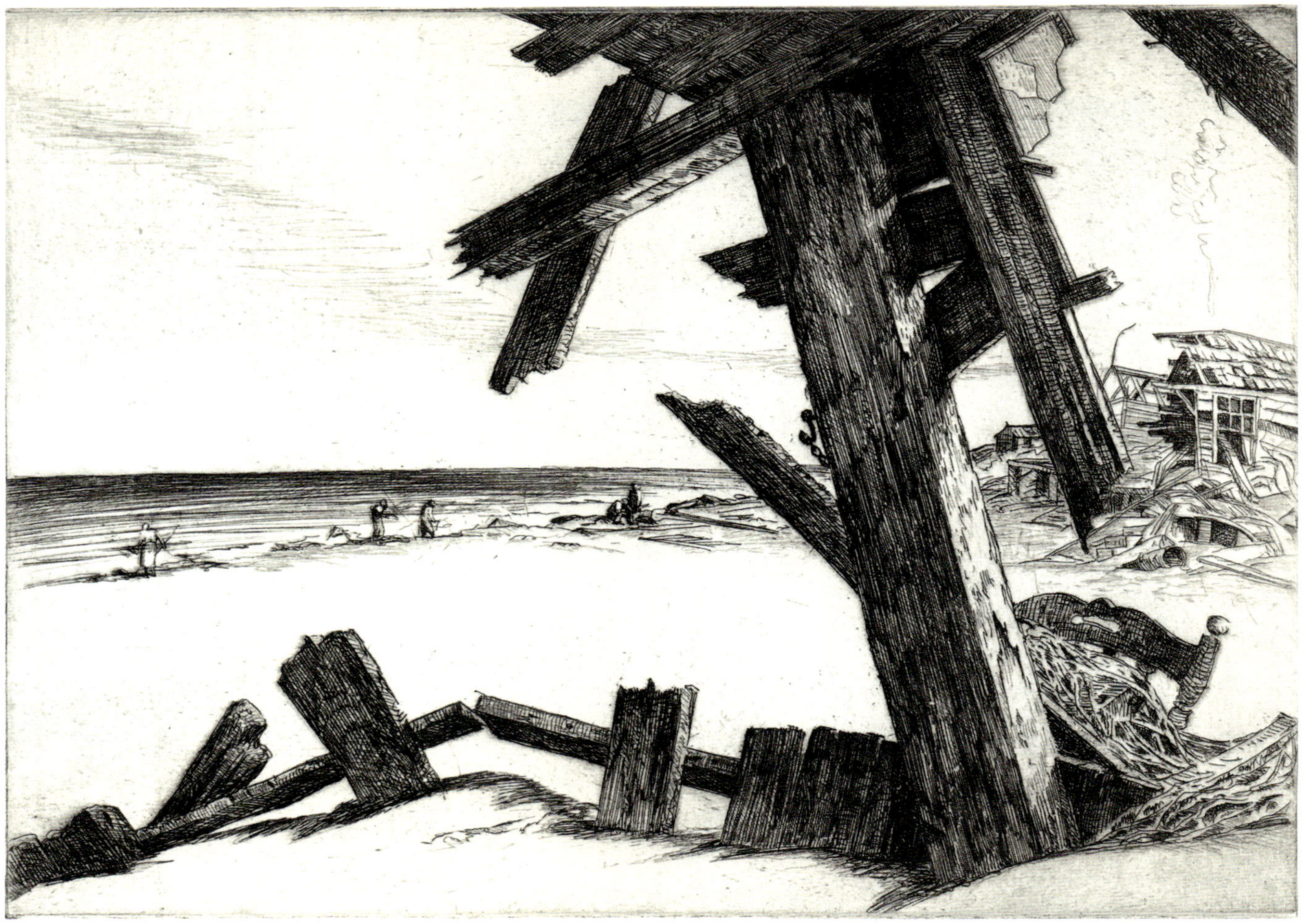

James Fowler Cooper, *Aftermath,* etching

expected to be one of the families that had a place on Pawleys. Cooper designed a beach house, and it was built by a carpenter and his son who worked for small wages and groceries. It was then whitewashed with brushes made from pine needles. That beach house is still a very sturdy, graceful, and functional structure. [44]

The North Bridge, Pawleys Island "The refinement of draftsmanship and subtlety of bite are remarkable and result in jewel-like elegance. Notice again those technical abilities in the overshadowed supporting poles [or pylons] under the bridge, in whose structure he shows almost the kind of interest an engineer might take."[45]

Back Beach, Pawleys Island "This work reflects a skillfully measured depth of implied space."[46]

Aftermath "This depicts the beach at Pawleys after it had been hit by Hurricane Hazel in October 1954. The five people at the water's edge are like ghosts."[47]

ALFRED HUTTY AND THE CHARLESTON RENAISSANCE

The above work represents Boyd Saunders's second book project aimed at preserving the life and art in the prints of an accomplished printmaker who lived in, and documented, or interpreted aspects of South Carolina's topography, architecture, and common folk. The Hutty catalog also marks the second collaborative authorship for Saunders, this time with the writer Ann McAden.

Alfred Hutty was born in Grand Haven, Michigan, on September 16, 1877. Grand Haven, said to be essentially a village at the time, whose inhabitants worked in logging and lumber enterprises, is a short distance south of Muskegon on the eastern shore of Lake Michigan.[48] Seeking other opportunities his family moved west, first to Kansas City, Missouri, and then northwest to Leavenworth, Kansas. The latter has been described as a frontier town in the 1880s and a rough or difficult place for young Hutty to grow up.[49]

In 1892 a Leavenworth public school awarded Hutty a scholarship to the St. Louis School of Fine Arts for producing the winning drawing, that is, "the most original drawing," in a competition. At the St. Louis school, Hutty benefited from more professional instruction and from being around more advanced students, some of whom were able to study further in Europe.[50] However apparently Hutty's scholarship was insufficient to cover all his living expenses. He left St. Louis and moved west again to Kansas City, where he found employment as a designer and painter in a studio that produced stained glass, especially figure and landscape windows.[51]

Ten years later Hutty married Bessie Burris Crafton from Liberty, Missouri, and he was working again in St. Louis in the same field as he had prior in Kansas City. Hutty thoroughly enjoyed all aspects of the stained glass technique at the St. Louis firm, but after attending a large exhibition of paintings there by East Coast painter Lowell Birge Harrison, he began to yearn to be a painter.[52] Hutty was twenty-seven and not at all settled. Nevertheless he was determined to travel to New York State (which he did) and enroll in a summer school for landscape painting taught by Harrison himself. That summer school was a new feature of the well-known New York Art Students' League but was located north of New York City in the Woodstock community. After just two months there, in 1907 Hutty boldly declared that he would spend the rest of his life as a painter . . . maybe forgetting he had a family for which to provide. Then reality struck, and he went south to New York City looking for part-time work. He later recalled: "We had not quite $300. I tried all the places where there might be stained glass work, but no luck. They almost convinced me that no one from the Middle West could possibly be any good."[53]

Then Hutty's luck turned thanks to a chance encounter. One day he walked by Tiffany's and stopped to look into the display windows at the large Roosevelt stained glass window that would later be placed in the chapel of the West Point Military Academy.[54] "I stopped to look at it. A man came up behind me and said, what do you think of it? It's not very good, I said. Do you know anything about stained glass? Why isn't it good, asked the stranger? In his reply Hutty explained his ideas about the technique used and was amazed to find that he had talked himself into a job with [the famous] Tiffany Glass Studios. For the next ten years he lived in Woodstock, did stained glass work on a commission basis, studied at the Art Students League and painted."[55]

In those ten years the Huttys purchased a farm in the Woodstock area, which they named Broadview, and converted one of its two barns into the "Studio on the Hill."[56] Hutty was enjoying increasing success exhibiting his paintings in many galleries and once again dreamed of painting full time, but once again he was thwarted when, in 1917, America entered World War I. Hutty, along with several other artists, painted camouflage patterns on U.S. Navy vessels for two years.[57]

Alfred Hutty's connection with Charleston, South Carolina, began in 1919 after the end of hostilities in Europe. Hutty, then forty-two, set out by train for Florida seeking a warm winter climate in which to paint and accidently found a South Carolina seaport much to his liking. Excitedly he telegraphed his wife in Woodstock of his discovery: "Come quickly, have found heaven!"[58]

In addition to his first short walking expedition, Hutty had the good fortune to meet members of the Carolina Art Association who invited him to teach at the Gibbes Art Memorial Art Gallery. "Since I had no preconceived idea of Charleston, and having seen no pictures of it at any time, knowing little, if anything, of its history or traditions, it was with open vision that I first beheld its quaintness and beauty and tested the full charm of its old world flavor." [59]

Could Hutty's first impressions, in fact, have been describing the actual city of Charleston in the post–World War I era? Saunders and McAden found assessments of Charleston starkly different from Hutty's first impressions:

> In the 1920s and 1930s, Charleston, in spite of the mystique that love and legend has accorded her, was a most unlikely place for an artist to expect to find the base of support (financial or otherwise) to sustain a serious professional career. The population numbered approximately 65,000, divided more or less between whites and African-Americans. The rice culture and market had, for all serious purposes, disappeared. The highly prized long-staple sea-island cotton had been wiped out by the boll weevil, and the upland short-staple cotton was no longer being marketed through Charleston as it once had been. The phosphate-mining industry, which had enjoyed something of a boom after the War Between the States, had exhausted itself, and there was little in the way of new industry to take its place.
>
> While other Southern ports such as New Orleans, Mobile, and Savannah had managed to flourish somewhat during the preceding years, the seaport of Charleston had lost the prominence it had enjoyed before the war. In short, Charleston, at the time, had no significant economic base and was a seriously depressed area.[60]

Patricia Robinson, a Charleston playwright, summarized Charleston's plight: "Charleston was a gentle town, far from prosperous and not yet recovered from the ravages of Civil War and Reconstruction. There was little money, no industry to speak of and the old saying, 'too poor to paint, too proud to white-wash' was a way of life. The old town seemed to slumber."[61]

How then, could anyone have predicted a Charleston Renaissance? . . . Right, but it happened anyway . . . a Cultural Renaissance! Robinson had this to say: "There was a flowering of art, literature, drama, and music. Dubose and Dorothy Heyward, John Bennett, Hervey Allen, and Josephine Pinckney were writing their books and plays. Alfred Hutty, Alice Ravenel Huger Smith, Minnie Mikell, and Beth Verner were at work in their studios. Susan Frost began the work of Charleston preservation. It was the beginning of the Poetry Society of South Carolina, The Footlight Players, and the Charleston Symphony. There was no money from foundations or government. What happened was spontaneous, growing out of people's will to answer their own cultural needs; the lives of these creative people touched constantly. They enriched an encouraged each other. They gave the town vitality and an identity which even the onslaught of *Progress* failed to destroy."[62]

In February 1920 Hutty returned to Charleston, where in a year or so he began teaching etching and other techniques at the Gibbes Memorial Art Gallery. He repeated that for three more years but seems to have taught mostly at his home studio thereafter.[63]

For the first few years that Hutty came to Charleston as a seasonal resident, he was a guest in the homes of newfound friends. One of his hosts was Susan Pringle Frost, who led the successful effort to save the Joseph Manigault House (built c. 1803, and an excellent example of the elegant Federal Style) from being demolished to make way for a gas station. Her actions led to the formation of the Society for the Preservation of Old Dwellings in 1920. In 1928 that organization was restructured as the Preservation Society of Charleston.[64] Upon Hutty's first visit to Charleston, he had been immediately impressed by the number and variety of eighteenth-century churches, commercial buildings, and homes. He quickly learned of their precedents in Barbados and other exotic locations and, just as quickly, realized, with pleasure, that most of Charleston's architecture was created on a human scale. He was clearly smitten by Charleston's single houses with their multitiered balconies and their high-walled gardens and by the Georgian mansions, which were once grand, but by his first visit many evidenced neglect and decay.[65]

Perhaps Bessie Hutty was as graciously welcomed to Charleston and, charmed by its quaintness as her husband was, they decided to purchase a vintage home located at 46 Tradd Street. Having caught the preservation spirit, the Huttys also set about restoring it. From the beginning Hutty was impressed with the potential for the separate kitchen to become his studio. A features writer for a local newspaper wrote about his visit to Hutty's kitchen-studio: "The ancient kitchen with the brick floor and raftered ceiling was given a skylight. Between the huge fireplace and the mezzanine, he kept his press and made his prints there. The fireplace in the Studio is one of the oldest in the city, believed to have been built in 1740. Friends from the North have told Mr. Hutty that the fireplace is a genuine Dutch hearth . . . used in the

18th century for cooking and heating. The structure is made entirely of uneven English handmade brick which was covered with a thick plaster of oyster shell composition. The fireplace's opening is 4 × 6 ft. and 3 ft. deep. There are compartments for fuel storage and baking. The draft is perfect and fires burn as well as they did 196 years ago."[66]

Many people visited the Hutty home and studio over the decades, especially from outside the South. "Bessie entertained a steady stream of the well-known and the lesser known. Booth Tarkington came and Mrs. Joseph Kennedy, as well as many others. They signed the guest book, bought prints and paintings, and many times wrote back for more."[67]

Alfred Hutty's exposure to and competence in printmaking techniques in Charleston in 1919 is not clear. It is certain that he already possessed enviable abilities as a draftsman, designer, and painter, and there is speculation by Saunders and McAden that "he was trained as an engraver during his tenure with the Tiffany Glass Studios. The term 'engraver': used in this context has a meaning more general than specific, and could even imply experience with various acids and mordant used in etching designs into glass and metal."[68]

Louisa D. Stoney, writing for the *Charleston News and Courier,* reflected about Hutty's grounding in the etching process: "Mr. Hutty's career as an etcher began in Charleston. Mrs. Earle (Witte) Sloan, after seeing the clear expressiveness of his pencil drawings, encouraged him to learn the technique of etching."[69]

An etching titled *In Bedon's Alley* is said to be Hutty's first and to be dated 1921. More important though are other early etchings/drypoints, for example those of St. Philip's Church (1761) and St. Michael's Episcopal Church (1761). The design of that colonial era church has been attributed to a possible student of Sir Christopher Wren. The work titled *St. Michael's Portico* is referred to as Hutty's second print and was given the same date as *Bedon's Alley.*

Charles Lemon Morgan, a columnist for *Prints* magazine, was also impressed with Hutty's early etchings: "It was Charleston architecture which induced him to use the needle and it was two years before he did other subjects. These architectural subjects marked the beginning of his important contribution to American graphic art and of etching."[70]

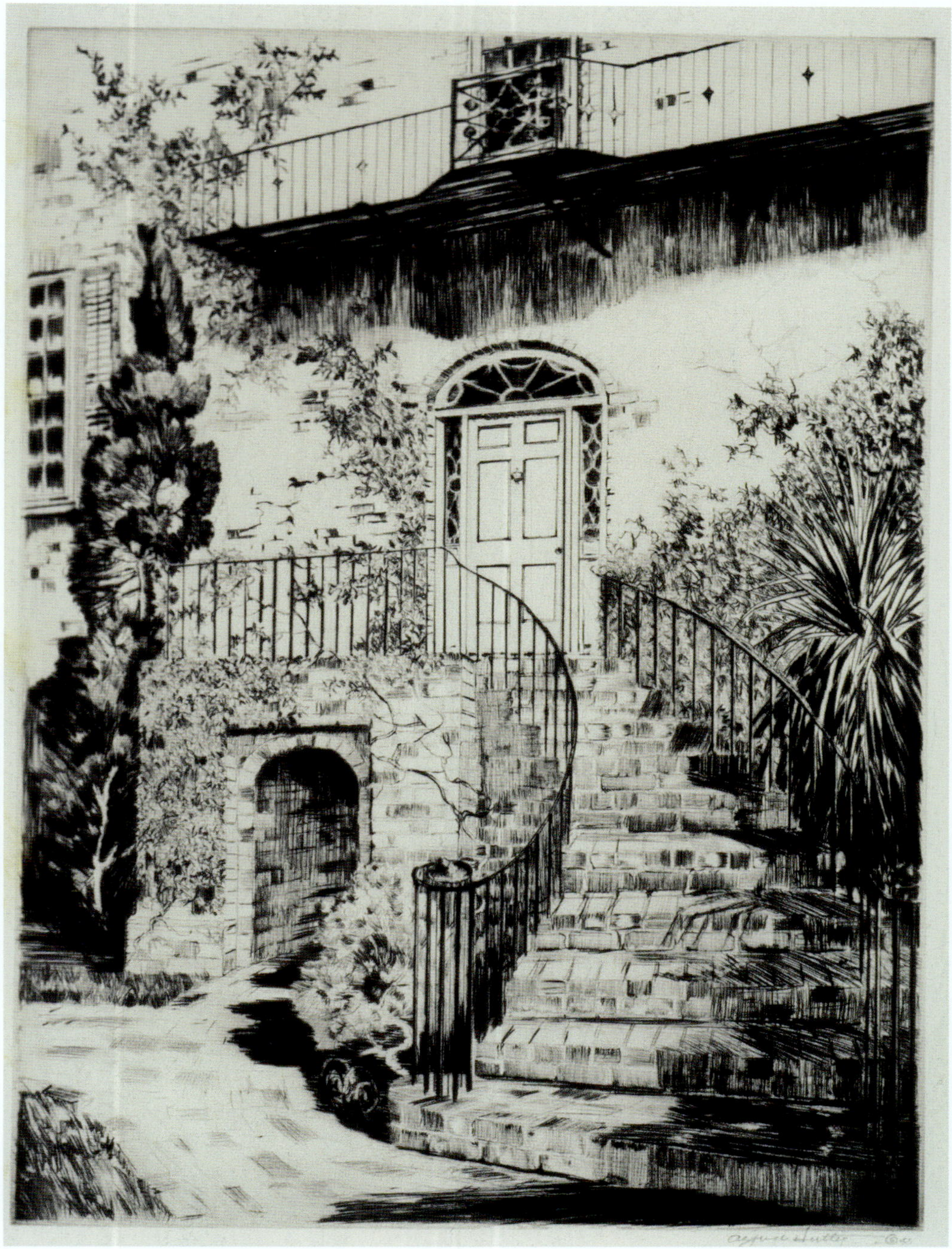

Alfred Hutty, *Doorway on Tradd Street* (the artist's home), drypoint

Upon seeing Hutty's prints of Charleston at that time, art collector and critic Duncan Phillips praised the artist for "an amazing reliance upon line rather than tonal values for giving specific character but also spatial existence to trees and buildings and figures."[71]

Saunders and McAden echoed Phillips's assessment: "Hutty enjoyed a wide reputation for his ability to depict the elegance and the sweep of trees. In Charleston, he realized as well the rightness of the

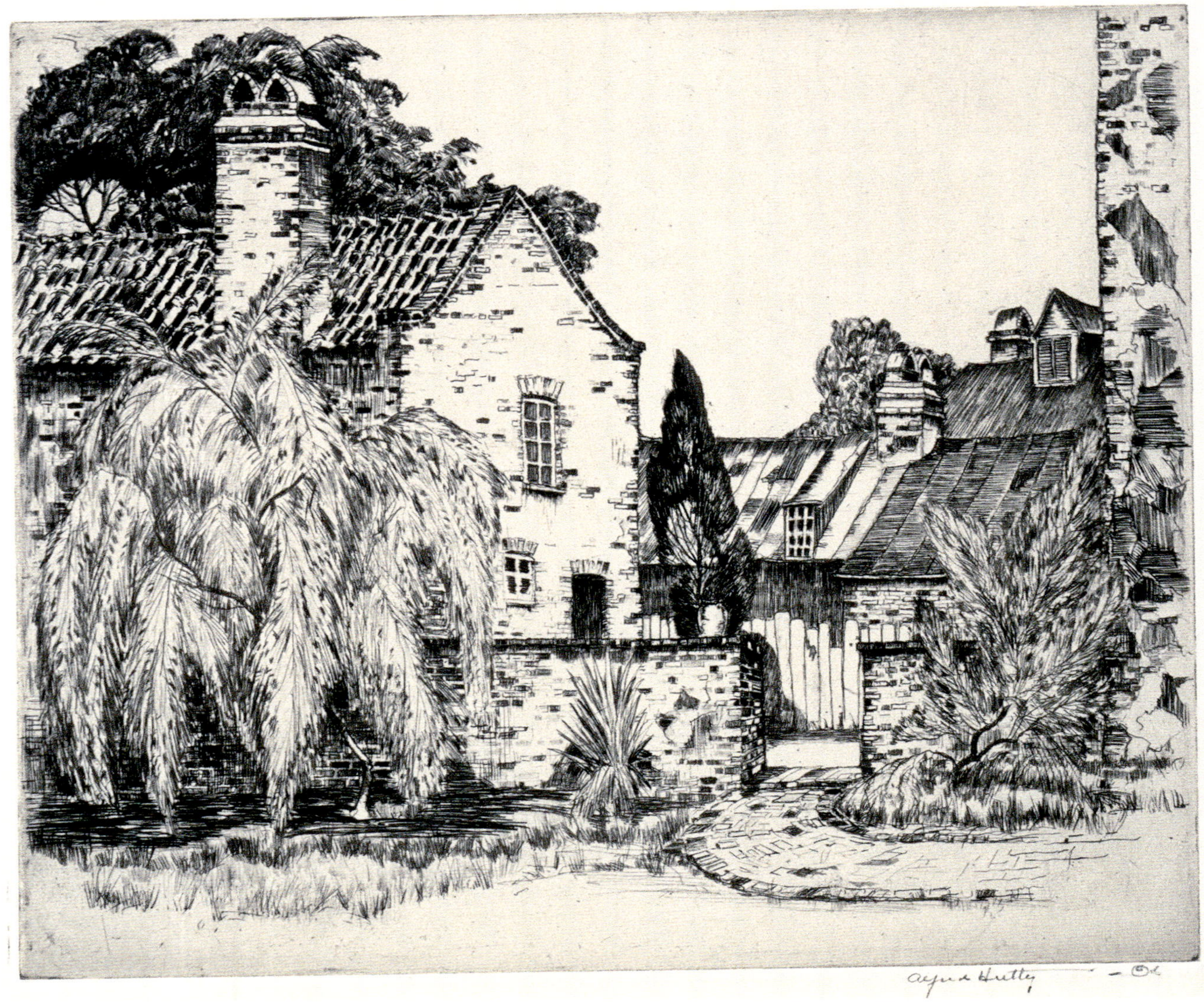

Alfred Hutty, *My Charleston Studio,* etching

bitten line for expressing the linear grace of that city's architectural forms."[72]

There is no doubting Hutty's fondness for Charleston's historic architecture, and the Hutty catalog contains several reproductions of prints to confirm his interest. However, of the fifty-seven plates in the catalog section, the majority of images are figurative, and most of those are of African Americans. Surely the most animated figurative composition is *The Jenkins Orphanage Band.* The body language and the facial features represent a mannerism not unlike that used by the Midwest regionalist painter Thomas Hart Benton for his illustrative painting for Steinbeck's book *The Grapes of Wrath* in the 1930s. Saunders and McAden made enriching connections between a wonderfully descriptive event from Dubose Heyward's 1926 novel *Porgy* involving an extraordinary annual parade in Charleston and an orphanage youth band, all as another example of a renaissance of music in Charleston during the 1920s and 1930s.

According to Saunders and McAden, "the Jenkins Orphanage Band was founded by Reverend Daniel Jenkins, an African-American Baptist minister who started it to help raise funds for an orphanage after he found four homeless young African American orphans shivering in a railroad yard on a cold winter day. After the orphanage opened in 1892, funded by local and northern contributions, and the band's earnings, the band (or bands because there were as many as four at the time) continued to play regularly on the streets

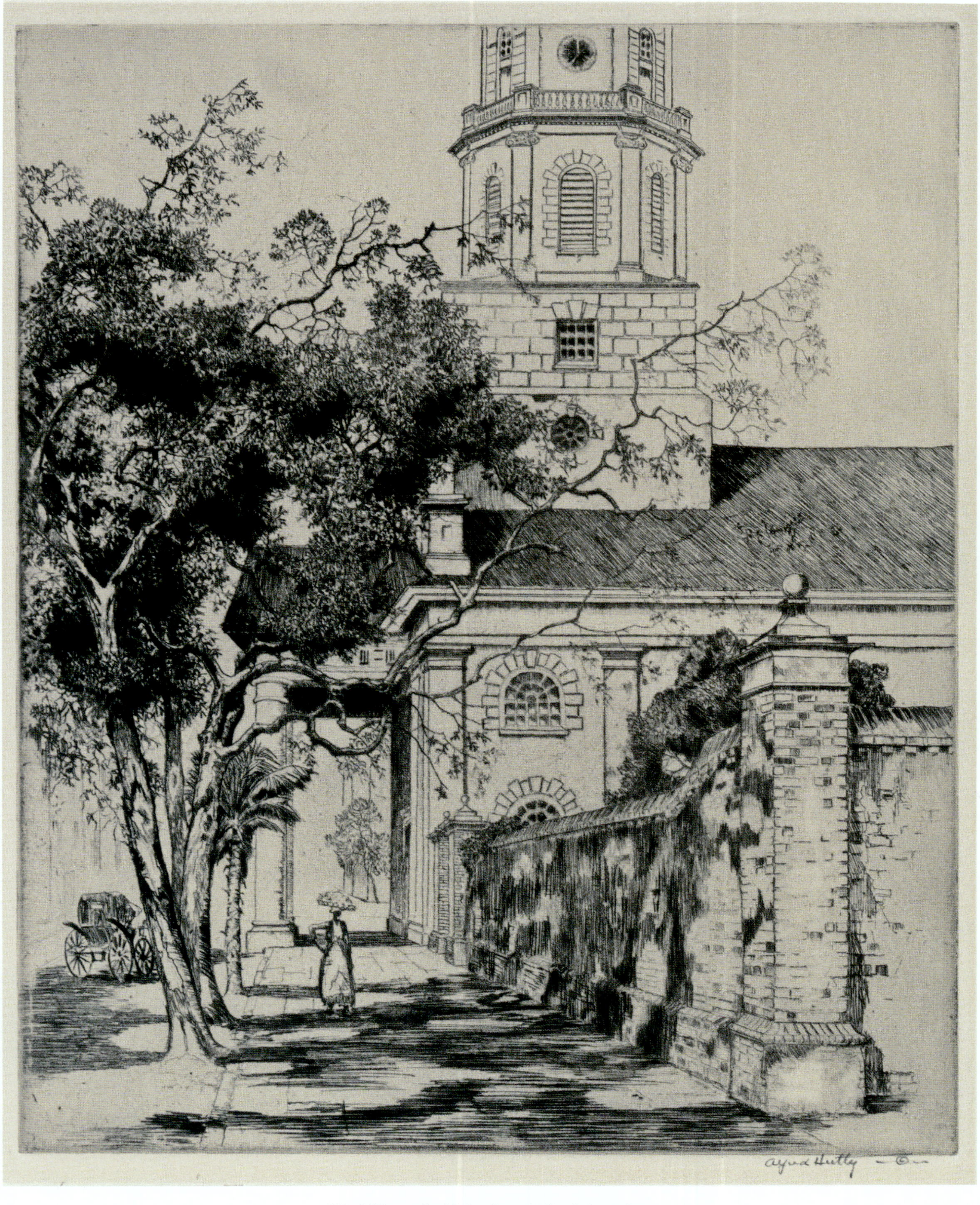

Alfred Hutty, *St. Michael's in the Sunlight,* etching

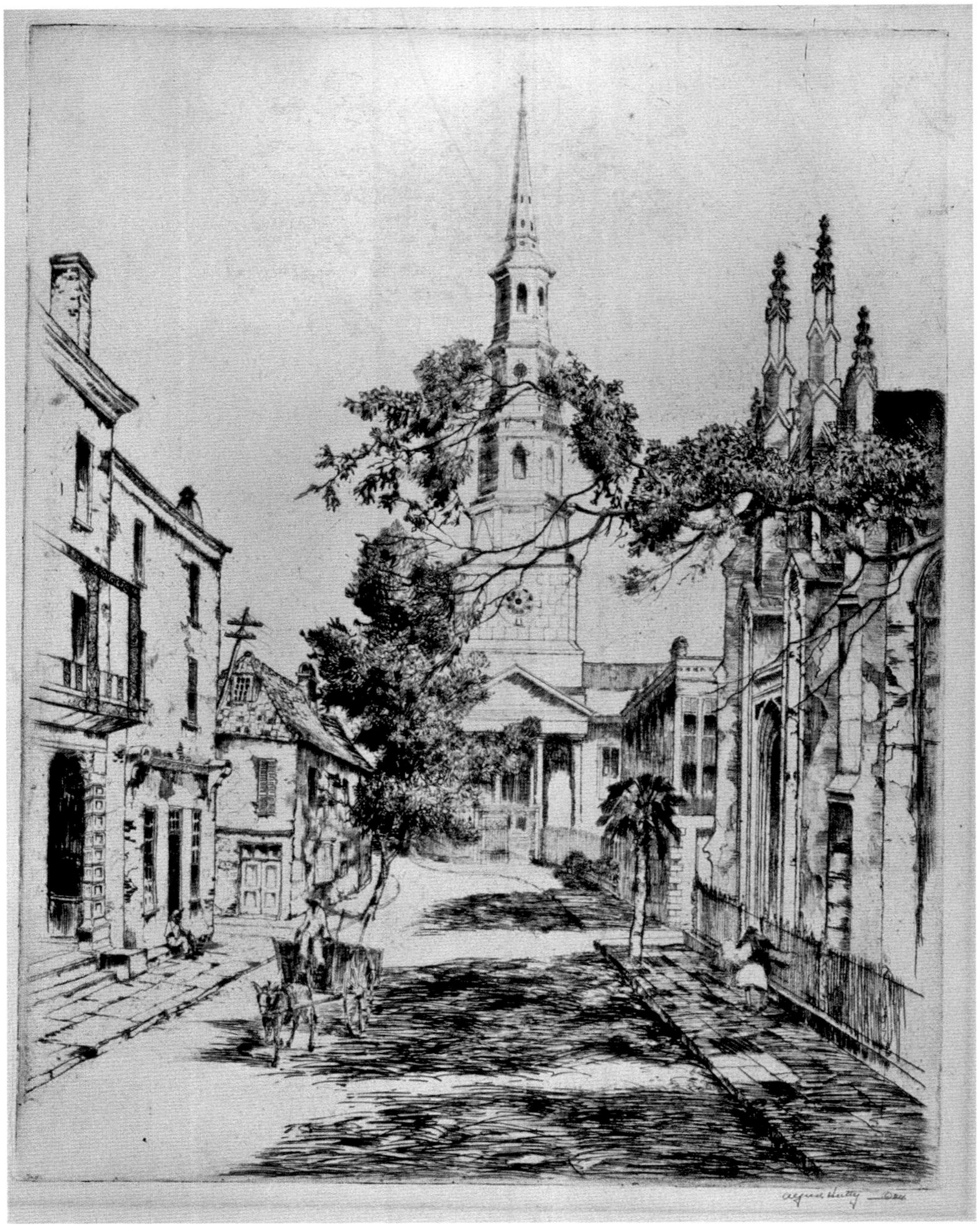

Alfred Hutty, *St. Philip's Church,* etching/drypoint

of Charleston, passing the hat after performances, and traveled throughout the United States, Canada, and abroad. They were in the inaugural parade for President William Howard Taft, and the band starred in the openings of the play *Porgy* in New York (1927, and in London, where they performed in 1905 and 1914)."[73]

According to Saunders and McAden, Alfred Hutty attempted to present the magic and vitality of the Jenkins Orphanage Band in his drypoint of the same name. "Perhaps close examination will reveal a youthful 'cat' Anderson, who went on to play with Duke Ellington's band, or 'Jabbo' Smith, who later joined Louis Armstrong's band."[74]

Additionally Saunders and McAden felt there was an important connection between the Jenkins Orphanage Band and a particular passage in Dubose Heyward's book *Porgy,* which follows below:

> There are also the daily dramas of two cultures, simultaneous in time and place, yet vastly different. One such drama Heyward incorporated into *Porgy* with particular resonance. It is set at the first sunlight of morning on the day of the grand parade of "The Sons and Daughters of Repent Ye Saith the Lord" lodge:

> The drowsy old city had scarcely commenced its day when, down through King Charles Street, the procession took its way. Superbly unselfconscious of the effect that it produced, it crashed through the slow, restrained rhythm of the city's life like a wild, barbaric chord. All of the stately mansions along the way were servantless that day, and the aristocratic matrons broke the ultimate canon of the social code and peered through front windows at the procession as it swept flamboyantly across the town.
>
> First came an infinitesimal Negro boy, scarlet-coated, aglitter with brass buttons. Upon his head was balanced an enormous shako; and while he marched with left hand on hip and shoulders back, his right hand twirled a heavy gold-headed baton. Then the band, two score boys attired in several variations of the band master's costume, strode by. Bare, splay feet padded upon the cobbles; heads were thrown back, with lips to instruments that glittered in the sunshine, launching daring and independent excursions into the realm of sound. Yet these improvisations returned always to the eternal boom, boom, boom of an underlying rhythm, and met with others in sudden weaving and raveling of amazing chords. An ecstasy of wild young bodies beat living into the blasts that shook the windows of the solemn houses. Broad, dusty, blue-black feet shuffled and danced on the many-colored cobbles and the grass between them. The sun lifted suddenly over the housetops and flashed like a torrent of warm, white wine between the

staid buildings, to break on flashing teeth and laughing eyes.

After the band came the men members of the lodge, stepping it out to the urge of the marshals who rode behind them, reinforcing the marching rhythm with a series of staccato grunts, shot with crisp, military precision from under their visored caps. Breasts cross-slashed with the emblems of their lodge, they passed.

Then came the carriages, and suddenly the narrow street hummed and bloomed like a tropic garden. Six to a carriage sat the sisters. The effect produced by the colors was strangely like that wrought in the music; scarlet, purple, orange, flamingo, emerald; wild, clashing, unbelievable discords; yet, in their steady flow before the eye, possessing a strange, dominant rhythm that reconciled them to each other and made them unalterably right. The senses reached blindly out for a reason. There was none. They intoxicated, they maddened, and finally they passed, seeming to pull every ray of color from the dun buildings, leaving the sunlight sane, flat, dead.

For its one brief moment out of the year the pageant had lasted. Out of its fetters of civilization this people had risen, suddenly, amazingly. Exotic as the Congo, and still able to abandon themselves utterly to the wild joy of fantastic play, they had taken the reticent old Anglo-Saxon town and stamped their mood swiftly and indelibly into its heart. Then they passed, . . . those whom the ages had rendered old and wise.

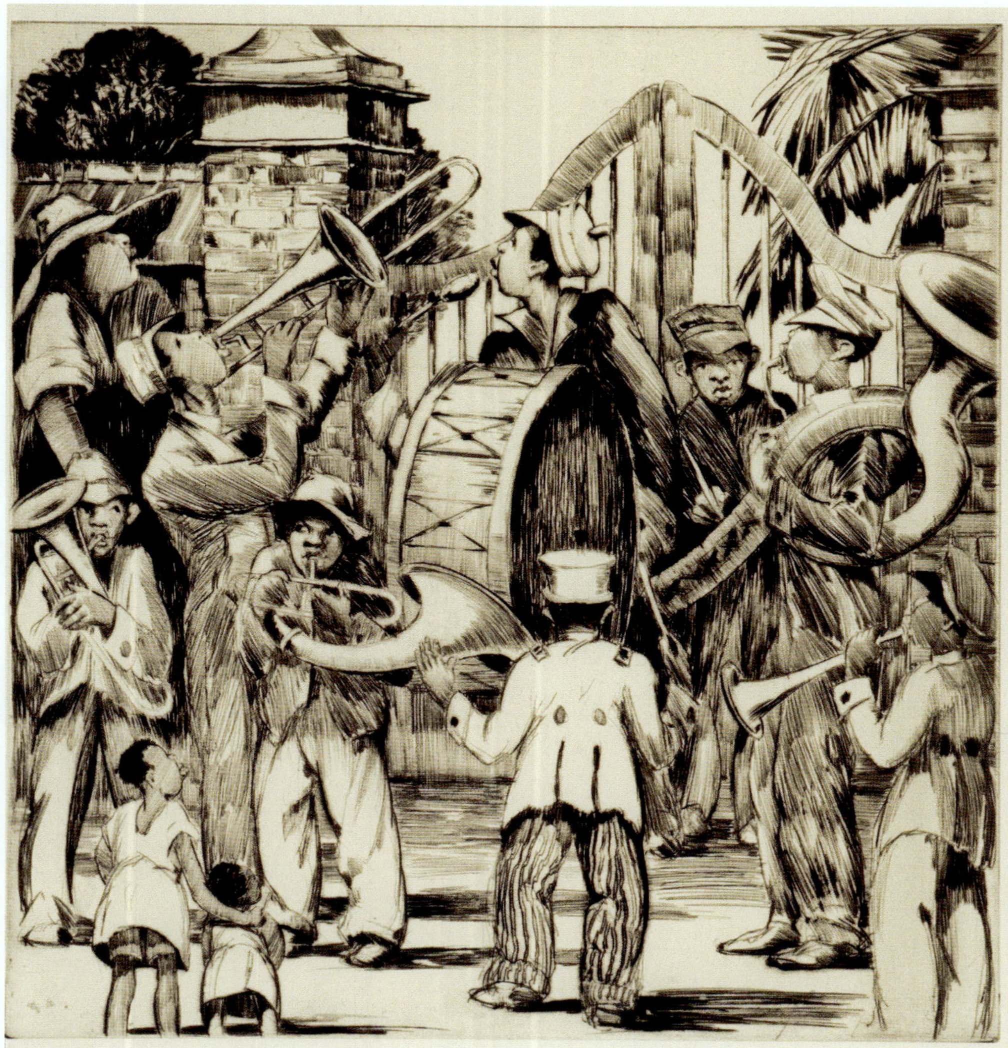

Alfred Hutty, *Jenkins Orphanage Band,* second version, drypoint

In such a setting, with such an appeal to the senses, it is easy to understand how an artistic renaissance such as Charleston experienced could have taken place. It is also easy to understand how the look and feel of such a place could have figured so prominently in its art. The parade is, by no means, pure invention. Clearly, the inspiration for this passage was the Jenkins Orphanage Band.[75]

Saunders and McAden were also able to find credible information about Hutty's ways of printing, exhibiting, and marketing his etchings and drypoints. "Hutty was very disciplined about inking and printing his plates, for he was a craftsman as well as an artist. Any vagueness on his part extended only to details that could well be proved irrelevant in any final appraisal of his work. He was definitely objective and clear sighted in addressing his own pictures. As he pointed out in appraising one of his works, "there I came close to what I was trying to express; that is good, but here, this is a little muddled. I would not do it that way now."[76]

According to Saunders and McAden, "if an image was popular and seemed destined to be printed in some quantity, the plate (especially if it was a drypoint) was sent North to be steel-faced to help withstand the rigors of extensive printing. Usually, he made seventy-five prints of each plate."[77]

However, remembering a few of James Fowler Cooper's unorthodox approaches to procedures, Hutty had his quirks, too. Said Saunders, "He was rather casual about dating and numbering them, though,

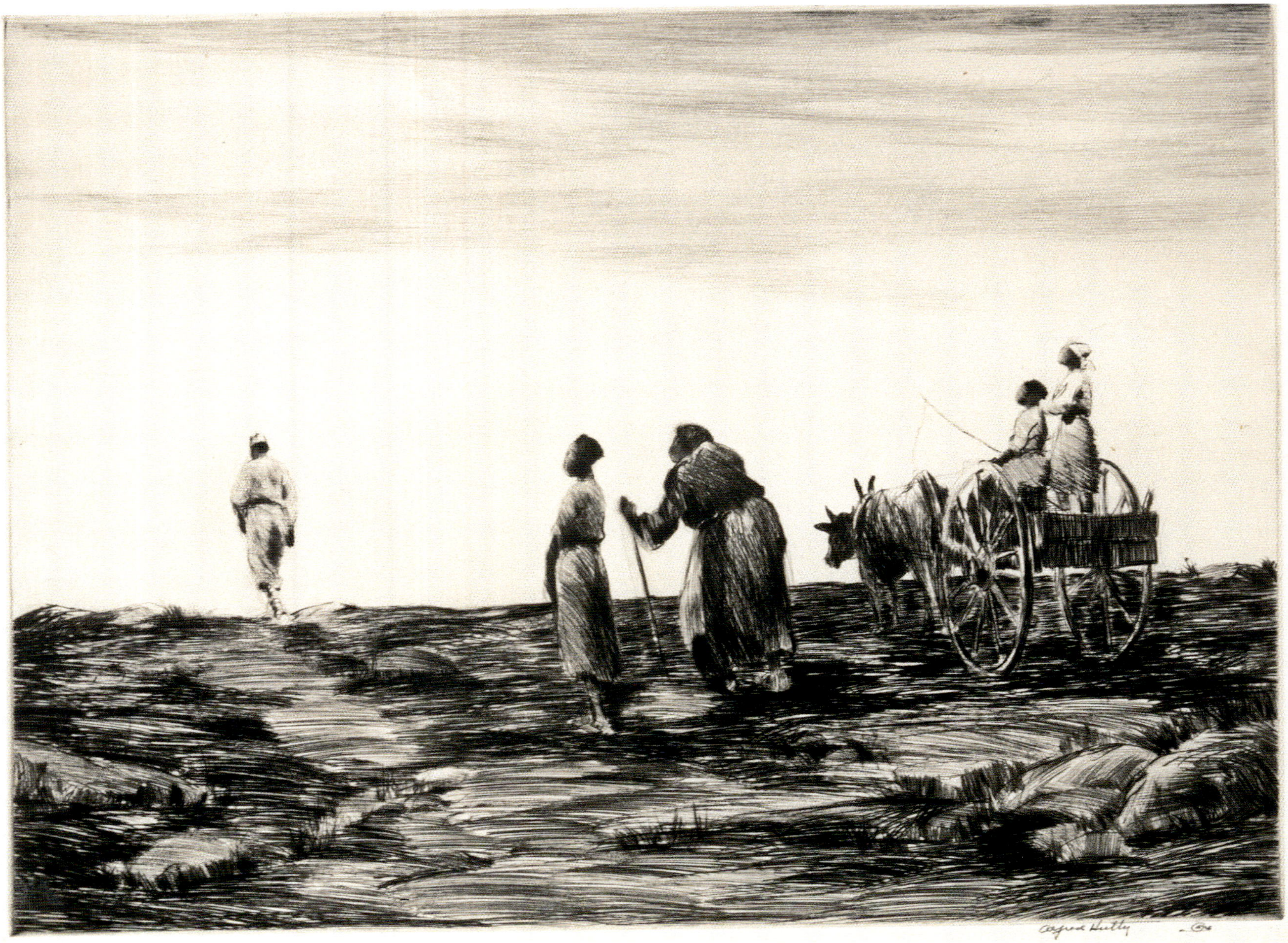

Alfred Hutty, *Toward a New Day,* drypoint

sometimes to the point of exclusion altogether. Titles were subject to change, and a few plates have more than one title."[78]

Hutty was also not without a sense of humor at his own expense. According Saunders and McAden, "because he had waited until late in life to start this new career, he adopted the snail as an emblem to follow his signature on most of his prints."[79]

Hutty was fortunate to have an interested and capable wife to serve as his business manager. Saunders and McAden even believe she should be credited for much of Hutty's professional success. Furthermore Hutty, unlike Cooper, exhibited his works aggressively and almost immediately won honors. Simultaneously he sought and quickly acquired a network of gallery affiliations mostly along the eastern seaboard, especially in Massachusetts and New York.

From the early 1920s until the early 1950s, the Huttys spent winters in Charleston, South Carolina, and summers in Woodstock, New York. Until 1951 he continued to paint and make prints. He died on June 27, 1954, at his Woodstock farm, Broadview, at age seventy-six.[80] On the occasion of a memorial exhibition in Hutty's honor at the Gibbes Art Gallery

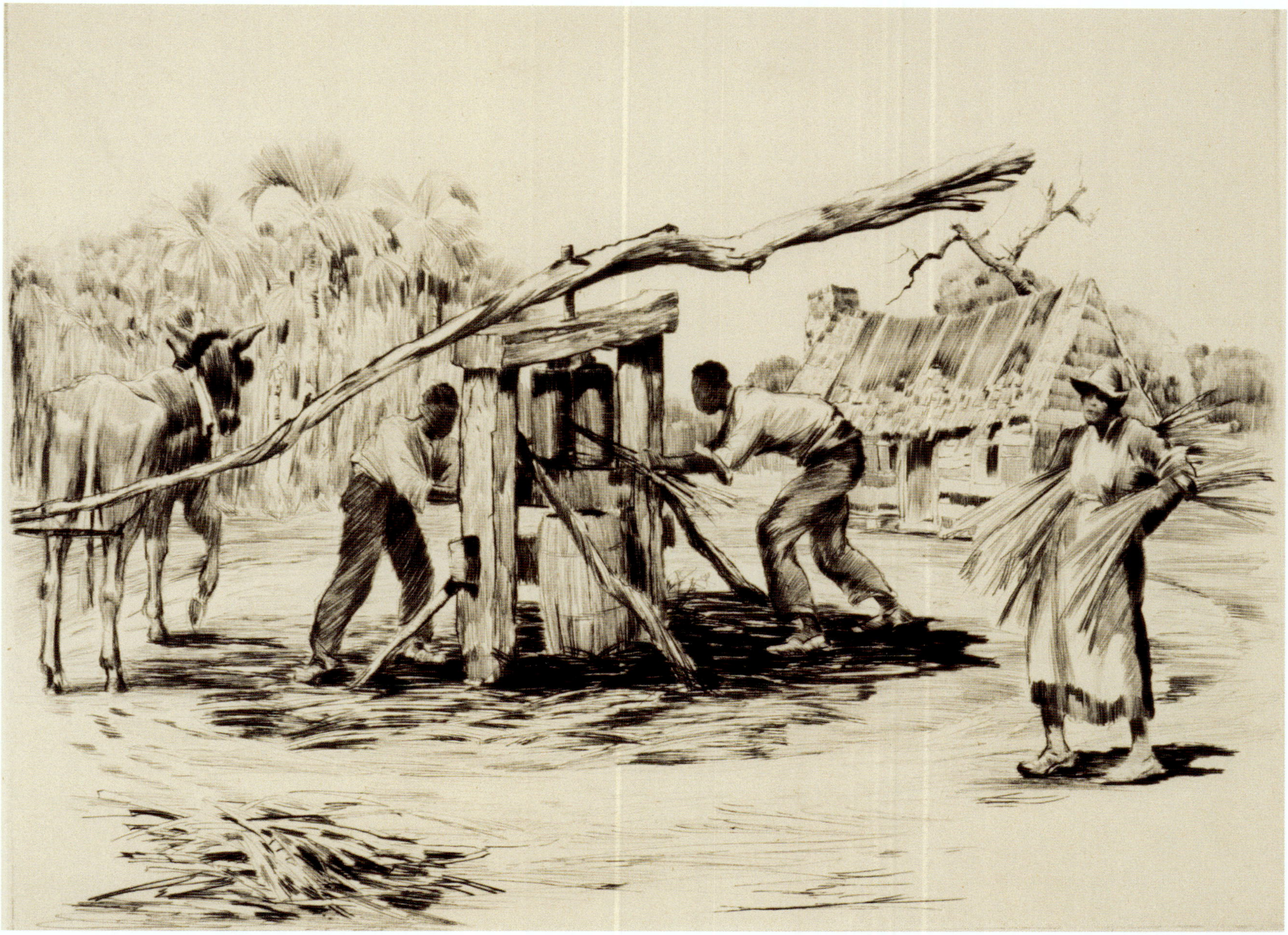

Alfred Hutty, *Pressing Sugar Cane,* drypoint

in 1956, friend Selma Dotterer Furtwangler reviewed the exhibition for the *Charleston Evening Post* and offered a tribute, a portion of which follows: "He had no pretensions about his own importance, he never felt that he had important messages or interpretations to swath obscurely in art for the good of, or for the edification of, mankind—he felt simply that he was an instrument through which a talent passed on, a talent surging from a source greater than himself."

"In 1959, Warren Hutty set up a memorial gallery for his father's work in Woodstock. Although Hutty had printed in New England, New York, France, and England, Warren was aware that his father was more proud of the work he did in the low country [of South Carolina] than any other he ever did. Of the low country work, his favorite composition was *Toward a New Day.*"[81]

Remembering playwright Patricia Robinson's declaration mentioned earlier about a flowering of the arts contributing a wider Charleston Renaissance during the 1920s and 1930s, that phenomenon definitely included printmaking, and certainly Alfred Hutty helped establish quite possibly the first printmaking group in Charleston. "The formation of the

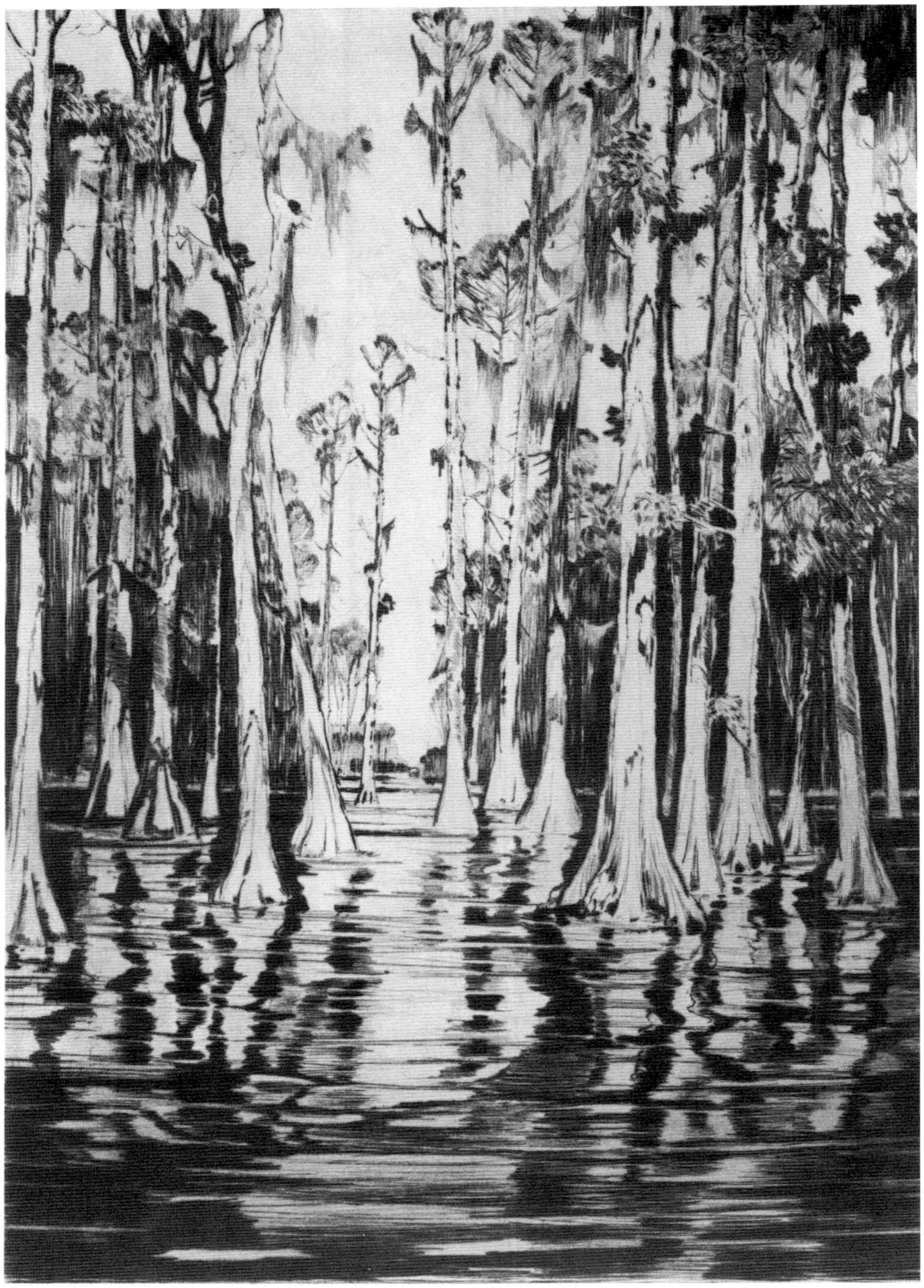

Alfred Hutty, *Cypress Gardens,* drypoint

Charleston Etchers Club, a group of nine artists in 1923, is an event of considerable significance in the history of American printmaking. The founding members were: Alfred Hutty, Alice Ravenel Huger Smith, Gabrielle de Veaux Clements, Ellen Day Hale, Elizabeth O'Neill Verner, Alexander B. Mikell, Arthur Rhett, Leila Waring and John Bennett. Within a short time there were two new members, Selma Dotterer and Robert Whitelaw."[82]

Even before the launch of this club there was interest in print collecting and connoisseurship.

> [Patricia Robinson] Anna Heyward Taylor and her friend Alice R. H. Smith had both fallen under the spell of Japanese woodcut prints. Some years earlier, Smith's interest in Japanese prints had begun under the instruction and encouragement of Helen Hyde who had spent time in Japan (1905–1913), had studied Ukiyo-e woodblock methods closely, and brought them back to the United States. She quickly equipped herself with [the appropriate tools and supplies]. She also [studied an extensive collection of more than six hundred Japanese color prints as well as blocks, tools, and color registration devices, which belonged to her cousin, Motte Alston Read, a retired Harvard professor]. Smith experimented with printing from some of the blocks in the traditional manner, then proceeded to design and cut her own blocks in the same manner. By the middle 1920s Smith was exhibiting her prints in prestigious American and international shows.
>
> Anna Heyward Taylor also achieved considerable recognition as a block printer during the 1920s, and she, too owed much of her artistic development to her contact with Japanese prints.[83]

Chapter 12

A Gallery of Saunders's Drawings

While documenting the art in the preceding chapters, it became quite apparent that Saunders is not just an adequate renderer; he is a consummate draftsman and for the most difficult of subjects—the human figure. Figurative images permeate the run of subjects he has addressed from Faulkner's fiction to a Revolutionary War battle in the South Carolina upcountry. It was, in fact, when I saw many graphite studies for the painting *The Battle of Hanging Rock, South Carolina, 1780* (installed in the South Carolina State Museum), that I immediately exclaimed, "Some of these just have to be in the book!," and some of them are.

Those realizations probably should have satisfied me, but I desired to see more . . . more sketches and drawings. I love drawings as much as I love prints. Just think, the first mark made on a piece of paper, a metal plate, or a LCD monitor might be an artist's first visualization of an idea; that thought, that spark that travels from the brain down an arm to a handheld stylus or mouse may begin a network of marks that become something or . . . become nothing. Obviously sketches and drawings can be wonderful incubators for visual art in general or stand alone as art.

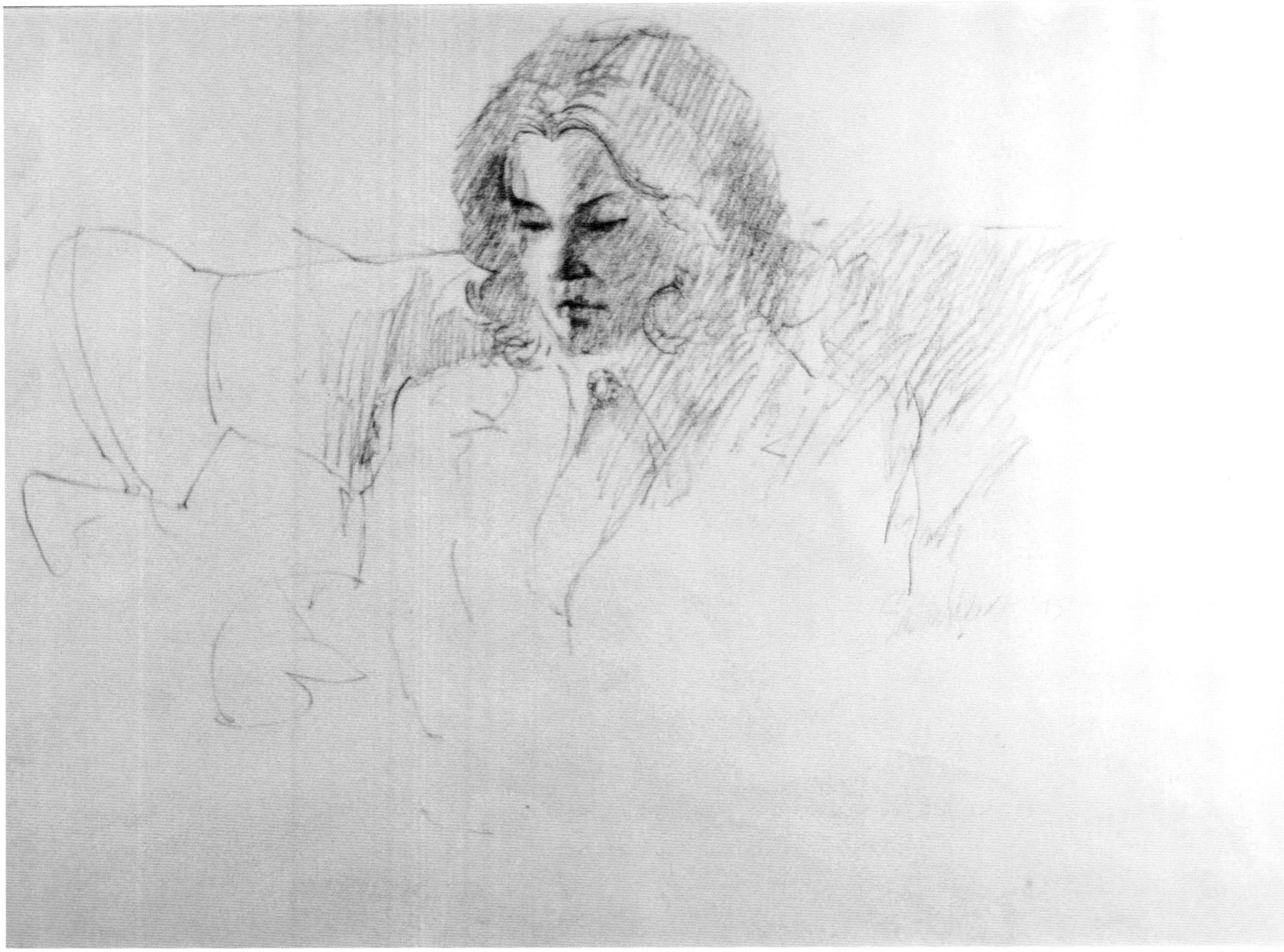

Stephanie (wife of artist), graphite

At some point I proposed a "Gallery of Drawings" section for this book. Boyd considered the idea, searched through many flat files, warmed greatly to the concept, and sent me about twenty reproductions of drawings ranging from light contour figural studies to complex, multimedia compositions. A selection of those pieces makes up this section of the book. They are presented with captions but without individual commentaries, thus just as they might be shown in a commercial gallery or a museum.

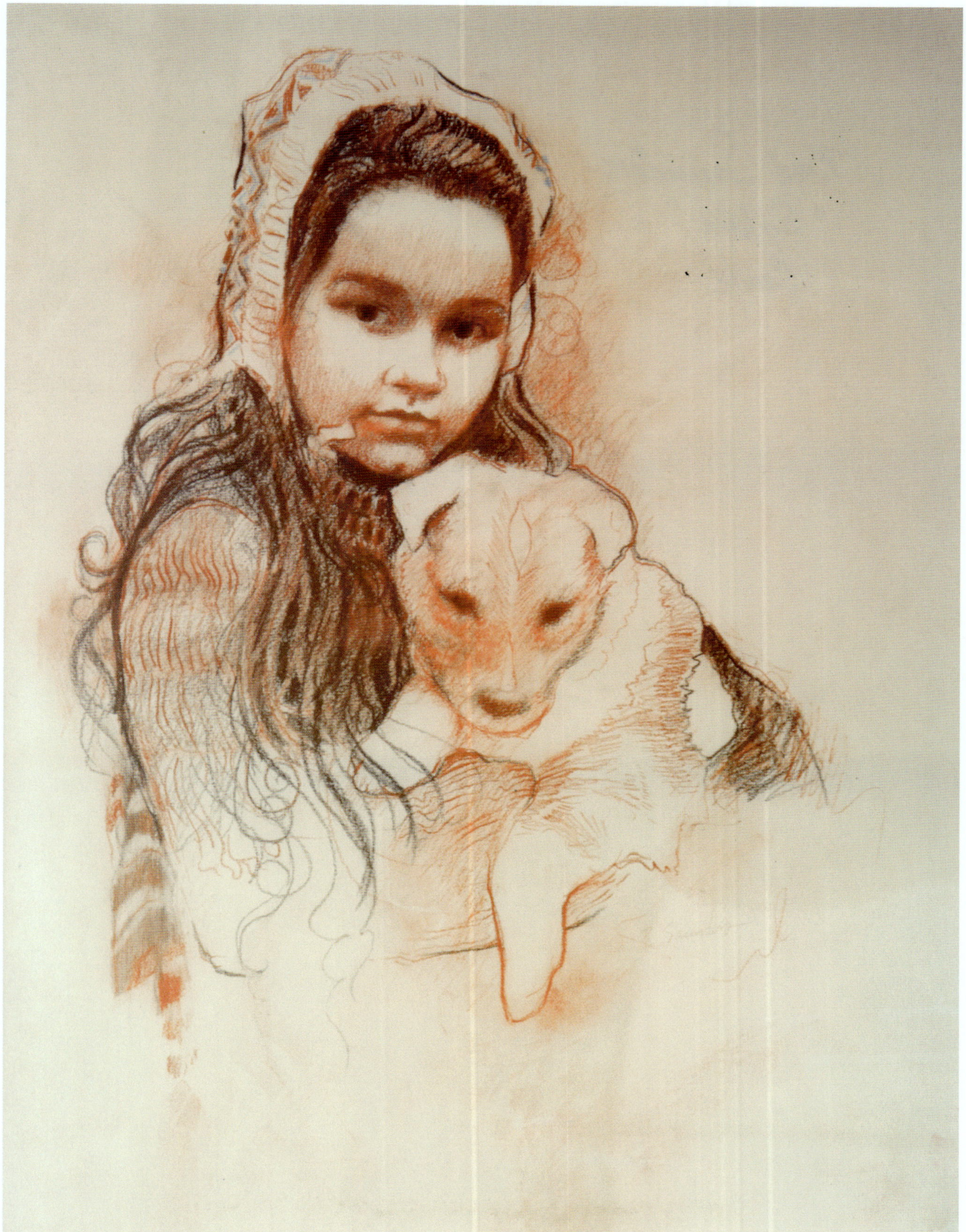

Sylvia (one of Saunders's daughters), conté

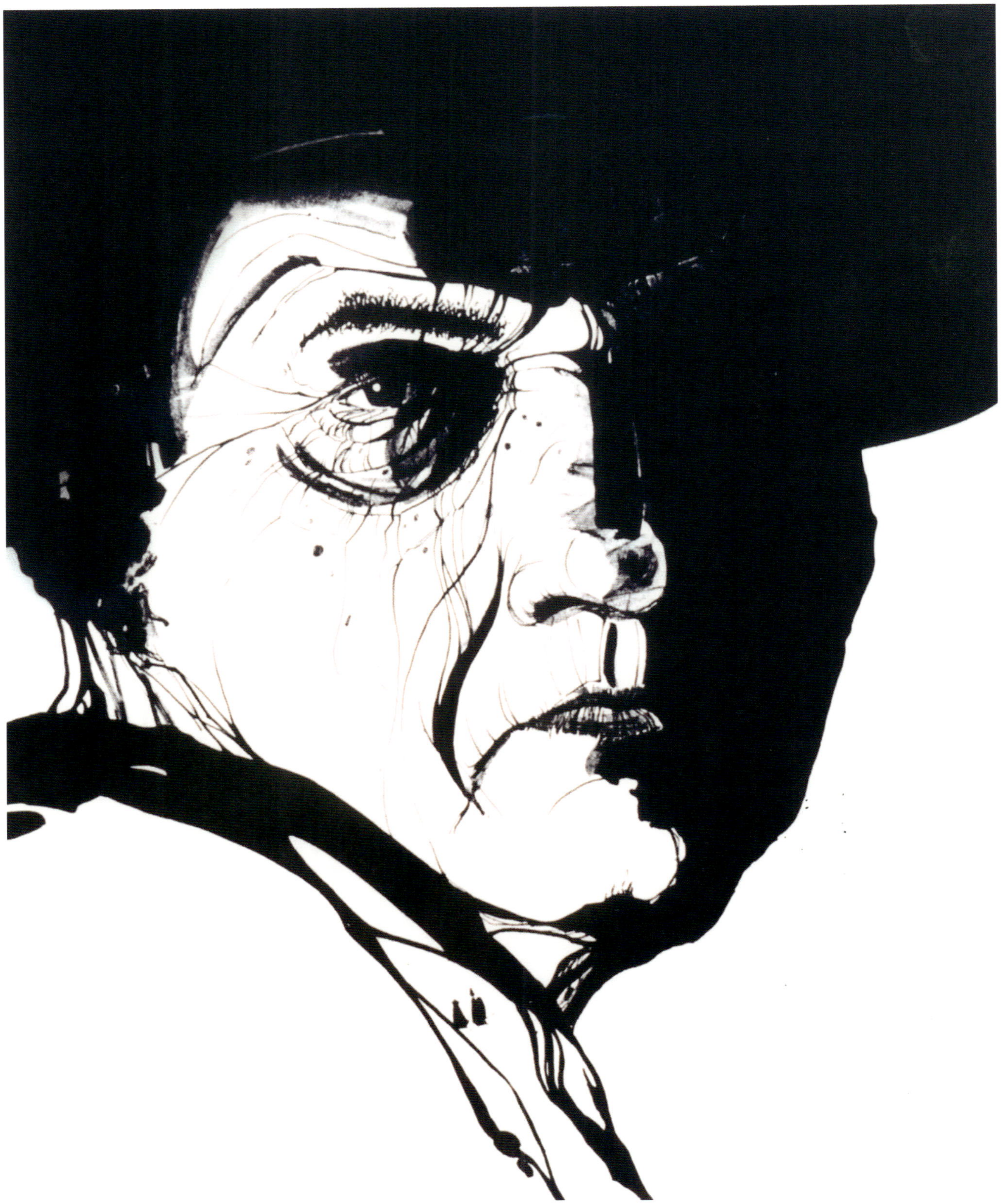

Harridan, ink wash

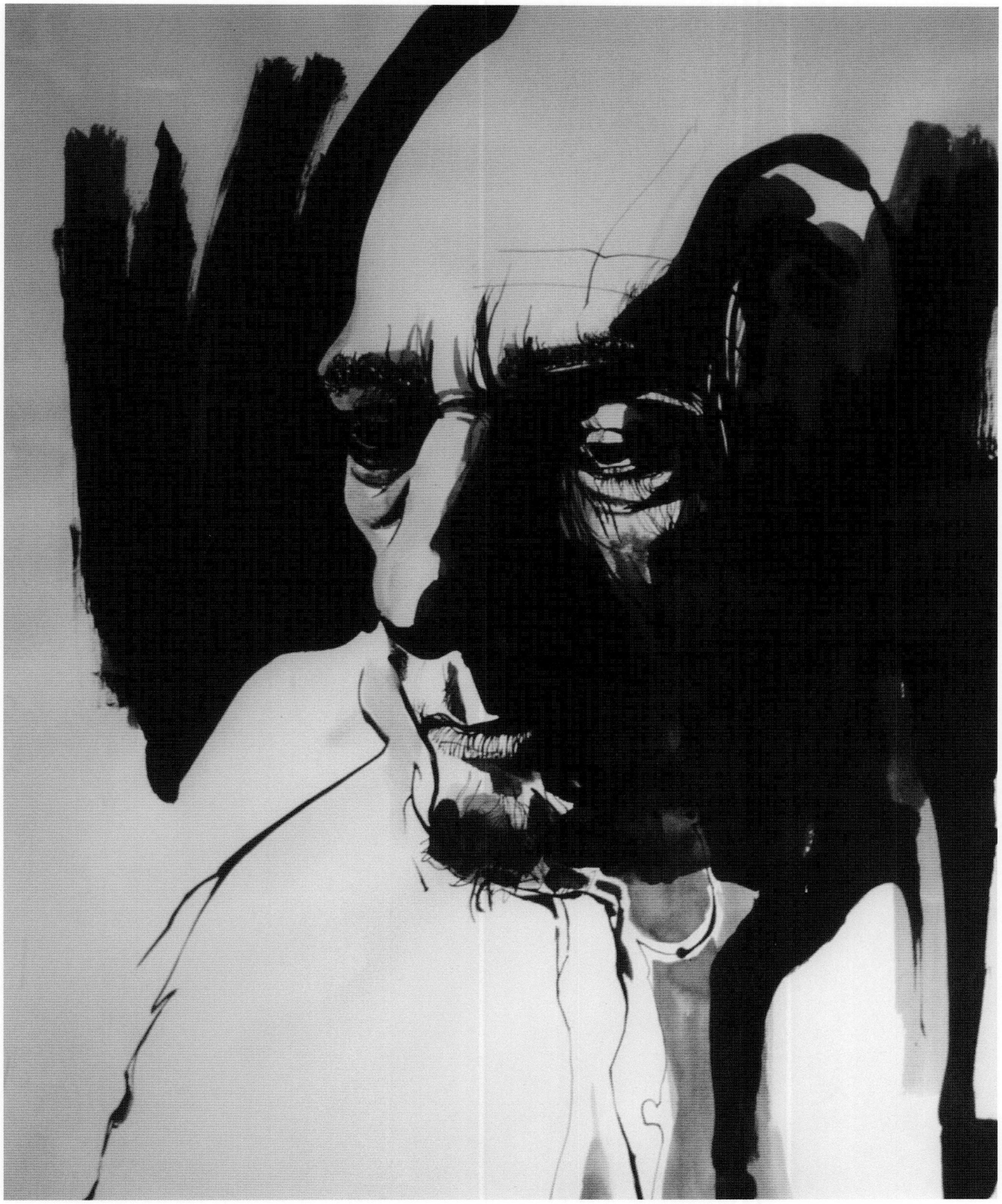

Rabbi, ink wash

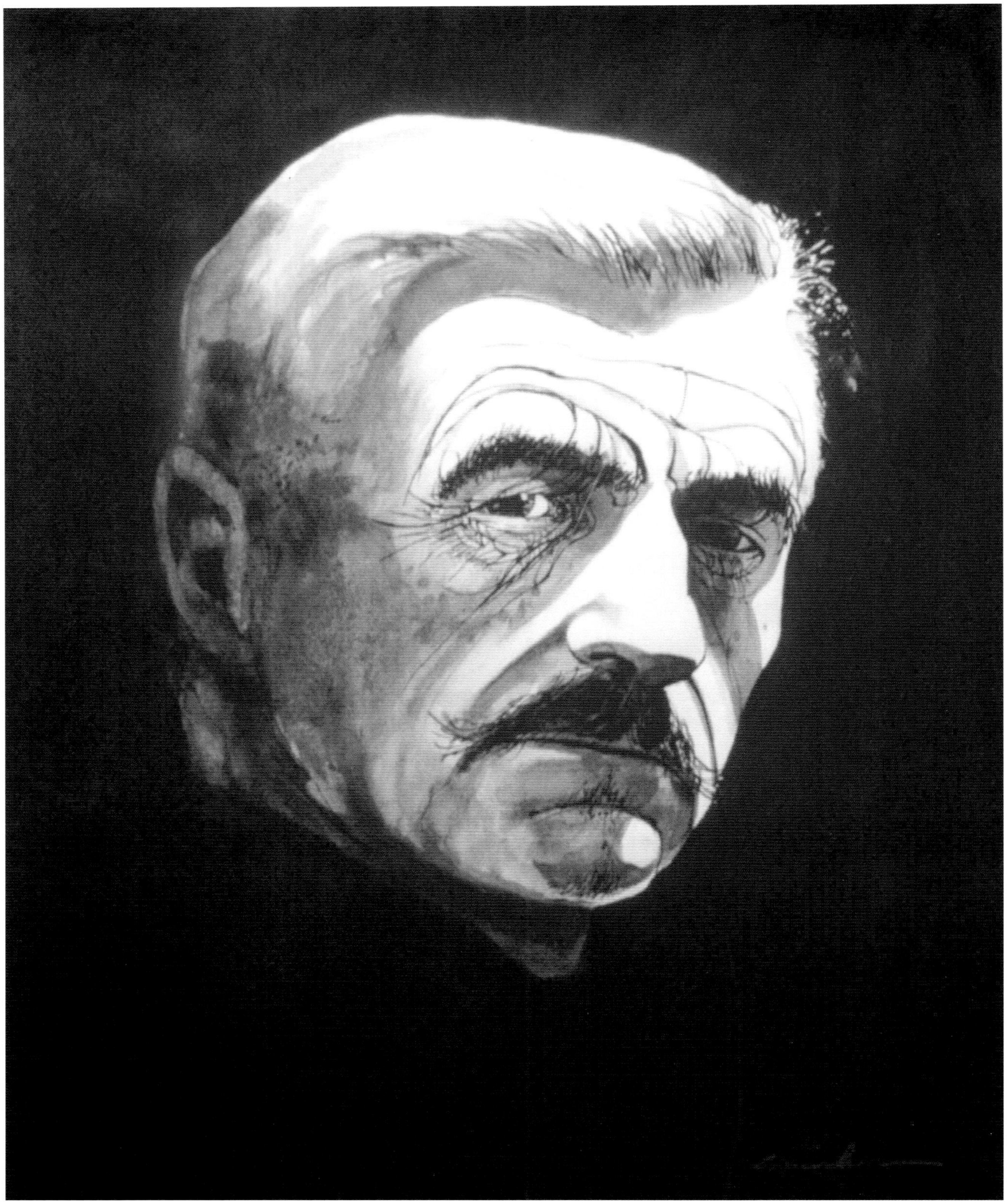

Faulkner, ink wash

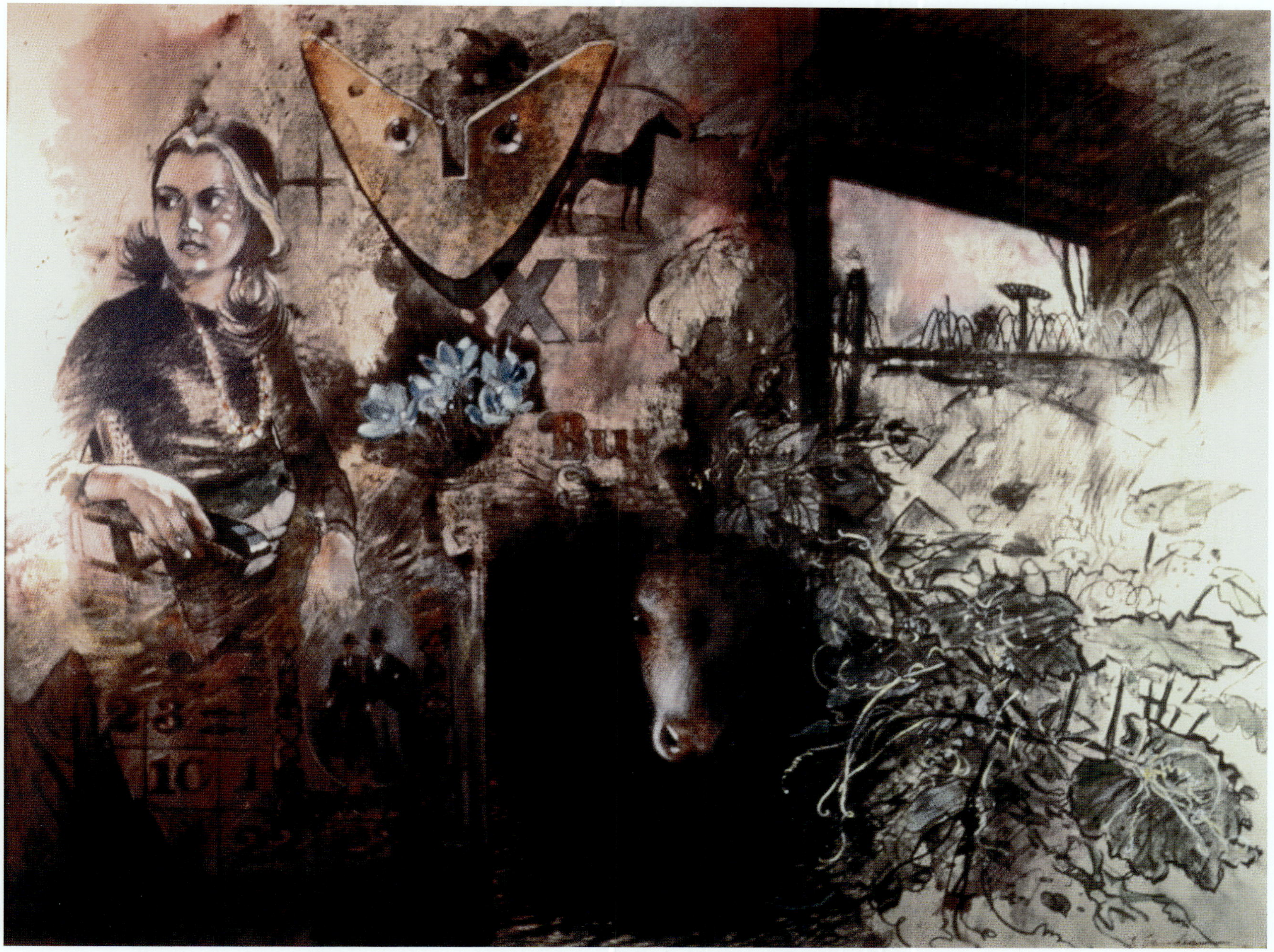

The Spring Calf, charcoal, pastel, and watercolor

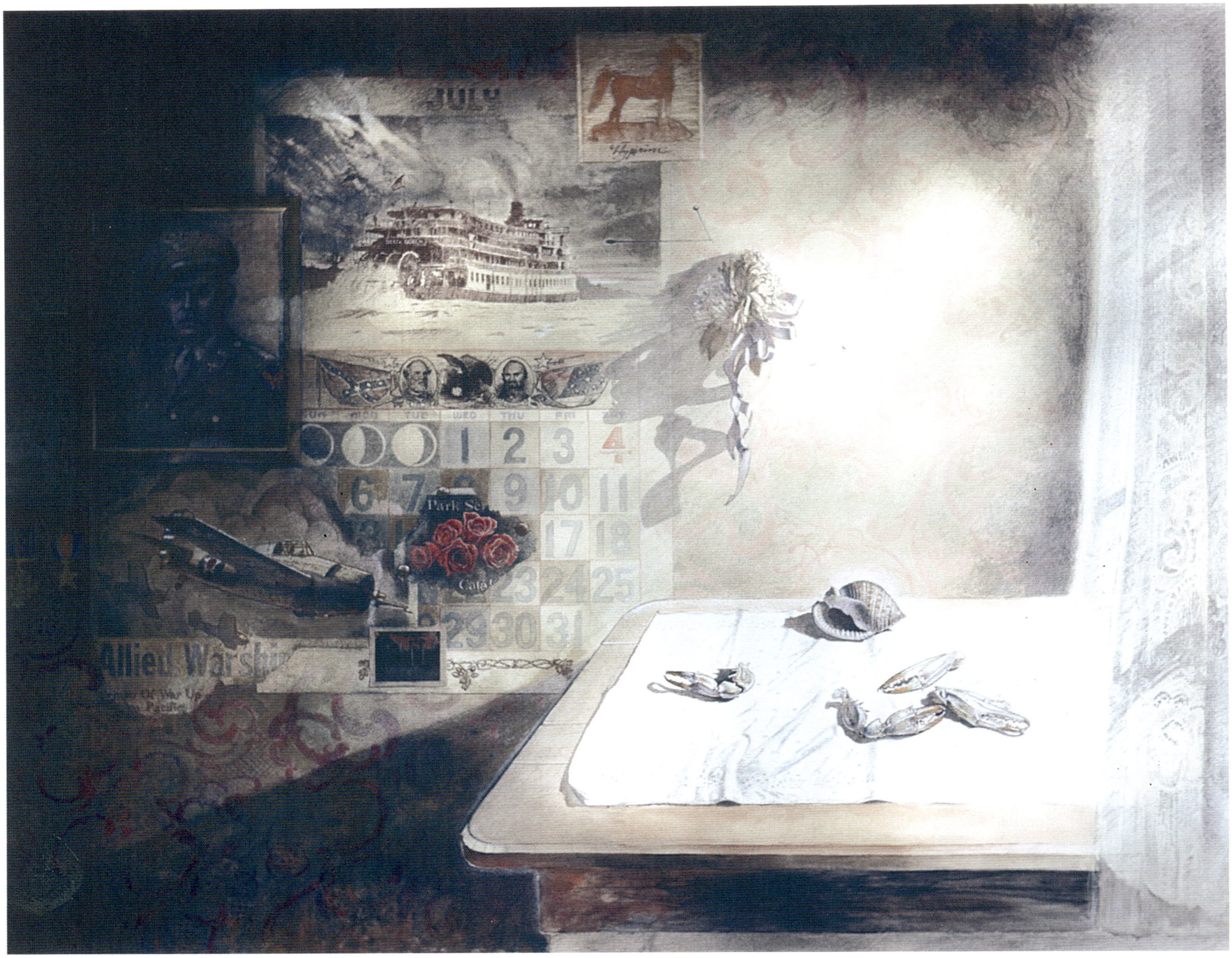

Threnody for Heroes and Dreams, graphite, charcoal, and watercolor

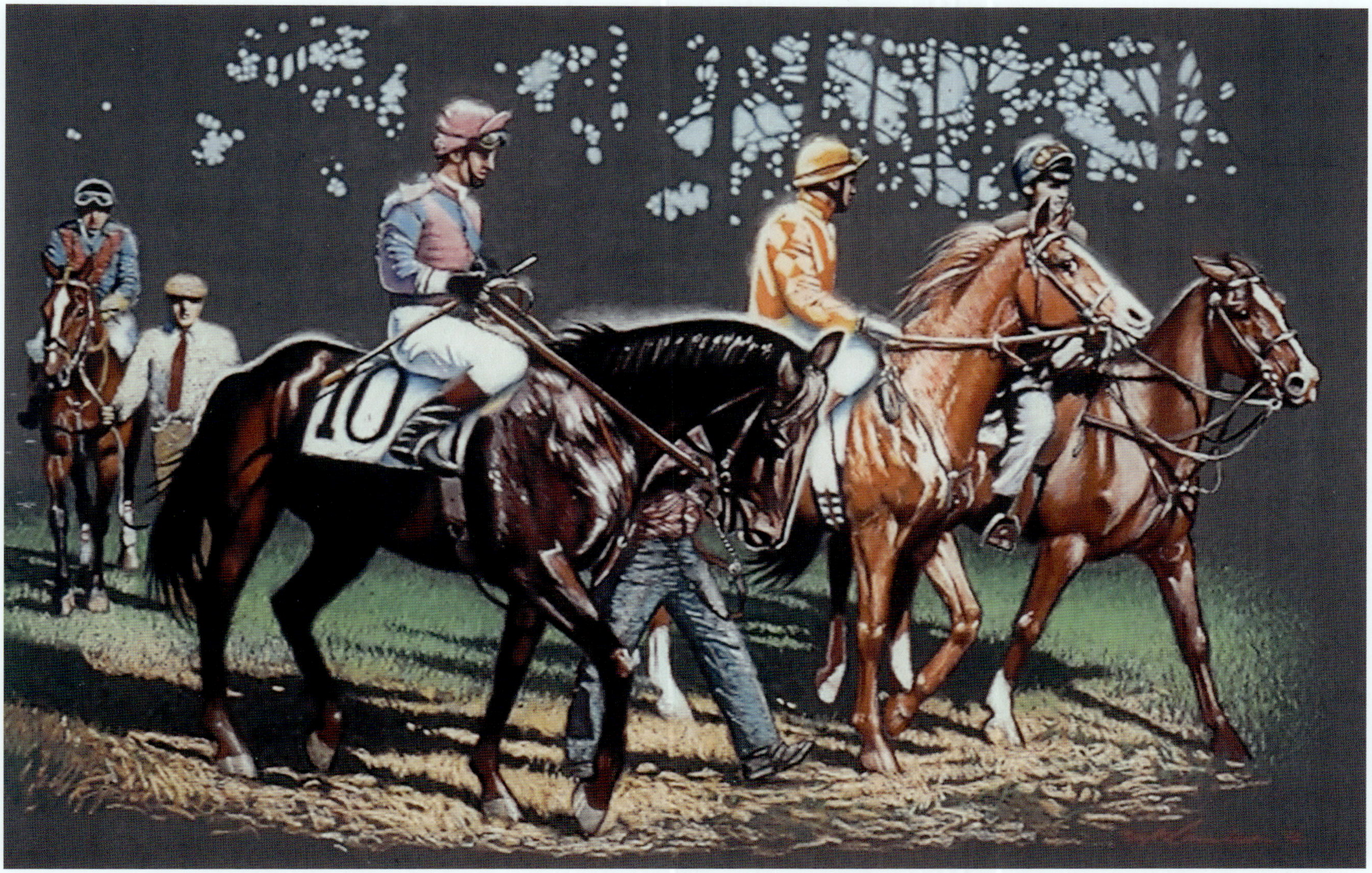

Saturday Centaurs, pastel

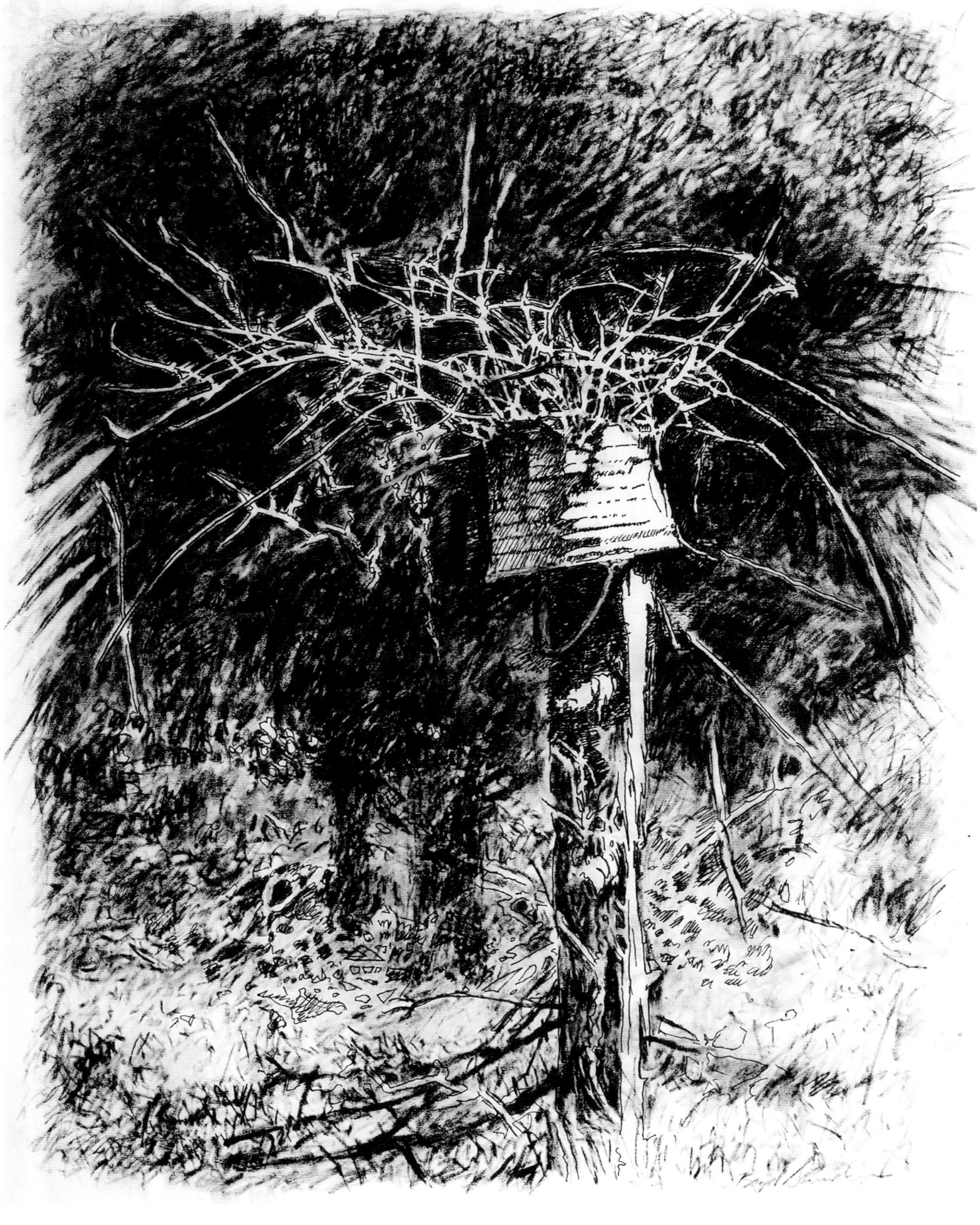

Sentinel I (study for *Summer Solstice*), ink wash

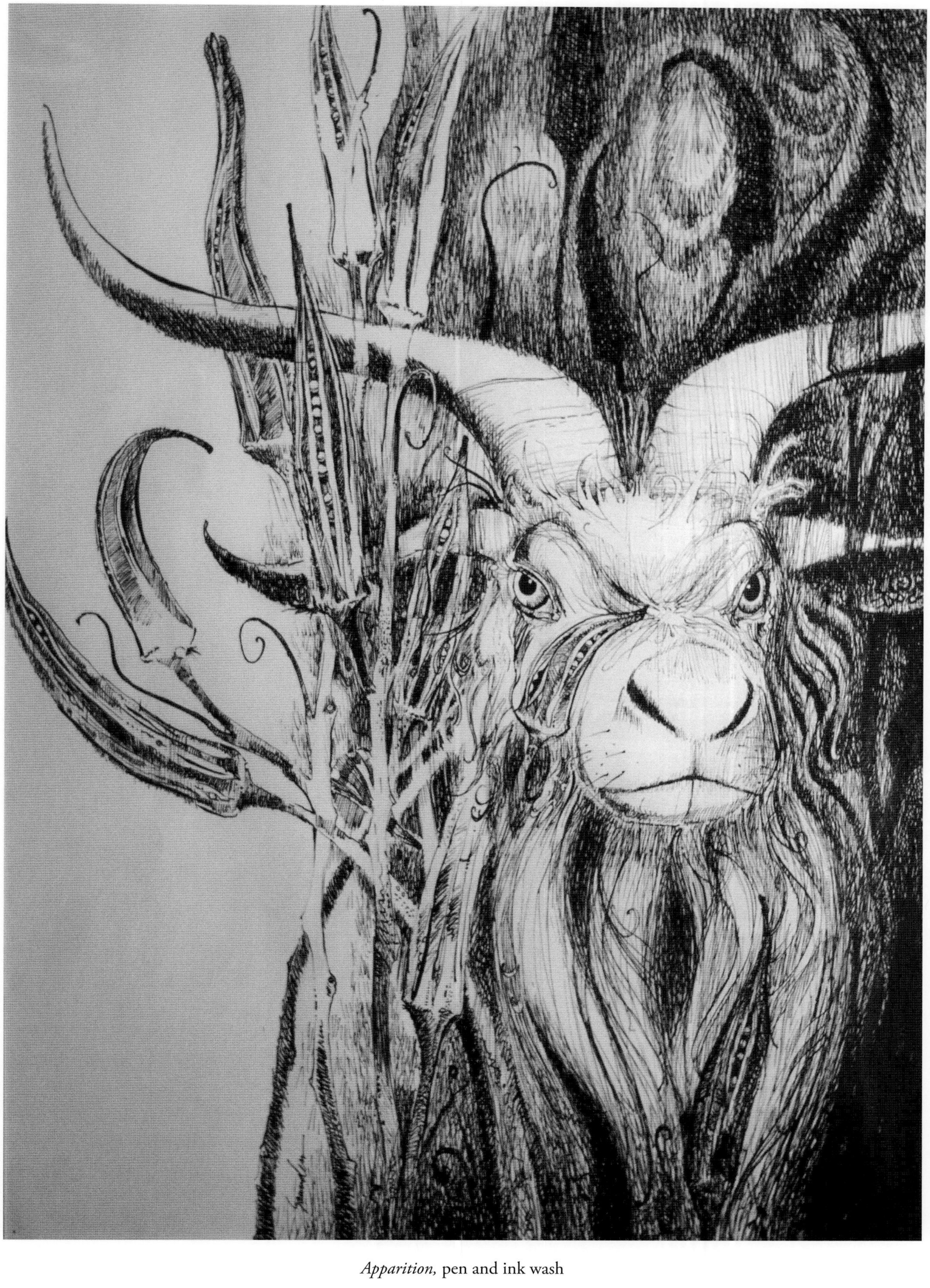

Apparition, pen and ink wash

Chapter 13

Saunders and Music

As with reading and drawing, Boyd Saunders was seemingly born with an affinity for music. Those qualities were nurtured early on by the artist's mother, who was an especially competent musician and inspired teacher (see chapter 2). Boyd's father was an amateur singer as well. Irene Saunders began teaching music to her four sons when they were young. For example, before the boys were teenagers, she had formed them into a gospel quartet, then both directed and accompanied them at the piano. As a group they performed at social events and church functions throughout southwest Tennessee. Those same brothers played in their high school band, and Boyd was a percussionist with a small dance band. In addition he built a competency on the piano, performing often at local venues. Following his mother's example, he learned to play the organ and served as organist at churches in Rossville and Collierville, Tennessee.

While at Memphis State University as an undergraduate, Saunders intensified his involvement with music by adding a minor in it. He was a member of more than one chorus and glee club and even performed in several operas. Related coursework included music theory, composition, music history, and conducting. Student Saunders also studied pipe organ under

Dr. George Harris and simultaneously served as music director for a Methodist church in Memphis.

After completing academic degrees at Memphis State and the University of Mississippi, Saunders continued his passion for vocal music by studying voice under Professor John Belisle at Southwest Texas State University–San Marcos, which was, once again, Saunders's first teaching post. After he accepted a teaching position in 1965 at the University of South Carolina, and had sufficiently settled in, he began inquiring about choral groups in the area. Relatively soon Saunders became a member of the Columbia Choral Society, founded in 1930, and joined the Washington Street Methodist Church choir about the same time. Then in 1985 Professor Saunders was accepted into the Palmetto Mastersingers, one of the most prestigious male choral groups in the state of South Carolina. The Palmetto Mastersingers was begun in 1981 by Professor Arpad Darazs, who was also director of choral studies at USC-Columbia. This group is said to be the realization of his vision. "He saw the wonderful possibilities of a men's chorus to provide an opportunity for men from all walks of life who love to sing together, to do so, but he also saw the greater purpose of the rich service such as a group could provide to many people by enhancing the cultural life of the community. Commencing our next twenty-five years bears witness to the fact that others caught the vision, provided the leadership, and made the commitment to fulfill it."[1]

The Twenty-Fifth Anniversary Concert Season–reunion logo (1981–2006) sports a banner proclaiming this organization collectively as "South Carolina Musical Ambassadors."[2] "Over the past 25 seasons, The Palmetto Mastersingers have promoted the unique sound of a male chorus throughout South Carolina, throughout other parts of the United States and across the globe. It is through the many thousands of hours of volunteered time that we have been fortunate to do this."[3]

Saunders certainly echoed those statements by an anonymous spokesman when he wrote: "We have had an impressive run, have performed in a wide variety of local, national and international venues, have joined forces with a number of international celebrities, have produced several popular CDs, and have received high critical acclaim."[4]

The Palmetto Mastersingers thirty-eight-page booklet for the 2005–6 concert season listed its participants in groups of columns, that is, first tenor, second tenor, baritone, and bass, totaling almost eighty voices. Saunders's name was listed in the baritone section, and he continues to sing with that distinguished organization.

During the twenty-fifth anniversary season, this choral group's itinerary included singing with Grammy Award winner Melissa Manchester, a radio appearance on *Walter Edgar's Journal,* performing with the U.S. Army Field Band as part of its southeastern states U.S. tour, singing with the South Carolina Philharmonic Orchestra for a special reprise of *Mark Twain Remarks,* participating in the welcoming activities for the South Carolina legislature as it began the 2006 session at the statehouse in Columbia, and touring in China.[5]

In 2009 the Palmetto Mastersingers presented concerts in eastern Canada beginning in Montreal, Quebec, in a joint performance with the Welsh Men's Choir. Soon the South Carolina choir boarded a Holland American cruise ship, *The Maasdam,* and traveled east, northeast along the St. Lawrence Seaway presenting concerts at Charlottetown on Prince Edward Island, and Sidney and Halifax in Nova Scotia, ending down the New England coast at Boston, Massachusetts. This same troupe even presented a concert on the cruise ship for their sixteen hundred fellow passengers.

Since its formation in the early 1980s, the Palmetto Mastersingers have performed in premier venues in the United States including the National Cathedral, the White House in Washington, D.C., and Carnegie Hall, New York City. International concerts beyond the already mentioned eastern Canadian venues include several concert tours in Europe, at stellar sites or institutions, for example Chartres Cathedral, Chartres, France; Notre Dame Cathedral, Paris; the Cathedrals of Ulm and Cologne in Germany; St. Mark's Cathedral in Venice, and St. Peter's Basilica, Rome.[6]

In addition concerts were presented in Vienna, Austria; Budapest, Hungary; and Moscow and St.

Petersburg, Russia after the end of the Cold War. Not to be overlooked are the number of successful recordings, and the number of commissioned and premiered original choral compositions from prominent contemporary composers, or for that matter the number of performances with such musical notables as the Kingston Trio and the Four Freshman, as well as the above mentioned Melissa Manchester.[7]

Chapter 14

Saunders and the Loblolly Society of Columbia, South Carolina

The Loblolly Society of Columbia, South Carolina, originated in late 1981 as a way of nurturing more interaction between University of South Carolina faculty and staff plus city and county individuals who had more varied professions. It was hoped those persons would regularly come together for fellowship and intellectual stimulation and perhaps in a dining setting.[1]

The founder of the infant organization was Dr. James B. Meriwether, a USC professor of English and an eminent William Faulkner scholar. Gail Morrison, a graduate student in 1981, suggested that Dr. Meriwether's original notion had a more modest goal, that of establishing a forum in which he and several of his Ph.D. candidates could explore scholarship on broader topics in more relaxed circumstances than a classroom or seminar room. Other long-term members tend to concur with the preceding statements, albeit with varied details, though Dr. Meriwether did have an additional goal in mind. He had formerly belonged to a similar organization in the area but then regretted that it was a male-only group. Hence one of the organizational planks for the Loblolly Society was that it be of mixed gender and, for that matter, not discriminatory in any other way. To his credit five of the original nine members were women, including USC graduate students and, during those early years, a number of the male members' wives. The Loblolly Society grew at a modest rate to twenty-five or thirty members and then leveled off.

The membership process in general has involved a member recommending another person or persons for consideration, followed by a background check, request for credentials, a visit by invitation to one of the organization's regular meetings, introduction, conversations with the regular membership, and at a later date a formal nomination, discussion including the important element of collegiality, and finally a vote by secret ballot.[2]

Though the word "loblolly" may be a household term in South Carolina, the majority of people outside the region might be unfamiliar with it. Loblolly makes a curious sound when spoken. It has also had a curious history or etymology over the centuries with a couple of connotations that could hardly have been the association desired by the newly formed group in Columbia, South Carolina, in 1981. For example a popular American 1970s dictionary defined the word in question as follows: "loblolly n., *pl,* lies, *Regional.* 1. A mudhole; a mire. 2. A lout. ["Originally a thick gruel: perhaps dialectal *lob,* to bubble, boil + *lolly,* broth."][3]

The American Heritage Dictionary of the English Language (2006) provides an expanded clarification with a more local focus: "Regional Note: Loblolly is a combination of *lob,* probably an onomatopoeia for the thick, heavy bubbling of cooking porridge, and *lolly* an old British dialect for broth, soup or any other food boiled in a pot; Thus loblolly originally denoted thick porridge or gruel, especially that eaten by sailors aboard ship. In the Southern United States, the word is used to mean 'a mudhole; a mire, a sense derived from an allusion to the consistency of porridge.'"[4]

In the twenty-first century the word "loblolly" is most likely a botanical reference for which the already quoted regional note is helpful: "The name *loblolly* has become associated with several varieties of trees as well, all of which favor wet bottomlands or swamps in the Gulf and South Atlantic states":[5] "Loblolly pine: A pine (pinus taeda) [tree] of the southeast United States, having needles in fascicles of three, oblong cones and strong wood used as lumber and for paper pulp."[6]

Dr. Meriwether is said to have chosen loblolly as the name for his modest-sized town-and-gown group and briefly for two reasons: "He liked the association of the loblolly pine because it is a familiar South Carolina species and the greatest lumber producing southern conifer in South Carolina."[7]

The conifer is indigenous to South Carolina, easily recognizable and important to the state's economy. The other appeal of loblolly for Dr. Meriwether involved a whimsical association. He apparently surmised that loblolly, an obscure eighteenth-century term for "commodious miscellany," could be translated loosely as "an all embracing definition of something that could deal with a variety of subjects."[8] Loblolly Society members have presented papers on widely diverse subjects, and they enjoy discussing their presentations "over some pretty fancy stew."[9]

The primary academic function of the Loblolly Society has been the preparation of engaging, provocative papers that are presented and discussed collegially during question and answer sessions. Copies of about fifty papers presented at Loblolly Society meetings over the years are housed at the USC Caroliniana Library in Columbia. As luck would have it, the earliest paper in the collection (which dates back to April 9, 1984) has an art topic. It was titled *The Early Work of J. Bardin,* who was also the author. Artist J. Bardin was a USC classmate and friend of fellow South Carolina artist Jasper Johns before the latter became internationally renowned for his experimental, mixed-media work and bold lithographs, some of which are emblematic of pop art.

It is not surprising that Boyd Saunders, now a USC distinguished professor emeritus, but still very much an active artist, along with Tommy Stepp, secretary to the board of trustees of the University of South Carolina, were noted in Curtis Clark's short history presentation as the longest-serving current members of the Loblolly Society, which they joined in 1984. Finally it was at a Loblolly Society monthly meeting in 2000 where Saunders presented his carefully researched, written, and illustrated paper on the subject of his mural-size painting *The Battle of Hanging Rock, SC, 1780.* The location of the meeting was the South Carolina State Museum, where the installed painting was formally unveiled to the public on that occasion. The Loblolly Society's thirtieth anniversary was celebrated in 2011.

About fifty Loblolly Society paper topics and their authors are listed at the online source USC South

Caroliniana Library Catalog, http://library.sc.edu/socar/. A sampling of those titles reveals a breadth of subjects and the members' willingness to tackle unpleasant issues:

Nancy C. Meriwether, "Southern Pottery: Form Follows Function," 1988

Lynn S. Barron, "Japonisme" and Its Influence on the Work of Two South Carolina Artists: Alice Ravenel Huger Smith and Anna Heyward Taylor," 2003

J. Bardin (Jesse Redwin), "Anna Wells Rutledge, William Aiken Walker and the Summer of '88 [1888]," 1988

John J. Winberry, "Kudzu: The Vine That Almost Ate the South," c. 1996

Jim Welch, "Sojourns, Saunters, Treks and Odysseys: Encounters with Nature in South Carolina, 1540–2000," 2000

John J. Winberry, "Profitable as the Mines of Mexico or Peru: Indigo in South Carolina," 2002

Bruce Estes Rippeteau, "Southern Dirt: The Literate Archaeology of a Loblolly Menagerie, or The Name of the Rose Redux," 2001

William Shepherd McAnich, "A Brief History of Capital Punishment in South Carolina (with Some Emphasis on Race)," 2000

Warner Miller Montgomery, "The Desegregation of Richland County School District One, 1970–1973," 2006

Kevin Lewis, "Lynching, Prophecy, and Poetry," 1994

Thomas L. Stepp, "Controversy in the Management Environment of Previous South Carolina Performing Arts Institutions," 1985

Lynn S. Barron, "Book Banning in South Carolina," 2000

Jerry Burford McAninch, "John Ehle and the Settlement of Western North Carolina," 2000

Gary J. Miler, "No Matter How You Slice It, There Are Always Two Sides: A Review of Banastre Tarleton's Affect on American History," c. 2001

John Hammond Moore, "Founding and History of Columbia and Richland County, SC," 2003

O'Neal Smalls, "Reconstruction Lawmaking," 2000

Becky Wingard Lewis, "The Girl behind the Counter, the Boy of the Cake, and the Steel Wasp: Themes in Owen Wister's Lady Baltimore," 2002

Quitman Marshall, "The Swamp: Excerpts from a Work in Progress," 1999

Ronald E. Bridwell, "The Coming of Commercial Radio to South Carolina and the Evolution of 'Hillbilly Music' in the 1930s," 2008

Boyd Saunders, "Familiar Tracks: A Circular Journey," 2002

Ceille Baird Welch, "James Dickey in 4 Parts," 2006

Ronald E. Bridwell, "The Library (and Life) of a South Carolina Scholar: George Calvin Rogers, Jr.," 1999

Chapter 15

The Storyteller's Art

As stated in the chapter "Early Life," I was born on a farm in west Tennessee and have lived in the South all my life. It has been quite natural for me to assume the southern affinity for literature and storytelling: whether from the Bible stories that were read to me as a child, the accounts of hunters around evening campfires, raconteurs spinning yarns to pass the time while working in the fields, preachers and politicians mastering the art of oratory, or that great army of southern literary giants, too vast to list, who have dominated the world of modern literature.

Indeed most of the visual art that I saw and loved as I was growing up was intended to illustrate many of these narrative vehicles. It should be pointed out that none of those tellers of tales were under any burden to confine themselves to strict scientific accuracy in their utterances. In fact magic, miracles, fantasy, and superstition were a vital and integral part of the consciousness of the times, whether as a matter of absolute belief or simply a literary diversion to add texture to a tale. Ghosts regularly haunted graveyards or abandoned houses, angels and demigods walked about on the earth, conjurers cast spells, and animals sometimes talked and acted like humans. Preaching and political oratory were filled with hyperbole, exaggeration, and, in the case of politicians, downright lies.

In that world, in which the divinity and ultimate sacrifice of Christ, the violence of his death, and the mystical transformation of his resurrection were paramount and all pervasive, it was perhaps inevitable that human redemption was often found in self-destruction, violent retribution, horror, and magic. It was equally inevitable that any man who wished to take himself seriously felt compelled to raise himself to the level of the hero or superhuman. (It is significant that a large majority of the men who have been awarded the American Congressional Medal of Honor for courage in battle have been southerners.)

It is easy to understand why much southern visual art, mine included, has tended to weave a richly evocative texture of narrative and surreal fantasy. From infancy onward I was read to extensively by parents and relatives alike. The words had a powerful and evocative effect on me, and my imagination easily turned the descriptive phrases into rich and colorful images. It was of little concern to me whether or not the Mother Goose stories were based on historical fact, nor was I bothered by the concept of humanized animals who could talk and wear clothes. I was terrified that the Little Red Hen might be eaten by the hungry fox and extremely pleased that she just happened to be carrying needle and thread and scissors to facilitate her escape. The great Bible stories were memorable and did not move me to ponder exactly when or how far away they might have taken place. I never saw a huge difference between the great Bible stories and the fairy tales in children's books. For me the epic Bible tale of David and Goliath was, for instance, quite similar to the tale of Jack and the Beanstalk, and it could be enjoyed for many of the same reasons. A good tale was a good tale.

As I listened to radio during its golden era, my mind easily took the words from the old cathedral radio set and provided pictures to accompany them.

When adult kinfolk came to visit, I heard countless stories of ancestors or distant relatives that I would never in my life lay eyes on. Thus unburdened by fact, my mind could paint them any way it pleased.

On soft summer evenings my family gathered after supper on the front porch. My brothers and I would "play out" in the gathering dusk, often joined by neighbor kids, which provided a blood feast for every ravenous mosquito or chigger in the county, until the darkness was complete; then we would join the adults on the porch. There we migrated from lap to lap or lay on pallets while we watched lightning bugs in the orchard or listened to the adults talk in relaxed cadence of the farm events of the day, or the war in Europe or the Pacific, or who else had just been drafted, or the local soldier boy who was missing or dead and would not be coming home.

Around 9:30 P.M. the Streamliner "fast train" would pass across our view on the Southern Railroad, a mile away down in the river bottom, looking exotic and mysterious, its stentorian baritone horn proclaiming its presence and announcing its rapid progress toward places unknown. This was my grandfather's traditional signal that it was time for us to go inside and to bed. While my mother read to her sons from the big Bible storybook about Noah and the Flood or Samson slaying the Philistines with the jawbone of a donkey, my father listened to the radio as H. B. Kaltenborn or Bill Stern talked about the progress of the war.

Then there was the rainy evening when a neighbor gentleman came calling on my father, and after some perfunctory palaver, the two retired to the porch for obviously more important and probably more confidential conversation. Sensing the gravity of their demeanor, I slipped out and hid behind a potted fern. From this vantage point I heard them speak in low and somber tones about the relative who had finally succumbed to his despair and killed himself.

I consider myself a product of a long southern tradition of storytelling, preaching, and oratory. As if being a narrative artist were not bad enough, I am also a printmaker. This too seems to mystify and confuse the unenlightened. Certainly throughout history the printed word and the printed image have been closely associated with one another. Sometimes my art is dismissed as narrative or illustrational. I am afraid I never have any real snappy comeback . . . because maybe it's true. However, most of the art in our common artistic heritage could be described in the same manner.

I have a special affinity for humor. Jokes, pranks, and ribald anecdotes (many with language too raunchy for polite society) were a regular part of the world I once knew and composed much of the dialogue of my high school classmates and myself. There seemed to be a constant competition to see who could be the funniest or most outrageous. It was sort of a means of achieving status. Some of the pranks we pulled became legendary.

As I grew up I found myself working with youth groups in one capacity or another: camp counselor, ball coach, recreation leader, and so on. It seemed that some of my specialties were campfire storytelling and skit productions. This may have reached some sort of high (or low) point during my college days with the production of several Halloween parties for my college friends out in the Saunderses' farm woodlot. The last and most notorious of these (with me as the master of ceremonies, of course) featured a large campfire, magic tricks, stories, Indian dancers, a fabulous haunted house, a headless horseman, and—the crème de la crème—burning my baby brother Lee alive before the startled eyes of one and all. My mother never quite forgave me for that one, although baby brother Lee is still very much alive and well. The event was a legend thereafter.

After Stephanie and I married, we had no television and very little money, so many evenings were spent reading to one another. After our children were born we made it a point to remain televisionless for several years and chose, instead, to spend our evenings with our children in other ways; reading aloud, telling stories, and playing games, or sometimes I played monster out in the yard in the gathering dusk with our offspring and the neighborhood kids.

Our daughters learned to read early and well and had very fertile imaginations. Some of our most cherished family possessions were big, lavishly illustrated storybooks. Our children were introduced to the fine art of storytelling while looking at pictures created by artists such as Johnnie Gurelle, Beatrix Potter, Nancy Eckstrom-Burkert, the Provensens, or N. C. Wyeth. I must confess that many of the books just may have been selected for acquisition more because of their appeal to my wife and myself than for the children's needs, although no one would have ever admitted it.

One night, somewhat after bedtime, daughter Sylvia discovered to her considerable terror that there was a bear under her bed. My assurances to her that there was no bear under her bed were of no avail; she had most certainly seen him reach his claw out and drag one of her shoes under the bed, where she could hear him eating it.

Deciding to fight fire with fire, I looked under the bed, agreed that there was indeed a very large bear under there, and declared that I would get him out. While Sylvia hid her head under the covers, I grabbed a nearby broom, shoved the end of it under the bed, and with much noise and clattering about, drove the bear out from under her bed, down the hall, and out into the darkened backyard where I had a loud and violent fight with him before driving him off into the woods.

I then returned to her room breathless and disheveled and covered with dirt and pine straw and claimed that I had vanquished the bear, taught him a lesson, and was sure he would not return. Whatever else, it was great theater. She seemed satisfied with the outcome, settled down, and went to sleep. Feeling somewhat smug and smart, I showered and went back to bed.

Strangely enough, about a week later, the bear was back, so the performance had to be repeated. Then again, and again, and so on. Belatedly I began to realize that she had long ago figured out the scam, and whenever she had done the drink-of-water thing and the potty thing and wanted to stall bedtime, or was just plain bored, she would play the bear card and watch her simpleminded father play out the "Banishing the Bear" skit and again make a complete fool of himself for her amusement. It was great theater!

Her younger sister, Rachel, on the other hand, received frequent nocturnal visits from the "Night Mary," whose red eyes could be seen glowing, even through the drawn curtains, as she peered into Rachel's bedroom, perhaps intent on eating the child. By the time the resulting outcry had awakened her parents and we had arrived to the rescue, the night visitor had vanished.

It took many of these episodes for us to realize that when the teenage neighbor boys across the street arrived home late at night, drove into their parents' carport, and pressed the car's brake pedal, the glowing tail lights would shine across the street, through the red plaid curtains, and into Rachel's bedroom. When we came in and switched on the light, the red eyes vanished.

That, of course, still did not explain the child's asking one morning why we had already repainted her door jamb and covered over the claw marks where "Night Mary" had been clawing at her door trying to gain entrance to Rachel's room the previous night.

Perhaps a fertile imagination is not always a good thing. Maybe a crazy father isn't either.

It was some years later I learned that my young niece and nephew back in Tennessee had been long afraid of the "Great Fearsome Hide-Behind" as described by their Uncle Boyd. The Hide-Behind could not be seen because he was always hiding behind something, and no one had ever seen him and lived to tell the tale. Maybe a crazy uncle is as bad as a crazy father.

Early on, E. B. White's classic work *Charlotte's Web* became a part of our family legend. This whimsical tale of the garden spider (also known as a scrivener spider) who saved the life of Wilbur the pig, by weaving mysterious messages into her web, was a top favorite in our house. Shortly after one of the readings of this story, a real, live garden spider took up residence on the terrace just outside Rachel's bedroom, where we could watch her daily as she went about her duties of weaving a huge web with the mysterious writing in the middle of it, catching unwary insects in the web, immobilizing them in her cocoon, then sucking the life out of them.

Rachel was fine with this arrangement as long as there was a double pane sliding glass door between this drama and her, and she followed it with some fascination. On those occasions when a spider was discovered in her room, however, it was an entirely different matter, and Daddy was quickly summoned to the rescue.

We all watched as our Charlotte built and filled several egg sacks then began to grow listless and transparent. Then came the day, as summer was turning into autumn, when our Charlotte stopped moving and shriveled to near nothing, and the long gossamer parachutes attached to the egg sacks, caught the breeze and sailed away over the trees, carrying their egg sack cargoes away to another place and another season of life.

University life provides a wide range of cultural opportunities, and my family spent many happy hours at musical and theatrical events. Both Sylvia and Rachel were active in dramatic programs while they were in high school, and as they grew into young women, we had an especially treasured family tradition of enjoying summer repertory theater. For a number of years the University of South Carolina Theater Department presented an outstanding summer rolling rep series in a wonderfully intimate theater-in-the-round setting. We subscribed to all the offerings. Stephanie, Sylvia, and Rachel and I would have dinner out together, go to the play (with seats so close we could almost hold hands with the actors), and then stop for dessert somewhere on the way home where we would discuss the play.

When I first arrived at the University of South Carolina in 1965, the first person I met was a big, burly, straight-talking Irishman named John O'Neil. For the next four decades we were close friends and colleagues, and for much of that time he was also my department chairman.

The USC Art Department that I joined in 1965 had fewer than a half dozen faculty members and a modest student enrollment. Over the ensuing years the department changed profoundly as it struggled to keep up with the changing times and a rapidly expanding university.

During those days some very interesting characters, some with quirky personalities, others with, let's face it, serious mental disorders, passed through our midst. John and I seemed destined to deal with all of them. Over the years we developed a litany of stories about those encounters that a similar circumstance or a glass of whiskey might well precipitate.

Most of those tales we could each tell alone quite credibly, but some of them we could best relate as a team. We both subscribed to the theory that if a story is worth telling, it is worth telling well. We also believed that if something didn't actually happen exactly that way, maybe it should have, so absolute factual accuracy was not necessarily a high priority in those accounts. Indeed, like fine wine or cheese, most of those narratives seemed to improve with age and repetition.

From time to time it was suggested by several friends that this body of legend should be preserved for future generations, that he and I should sit down one day with a tape recorder, a bottle of good Tennessee bourbon, and a few like-minded friends who would ask key questions and laugh at appropriate times, and thus record these treasures for posterity, perhaps turn it into a book or something. The resultant tone might have been titled "An Unauthorized and Occasionally Factual History of the USC Art Department," or perhaps a simpler title might have been "Lunatics We Have Known." Unfortunately we never got around to it. John died in December 2004. Now, sadly, that will never take place.

Then there was the Rembrandt Memorial Light Cavalry, Chili, Perloo and Literary Society, Dismounted, a motley crew of a half dozen or so advanced printmakers, student helpers, and assorted friends who would convene for a social moment from time to time in my office at the university after a Friday seminar or critique. A bottle of Jack Daniel's finest or some Glenlivet scotch was sacrificed, and the B.S. and ballyhoo flowed. We pretended to be some gathering of eccentric scholar-adventurers regaling and attempting to outdo each other with accounts (spurious and always outrageous) of our exploits and adventures defending crown and country in far-off India, or discovering long-lost scrolls in Ur, or extricating ourselves from an unfortunate incident in a Paris bordello.

Each of us had multiple honorific titles in the society: "Master of Hounds," "Bung Starter," "Keeper of the Condom," "Procuress in Residence," and so on. Some members occasionally wore folded newspaper hats or brought makeshift wooden swords. We usually opened the meeting with a ceremonial reading from *Ole Man Adam and His Chillun* or maybe Boccaccio's *Decameron* tales, and offering a toast to the long life of the Queen or to secession, or perhaps to free love.

After that it was freeform and extemporaneous. Occasionally John O'Neil joined us. He could be counted on to hold his own. Especially rewarding were the times when the congenial, humorless, Yankee art historian from down the hall blundered in, intent on speaking with me about some arcane matter, and be caught in up in the middle of this madness.

Not surprisingly no one ever slipped out of character or gave an inch. After trying hopelessly to figure what was happening or become a party of it, he would flee down the hall, babbling to himself and glancing furtively back over his shoulder. It was great fun. It was great theater.

For a number of years I served as master of ceremonies for a country music festival and barbecue picnic that was organized and hosted by my friends Doug and Bunny Williams. It began as an annual Sunday afternoon gathering at their house in the country, but it expanded year by year and finally migrated to the stage of the Newberry Opera House. It pretended to be an old-time radio show in the manner of *The Grand Ole Opry,* or perhaps *The Prairie Home Companion,* and was called *A Carolina Jubilee.*

As master of ceremonies, I introduced the different acts, provided filler between acts, and told homespun yarns and jokes, usually at the expense of various members of the troupe. It was there that I had the good fortune to make the acquaintance of two dynamite women with extraordinary literary talent, Sue Summer and Andy Hawkins. They each have a separate life with home and family and all that, but when they get together, they function like a well-rehearsed dance team, at both the personal and professional levels. Sue lives in Newberry, South Carolina; Andy resides in nearby Prosperity.

Both have a wide variety of literary credentials, including a weekly radio show on a Newberry A.M. radio station, and Sue writes a column in the local weekly newspaper. Andy is public relations director for a local hospital, and Sue has recently completed a novel. Both are world-class storytellers and have been the authors of many of the skits and fake commercials on the *Carolina Jubilee* show.

Their humor is quick, often ribald, and relentless and can turn on a dime to heartbreaking pathos. They are big on telling and performing stories and from time to time attend national storytelling conclaves such as the one in Jonesboro, Tennessee.

Over time they have created an alternative world, part fact and part fiction, built on the lives and goings-on of the inhabitants of "the Berry"; the more outrageous, the better.

My life and outlook have been vastly enriched by knowing them, and my artistic and literary skills have been profoundly informed by their input. Twice I have appeared as a guest on their morning show on radio station WKDK in Newberry, South Carolina, to spin a yarn (in the guise of a columnist or commentator) about some fictional character or happening in the Dutch Fork community. Surprisingly, I have not yet caused the station to lose its FCC license.

When Stephanie was recuperating from a broken hip, I read to her at bedtime; maybe Faulkner, maybe Uncle Remus, maybe Winnie the Pooh or Raggedy Ann. And when I was nearly blinded by the wrong prescription drugs and struggling to save what was left of my eyesight, she read to me every evening.

Even now, under much improved circumstances, she frequently reads to me from her book club selections. Some of our favorite writers are Thomas Friedman, Karen Armstrong, and Thomas Cahill.

On long road trips we frequently listen to books on tape, and at home we listen to Dick Estelle's *Radio Reader* show on National Public Radio (NPR). Through the magic of radio, John Grisham is a frequent visitor at our breakfast table.

As stated earlier in this book, most of my artistic output has been involved with producing a body of prints, paintings, sculptures, and drawings that serve as a sort of epic visual poem about a fictional agrarian community in the American South. Each piece is designed to stand alone or be experienced as a part of this larger collective body of work. In differing contexts several titles have been used: *Southern Cross/A Trilogy, St. James Crossing,* and *Return of the Wanderer.* From time to time I have incorporated the written word into my compositions. At other times I have written or narrated short fictional stories, often humorous, that convey ideas that I do not possess the skill to realize in purely visual form.

Most recently the *Return of the Wanderer Suite* served as inspiration for the short, humorous written tale "The Return of Miss Dixie," which was preceded by another short written tale "Henry the Mule."

Of course in this context the literal truth or veracity of a humorous anecdote becomes relatively unimportant. *"If it didn't happen that way, it should have."* Good stories, like fine wine or cheese, can often improve with age. With repeated telling, stories tend to edit themselves. Insignificant extraneous details can often be replaced by much better extraneous details. As one might guess, the comic pages and editorial cartoons have always been my favorite part of any newspaper. But there are many fine visual artists who have served as models for my own efforts; some of them have been illustrators and "commercial" artists. I have also drawn much inspiration from writers of prose and poetry; the novels and short stories of William Faulkner or Edgar Lee Masters's *Spoon River Anthology* come quickly to mind. Additionally I have used the music of Charles Ives (1874–1954) as an inspiration for many of my own visual compositions. More recently I have learned much from the work of such southern artists as Terry Allen and Ke Frances, both of whom often weave the written and spoken word and visual imagery together in virtually seamless artistic statement.

Again, in spite of my high regard, yea, even reverence, for the written word, many stories just need to be *told* and *told well* in order to be fully appreciated.

THE WOOD LOT

Christopher Robin had a special, enchanted place called "the Hundred Acre Wood." There his stuffed toys, Winnie the Pooh, Tigger, Eeyore, Small, Wol, and their friends, were magically transformed into living beings who walked and talked and became the players in a series of wonderful and charming stories. These accounts, written by A. A. Milne, have captured the fancies of children and adults alike for almost a century. Ancient mystics had their sacred groves; Christopher Robin had the "Hundred Acre Wood" in which reality could be transformed into magic.

My brothers and I also had such a place. "The Wood Lot," as it was called, was a grove of ancient hardwood trees that lay beyond the barn on the Saunderses' farm in west Tennessee where we grew up. It was not much more than two acres in size; it was bordered on the west side by an ancient sunken road, and in other places by fields, barns, and a couple of tenant houses. The wood lot had often served as a pig pasture and thus contained a few small ponds and a couple of secluded animal shelters. The dominant feature of this place was the collection of gnarled and weather-beaten centenarian oak and hickory trees. Those trees provided a majestic towering canopy of cover that dimmed summer sunlight and provided fertile fields for the imagination to run wild.

The huge roots of these trees spread out, half in, half out of the ground in a maze of twisting and looping forms that created arches and tunnels and bridges and caves and bowers that could excite the imagination of any childlike person. Small, furry animals dined on the acorns and hickory nuts and often made their dens here. Add some toys with wheels, or metal miniature soldiers, and it became a toy land to rival any department store Christmas window. Add some little girls with dolls, and these nooks became perfect dollhouses or nests. Occasionally one of those artifacts would be left unnoticed, wedged into a secluded crotch of these roots. Over time the roots would slowly encase the toy in the wood, making it impossible to remove. In this way toy fragments, even from previous generations of children, long since grown, remained as markers of those children's passage this way. In much the same way that Raggedy Ann had a candy heart hidden in her body, some of those trees actually had small children's toys buried inside them.

In that enchanted grove, my brothers and I could become Robin Hood and his merry men; or perhaps Hopalong Cassidy, or maybe American Marines storming a Japanese fortification. We learned to transform the hickory wood into bows and arrows of remarkable sophistication. These bows were sturdy and symmetrical, and the arrows were tipped with steel and fletched with chicken feathers. On occasion one of those marvelous projectiles would be launched into the air on a test flight. Our feelings would quickly go from exhilaration to despair as we watched it sail high in elegant trajectory and impale its point into one of the topmost branches of an ancient oak tree, sixty feet high and completely inaccessible, there to remain forever.

There was a lesson in life there; hours of painstaking work for this one brief flight, one fleeting instant of ecstasy. We have all been there at one time or another. When our mother learned of those dangerous projectiles, she invoked her version of the Geneva Conventions and banned them forever. In those woods we could build tree houses with elaborate arboreal approaches, via rope ladders and swinging bridges and such, which required simian agility and human foolishness to traverse. In those upper reaches we became as one with the raucous crows and sinister hawks who built large nests in those places.

When a beloved pet died, it was buried there in a special place with the twin girls from across the road joining us and singing a moving rendition of "Sioux City Sue" as part of the ceremony. In that enchanted place we not only could become invisible to our parents' scrutiny but were magically rendered unable to hear them calling us to more mundane duties. (In bad weather the hay loft of the barn also served this function quite well.) In the grove neighbor kids would join us for mock battles that would sometimes spill out over the surrounding fields and up and down the wooded banks of a nearby creek. As Tarzan of the Apes, we would swing from tree to tree on long ropes or muscadine grapevines.

Over the years that grove often served as the venue for groups of other kids from school or church who would gather around campfires there for "weenie roasts" or other social events. This continued into my college days when elaborate Halloween parties were staged there for my college friends. Those events became quite extensive and even included turning a nearby abandoned tenant house into a first-rate haunted house with many delightful features, including a headless body writhing about on the floor while his nearby severed head moaned and gasped and wallowed in a pool of its own blood. It was all damn good theater.

I remember with great fondness taking one of my brothers and a boyhood friend to the haunted house for a preview one afternoon before a party. As we stood in a dim room and talked, from across the room I magically caused a piece of bed sheet to rise from beneath a pile of rags and clutter in a corner to ascend toward the ceiling. Instantly a strange noise came from the throats of my brother and our friend, and in great haste they simultaneously proceeded to leave the building. As it turned out they each tried to go through the door at the same time, and momentarily both became stuck there. It was classic Three Stooges.

A couple of city kids were so unnerved by their Halloween experience in the dark and sinister woods that they freaked out and had to leave early and drive back to more familiar surroundings, poor things.

Some years later most of the family was gathered at the home place for Thanksgiving. The clan had, by then, increased to include another generation of small offspring. After dinner brother Lanny led everyone out to the edge of the wood lot and announced that it was now time to get the Thanksgiving turkey. He positioned everyone a little distance away from the edge of the woods, demanded absolute stillness and silence, then took his shotgun and disappeared into the woods, making turkey gobbling sounds as he went.

A short time later there came a loud bang from the gun, then to the astonishment of everyone, young and old alike, brother Lanny came walking out of the woods, his still-smoking gun in one hand and a very large, very alive turkey gobbler in the other. I suppose if one had looked closely, the remains of a tether might have been seen on one of the turkey's legs. After much ado, the bird was ceremonially presented to our friend Floyd, who took him home, fattened him up, and ate him for Christmas dinner. The caper was such a hit that it became a family tradition that had to be repeated every Thanksgiving for many years thereafter. Some members of my family catch on very slowly. Many traditions, like heroes, are made, not born.

The wood lot continued to be a magical and enchanted place. After all it was there that the Great Fearsome Hide-Behind was believed to reside. As Uncle Boyd had pointed out to unfortunate youngsters, he usually hid behind large trees and such, and no one had ever seen him and lived to tell of it. Many years later, when brother Lanny's eldest son was a grown man, with small children of his own, he and his father decided to raise the mother of all vegetable gardens at the Saunders's homestead. It was a truly noble endeavor; tomatoes, corn, beans, squash, carrots, a veritable cornucopia of the fruits of the good earth.

Just as these plants were reaching maturity, a marauding band of large, dark, hairy creatures came forth out of the wood lot in the night and laid total waste to the garden. They pulled down stalks, they dug up roots, and they plundered the produce. The devastation was complete in a few overwhelmingly destructive nocturnal raids. The dark, hairy creatures turned out to be groundhogs (also known as woodchucks). Those grossly oversized and gluttonous rodents (or whatever) had surreptitiously moved into the wood lot and taken up residence in elaborate burrows under the roots of the same old centenarian oak trees that we once had the temerity to consider ours. Those animals had never been there before. Indeed no one around there had ever seen such a creature, but there they were, and nothing could stand before them.

The magic of that old enchanted grove could indeed take strange forms. The barns and buildings are all gone now, having succumbed to the ravages of time and change. The surrounding fields and pastures are becoming streets with upscale houses. Many of the old patriarchal oaks have been felled by age or lightning, but a remnant of the old wood lot still stands. And on many Sunday afternoons, my nephew and his small sons drive out from Memphis to engage in paint-ball battles or roar through the trees on an ATV. And the Great Fearsome Hide-Behind remains unseen.

HENRY THE MULE

Hello, dear hearts! This is Boyd the Bodacious, and it is time once again for the latest social news from the Dutch Fork. We are happy to report that Miss Maybelle Shealy has recently returned home to "the Fork" after an extended visit with her daughter in Orangeburg. She has been there for a right good while trying to recover from an attack of the nerves.

It all started with Miss Maybelle's mule named Henry. Henry was a fine, high-spirited, long-legged mule that Miss Maybelle had kept around for occasional light work after her husband, Elwood, had quit farming and run off with Gail, the hairdresser.

Miss Maybelle had a nephew named Purvis. Now Purvis was a good enough old boy, but he didn't always fire on all eight cylinders, if you know what I mean. He had been a little strange ever since that time, oh, years ago, when his uncle Vander, a schoolteacher, had given him a book entitled *Classic Tales of Antiquity.*

Purvis was real taken by the tale of Daedalus and Icarus, how they built wings and flew and all. So he and his brother Leonard tried to do the same thing. They built wings out of broomsticks, burlap, baling wire, and some chicken feathers and proceeded to launch Purvis into the air from the top of the barn. Unfortunately he dropped like a stone and landed on his head. After that he was never quite right.

One day he borrowed his Aunt Maybelle's mule, Henry, to put in a little garden for his mama out behind her house, over on the other side of town.

As he was plowing with Henry, a sudden thunderstorm came up, and Purvis unhitched Henry from the plow and led him, still in harness, to the edge of the garden, where he quickly looped the ends of the plow lines around an iron fencepost. Then our boy ran to seek shelter from the rain under a large sassafras tree nearby.

Before Purvis could get to the tree, a bolt of lightning struck the tree, then ran, hissing and sparking, along the top wire of the fence to the iron fencepost, which suddenly began to spit sparks, hum, and glow with a strange, unearthly light.

Henry the Mule took one look at that spectacle and immediately decided that he needed to be someplace else, preferably back at his home barn, so he turned and bolted for home, never mind the fact that the far end of that sixteen-foot cotton rope plow line was still fastened to that iron fencepost. When Henry hit the end of that plow line, honey, it twanged like a plucked bowstring, and the fencepost on the end of it popped out of the ground like a cork out of a bottle and, quite naturally, proceeded to follow Henry home, bringing along a few stray strands of barbed wire just for company.

The plow line was hopelessly entangled in Henry's harness on the front end, and that iron fencepost, which was still glowing and spitting sparks, at the other. Not only that but it was careening wildly from one side of the road to the other, occasionally bouncing high into the air and making loud-clattering noises and striking sparks whenever it came down on the pavement. By this time the rain was coming down in sheets, and thunder and lightning were crashing all about.

Well, Henry, who was already running like a racehorse, did not particularly want company on this trip. Every time he looked back over his shoulder and saw that noisy nightmare following him, he would redouble his efforts and increase his speed, trying to run off and leave that beast. But it still followed him. Soon every dog in town was noisily chasing hysterically after this procession. The few motorists who were out and about quickly abandoned the pavement when they were approached by this moving bedlam. Some actually blew their horns at it, for whatever good they thought that might do.

Miss Maybelle was holding a meeting of the Women's Christian Missionary Society at her house that day. She had just served the little triangular pimiento cheese sandwiches and coffee when she heard the racket coming up the road to her house. She looked out the front window and saw the contingent sweep through her front yard, ripping out her prize gardenia bush and taking it along for the ride. As Henry and his retinue flashed around the corner of the house, she and the other ladies all rushed to the back windows just in time to see the flying iron fencepost leap into the air and catch her clothesline, bringing all her fresh wash along on this final push to the barn.

Just before Henry reached the safety of the barn, the plow line, burdened far beyond its intended capacity, broke, allowing Henry to find solitary comfort in the barn, leaving the tangle of fencepost, barbed wire, honeysuckle vines, gardenia bush, clothesline, and a mass of Miss Maybelle's unmentionables for the still hysterical dogs to throw themselves at and fight over, each one carrying off his own prize garment as if it were a trophy of the hunt.

The Missionary Society Meeting disbanded hastily, and Miss Maybelle felt a sudden need to go in and lay down for awhile. Next day she ran an ad in the *Chapin Times Newspaper* that simply said, "Mule for sale, cheap." And Purvis? Well that lightning bolt that struck that tree, knocked him out cold as a mackerel. When he came to, his clothes were scorched and smoking, all his hair was singed off, and he had a strange ringing in his ears. But his mind, dear hearts: yes, his mind was as clear and sharp as new paint. It was a miracle! He was healed! Praise the Lord! He decided then and there that he would devote the rest of his life to preaching the gospel.

He has now converted an old abandoned dairy barn into a church where he holds weekly Friday night healing services for the throngs who arrive from near and far. The high point of each service comes when the barn (turned tabernacle) is suddenly darkened and a brilliant electric charge flashes across between two lightning rods in front of the pulpit. When the lights return, the band unleashes all its volume while Purvis, resplendent in his white-and-sequined costume and bathed in a spotlight, comes down the aisle, riding . . . on Henry the Mule.

This is Boyd the Bodacious,
and that, dear hearts, is the news from the Fork,
where the tomatoes are home grown,
the road kill is fresh,

and
the fish is always fried!

THE RETURN OF MISS DIXIE

Well, folks, this is Boyd the Bodacious, and it's time for the latest social news from the Dutch Fork.

We are happy to report that Miss Dixie Doodahday Dalrymple has returned to the Fork after an extended absence. She invites all her friends, old and new, to drop by for a chat and a do real soon.

Miss Dixie was a senior in high school the year the new highway bypass clipped off a corner of her daddy's south pasture, and he responded by selling the rest of the pasture for a hefty chunk of change to a real estate developer who had dreams of putting a shopping center there.

That was the year that Miss Dixie was elected homecoming queen at the high school and named Miss Squash Blossom in the Annual Summer Garden Festival.

She was also named Miss Happy Heifer at the Dairy Month Festival.

As news of Daddy's financial windfall spread, he found himself the recipient of an unaccustomed amount of attention and popularity. It was almost enough to turn a body's head.

One day two men in expensive suits and claiming to be from Clemson College came for a visit. They sat with Daddy on the porch sipping iced tea, and after chatting for a time about the weather and the crops, they started urging Daddy to send Miss Dixie to Clemson.

The school had not long been coed, and they were looking for highly qualified women like Miss Dixie who would bring much to the school and, most certainly, gain much from it, and maybe Daddy would like to make an additional financial contribution to the school, while they were on the subject. Maybe an athletics scholarship or something.

Well, Daddy allowed that he was indeed planning on using some of his newfound prosperity to send his daughter to college. She would, after all, be the first person on either side of her family to go to college; but he had rather thought he would send her to the University of South Carolina. It was, after all, the state university and had a long and venerable reputation as an academic institution.

The two strangers glanced briefly at one another, looked furtively around, then leaned in toward Daddy. "I suppose that's all right for some folks," said one, "but I guess you have heard what they say about THAT PLACE haven't you?"

"They say," said the stranger, speaking slowly and shaking his head in disbelief, "that the boys and girls down there use the SAME CURRICULUM."

"You can't mean it!" exclaimed Daddy, incredulously.

"Oh yes," affirmed the stranger.

"And not only that," chimed in his companion, "but I have heard from reliable sources, that the boys and girls at that place MATRICULATE TOGETHER."

"Say it ain't so," pleaded Daddy, and before anyone could draw a second breath, the first stranger leaped back in to the fray.

"Listen," he said, "that ain't nothing. I have heard that before a female student can graduate from that institution, she has to have a MALE PROFESSOR EXAMINE HER THESIS!"

"My God!" bellowed Daddy. "I ain't sending no daughter of mine to such a den of iniquity. She is going to Clemson where decent Christian folks like you two will look after her."

And that was that!

The following fall Miss Dixie was a coed at Clemson. She joined the marching band, playing the clarinet like she had in high school, but soon found herself in the coveted role of majorette. The role was her, and she was it.

When the band marched onto the gridiron at halftime Miss Dixie Doodahday Dalrymple was strutting and prancing back and forth out front in her shimmering sequin-covered short shorts and halter and white high heel boots.

With her luxuriant mane of red hair flowing and flapping like the flame of an Olympic torch and her silver baton whirling and flashing like a dervish scimitar, no one, in the stands or on the side lines, or in the press box, had any interest in anything else that was going on in the stadium at that moment: not the concession venders, not the music the band was playing, nor even the score of the game.

It was powerful magic indeed.

Miss Dixie also did well in her studies, joined the debate society, and was named to the dean's list by the end of her first semester.

Of course all that was before Billy Bob.

Billy Bob Bohicket stepped off the Greyhound bus at the college station with a cardboard suitcase of clothes, a tailor-made cue stick, and five dollars in his pocket.

He was also the recipient of a scholarship to play wide receiver for the football team. Billy Bob was tall and lanky with long arms and very talented hands that could snag and pull down just about any football that was flung anywhere in his general direction.

His background was a nebulous and fluid narrative that seemed to change from one accounting to another, depending on the circumstances and the audience and Billy Bob's mood at the time. One consistent theme, however, related a history as a part-time rodeo clown and bull rider.

At any rate one souvenir of those days that seemed to be his most prized possession was a large solid-bronze belt buckle with the head of a longhorned bull sculpted in high relief. The eyes of this belligerent bovine were made of a pair of rubies or garnets or maybe just red bottle glass; it really didn't matter.

How Billy Bob had come by it was also a story that seemed to change and improve with subsequent tellings. He wore that buckle most all the time.

In the spring, when there was no football on weekends, there was not a lot to do for amusement. In those simpler times the closest the campus usually came to a disturbance was the occasional panty raid.

These events usually began at a juke joint and pool hall near campus that was officially named Bubba's Place but was always referred to by the college boys as "THE FLATULENT PIG."

Regular customers thought of themselves as something of a club and generally greeted each other with loud and lugubrious armpit farts. They were very talented young men.

On special occasions, after indulging in large quantities of beer and bluster, a motley crew of these geniuses would sally forth and nosily head for the women's dormitories, picking up new recruits along the way.

To add to the mob scene, some scholars fashioned makeshift torches, most of which kept going out, while others managed to stay alight long enough to set their owners' clothing or hair on fire.

When the raiding party reached the women's dormitory, they would mill about noisily outside until the coeds, having made the obligatory expressions of shock and disgust, would relent and begin tossing undergarments out the upstairs windows to the mob below. Many of these undergarments just happened to be adorned with their owners' names.

As these fanciful fetishes floated down through the evening air, like manna from Heaven, they would be grabbed and frantically fought over by the assembled geniuses, then carried off like pillaged plunder to the scholars' rooms.

There they would be proudly displayed like trophies of the hunt in such imaginative and tasteless ways as to defy description in this telling.

On many weekends Billy Bob could be found at the Flatulent Pig, holding court by the pool table while he used the aforementioned custom-made cue stick to increase his financial holdings.

As the first panty raid he had ever experienced began to take form, he tagged along, mostly out of curiosity, but also out of the fact that he never could pass up a good party (or a good fight, for that matter). It seemed to be a weakness of his.

The next such event, some weeks later, was a slightly different matter. When the sortie seemed to flounder for want of leadership, Billy Bob found himself, quite unexpectedly and most involuntarily, in the role of a leader, or general or field marshal or whatever you care to call it.

The spirit of the moment took over with both Billy Bob and the raiders rising to heights of foolishness that surprised even them.

Earlier the dean of women had ordered the women's dormitories to be locked down, and the women were sternly admonished to stay absolutely away from the windows.

When the mob of scholars arrived to such callous inhospitality, their determination intensified, and a commando quad, led by Billy Bob himself, managed to gain access to the citadel interior and was shortly racing through the halls wreaking havoc, bursting into the girls' rooms and throwing clothing out the windows.

Miss Dixie and her roommate watched in horror and disbelief as Billy Bob and his buddies snatched clothing out of the closet, garments that Miss Dixie and her mama had shopped for so carefully, and tossed them out the window to the assembly of scholars convened on the lawn below, to be most disrespectfully fought over.

The arrival of the campus police and their newly acquired tear gas sent the scholars scattering like dry leaves before an autumn wind, and the lingering odor of tear gas made the area uninhabitable for days afterward.

Before many weeks had passed, however, boredom and beer had sent these valiant crusaders off on another such sortie toward the girls' dormitories.

By then Billy Bob Bohicket had decided that he quite enjoyed the field marshal thing and found that, under the right circumstances, he possessed a remarkable amount of leadership charisma.

His sturdy minions, none of them exceptionally bright, responded to his leadership with enthusiasm.

This time all downstairs doors and windows in the girls' dormitories were firmly secured and inaccessible. After a bit of milling about, Billy Bob and a couple of his buddies managed to get onto the roof of the front porch, then proceeded to pry open the window to Miss Dixie's room and climb in, Billy Bob going first.

Miss Dixie had no interest in a repeat performance of the previous event and took matters in hand.

As Billy Bob thrust his head and shoulders through the window and into the room, his eyes fixed on Miss Dixie's roommate cringing against the far wall in her baby-doll nightie; Miss Dixie was standing against the front wall, just beside the window, with her majorette baton poised high above her head. Then, with a move perfected swinging a six-pound double-bit axe cutting wood back on Daddy's farm, she brought it down on the back of Billy Bob's head.

In a word she flat coldcocked that boy, and he fell into the room and landed in an unconscious heap on the floor.

His ardent followers, upon seeing their fearless leader disappear upside down into the darkened room, quickly lost interest in the adventure, turned, and retreated in full rout away from the now noisily approaching campus security forces and their wonderful tear gas grenades.

Meanwhile Miss Dixie and her roommate paused to gather themselves and assess the situation. First they dressed themselves, then, concluding that this whole thing seemed to be about clothing, they proceeded to separate the unconscious Billy Bob from his.

The roommate was a mite reticent at first. Miss Dixie, having grown up on a farm around notoriously immodest farm animals, was much less hesitant. However after a few drinks of the potent potion in the silver flask they found in their victims' hip pocket, they addressed themselves to the task at hand with considerable enthusiasm.

They stripped Billy Bob right down to his absolute nothings, pausing occasionally to take photographs from many angles and points of view. After stripping him down to his purely natural state, they tied a pink ribbon in a lovely bow knot onto his essential male member, took more photos, then dragged his inert and naked form into the hallway, wearing nothing but the pink willy-bow, then returned to their room and locked the door.

All of Billy Bob's clothing was folded neatly and stored in a cardboard box under Miss Dixie's bed. The red-eyed bull belt buckle was placed carefully on top of the other clothing in the box.

Meanwhile the commotion of the raid having died away, some of the coeds were venturing from their rooms and headed for the bathroom when they discovered a male visitor lying naked in the hall. They were relieved to see that he was breathing and beginning to stir.

The word spread quickly, and soon a sizable crowd of girls had gathered at a safe distance to witness this wonder of nature, giggle, and offer wry commentary.

When his consciousness returned, Billy Bob fled in confusion down the nearest fire escape into the custody of the campus police, who gave him ample opportunity to explain his strange circumstances.

The following week Billy Bob received a letter from Miss Dixie, delivered by a special messenger. It was on fine personal stationary, and in elegant cursive script it thanked Billy Bob for unexpectedly dropping in for a visit the previous week, mentioned how entertaining she and her friends had found him, and reminded him that when he departed he had left behind his clothing.

She went on to point out that she had been mightily offended by his callous treatment of her on that and previous visits and that she expected a full and sincere apology from him if he expected to get his raiment returned.

Enclosed therewith were two photographs; one showing the open cardboard box, clearly containing his clothing, all neatly folded and with the bull head belt buckle prominently displayed on top. The other was a fine full-length photo of Billy Bob lying naked and unconscious on her bedroom floor with his hoodickapippy festively adorned by a pink bow ribbon.

After a brief reflection, Billy Bob called her on the telephone, acknowledged his contrition, and asked for the opportunity to deliver his apology to her in person. She agreed.

The next day they met for coffee at the student union. Billy Bob honestly and sincerely apologized for his previous behavior; said it was a product of a mixture of beer, bravado, and bad judgment; a college prank that got out of hand.

He declared that he was not brought up that way, vowed that he was very, very sorry, and hoped she could forgive him.

Now Miss Dixie was not a person easily swayed, and she was still mad about her treatment at the hands of those clowns from the Flatulent Pig, led by the person sitting across the table from her.

Still he did seem sincerely repentant, and he did have a certain open, rural, boyish charm. He also had a merry twinkle in his eye and a sort of lopsided, easy smile.

And he was certainly a fine, robust example of young manhood. She blushed to herself to realize that she probably knew this better than most.

So she relented and started to forgive him . . . sort of.

"Maybe," she said. But there was still the matter of her vandalized clothing. How was she supposed to have a decent social life without anything to wear? And what was he going to do about it? Well, he ventured, how about if he were to take her shopping for new garments?

That sounded like a plan. So, come Saturday, they went on a shopping trip. They had fun, and at the end of the day they had supper together. Then again the next Saturday, and the next, all paid for by Billy Bob and financed by the aforementioned custom-made pool cue stick.

After the first shopping day, Miss Dixie returned the box of Billy Bob's clothing to him, also the photographs. Well, most of them, anyway.

After a while they were not shopping anymore and needed no excuse to spend every available moment with each other.

During those times she learned that he had previously spent time in Alaska doing construction work on the Alaska Pipeline . . . probably. One always took his stories with a grain of salt, although they usually turned out to be true. Mostly. At any rate he seemed to have read everything Robert Service ever wrote and could quote many lines by heart. But then he could also quote Robert Frost with equal ease.

One Saturday night Miss Dixie returned after curfew time to the receiving parlor of the dormitory, somewhat disheveled, and pleasantly inebriated and twirling her panties around her upraised index finger like a flag or pennant.

The house mother arose from her desk and started across the room to chastise her and invoke the rules of the house. However when she saw the strange new gleam in Miss Dixie's eyes, some sixth sense, some primordial survival instinct, caused her to look away, change course, and just walk on by.

The few girls remaining in the parlor suddenly found themselves busily engaged reading magazines or playing cards.

From that time forth Miss Dixie was a changed person.

One day the bachelor uncle who raised Billy Bob passed on to his eternal heavenly reward. Billy Bob returned from the funeral with several items that he had left there for safekeeping. Among them were a couple of things that were part of his other life as a rodeo clown. They were a magnificent 1937 Packard sedan and a chimpanzee named Stonewall.

Stonewall was a creature of a certain age, an endless bag of tricks, and a generally foul disposition.

The Packard had been lovingly and carefully restored to near mint condition with white sidewall tires, replated chrome, and a silver-gray paint and wax finish that you could comb your hair in. The powerful eight-cylinder engine and resonator muffler gave it a most commanding sonic presence as well.

Everything was like original except for one thing. All the control devices—steering wheel, pedals, gear shift, et cetera—had been relocated to the left back seat, leaving only a now inoperable steering wheel in front of what had been the driver's seat, so that the driver, meaning Billy Bob, could sit in the back seat and drive the car, virtually unseen from the outside, while Stonewall would sit in the front seat, holding onto the useless steering wheel and pretending to drive the car.

It was a good act in the rodeo ring but a lot more fun out on the street among unsuspecting civilians.

Billy Bob and Miss Dixie took the Packard and Stonewall for special outings, usually to nearby towns, and only occasionally closer in. They sat in the back seat with Billy Bob driving. The relocated steering wheel in the back was small and low so that it was practically out of sight from outside the car, and the back seat was set so far back that it was hard to see if anyone at all was in it anyway.

Stonewall would be in the original driver's seat, wearing his leather vest and bomber pilot cap with the fifty-mission crush. As the car cruised along he would bounce around in the seat, blow the horn (that still worked up front), lean his head and shoulder out the window, grimace, and wave a long, hairy arm at startled passing motorists and terrified pedestrians, leaving behind a wake of confusion and disorder and other cars that had run into each other or off the road. Billy Bob and Miss Dixie found it all extremely amusing and entertaining.

They were making their first venture near the campus one evening when Deputy Dingle pulled them over. Maybe it was the very unusual license tag, maybe it was the fact that one tail light did not work, or maybe it was the very strange driver in a very unusual car that got his attention.

He got out of the patrol car and approached the strange, unmoving dark vehicle cautiously. He realized at the last minute that he did not have his flashlight; he must have left it at the motel last night. Still by the lights of the patrol car and a distant street light he could see the dark form of the driver of the car in the front seat.

He stood a few feet away from the car and demanded that the driver get out and show some identification. When the driver did not respond, he stepped closer and repeated his demand, this time louder and with more authority. And, like the wonderful tar baby, the driver still made no response. This thoroughly angered the deputy, so in his rage he stepped forward, opened the door of the car, and proceeded to grab the driver by the arm and pull him from the car, at the same time snatching off the driver's cap, the better to see his face.

Suddenly, with a primal scream, Stonewall leaped from the car straight onto Deputy Dingle's chest and face and bit him savagely on the nose. As the deputy staggered back, still trying to comprehend the nature of this monster in his face, he managed to fumble his pistol out of its holster, only to have a prehensile primate foot snatch the pistol from his hand.

It was all very much like the comic routine that Stonewall had learned to perform with Billy Bob and the car and a toy gun in the rodeo ring; only now it seemed much more real. The terrified deputy stumbled backward, tripped over something, and fell sprawling to the ground. Stonewall leaped away from him, snatching up the pistol and his cap in the same motion. As his hand closed around the handle of the big .45 caliber Smith and Wesson handgun, he somehow managed to squeeze off a round into the night air. The great noise and recoil startled him, and he fled for safety through the upper reaches of a nearby grove of trees, still in possession of the pistol and cap, but escaping once and for all from this human foolishness, never to look back.

It had all occurred so quickly that Deputy Dingle was not quite sure what had happened or what to make of the dark and hideous apparition that had leaped out of the Packard and into his face, disarmed him, then bounded off into the night. He did know that his gnawed-on nose was hurting mightily and bleeding profusely, so he got to his feet and staggered to his patrol car to call for backup.

It had also never come to his attention that Billy Bob and Miss Dixie were sitting in the darkened back seat of the Packard throughout the episode.

They, meanwhile, were almost as startled as he was by this strange and sudden happening, but when they heard Deputy Dingle calling for help, Billy Bob knew absolutely that it simply would not do for Smokey the Bear to be searching through the Packard, so he did about the only thing left. As the sound of approaching police sirens grew louder, he started up the car and drove away as quickly as possible.

Deputy Dingle then had the unsettling experience of watching an unoccupied car start up and drive itself off into the night.

All his instincts and training said he should give chase, but to what? The Packard, with no lights showing, had disappeared into the darkness, and if he should catch it, then what? Arrest a car? Maybe a ghost car? And on what charges? Besides who knew what other evil tricks such an unearthly contraption had up its sleeve? Deputy Dingle was surely in no hurry to find out.

And the strange and terrifying monster that had attacked him was somewhere in the treetops with a bad disposition and a gun: the deputy's gun, which he did not have anymore. That seemed like an impossible situation any way one looked at it.

He was still sitting in his patrol car, alone on a dark and empty stretch of road, studying the situation and nursing his bleeding proboscis, when the backup forces arrived.

Deputy Dingle had grown up well back in the tall and uncut and found it easy to accept the idea of a world abundantly inhabited by "Ghosties and Ghoulies, Long Leggitie Beastiess, and Things That Go Boomp in the Night."

As he tried to tell his incredulous comrades what had befallen him that evening, and, for that matter, to understand it himself, the story began to take on rather supernatural overtones.

Some of his fellow officers did not believe it; others embraced the story and, indeed, enhanced the supernatural qualities of it as they later went on to retell it themselves. Soon it took on a life of its own and blossomed into a richly embellished myth.

Certainly these sturdy minions of the law did not find such a strange story, even with its hobgoblins, much more implausible than the behavior of weird college students and the even weirder professors they had to endure regularly.

Billy Bob and Miss Dixie realized that, once again, a simple college prank had gotten a bit out of hand. This time it was serious and seemed like a situation from which there was no turning back. They quickly concluded that they would be better off someplace else.

They went first to Billy Bob's room, then to Miss Dixie's dormitory, gathered up their belongings, and threw them into the Packard. At sunup they were headed west across the mountains toward the bright lights of Hollywood.

It was a pleasant trip. They kept mostly to roads less traveled and, for years afterward, in small towns all the way across America, folks were telling the wondrous tale of the great gray ghost car that cruised out of the darkness and off into the unknown, with no driver and no passengers, never to return. Fortunately the legend expanded and improved with repetition and age. Meanwhile it seems that the fugitive Stonewall, after a time of wandering about, took up residence in the barn loft of an abandoned farm not far outside of town. From there he would venture forth in the dim light of early dawn and late dusk to forage for food in vegetable gardens and garbage cans. He was usually able to accomplish this without being seen by the townsfolk, but occasionally some startled citizen would catch a dim and fleeting glimpse of him, still wearing the vest and military cap and usually carrying Deputy Dingle's purloined pistol.

Such rare sightings always prompted frantic phone calls to someone in authority and generally featured wildly, improbably, and fantastic descriptions and ludicrous attempts at identification of this dark apparition. Soon his legend had grown to hysterical and monstrous proportions, rivaling Bigfoot, Swamp Thing, and the Abominable Snowman.

In Hollywood, Miss Dixie soon figured out how things worked and managed to start picking up bit parts and minor roles in generally forgettable films. Billy Bob got work occasionally as a stunt double in other forgettable films, usually B-grade westerns, but was soon also working the rodeo circuits as a clown and sometimes bull rider. Whenever things got lean, the tailor-made cue stick could be counted on to pay the rent.

Although Miss Dixie's movie career was modest at best, back home in Dutch Fork she was hailed as a celebrity, and any movie in which she appeared, however briefly, was well attended at the local movie theater. All her kin were very proud of her success.

All this took a rather dramatic turn when Miss Dixie was featured in a three-page centerfold pictorial presentation in *Playboy Magazine.* The ink was still fresh on the pages when the picture appeared, as if by magic, on the bulletin board of the choir room of the Baptist church back home where she used to sing in the choir.

No one knew where the picture came from, but when the choristers arrived for choir practice one Wednesday night, there she was, pictured in a three-page, foldout, rotogravure image, in full and glorious color, in her purely natural state, dazzling in her youthful beauty, and wearing nothing but a big, happy smile.

When the preacher saw it, he immediately retreated to his study and changed the topic for his upcoming Sunday sermon. He had planned to preach on the parable of the Prodigal Son but abandoned that in favor of a sermon entitled "Wake Up, America!"

On that Sunday he delivered a passionate, spittle-spewing diatribe on moral decline in America, how lust and carnal desire and a turning away from God were destroying the moral fiber of the country.

Without naming names, but everyone knew the names, anyway, he made it known that his asperity was prompted by the choir room thing. He spoke with a special vehemence whenever he thundered the phrase "Nekkid as a Jay Bird."

Caught up in the moment, he went on so long that he caused many of the worshipers to be late for the Sunday Special at the Bon Ton Sanitary Cafeteria.

The following week Miss Dixie's mama quietly withdrew her membership and financial support from that church, never to be seen there again.

The rumor was circulated at the next meeting of the Women's Bible Study that she had even gone so far as to become a, well . . . a Unitarian. The word was spoken in hushed, whispered tones, with hands half covering the ladies' mouths, and this utterance was generally accompanied by a rolling of eyes and wagging of heads in expressions of shock and disbelief.

The appearance of *Playboy Magazine* in the Fork was somewhat amazing. No one there admitted to reading or even knowing about the magazine, but suddenly there it was. Not only did the offending abomination appear at church, but another one turned up at the barber shop, and two were confiscated and destroyed by alert teachers at school. The three-page foldout was carefully removed from the magazine and tacked to the wall of the service bay down at the Gulf station, where it remains in all its faded glory even today.

With the passage of time and the maturing of Miss Dixie's face and figure, the movie roles, modest as they had been, seemed to dry up and slowly disappear before her eyes. She then turned her attention to the business of movie makeup and hair styling.

Turns out she was very good at it. Before long she was one of the most sought after cosmetic styling artists in Hollywood. It seemed like all the stars wanted her to "Do" them. Many claimed that she could make them look better than Mother Nature ever had. The big studios clamored for her services, and aging stars turned to her as a last defense against the ravages of time. For the rest of her days in Hollywood she was much more successful as a cosmetic stylist than she had been as an actress.

Well, now Miss Dixie Doodahday Dalrymple has moved back home to the Dutch Fork. She has returned for occasional brief visits over the years, but now she is back home to stay. She has moved back into the old home place, which had stood vacant ever since the passing of her mama and daddy, and she has opened a beauty parlor on Main Street in what used to be a sandwich shop. Her daughter, a fashion designer from Atlanta, has spent the last several weeks helping her move in and get set up.

She is eager for all her friends, old and new, to stop by for a chat and a "Do." It has been some time since she left here. The once flame-red hair is a soft, rosy shade of gray now, almost white, and shorter. She has a few extra pounds here and there, and there are gentle laugh lines around the sparkling gray-green eyes. She always has a smile and a friendly word for everyone.

The beauty shop is attractive and shining under new paint. Over the door is a sign saying "The Dixie Doo/Beauty Secrets of the *Stars.*" Inside there is the necessary beautician's chair, mirrors, fresh flowers, and potted plants and a perpetually simmering coffee pot. On the walls are framed and autographed pictures of Hollywood stars, many photographed with her. There is also a big framed photo of Miss Dixie in her college majorette costume, strutting in front of the band, and a framed copy of the infamous Playboy foldout.

And above the light switch right beside the door is a small polished walnut wood plaque. On it is mounted a large, ornate bronze belt buckle containing the head of a long-horned bull sculpted in high relief. The eyes of this belligerent bovine are made of a pair of rubies, or garnets, or maybe just red bottle glass.

It really doesn't matter.

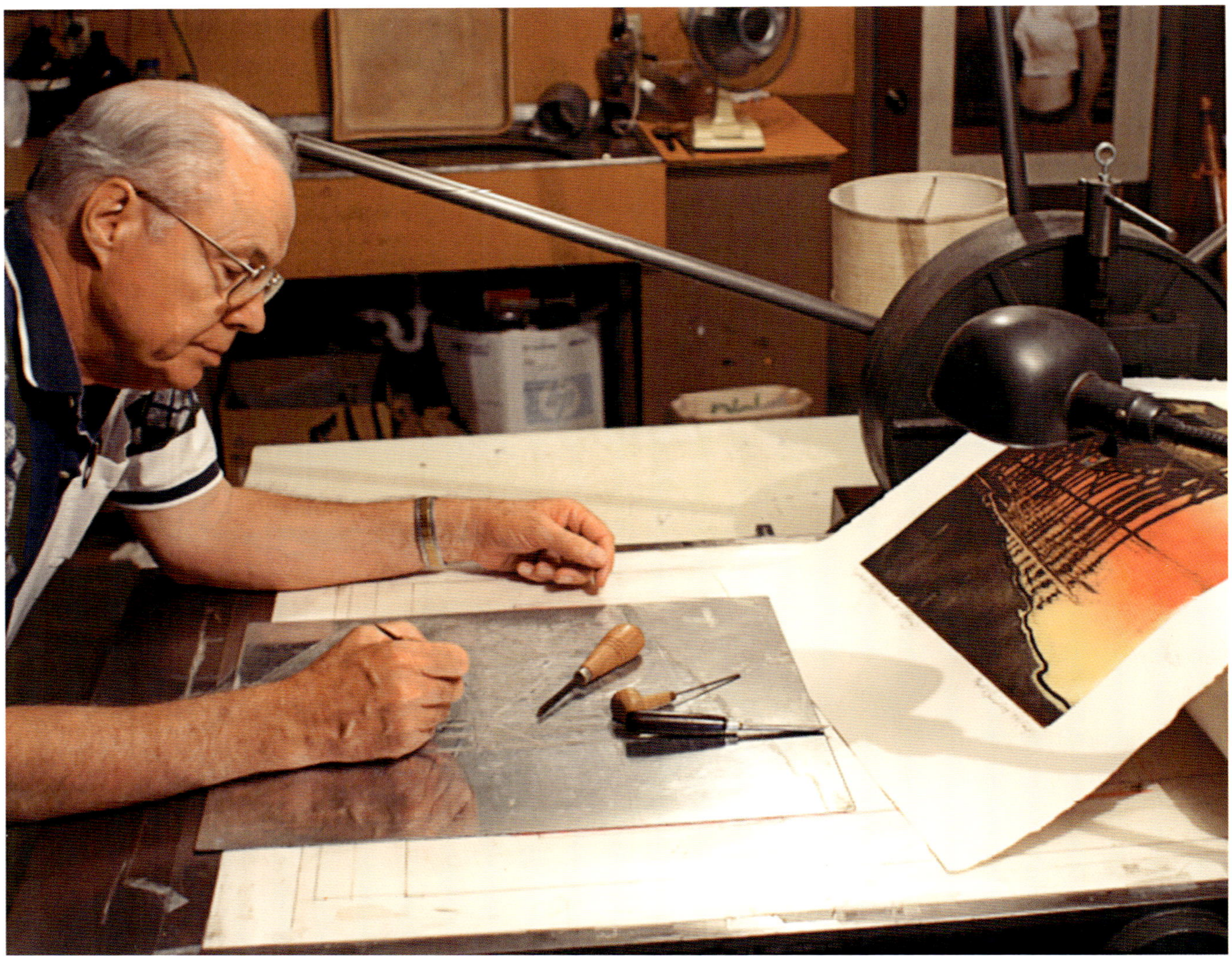

The artist at work

Afterthoughts

In chapter 10 Saunders expressed his admiration for the long-standing tradition in Japan of officially recognizing "certain highly skilled senior artisans" as treasures. As a fitting closing to the individual whose life, artwork, and stories make up this book, I propose the designation "Boyd Saunders: Southern Master/National Treasure."

Notes

Chapter 1. Fateful Introductions and the Beginnings of This Book Project

1. For the record I was not the first Dewey to venture south into Mississippi. My great grandfather Theron Stephens Dewey "visited" Vicksburg during the 1863 siege as a member of the Third Illinois Cavalry. Though wounded, he survived, returned to southern Illinois to farm, marry, and rear a family that included three boys and one girl. One of his sons, William Jonathan Dewey, was my beloved grandfather. My father and I inherited my great grandfather's first name.

2. Southeastern Graphics Council, Annual Conference, Florida State University–Tallahassee, February 18–20, 1977, program.

3. The pewter medallion carried a profile relief image of the recipient's head on one side and the announcement of the award on the other side. The medallion was crafted by Lewis Chapman of Camden, South Carolina, in 1978.

Chapter 2. Boyd Saunders

1. Boyd Saunders, "Funeral of Mrs. Irene Saunders Tribute," February 2006, transcript, 1.

2. Ibid., 1–2.

3. Ibid., 2.

4. Boyd Saunders, *Familiar Tracks/A Circular Journey,* presentations; overview of the artist's life and career in art, Greenville, S.C., October 11, 2002, videocassette (VHS) 9, transcript 3.

5. Ibid., 4–5.

6. Boyd Saunders, journal entry, n.d.

7. Boyd Saunders, *Familiar Tracks/A Circular Journey,* presentations; overview of the artist's life and career in art, Greenville, S.C., October 11, 2002, videocassette (VHS) 9, transcript 3–4.

8. Ibid., 4.

9. Boyd Saunders, presentation regarding his *Retro Spectus Exhibition,* McKissick Museum, University of South Carolina–Columbia, September 2001, videocassette (VHS) 6, transcript 2.

Chapter 3. Saunders's Early Career

1. Boyd Saunders, transcript of audiotape discussion at the artist's home near Chapin, S.C., August 2006.

2. Boyd Saunders, "Bosque Territory Commentary," November 5, 2008, 1.

3. Ibid., 3.

4. William C. Pool, *Bosque Territory: A History of an Agrarian Community* (Kyle, Tex.: Chaparral, 1964, 7.

5. Ibid., 1.

6. Ibid., 65.

7. Ibid., 131, original source Tax Rolls, Bosque County, Ad Valorem Tax Division, State Capital Building, Austin, Tex., n.d.

8. Ibid., 133–34, original source W. W. Baldwin, ed., "Driving Cattle from Texas to Iowa 1886," *Annals of Iowa* 14 (April 1924), 243.

9. Boyd Saunders, 2002 Printmaker Emeritus Award acceptance speech, Southern Graphics Council Conference, New Orleans, La.

10. Ibid.

11. Ibid.

12. Fred S. Kleiner, *Gardner's Art through the Ages: A Global History,* vol. 2, 13th ed. (Boston: Thompson Wadsworth, 2008), 555.

13. Boyd Saunders, "The Gorge Commentary," a commentary regarding the print on onion skin paper, possibly as a carbon copy, n.d.

14. Linda Hults, *The Print in the Western World: An Introductory History* (Madison: University of Wisconsin Press, 1996), 85.

Chapter 4. Saunders and Faulkner

1. Videocassette 8, October 2, 2001, Boyd Saunders speaking to an assembled group of patrons on the occasion of *Retro Spectus,* a retrospective exhibition of the artist's work which filled several galleries and halls. Saunders also led a large number of the attendees through the various galleries addressing intentions, themes, sources, formal qualities, and other considerations for his work on view at the McKissick Museum, University of South Carolina–Columbia.

2. Ibid., transcript 2.

3. Ibid.

4. Ibid., 3–4.

5. Ibid., 2.

6. Ibid., 5–6.

7. William Faulkner's acceptance speech for the Nobel Prize in Literature, delivered in Stockholm, Sweden, December 10, 1950, Copyright ©The Nobel Foundation (1950), Nobelprize.org, accessed November 9, 2015.

8. *Retro Spectus,* videocassette (VHS) 8, transcripts 7–8.

9. Ibid., 8.

10. William Shakespeare, *The Tragedy of Macbeth,* act 5, scene 5, in *The Tragedy of Death,* edited by Nicholas Brooke, 1990, 204.

11. *Retro Spectus,* videocassette (VHS) 8, transcript 8–9.

12. Ibid., 9.

13. Ibid.

14. Ibid., 9–10.

15. Ibid., 10, 14.

16. Ibid., 10.

17. Ibid., 9.

18. David Paul Ragan, "Reflections on Faulkner's *The Sound and the Fury,*" introductory essay. William Faulkner's *The Sound and the Fury: A Suite of Eight Etchings by Boyd Saunders* (Chapin, S.C.: Hubris, 2004), 7. Ragan's nine–page commentary accompanied Saunders's etchings as a boxed set in 2004.

19. Videocassette (VHS) 8, transcript 15.

20. Ragan, "Reflections on Faulkner's *The Sound and the Fury,*" 8.

21. Videocassette (VHS) 8, transcript 12.

22. Ibid., 12.

23. Ragan, "Reflections on Faulkner's *The Sound and the Fury,*" 7.

24. Videocassette (VHS) 8, transcripts 11, 15.

25. Ibid., 11–12.

26. Boyd Saunders, "Notes and Reflections," *Spotted Horses,* 1989.

27. Videocassette 5, Boyd Saunders explaining the creation of the illustrated book *Spotted Horses* to an assembly of people, January 24, 1995.

28. Ibid., Transcripts 1, 3

29. Ibid., 3.

30. George Reeves, commentary on *Spotted Horses by William Faulkner with Original Lithographs by Boyd Saunders* (Columbia: University of South Carolina Press, 1989), promotional brochure, n.pag.

31. Videocassette 5, transcript 4.

32. Ibid., 5.

33. Ibid.

34. Ibid.

35. William Faulkner, *Spotted Horses Illustrated with Original Lithographs by Boyd Saunders,* a deluxe, limited edition book illustrated with thirty-four original hand created and printed lithographic color images by Boyd Saunders (Columbia: University of South Carolina Press, 1989), n.pag. *The Faulkner Reader* (New York: Random House, 1954), 447–49.

36. Videocassette (VHS) 5, transcripts 5–6.

37. Ibid., 8.

38. Reeves, commentary on *Spotted Horses by William Faulkner,* n.pag.

39. Jim Meriwether, "Notes and Reflections," *Spotted Horses,* 1989 (itself a large part of *The Hamlet,* 1931) Columbia: University of South Carolina Press, 1989, n.pag.

40. Reeves, commentary on *Spotted Horses by William Faulkner,* n.pag.

41. Ibid.

42. Videocassette (VHS) 5, transcripts 8–9.

43. Ibid., 9.

44. Ibid.

45. Ibid.

46. Ibid., 9–10.

47. Ibid., 7.

48. Reeves, commentary on *Spotted Horses by William Faulkner,* n.pag.

49. Saunders, "Notes and Reflections," 11.

50. Ibid.

51. Faulkner, *Spotted Horses Illustrated with Original Lithographs by Boyd Saunders*, n.pag.; Faulkner, *Faulkner Reader*, 478.

52. Faulkner, *Faulkner Reader*, 479.

Chapter 5. Southern Cross/A Trilogy—The Farm, Blackberry Winter, and *Late Light*

1. Videocassette (VHS) 9, B. Saunders's presentation at Greenville, S.C., October 11, 2002, transcript 6.

2. Boyd Saunders, journal entry, n.d., 5.

3. Interview, *Verve,* South Carolina ETV, September 2001, videocassette (VHS) 10.

4. Videocassette (VHS) 9, transcript 2.

5. *Southern Cross/A Trilogy,* exhibition catalogue (Atlanta, Ga.: Fine Art and Publishing, Transart, WLC Industries, 1984), n.pag.

6. Phone conversation with Boyd Saunders, June 2008.

7. *Southern Cross/A Trilogy,* exhibition catalogue.

8. Videocassette (VHS) 6, Boyd Saunders speaking in front of his artwork at *Retro Spectus,* a large one-person exhibition, McKissick Museum, University of South Carolina–Columbia, dated September 8, 2001, transcript 12.

9. Nina Parris, "A Sense of Place—the Art of Boyd Saunders," in *Southern Cross/A Trilogy,* exhibition catalogue (Atlanta, Ga.: Fine Art and Publishing, Transart, WLC Industries, 1984), n.pag.

10. Videocassette 6, transcript 13–14.

11. Steve Harris addressed several features of *The Orchard,* from Boyd Saunders's series *The Farm Suite,* in "The Cistern" and "Features of the Orchard," commentary from *The Farm Suite* Series, 1980, promotional brochure, n.pag.

12. Videocassette 6, transcript 17.

13. Boyd Saunders, "The Guardian Commentary," June 16, 2008.

14. James Snyder, *Northern Renaissance Art: Painting, Sculpture and the Graphic Arts from 1350 to 1575* (Upper Saddle River, N.J.: Prentice Hall, 1985), 94, and 332–34.

15. Saunders, "The Guardian Commentary."

16. Boyd Saunders, Commentaries for *The Stable, The Commissary,* and *The Wedding Party,* in *Southern Cross/A Trilogy,* exhibition catalogue (Atlanta, Ga.: Fine Art and Publishing, Transart, WLC Industries, 1984), n.pag.

17. Gita Maritzer Smith "Capturing the Late Light: The Storyteller's Art of Boyd Saunders," in *Southern Cross/A Trilogy,* exhibition catalogue (Atlanta, Ga.: Fine Art and Publishing, Transart, WLC Industries, 1984), n.pag.

18. Harris, "The Cistern," commentary from *The Farm Suite* Series, 1980, promotional brochure, 1980, n.pag.

19. Boyd Saunders, journal entry, "The Old Nuckhall Place," revised November 2010.

20. Videocassette (VHS) 10, transcript 3.

21. "Capturing the Late Light: The Storyteller's Art of Boyd Saunders," n.pag.

22. Boyd Saunders, "The Dogtrot Commentary," June 16, 2008.

23. Videocassette (VHS) 6, transcript 15–16.

24. Ibid., 16.

25. Ibid.

26. Boyd Saunders, commentary for *The Wagon Shed,* typescript, 2009, 1.

27. Saunders, commentary for *The Scarecrow,* typescript, 2009, 1.

28. Ibid., 1–2.

29. Ibid., 2.

30. Ibid.

31. Saunders, commentary for *The Tobacco Auction,* typescript, 2009, 1–3.

32. Saunders, commentary for *The Forge,* typescript, 2009, 1–3.

33. Saunders, commentary for *The Commissary,* in *Southern Cross/A Trilogy,* exhibition catalogue (Atlanta, Ga.: Fine Art and Publishing, Transart, WLC Industries, 1984), n.pag. The large World War II poster shows the body of a sailor washed up onto a beach. The message below the image, which is partially blocked from view, reads: *A Careless Word, A Needless Loss.* Sailors on shore leave and civilians working for defense contractors were warned not to discuss sensitive information around strangers because of the threat of spies.

34. Saunders, "The Old Pony," commentary, June 16, 2008.

35. Boyd Saunders, commentary for *The Gathering,* 2009, 1–2.

36. Saunders, commentary for *Early Easter,* 2009.

37. Saunders, commentary for *The Wedding Party,* in *Southern Cross/A Trilogy,* exhibition catalogue (Atlanta, Ga.: Fine Art and Publishing, Transart, WLC Industries, 1984), n.pag.; and

a journal entry for *The Wedding Party,* 2009.

38. Saunders, commentary for *Air Battle,* 2009.

39. Saunders, commentary for *The Vixen,* 2009.

40. Saunders, commentary for *Mollie's Table,* by 2009.

Chapter 6. The Return of The Wanderer, Railroad Muses, and *September Folly*

1. Interview regarding Saunders's *Retro Spectus Exhibition,* the McKissick Museum, University of South Carolina–Columbia, fall 2001, transcript of videocassette, 16.

2. Saunders, "Return of the Wanderer Commentaries," March 2010.

3. Ibid.

4. Ibid.

5. Jessie Poesch, *The Art of the Old South: Painting, Sculpture, Architecture, and the Products of Craftsmen 1560–1860* (New York: Alfred A. Knopf, 1983), 196.

6. Ibid.

7. Saunders, "Return of the Wanderer Commentaries."

8. Telephone interview with Howard Shepherd, member, board of trustees, South Carolina Railroad Museum, Winnsboro, July 15, 2010.

9. Saunders, "Return of the Wanderer Commentaries."

10. Folly Beach Carolina Tourism History Timeline, http://www.follybeachsouthcarolina.org/index.aspNID=70&PREVIEW=YES.

Chapter 7. The Aikenhead Collection

1. *The Aikenhead Collection,* exhibition catalogue (Aiken, S.C.: Aiken Partnership, n.d.).

2. Nicole Kraft and Kelly Rucker "Gaits," Harness Racing, United States Trotting Association, http://www.ustrotting.com.

3. Ibid., General Terms.

4. Ibid.

5. Ibid.

6. *The American Heritage Dictionary of the English Language,* 4th ed., s.v. "frog," 706.

7. Ibid., s.v. "pasterns," 1286.

Chapter 8. The Shanghai Etchers Workshop

1. Boyd Saunders, "The Shanghai Etcher's Workshop." Report to the Art Department and University of South Carolina–Columbia, 1995. This draft copy was given to me during a three-day interviewing session at the artist's home and studio near Chapin, S.C., August 13–15, 2006, 1.

2. Ibid., 3, 4, 7.

3. Ibid., 7, 8.

4. Ibid., 8, 10.

5. Ibid., 10.

6. Ibid., 10–11.

7. Ibid., 10.

8. Ibid., 11.

9. Ibid., 12.

10. Ibid., 13.

11. Ibid., 15.

12. Ibid., 18.

13. Ibid., 20.

14. Ibid., 21.

15. Boyd Saunders, "Familiar Tracks/A Circular Journey, Printmaker Emeritus Award Acceptance Speech at the Annual Southern Graphics Council Conference, New Orleans, La., March 2002.

16. Ibid.

17. Saunders, "The Shanghai Etcher's Workshop," 16–18.

18. Saunders, "Familiar Tracks/A Circular Journey."

Chapter 9. The Battle of Hanging Rock, South Carolina, 1780

1. Boyd Saunders, "The Battle of Hanging Rock," illustrated research paper presentation, Loblolly Society, Columbia, S.C., meeting in 2000, recounting the artist's commission to execute a 4 × 8 ft. painting of the 1780 battle, transcript, 1.

2. Ibid., 2.

3. Ibid., 2–6.

4. Walter Edgar, *Partisans and Redcoats: The Southern Conflict That Turned the Tide of the American Revolution* (New York: Perennial/Harper Collins, 2001), 101–2.

5. Edgar, *Partisans and Redcoats,* 103–4.

6. Saunders, "The Battle of Hanging Rock," 2–6.

7. Ibid., 6.

8. Ibid., 9–10.

9. Ibid., 11, 13.

10. Ibid., 10–11.

11. Ibid., 8–9.

12. Ibid., 9–10.

13. Ibid., 16.

14. Ibid., 11–12.

15. Ibid., 14–15.

16. Ibid., 15.

17. Ibid., 16.

18. Ibid., 15.

19. Ibid., 13.

20. Ibid., 16–17.

21. Ibid., 11.

22. Ibid., 18.

Chapter 10. Service to the Field

1. Boyd Saunders Early History of the Southern Graphics Council.

2. Boyd Saunders, "Information Exchanges and False Voices," Printmaker Emeritus Award Presentation Speech at the Annual Southern Graphics Council Conference, University of Texas at Austin, March 7–11, 2001.

3. All data appearing in the lists "Southern Graphics Council International" and "Southern Graphics Council Presidents" are from the Southern Graphics Council International Archives, University of Mississippi, Oxford. Southern Graphics Council International began as the Southeastern Graphics Council (1972–78) and the Southern Graphics Council (1979–2010) and officially became known by its present name at the council's 2010 conference in Philadelphia, Pa., March 2010.

Chapter 11. More Service to the Field

1. Boyd Saunders and Stephanie Saunders, *The Etchings of James Fowler Cooper: An Illustrated Catalog* (Columbia: University of South Carolina Press, 1982), introduction, xi.

2. Ibid.

3. Ibid., xii.

4. Ibid.

5. Ibid.

6. Ibid., xiii.

7. Ernest Stephen Lumsden, *The Art of Etching* (London: Seely, Service, 1925).

8. Saunders and Saunders, *Etchings of James Fowler Cooper,* xiii.

9. Ibid.

10. Ibid.

11. Ibid., xvi.

12. Ibid., xii.

13. Ibid., xvi.

14. Ibid., xxi.

15. Ibid., xxii.

16. Ibid., xxii, xiii.

17. A one-page document or statement that briefly clarifies the efforts by Boyd Saunders and his technical assistants to make ready for the printing of copper plates carrying images made by J. F. Cooper for the purpose of illustrating this book project . . . but not for selling the prints. Undated.

18. Saunders and Saunders, *Etchings of James Fowler Cooper,* 185.

19. Ibid., xxii, xiii.

20. Ibid., 185

21. Saunders, 186.

22. Ibid., 187.

23. Ibid., 188.

24. Ibid., 187.

25. Ibid.

26. Ibid.

27. Ibid.

28. Ibid., 188.

29. Ibid., xx.

30. Ibid., 188.

31. Ibid., ix.

32. Ibid., 189.

33. Ibid., ix.

34. Ibid., 189.

35. Ibid.

36. Ibid., 189–90.

37. Ibid., 190.

38. Ibid.

39. Ibid., 191.

40. Ibid., 192.

41. Ibid., 193.

42. Ibid.

43. Ibid.

44. Ibid., xvii.

45. Ibid., 195.

46. Ibid., 196.

47. Ibid., 197.

48. Boyd Saunders and Ann McAden, *Alfred Hutty and the Charleston Renaissance* (Orangeburg, S.C.: Sandlapper, 1990), 14.

49. Ibid.

50. Ibid.

51. Ibid.

52. Ibid.

53. Ibid.

54. Ibid., 14–15.

55. Ibid., 15.

56. Ibid.

57. Ibid., 15–16.

58. Ibid., 13.

59. Ibid.

60. Ibid., 19.

61. Ibid.

62. Ibid., 19–20.

63. Ibid., 16.

64. Ibid., 34–35.

65. Ibid., 18, 31.

66. Ibid., 35.

67. Ibid., 36.

68. Ibid., 51.

69. Ibid., 50–51.

70. Ibid., 50.

71. Ibid., 51.

72. Ibid.

73. Ibid., 36.

74. Ibid., 33.

75. Ibid., 32–36. Dubose Heyward's book *Porgy* (1926) was successful, and soon he collaborated with his wife, Dorothy, to turn the book into a play by the same name. It too was successful, but the most historical development came when Dubose and Dorothy Heyward collaborated with George and Ira Gershwin to create the now immortal folk opera *Porgy and Bess* by 1935.

76. Saunders and McAden, *Alfred Hutty and the Charleston Renaissance*, 51–52.

77. Ibid., 52.

78. Ibid., 51.

79. Ibid.

80. Ibid., 60.

81. Ibid., 61.

82. Ibid., 43–44.

83. Ibid., 44.

Chapter 13. Saunders and Music

1. Anon. untitled, brief, historical remarks regarding the founding of the organization, in *The Palmetto Mastersingers 2005–2006 Season 25th Anniversary Booklet* (Columbia: University of South Carolina, 2006), 32.

2. Ibid.

3. Ibid.

4. Boyd Saunders, Music, typescript, dated September 14, 2008, 1–2.

5. David Stewart, "An Anniversary Note," *The Palmetto Mastersingers 25th Season Anniversary Booklet* (Columbia: University of South Carolina, 2006).

6. Boyd Saunders, additional information regarding the Palmetto Mastersingers concert tours and accomplishments, typescript, postmarked October 12, 2010.

7. Ibid.

Chapter 14. Saunders and the Loblolly Society of Columbia, South Carolina

1. Curtis Clark, "The Non-academical Gumshoe: Curtis Clark and the Elusive History of the Loblolly Society," paper presented at the January 2010 meeting of the Loblolly Society, Columbia, S.C. Clark volunteered that he borrowed "Academical Gumshoe" from a paper title by fellow Loblolly Society member Paul Ragan, whose paper, "The Academical Gumshoe: James B. Meriwether and William Faulkner," was presented at an earlier Loblolly Society meeting in late 2009 or early 2010, 1.

2. Clark, "Non-academical Gumshoe," 2, 8.

3. *The American Heritage Dictionary of the English Language*, 4th ed., s.v. "loblolly," 1026.

4. Ibid., s.v. "onomatopoeia," 1230.

5. Ibid., s.v. "loblolly."

6. Ibid.

7. Clark, "Non-academical Gumshoe," 7.

8. Ibid.

9. Ibid.

Bibliography

The Aikenhead Collection, exhibition catalogue. Aiken, S.C.: Aiken Partnership, n.d.

Anon. Untitled, brief historical remarks regarding the foundation of the organization. *The Palmetto Mastersingers 25th Season Anniversary Booklet.* Columbia: University of South Carolina, 2006, 32.

Clark, Curtis. "The Non-academical Gumshoe: Curtis Clark and the Elusive History of the Loblolly Society." Paper presentation to the Loblolly Society, Columbia, University of South Carolina, 2010.

Edgar, Walter. *Partisans and Redcoats: The Southern Conflict That Turned the Tide of the American Revolution.* New York: Perennial/Harper Collins, 2001.

Faulkner, William. "Acceptance Speech for the Nobel Prize in Literature." Stockholm, Sweden, December 10, 1950. Copyright ©The Nobel Foundation (1950), nobelprize.org.

———. *The Faulkner Reader.* "Spotted Horses." New York: Random House, 1954, 447–49, 478–79.

———. *Spotted Horses Illustrated with Original Lithographs by Boyd Saunders,* a deluxe limited edition. Columbia: University of South Carolina Press, 1989.

Folly Beach South Carolina Tourism. "History Timeline." http://www.follybeachsouth Carolina.org/index.aspNID-70&PREVIEW -YES.

Harris, Steve. "The Cistern" and "Features of the Orchard," commentary from *The Farm Suite* Series, 1980. Promotional brochure, n.pag.

Hults, Linda. *The Print in the Western World: An Introductory History.* Madison: University of Wisconsin Press, 1996.

Kleiner, Fred S. *Gardner's Art through the Ages: A Global History.* Vol. 2, 13th ed. Boston: Thompson Wadsworth, 2008.

Kraft, Nicole, and Kelly Rucker. "Gaits," Harness Racing. United States Trotting Association. http://www.ustrotting.com.

Lumsden, Ernest Stephen. *The Art of Etching.* London: Seely, Service, 1925.

McKissick Museum, University of South Carolina–Columbia.

Meriwether, Jim. "Notes and Reflections," *Spotted Horses,* Columbia: University of South Carolina Press, 1989, n.pag.

Palmettomastersingers.org.

The Palmetto Mastersingers 25th Season Anniversary Booklet. Columbia: University of South Carolina, 2006.

Parris, Nina. "A Sense of Place—the Art of Boyd Saunders," in *Southern Cross/A Trilogy,* exhibition catalogue. Atlanta, Ga.: Transart, WLC Industries, 1984, n.pag.

Poesch, Jessie. *The Art of the Old South: Painting, Sculpture, Architecture, and the Products of Craftsmen 1560–1860.* New York: Alfred A. Knopf, 1983.

Pool, William C. *Bosque Territory: A History of an Agrarian Community.* Kyle, Tex.: Chaparral, 1964, 65; 131 (original source: Tax Rolls, Bosque County, Ad Valorem Tax Division, State Capital Building, Austin, Tex., n.d.); 133–34 (original source W. W. Baldwin, ed., "Driving Cattle from Texas to Iowa 1886," *Annals of Iowa* 14 [April 1924], 243).

Ragan, David Paul. "Reflections on Faulkner's *The Sound and the Fury,*" introductory essay. William Faulkner's *The Sound and the Fury: A Suite of Eight Etchings by Boyd Saunders.* Chapin, S.C.: Hubris, 2004, 6–8.

Reeves, George. Commentary on *Spotted Horses by William Faulkner with Original Lithographs by Boyd Saunders.* Columbia: University of South Carolina Press, 1989. Promotional brochure, n.pag.

Saunders, Boyd. "The Battle of Hanging Rock," illustrated research paper presentation. Loblolly Society, Columbia, S.C., 2000.

———. "Bosque Territory Commentary." November 5, 2008.

———. Commentaries for *Air Battle, Early Easter, The Gathering, Mollie's Table,* and *The Vixen,* 2009.

———. Commentaries for *The Forge, The Scarecrow, The Tobacco Auction,* and *The Wagon Shed,* 2009.

———. Commentaries for *The Stable, The Commissary, and The Wedding Party*, in *Southern Cross/A Trilogy,* exhibition catalogue. Atlanta, Ga.: Fine Art and Publishing, Transart, WLC Industries, 1984, n.pag.

———. "The Dogtrot Commentary," June 16, 2008.

———. "Familiar Tracks/A Circular Journey." Presentation. University of South Carolina, Columbia, 2002. Videocassette (VHS) 9.

———. *Familiar Tracks/A Circular Journey,* presentations; overview of the artist's life and career in art, Greenville, S.C., October 11, 2002, videocassette (VHS) 9, transcript 3.

———. "Funeral of Mrs. Irene Saunders Tribute." February 2006. Transcript.

———. "The Gorge Commentary," n.d.

———. "The Guardian Commentary," June 16, 2008.

———. "Information Exchanges and False Voices," Printmaker Emeritus Award Presentation Speech at the Annual Southern Graphics Council Conference, University of Texas–Austin, March 7–11, 2001.

———. Interview. *Verve,* South Carolina ETV, September 2001. Videocassette (VHS) 10.

———. Music. Typescript, September 14, 2008. 1–2.

———. "Notes and Reflections," *Spotted Horses,* 1989.

———. "The Old Pony." Commentary, June 16, 2008.

———. Presentation. Greenville, S.C., October 11, 2002. Videocassette (VHS) 9.

———. Presentation explaining the creation of his illustrated book *Spotted Horses* to an assembly of people, January 24, 1995. Videocassette (VHS) 5.

———. "Retro Spectus Exhibition," presentation. McKissick Museum, University of South Carolina–Columbia, September 2001. Videocassette (VHS) 6.

———. "Retro Spectus Exhibition," presentation. McKissick Museum, University of South Carolina–Columbia, October 2, 2001. Videocassette (VHS) 8.

———. "Retro Spectus Exhibition," presentation. University of South Carolina-Columbia, 2002. Videocassette (VHS) 10.

———. "Return of the Wanderer Commentaries," March 2010.

———. "The Shanghai Etcher's Workshop." Report to the Art Department and University of South Carolina–Columbia, 1995.

———. "The Storyteller's Art," June 2008.

Saunders, Boyd, and Ann McAden. *Alfred Hutty and the Charleston Renaissance.* Orangeburg, S.C.: *Sandlapper*, 1990.

Saunders, Boyd, and Stephanie Saunders. *The Etchings of James Fowler Cooper: An Illustrated Catalog.* Columbia: University of South Carolina, 1982.

Shakespeare, William. *The Tragedy of Macbeth.* In *The Tragedy of Death,* Nicholas Brooke, ed. Oxford: Oxford University, 1990.

Smith, Gita Maritzer. "Capturing the Late Light: The Storyteller's Art of Boyd Saunders," in *Southern Cross/A Trilogy,* exhibition catalogue. Atlanta, Ga.: Fine Art and Publishing, Transart, WLC Industries, 1984, n.pag.

Snyder, James. *Northern Renaissance Art: Painting, Sculpture, the Graphic Arts from 1350 to 1575.* Upper Saddle River, N.J.: Prentice Hall, 1985.

Southeastern Graphics Council Annual Conference, Tallahassee. Florida State University, February 18–20, 1977. Program.

Southern Cross/A Trilogy, exhibition catalogue. Atlanta: Fine Art and Publishing, Transart, WLC Industries, 1984.

Southern Graphics Council International (formerly Southeastern Graphics Council and Southern Graphics Council) Archives. Zuckerman Museum, Kennesaw State University, Ga. (maintained at the University of Mississippi–Oxford, 1977–2013).

Stewart, David. "An Anniversary Note." *The Palmetto Mastersingers 25th Season Anniversary Booklet.* Columbia: University of South Carolina, 2006, 21.